CENTER STAGE 3

Express Yourself in English

Lynn Bonesteel **Samuela Eckstut-Didier**

Series Consultants

MaryAnn Florez

Sharon Seymour

PEARSON
Longman

Center Stage 3: Express Yourself in English

Pearson Education, 10 Bank Street, White Plains, NY 10606

Staff credits: The people who made up the *Center Stage 3* team, representing editorial, production, design, and manufacturing, are Andrea Bryant, Elizabeth Carlson, Dave Dickey, Shelley Gazes, Laura LeDréan, Melissa Leyva, Gabriela Moya, Robert Ruvo, and Barbara Sabella.

Cover art: Gilbert Mayers/SuperStock

Photo Credits: p. 5 Royalty Free/Corbis; p. 7 Banana Stock/Alamy; p. 8 Steve Cole/Getty Images; p. 9 Royalty Free/Jupiter Images; p. 10 Charles Gupton/Corbis; p. 11 Titus Lacoste/Getty Images; p. 12 Andersen-Ross/Corbis; p. 18 Iconotec Royalty Free/Fotosearch; p. 21 (top left) Robert W. Ginn/PhotoEdit Inc, (top right) Han Blossey/Peter Arnold, Inc. (bottom left) Mark Leibowitz/Masterfile Corporation, (bottom right) (c) PressNet/Topham/The Image Works; p. 24 Chris Andrews/ Getty Images; p. 25 Wolfgang Schmidt/Peter Arnold, Inc; p. 26 Bruce Forster/Dorling Kindersley Media Library/Bruce Forster (c) Dorling Kindersley; p. 27 Royalty Free/ Corbis; p. 35 Mike Blake/ Reuters/Corbis; p. 36 Vincent LaForet/Getty Images; p. 37 Omar Torres/Getty Images; p. 38 Monika Graff/The Image Works; p. 40 Lisa Blumenfield/ Getty Images; p. 41 Matthew Stockman/ Getty Images, (center) Royalty Free/Corbis; p. 43 (left) JT photo/Brand X/Corbis; p. 67 M Stock/ Alamy; p. 69 The New Yorker Collection 1979 George Booth from Cartoonbank.com; p. 74 Tanya Constantine/ Getty Images; p. 76 Digital Vision/Getty Images; p. 80 Royalty Free/ Corbis; p. 90 (top) Royalty Free/Corbis, (bottom) Photodisc/Getty Images; p. 92 (left) Royalty Free/ Corbis, (center) Royalty Free/Corbis, (right) Michael Goldman/Getty Images; p. 94 Medioimages/Getty Images; p. 95 Tom Grill/ Corbis; p. 98 Laura DeSantis/ Getty Images; p. 102 Viviane Moos/Corbis; p. 103 Digital Vision/Getty Images; p. 106 Royalty Free/Corbis; p. 108 Stewart Cohen/ Pam Ostrow/Getty Images; p. 120 Royalty Free/Corbis; p. 121 Images.com/Corbis; p. 123 Bruce Ayres/Getty Images; p. 124 Imagemore Co. Ltd/Getty Images; p. 130 (top) TouchLife Images/Getty Images, (bottom) Royalty Free/Corbis; p. 131 Stockbyte/Getty Images; p. 133 (top) Digital Vision/Getty Images, (bottom) Albane Naivzet/Corbis; p. 135 Blend Stock Images/Fotosearch; p. 137 (top) Monty Brinton/CBS Photo Archive, (bottom) Matthias Clamer/ Getty Images; p. 138 Keith Dannemiller/Corbis; p. 139 Keith Dannemiller/Corbis; p. 145 (top) Klaus Hackenberg/Zefa/Corbis, (bottom) Frank Krahmer/Zefa/Corbis; p. 148 (left) Juniors Bildarchiv/Alamy, (right) GK Hart/Vikki Hart/Getty Images; p. 150 (top left) Gallo Images/Corbis, (bottom left) Royalty Free/ Corbis, (top right) Juliet Coombe/Lonely Planet Images/Getty Images, (bottom right) Edmond Van Hoorick/ Getty Images; p. 152 Tom Brakefield/Corbis; p. 154 Dennis Scott/Corbis; p. 157 Royalty Free/Corbis; p. 161 McMillian Digital Art/Getty Images; p. 162 Image Source/Corbis; p. 165 Bettman/Corbis; p. 166 (top) Imagebroker/Alamy, (bottom) The Slow Food Movement; p. 168 photo Alto/Fotosearch; p. 172 Andrew Wakeford/Getty Images; p. 175 Peter Scholey/Getty Images; p. 180 VeriChip Corporation; p. 181 PhotoStock File/Alamy; p. 185 Photodisc Green/Getty Images; p. 188 Royalty Free/Corbis; p. 189 Royalty Free/Corbis; p. 191 Royalty Free/Corbis; p. 195 Royalty Free/Corbis; p. 204 (top left) Macduff Everton/Corbis, (top right) Royalty Free/Corbis, (bottom left) Royalty Free/Corbis, (bottom right) Dave & Les Jacobs/Corbis; p. 209 Digital Vision/Getty Images, p. 213 WP Simon/Getty Images; p. 222 Janine Wiedel Photolibrary/Alamy; p. 227 John Liend/Tiffany Schoepp/Getty Images; p. 228 (top) Keith Brofsky/ Getty Images, (bottom) Bob Krist/Corbis; p. 230 Howard Huang/Getty Images; p. 235 Sarah-Maria Vischer-Masino/The Image Works; p. 237 Photodisc Green/ Getty Images; p. 245 (top) Royalty Free/Corbis, (bottom) LWA-Shane Kennedy/Corbis; p. 250 Dave G Houser/Corbis; p. 251 Les Waslker/NewSport/Corbis; p. 256 Don Farrall/Getty Images; p. 265 Glowimages/Getty Images; p. 270 (left) Photographer's Choice/Getty Images, (right) Heritage/The Image Works; p. 273 Royalty Free/Corbis

Text composition: ElectraGraphics

Text font: 12 Minion

Illustrations: A Corazón Abierto (Marcela Gómez), Steve Attoe, Laurie Conley, Debby Fisher, Marty Harris, Christopher Hitz, Francisco Morales, Mari Rodríguez, Steve Schulman, Wendy Smith, Gary Torrisi, Meryl Treatner, Ralph Voltz

Library of Congress Cataloging-in-Publication Data

Frankel, Irene.
  Center stage. — 1st ed.
    p. cm.
  Contents: 1. Beginning / Irene Frankel — 2. High beginning / Lynn
Bonesteel and Samuela Eckstut — 3. Intermediate / Lynn Bonesteel and
Samuela Eckstut — 4. High intermediate / Lynn Bonesteel and Samuela
Eckstut.
  ISBN 0-13-170881-3 (student book : bk. 1 : alk. paper) — ISBN
0-13-187490-X (student book : bk. 2 : alk. paper) — ISBN 0-13-194778-8 (student book : bk. 3 : alk. paper) —
ISBN 0-13-194784-2 (student book : bk. 4 : alk. paper) 1. English language—Textbooks for foreign speakers. 2. English
language—Grammar—Problems, exercises, etc. 3. Vocabulary
—Problems, exercises, etc. 4. Life skills—United States. I. Bonesteel,
Lynn. II. Eckstut-Didier, Samuela. III. Title. PE1128.F67425 2007
428.2'4—dc22

                                    2006014957

ISBN: 978-0-13-194778-8; 0-13-194778-8

Printed in the United States of America

4 5 6 7 8 9 10-QWD-12 11 10 09

Acknowledgments

We would like to thank everyone at Pearson Longman for the time and effort they have put into seeing this project through. Specifically, we would like to thank our editors, Andrea Bryant, Julie Schmidt, and Kim Steiner, for their attention to detail and their insights; to Rhea Banker, for her considerable contributions to the design and visual appeal of the series; and to Laura Le Dréan, for her commitment to every phase of this complex project. Most importantly, we are grateful to Claudia and Robert for their support and encouragement and for always reminding us of the other worlds out there.

Lynn Bonesteel and Sammi Eckstut-Didier,
authors of Student Books 2, 3, and 4

The publisher would like to extend special thanks to MaryAnn Florez and Sharon Seymour, our Series Consultants, and to the following individuals who reviewed the *Center Stage* program and whose comments were instrumental in shaping this series.

Ruth Afifi, Fresno Adult School, Fresno, CA; **Janet L. Barker**, Tarrant Community College, Fort Worth, TX; **Sarah Barnhardt**, Community College of Baltimore County, Baltimore, MD; **Janet Bryant**, Truman College, Chicago, IL; **Rachel Burns**, New England School of English, Cambridge, MA; **Debby Cargill**, Prince William County Public Schools, Manassas, VA; **Veronique Colas**, Los Angeles Technology Center, Los Angeles, CA; **Dave Coleman**, Belmont Community Adult School, Los Angeles, CA; **Eleanor Comegys**, Los Angeles Community Adult School, Los Angeles, CA; **Ludmila Ellis**, Dutchess Community College, Poughkeepsie, NY; **Liz Flynn**, Centers for Education and Technology, San Diego, CA; **Gayle Forgey**, Garden Grove Unified School District, Lincoln Education Center, Garden Grove, CA; **Stephanie Garcia**, Gwinnett Technical College, Lawrenceville, GA; **Jennifer Gaudet**, Santa Ana College, Santa Ana, CA; **Sally Gearhart**, Santa Rosa Junior College, Santa Rosa, CA; **Jeanne Gibson**, Colorado State University, Pueblo, CO; **Anthony Halderman**, Cuesta College, San Luis Obispo, CA; **Cam Tu Huynh**, Banning Adult Learning Center, Los Angeles Unified School District, Los Angeles, CA; **Iordana Iordanova**, Triton College, River Grove, IL; **Mary Jane Jerde**, Price George's County Adult Education and Howard Community College, Bladensburg, MD; **Britt Johnson**, Albany Park Community Center, Chicago, IL; **Kathleen Krokar**, Truman College, Chicago, IL; **Xay Lee**, Fresno Adult School, Fresno, CA; **Sarah Lynn**, Somerville Community Adult Learning Experiences, Somerville, MA; **Ronna Magy**, Division of Adult and Career Education, LAUSD, Los Angeles, CA; **Dr. Suzanne Medina**, California State University, Carson, CA; **Dr. Diana Mora**, Fresno Adult School, Fresno, CA; **Jenny Moreno**, LAUSD, Los Angeles, CA; Meg Morris, Los Altos Adult Education, Mount View, CA; **John Nelson, Ph.D.**, Co-Director ESOL MA Program, University of Maryland, Baltimore County, MD; **Robert Osgood**, Westchester Community College, Valhalla, NY; **Judie Plumb**, Gwinnett Technical College, Lawrenceville, GA; **Barbara Pongsrikul**, Cesar Chavez Campus, San Diego, CA; Dr. Yilin Sun, Seattle Central Community College, Seattle, WA; **Alisa Takeuchi**, Garden Grove Adult Education, Chapman Education Center, Garden Grove, CA; **Garnet Templin-Imel**, Bellevue Community College, Bellevue, WA; **Lay Kuan Toh**, Westchester Community College, Valhalla, NY; **Marcos Valle**, Edmonds Community College, Edmonds, WA; **Carol van Duzer**, Center for Adult English Language Acquisition, Center for Applied Linguistics, Washington, DC; **Michele Volz**, Centennial Education Center, Santa Ana, CA; **Merari Weber**, Glendale Community College, Los Angeles, CA.

Scope and Sequence

Writing	Critical Thinking	CASAS	LAUSD Intermediate Low	FL. Adult ESOL Low Intermediate
Writing Tip: Use pronouns to avoid repeating nouns Prewriting: Answer questions Write a paragraph about making friends	Interpret a descriptive passage on an unfamiliar topic Utilize prior knowledge to analyze a text Infer word meaning from context Draw logical conclusions Support personal opinion with reasoning	0.1.2, 0.1.4, 0.2.1, 0.2.4	Competencies: 1, 3, 6, 48 Grammar: 1, 2a Language Skill Proficiencies: L: 1, 2, 5, 6; S: 1; R: 1; W: 5	4.05.01, 4.05.02, 4.14.02, 4.15.01, 4.15.03, 4.16.01, 4.16.02, 4.16.03, 4.16.04, 4.16.05, 4.16.06, 4.16.07, 4.16.08, 4.17.02, 4.17.03, 4.17.05
Writing Tip: Use correct subject-verb agreement Prewriting: Take notes Write a paragraph about a city you know	Make inferences from charts, maps, and illustrations Analyze and interpret population statistics Evaluate advantages and disadvantages Infer word meaning from context	0.1.2, 0.1.4, 0.2.1, 0.2.4, 2.6.1, 2.7.3, 5.6.1, 7.2.1	Competencies: 1, 3, 6 Grammar: 1, 24, 25e Language Skill Proficiencies: L: 1, 2, 5, 6; S: 1; R: 4; W: 5	4.05.01, 4.12.01, 4.13.01, 4.15.01, 4.15.02, 4.15.03, 4.15.06, 4.16.01, 4.16.02, 4.16.03, 4.16.04, 4.16.05, 4.16.06, 4.16.07, 4.16.08, 4.17.02, 4.17.03, 4.17.05
Writing Tip: Use commas with time clauses Prewriting: Use facts Write a paragraph about the history of a sport	Infer word meaning from context Support personal opinion with information from the text Hypothesize scenarios	0.1.2, 0.1.4, 0.1.6, 0.2.1, 0.2.4, 2.6.1	Competencies: 1, 3, 4, 6, 7 Grammar: 1, 5a, 22a, 22b Language Skill Proficiencies: L: 1, 2, 5, 6; S: 1, 2, 4, 7, 8; R: 1; W: 2, 5	4.05.01, 4.05.03, 4.15.01, 4.15.02, 4.15.03, 4.15.08, 4.16.01, 4.16.02, 4.16.03, 4.16.04, 4.16.05, 4.16.06, 4.16.07, 4.16.08, 4.17.02, 4.17.03, 4.17.04, 4.17.05
Writing Tip: Use different tenses to show when things happen Prewriting: Visualize Write a paragraph about an incredible or surprising event	Interpret and analyze diagrams Infer word meaning from context Compare and contrast different kinds of experiences	0.1.2, 0.1.4, 0.1.6, 0.2.1, 0.2.4, 8.2.3, 8.2.4	Competencies: 1, 2, 4, 7, 34, 35 Grammar: 5a, 6a, 6b, 22b Language Skill Proficiencies: L: 1, 2, 5, 6; S: 1, 2, 4, 7, 8; R: 1, 3; W: 2, 5	4.05.01, 4.05.03, 4.15.01, 4.15.02, 4.15.03, 4.15.08, 4.16.01, 4.16.02, 4.16.03, 4.16.04, 4.16.05, 4.16.06, 4.16.07, 4.16.08, 4.17.02, 4.17.03, 4.17.04, 4.17.05
List, prioritize, and organize ideas Writing Tip: Use and and or with verb clauses Prewriting: Use an outline Write a paragraph about the way something used to be and the way it is now	Compare and contrast different kinds of past experiences Compare and contrast customs in the present and the past Hypothesize past customs Evaluate changes in society Develop arguments Identify personal values and assumptions Interpret illustrations	0.1.2, 0.1.3, 0.1.4, 0.1.6, 0.2.1, 0.2.4, 1.7.4, 2.6.1, 3.5.7, 5.1.5, 5.1.6, 8.1.1, 8.1.4, 8.2.1, 8.2.2, 8.2.3, 8.2.4	Competencies: 1, 3, 6, 7, 50, 51 Grammar: 5a, 5b Language Skill Proficiencies: L: 1, 2, 5, 6; S: 1, 2, 4, 7, 8; R: 1, 2, 3, 4; W: 2, 5	4.05.01, 4.05.03, 4.07.02, 4.07.06, 4.14.04, 4.15.01, 4.15.02, 4.15.03, 4.15.08, 4.16.01, 4.16.02, 4.16.03, 4.16.04, 4.16.05, 4.16.06, 4.16.07, 4.16.08, 4.17.02, 4.17.03, 4.17.04, 4.17.05

Unit	Grammar	Listening	Speaking	Reading
6 **Busy Lives** Page 72	Future: *Will* for Decisions and Promises Future: *Be going to* and *Will* Future: Present Progressive for Future Arrangements	Listen to a conversation about busy lives Listen to conversations about everyday situations / activities Listen for main topics Listen for details	Talk about helping someone Talk about plans Ask and answer questions about schedules Ask and answer personal information questions Engage in small talk	Read a calendar Read an article about personal assistants Reading skill: Understand pronouns
7 **Education** Page 86	Future: *If* Clauses for Possibility Future: Time Clauses Future: *May* and *Might* for Possibility	Listen to a conversation between a teacher and a parent Listen to a comparison between the ideas of two mayoral candidates Understand the basic functions of local government Listen for main ideas Listen for details	Tell a story Work with peers to share information and solve problems Talk about future plans Talk about long-term and short-term goals Understand school structure and grading systems Understand how to communicate with school personnel	Understand authentic forms and applications Read a checklist Read an article about raising bilingual children Reading skill: Guess meaning from context
8 **Getting a Job** Page 100	Present Perfect: Regular Verbs Present Perfect: Irregular Verbs Present Perfect: *Yes / No* Questions	Listen to a conversation about jobs Listen to a conversation between an employer and a job applicant Identify relationships from context Understand how to inquire about jobs and participate in interviews Understand workplace communication	Ask and answer questions about jobs Talk about skills, personal qualities, and accomplishments Discuss job qualifications Ask and answer typical job interview questions Understand appropriate interview behavior	Read a classified ad Read an article about mystery shoppers Identify the main topic Understand time order Reading skill: Identify the main topic
9 **Relationships** Page 114	Present Perfect: *For* and *Since* Present Perfect Progressive: *For* and *Since* Present Perfect Progressive: Questions	Listen to a conversation about newlyweds Listen to a radio talk show about relationships Identify relationships from context Listen for details	Talk about family and friends Ask and answer personal information questions Engage in small talk Express opinions Work with peers to share information and solve problems	Read an article about China's one-child policy Reading skill: Scan for specific information
10 **Television** Page 128	Adverbs and Adjectives Adverbs of Manner Adverbs of Degree	Listen to a conversation from a soap opera Listen to scenes from different TV shows Identify location from context Listen for details Make inferences about speakers' emotions	Describe television shows Describe people Ask and answer questions Express opinions Work with peers to share information and solve problems	Read an article about telenovelas Reading skill: Understand examples

Writing	Critical Thinking	CASAS	LAUSD Intermediate Low	FL. Adult ESOL Low Intermediate
Writing Tip: Use *and* with verb clauses Prewriting: Answer information questions Write a paragraph about future plans	Infer information not explicit in the text Hypothesize scenarios Evaluate and classify information Interpret charts and illustrations Compare and contrast schedules	0.1.2, 0.1.3, 0.1.4, 0.1.6, 0.2.1, 0.2.4, 2.1.8, 2.3.1, 2.6.1, 2.7.3, 3.5.7, 7.1.1, 7.1.2, 7.1.4, 7.2.3, 7.2.5, 7.2.6	Competencies: 1, 3, 4, 5, 6, 7, 51 Grammar: 2b, 3, 9, 25e Language Skill Proficiencies: **L:** 1, 2, 3, 5, 6; **S:** 1, 2, 3, 4, 7, 8; **R:** 1, 2, 3, 4, 6; **W:** 2, 5	4.01.02, 4.05.01, 4.05.03, 4.05.04, 4.06.02, 4.08.01, 4.14.04, 4.15.01, 4.15.02, 4.15.03, 4.15.08, 4.16.01, 4.16.02, 4.16.03, 4.16.04, 4.16.05, 4.16.06, 4.16.07, 4.16.08, 4.17.02, 4.17.03, 4.17.04, 4.17.05
Writing Tip: Use correct tenses with time clauses Prewriting: Take notes Write a paragraph about learning a new language	Interpret illustrations, lists, and forms Infer information not explicit in the text Classify information Draw conclusions Hypothesize scenarios Support personal opinion with reasoning	0.1.2, 0.1.3, 0.1.4, 0.1.5, 0.1.6, 0.2.1, 0.2.2, 0.2.4, 2.1.7, 2.1.8, 2.5.5, 4.1.8, 4.1.9, 4.4.1, 7.1.1, 7.1.2, 7.1.3, 7.4.1, 7.5.1	Competencies: 1, 3, 4, 5, 6, 7, 9, 10, 12a, 12b, 12c, 48, 54, 57, 59, 60, 64 Grammar: 3, 4, 17, 22a Language Skill Proficiencies: **L:** 1, 2, 3, 5, 6; **S:** 1, 2, 3, 4, 7, 8; **R:** 1, 2, 3, 4, 6; **W:** 2, 4, 5	4.01.03, 4.01.02, 4.03.02, 4.05.01, 4.05.02, 4.06.02, 4.14.01, 4.14.02, 4.14.04, 4.15.01, 4.15.02, 4.15.03, 4.15.08, 4.16.01, 4.16.02, 4.16.03, 4.16.04, 4.16.05, 4.16.06, 4.16.07, 4.16.08, 4.17.02, 4.17.03, 4.17.04, 4.17.05
Writing Tip: Use business letter format Prewriting: Answer questions Write a formal letter of complaint	Interpret illustrations, advertisements, and charts Classify and order information Compare and contrast past experiences and accomplishments Hypothesize scenarios	0.1.2, 0.1.3, 0.1.4, 0.1.6, 0.2.1, 0.2.4, 2.4.1, 4.1.2, 4.1.3, 4.1.4, 4.1.5, 4.1.6, 4.1.7, 4.1.8, 4.1.9, 4.4.1, 4.4.2, 4.4.5, 4.4.6, 4.4.7, 7.1.1, 7.1.2, 7.2.1, 7.2.2, 7.3.1	Competencies: 1, 3, 4, 5, 6, 7, 9, 42, 43, 44, 46, 47, 48, 51, 52 Grammar: 1, 5a, 7a, 7b, 7d Language Skill Proficiencies: **L:** 1, 2, 3, 4, 5, 6; **S:** 1, 2, 3, 4, 7, 8; **R:** 1, 2, 3, 4, 5; **W:** 2, 4, 5	4.01.01, 4.01.02, 4.01.03, 4.01.04, 4.01.06, 4.02.01, 4.02.02, 4.02.05, 4.03.01, 4.03.02, 4.03.03, 4.05.01, 4.05.02, 4.05.03, 4.15.01, 4.15.02, 4.15.03, 4.15.08, 4.15.12, 4.15.13, 4.16.01, 4.16.02, 4.16.03, 4.16.04, 4.16.05, 4.16.06, 4.16.07, 4.16.08, 4.17.02, 4.17.03, 4.17.04, 4.17.05
Writing Tip: Use linking words to connect ideas Prewriting: List reasons Write a paragraph about a recent change in people's lifestyle in your country	Infer information not explicit in the text Draw logical conclusions Interpret illustrations Compare and contrast personal experiences Hypothesize scenarios Support personal opinions with examples	0.1.2, 0.1.3, 0.1.4, 0.1.6, 0.2.1, 0.2.4, 3.5.7, 3.5.8, 3.5.9, 7.2.2, 7.2.3, 7.2.5, 7.2.7, 7.3.1, 7.3.2, 7.3.3, 7.5.1, 7.5.2, 7.5.5, 7.5.7	Competencies: 1, 3, 4, 5, 6, 7, 9, 50, 51, 52 Grammar: 1, 2, 7a, 7b, 7d, 8a, 29 Language Skill Proficiencies: **L:** 1, 2, 5, 6; **S:** 1, 2, 3, 6, 7, 8; **R:** 1, 2, 3; **W:** 2, 5	4.05.01, 4.05.02, 4.05.03, 4.05.04, 4.15.01, 4.15.02, 4.15.03, 4.15.08, 4.15.13, 4.16.01, 4.16.02, 4.16.03, 4.16.04, 4.16.05, 4.16.06, 4.16.07, 4.16.08, 4.17.02, 4.17.03, 4.17.04, 4.17.05
Write a scene from a TV show List, prioritize, and organize ideas Writing Tip: Use examples to explain main points Prewriting: Use examples Write a paragraph about an effect of TV	Support personal opinions with examples Compare and contrast television shows Hypothesize emotions of speakers Hypothesize scenarios Analyze and describe characters in a story	0.1.2, 0.1.3, 0.1.4, 0.1.6, 0.2.1, 0.2.4, 2.6.1, 2.7.2, 2.7.3, 2.7.6, 3.5.8, 7.2.1, 7.2.2, 7.2.3, 7.4.1, 7.4.2	Competencies: 1, 3, 6, 7, 48, 50, 52 Grammar: 1, 2, 5a, 26b, 26d, 29 Language Skill Proficiencies: **L:** 1, 2, 5; **S:** 1, 2, 4, 7, 8; **R:** 1, 2, 6, 7; **W:** 1, 2, 5	4.05.01, 4.05.03, 4.15.01, 4.15.02, 4.15.03, 4.15.08, 4.15.13, 4.16.01, 4.16.02, 4.16.03, 4.16.04, 4.16.05, 4.16.06, 4.16.07, 4.16.08, 4.17.02, 4.17.03, 4.17.04, 4.17.05

Unit	Grammar	Listening	Speaking	Reading
11 **The Animal Kingdom** Page 142	Comparative and Superlative of Adjectives and Adverbs Comparative and Superlative of Nouns Equatives	Listen to a conversation about pets Listen to an interview comparing wild animals Make inferences Understand requests for clarifications Listen for numbers	Compare animals Ask and answer questions about animals Understand common sayings / expressions Compare and contrast information in order to express opinions	Understand time order Read signs Read an article about wolves and dogs Reading skill: Recognize similarities and differences
12 **Let's Eat!** Page 156	Reflexive Pronouns *One / Ones* *Other*: Singular and Plural	Listen to people ordering food in a restaurant Listen to a report about fast-food restaurants Make inferences about speakers' emotions Understand how to make requests and offers Understand appropriate restaurant behavior Listen for main ideas Listen for details	Compare food customs Ask and answer questions about food-related habits Identify and describe places Make inferences about new vocabulary Work with peers to share information and solve problems Ask for and give oral directions to places	Read charts Read an article about Slow Food Reading skill: Recognize conclusions
13 **Technology** Page 170	*Can* and *Be able to* *Could* and *Be able to* *Will be able to*	Listen to a technician assisting a customer Listen to a speech about "concept car" technology Listen for details Understand how to make requests and offer help Use clarification strategies to check for understanding and ask for meaning Understand a sequence of instructions	Talk about technology-related abilities Compare past and present daily routines Make predictions about future events and capabilities Express opinions	Read advertisements Read an article about radio frequency technology Reading skill: Skim
14 **A Kid's Life** Page 184	*Have to / Have got to / Must*: Affirmative Statements and *Have to*: Yes / No Questions *Does not have to* and *Must not* *Had to*: Statements and Questions	Listen to a conversation about family obligations Listen to a report comparing American and Japanese children Understand child rearing practices and parenting skills Listen for details Listen for main ideas	Compare school customs Understand the American school system Talk about appropriate behavior for children Talk about appropriate classroom behavior Talk about safety and emergency procedures Express opinions	Skim Read notes Read a letter to the editor about academic performance Reading skill: Recognize point of view
15 **Manners** Page 198	*Should (not)* + Verb *Should (not)* + *Be* + Present Participle *Should* and *Have to*	Listen to a mother give instructions to her son Listen to a report about table manners around the world Understand child rearing practices and parenting skills Listen for details	Talk about appropriate behavior Compare polite and impolite behavior in different countries Give and respond to advice Express opinions Make offers	Preview / Scan Understand appropriate behavior for different jobs Read an article about business etiquette Reading skill: Recognize supporting details

Writing	Critical Thinking	CASAS	LAUSD Intermediate Low	FL. Adult ESOL Low Intermediate
Writing Tip: Use *like* and *both* to compare two things Prewriting: Use a Venn diagram Write a paragraph comparing and contrasting two animals	Interpret illustrations and forms Infer information not explicit in the text Compare and contrast common expressions in different cultures Infer word meaning from context	0.1.2, 0.1.3, 0.1.4, 0.1.6, 0.2.1, 0.2.4, 2.6.1, 2.6.3, 6.0.1, 6.9.2, 7.2.1, 7.2.2, 7.2.3, 7.2.4, 7.2.5, 7.4.2, 7.4.4	Competencies: 1, 3, 4, 5, 6, 7, 49, 50, 51, 52 Grammar: 1, 23a, 23b Language Skill Proficiencies: **L:** 1, 2, 5, 6, 7; **S:** 1, 2, 4, 6, 7, 8; **R:** 1, 2, 3, 4, 6, 7; **W:** 1, 2, 5	4.05.01, 4.05.03, 4.05.04, 4.15.01, 4.15.02, 4.15.03, 4.15.08, 4.15.12, 4.15.13, 4.16.01, 4.16.02, 4.16.03, 4.16.04, 4.16.05, 4.16.06, 4.16.07, 4.16.08, 4.17.02, 4.17.03, 4.17.04, 4.17.05
Writing Tip: Use *in conclusion* and *to sum up* for conclusions Prewriting: List reasons Write a paragraph about food preferences	Interpret illustrations Infer information not explicit in the text Classify information Compare and contrast eating customs Infer word meaning from context Support personal opinions with examples	0.1.2, 0.1.3, 0.1.4, 0.1.6, 0.2.1, 0.2.4, 2.6.4, 2.7.2, 2.7.3, 3.5.2, 3.5.8, 3.5.9, 7.2.1, 7.2.2, 7.2.3, 7.2.4, 7.2.5, 8.1.3, 8.2.1	Competencies: 1, 3, 4, 5, 6, 7, 49, 50, 51, 52 Grammar: 1, 9, 25c, 25d Language Skill Proficiencies: **L:** 1, 2, 5, 6, 7; **S:** 1, 2, 4, 6, 7, 8; **R:** 1, 2, 4, 6, 7; **W:** 2, 5	4.05.01, 4.05.03, 4.05.04, 4.07.06, 4.11.03, 4.15.01, 4.15.02, 4.15.03, 4.15.08, 4.15.12, 4.15.13, 4.16.01, 4.16.02, 4.16.03, 4.16.04, 4.16.05, 4.16.06, 4.16.07, 4.16.08, 4.17.02, 4.17.03, 4.17.04, 4.17.05
List, prioritize, and organize ideas Writing Tip: Use time expressions Prewriting: Use a timeline Write a paragraph about a technology and how it has changed over the years	Interpret illustrations Support personal opinions with examples Hypothesize past and future customs and technological changes Evaluate technology-based changes in society	0.1.2, 0.1.3, 0.1.4, 0.1.6, 0.2.1, 0.2.4, 1.2.5, 1.7.3, 4.5.1, 7.2.1, 7.2.2, 7.2.3, 7.2.4, 7.2.5	Competencies: 1, 2, 3, 5, 6, 7, 49, 50, 51, 52, 53 Grammar: 1, 5a, 15, 28 Language Skill Proficiencies: **L:** 1, 2, 5, 6, 7; **S:** 1, 2, 4, 6, 7, 8; **R:** 1, 2, 3, 4, 6, 7; **W:** 2, 5	4.04.01, 4.05.01, 4.06.01, 4.15.01, 4.15.02, 4.15.03, 4.15.08, 4.15.12, 4.15.13, 4.16.01, 4.16.02, 4.16.03, 4.16.04, 4.16.05, 4.16.06, 4.16.07, 4.16.08, 4.17.02, 4.17.03, 4.17.04, 4.17.05
List, prioritize, and organize ideas Writing Tip: Use *the point is, in my opinion,* and *as I see it* to express point of view Prewriting: Brainstorm Write a letter about a community problem	Interpret illustrations and charts Infer information not explicit in the text Classify information Support personal opinions with examples Hypothesize and identify point of view in a text Develop arguments for or against an issue	0.1.1, 0.1.2, 0.1.3, 0.1.4, 0.1.5, 0.1.6, 0.2.1, 0.2.3, 0.2.4, 2.7.2, 2.7.3, 3.4.2, 3.5.2, 3.5.7, 3.5.8, 3.5.9, 4.6.1, 5.6.1, 7.2.1, 7.2.2, 7.2.3, 7.2.4, 7.2.5, 7.3.1, 7.3.2, 7.3.3, 7.3.4, 8.2.1, 8.2.2, 8.2.3	Competencies: 1, 3, 4, 5, 6, 7, 9, 10, 12c, 49, 50, 51, 52, 59, 64 Grammar: 1, 5a, 10a, 10b, 10c, 11 Language Skill Proficiencies: **L:** 1, 2, 5, 6, 7; **S:** 1, 2, 4, 6, 7, 8; **R:** 1, 2, 3, 4, 6, 7; **W:** 1, 2, 4, 5	4.03.02, 4.03.04, 4.05.01, 4.05.02, 4.05.03, 4.05.04, 4.07.06, 4.09.06, 4.13.03, 4.14.04, 4.15.01, 4.15.02, 4.15.03, 4.15.08, 4.15.12, 4.15.13, 4.16.01, 4.16.02, 4.16.03, 4.16.04, 4.16.05, 4.16.06, 4.16.07, 4.16.08, 4.17.02, 4.17.03, 4.17.04, 4.17.05
Writing Tip: Use words like *in fact* and *for example* to identify supporting details Prewriting: Use an outline Write a paragraph about business etiquette in your country	Compare and contrast polite and impolite behavior Evaluate statements Infer information not explicit in the text Support personal opinion with information from the text Hypothesize scenarios	0.1.1, 0.1.2, 0.1.3, 0.1.4, 0.1.5, 0.1.6, 0.2.1, 0.2.4, 2.7.2, 2.7.3, 3.5.5, 3.5.7, 3.5.8, 3.5.9, 4.4.1, 4.6.1, 4.8.2, 4.8.6, 4.8.7, 7.1.1, 7.2.2, 7.2.3, 7.3.1, 7.5.1, 7.5.2, 7.5.6, 8.1.1, 8.1.2, 8.1.3, 8.1.4	Competencies: 1, 3, 4, 5, 6, 7, 16, 49, 50, 51, 52, 64 Grammar: 1, 9, 11, 12, 22a Language Skill Proficiencies: **L:** 1, 2, 5, 6, 7; **S:** 1, 2, 4, 6, 7, 8; **R:** 1, 2, 3, 4, 6, 7; **W:** 1 ,2, 5	4.01.01, 4.01.02, 4.03.04, 4.05.01, 4.05.03, 4.05.04, 4.07.02, 4.14.04, 4.15.01, 4.15.02, 4.15.03, 4.15.08, 4.15.12, 4.15.13, 4.16.01, 4.16.02, 4.16.03, 4.16.04, 4.16.05, 4.16.06, 4.16.07, 4.16.08, 4.17.02, 4.17.03, 4.17.04, 4.17.05

x   Scope and Sequence

Writing	Critical Thinking	CASAS	LAUSD Intermediate Low	FL. Adult ESOL Low Intermediate
Writing Tip: Use questions to get reader's attention Prewriting: Use questions Write a paragraph about a problem in your country and a possible solution	Draw logical conclusions Hypothesize scenarios Compare and contrast past experiences Infer word meaning from context Evaluate the quality of arguments Identify problems and propose solutions	0.1.1, 0.1.2, 0.1.3, 0.1.4, 0.1.5, 0.1.6, 0.2.1, 0.2.4, 2.7.3, 3.5.7, 3.5.8, 3.5.9, 4.1.8, 4.4.1, 4.6.1, 5.6.1, 7.2.2, 7.2.3, 7.2.4, 7.2.5, 7.2.6, 7.3.1, 7.3.2, 7.5.4, 7.5.5, 7.5.6, 8.2.5, 8.2.6	Competencies: 1, 2, 3, 4, 5, 6, 7, 49, 50, 51, 52 Grammar: 1, 2a, 8a, 18 Language Skill Proficiencies: L: 1, 2, 5, 6, 7; S: 1, 2, 4, 6, 7, 8; R: 1, 2, 3, 4, 6, 7; W: 1, 2, 5	4.01.01, 4.01.03, 4.02.04, 4.05.01, 4.05.03, 4.05.04, 4.11.08, 4.13.03, 4.14.04, 4.15.01, 4.15.02, 4.15.03, 4.15.08, 4.15.12, 4.15.13, 4.16.01, 4.16.02, 4.16.03, 4.16.04, 4.16.05, 4.16.06, 4.16.07, 4.16.08, 4.17.02, 4.17.03, 4.17.04, 4.17.05
Writing Tip: Use synonyms to make your writing more interesting Prewriting: Use a cluster Write a paragraph about a common health myth in your country	Interpret illustrations and posters Compare and contrast health advice Compare and contrast past experiences and personal habits Hypothesize appropriate health advice for different groups Infer information not explicit in the text Draw logical conclusions Infer word meaning from context	0.1.1, 0.1.2, 0.1.3, 0.1.4, 0.1.6, 0.2.1, 0.2.4, 1.2.1, 1.3.8, 1.6.1, 2.6.4, 2.7.2, 2.7.3, 3.1.1, 3.1.2, 3.1.3, 3.2.3, 3.5.11, 3.5.2, 3.5.4, 3.5.5, 3.5.7, 3.5.8, 3.5.9, 4.6.1, 4.8.7, 7.1.1, 7.1.2, 7.1.3, 7.2.1, 7.2.2, 7.2.3, 7.2.4, 7.2.5, 7.2.6, 7.3.1, 7.3.2, 7.4.2, 7.5.2, 7.5.4, 7.5.5, 8.1.1, 8.2.1, 8.3.1, 8.3.2	Competencies: 1, 3, 4, 5, 6, 7, 36, 37, 38, 39, 49, 50, 51, 52 Grammar: 1, 5a, 5b, 9, 10a, 12, 20a, 20d Language Skill Proficiencies: L: 1, 2, 5, 6, 7; S: 1, 2, 4, 6, 7, 8; R: 1, 2, 3, 4, 6, 7; W: 1, 2, 5	4.02.03, 4.02.04, 4.02.05, 4.05.01, 4.05.02, 4.05.03, 4.05.04, 4.07.01, 4.07.02, 4.07.03, 4.07.06, 4.11.12, 4.14.04, 4.15.01, 4.15.02, 4.15.03, 4.15.08, 4.15.12, 4.15.13, 4.16.01, 4.16.02, 4.16.03, 4.16.04, 4.16.05, 4.16.06, 4.16.07, 4.16.08, 4.17.02, 4.17.03, 4.17.04, 4.17.05
List, prioritize, and organize ideas Writing Tip: Use logical order Prewriting: Use an outline Write a paragraph about a free-time activity	Interpret illustrations and charts Draw logical conclusions Compare and contrast personal experiences and interests Infer word meaning from context Support personal opinions with examples	0.1.1, 0.1.2, 0.1.3, 0.1.4, 0.1.6, 0.2.1, 0.2.2, 0.2.4, 2.6.1, 2.6.3, 2.7.2, 2.7.3, 3.5.8, 3.5.9, 7.2.1, 7.2.2, 7.2.3, 7.2.4, 7.2.5, 7.5.1	Competencies: 1, 3, 4, 5, 6, 7, 49, 50, 51, 52 Grammar: 1, 2, 5a, 19a, 19b, 20b, 20c, 23a, 28 Language Skill Proficiencies: L: 1, 2, 5, 6, 7; S: 1, 2, 4, 6, 7, 8; R: 1, 2, 3, 4, 6, 7; W: 1, 2, 5	4.05.01, 4.05.02, 4.05.03, 4.05.04, 4.15.01, 4.15.02, 4.15.03, 4.15.08, 4.15.12, 4.15.13, 4.16.01, 4.16.02, 4.16.03, 4.16.04, 4.16.05, 4.16.06, 4.16.07, 4.16.08, 4.17.02, 4.17.03, 4.17.04, 4.17.05
Writing Tip: Use examples when giving advice Prewriting: Use examples Write a paragraph about advice that experts give	Interpret illustrations Infer information not explicit in the text Hypothesize scenarios Support personal opinion with examples Identify problems and propose solutions	0.1.1, 0.1.2, 0.1.3, 0.1.4, 0.1.5, 0.1.6, 0.2.1, 0.2.2, 0.2.3, 0.2.4, 1.9.7, 2.1.2, 2.5.1, 2.7.2, 2.7.3, 3.4.2, 5.3.5, 5.3.7, 5.3.8, 5.5.6, 5.6.1, 7.2.1, 7.2.2, 7.2.3, 7.2.4, 7.2.5, 7.2.6, 7.2.7, 7.3.1, 7.3.2, 7.3.3, 7.3.4, 8.3.2	Competencies: 1, 3, 4, 5, 6, 7, 34, 35, 49, 50, 51, 52, 53 Grammar: 1, 5a, 6a, 9, 12, 20e, 21a, 21b Language Skill Proficiencies: L: 1, 2, 5, 6, 7; S: 1, 2, 4, 6, 7, 8; R: 1, 2, 3, 4, 6, 7; W: 1, 2, 5	4.05.01, 4.05.02, 4.05.03, 4.05.04, 4.06.03, 4.09.05, 4.09.06, 4.10.01, 4.10.02, 4.15.01, 4.15.02, 4.15.03, 4.15.08, 4.15.12, 4.15.13, 4.16.01, 4.16.02, 4.16.03, 4.16.04, 4.16.05, 4.16.06, 4.16.07, 4.16.08, 4.17.02, 4.17.03, 4.17.04, 4.17.05
List, prioritize, and organize ideas Writing Tip: Use quoted and reported speech Prewriting: Use quoted and reported speech Write a paragraph about a funny or interesting travel story	Interpret illustrations and charts Infer information not explicit in the text Hypothesize scenarios Compare and contrast past travel experiences	0.1.1, 0.1.2, 0.1.3, 0.1.4, 0.1.5, 0.1.6, 0.2.1, 0.2.4, 1.2.5, 2.6.1, 2.6.3, 3.4.2, 3.5.8, 4.8.3, 7.4.4, 7.5.6, 8.3.2	Competencies: 1, 3, 4, 5, 6, 7, 22 Grammar: 1, 2a, 5a, 9 Language Skill Proficiencies: L: 1, 2, 5, 6, 7; S: 1, 2, 4, 6, 7, 8; R: 1, 2, 3, 4, 6, 7; W: 1, 2, 5	4.05.01, 4.05.03, 4.05.04, 4.09.03, 4.09.04, 4.09.05, 4.15.01, 4.15.02, 4.15.03, 4.15.08, 4.15.12, 4.15.13, 4.16.01, 4.16.02, 4.16.03, 4.16.04, 4.16.05, 4.16.06, 4.16.07, 4.16.08, 4.17.02, 4.17.03, 4.17.04, 4.17.05

To the Teacher

Center Stage is a four-level, four-skills course that supports student learning and achievement in everyday work and life situations. Practical language and timely topics motivate adult students to master grammar along with speaking, listening, reading, and writing skills.

Features

- *Grammar to Communicate* presents key grammar points with concise charts and abundant practice in real-life situations.

- **Communicative activities**, such as *Time to Talk*, promote opportunities for meaningful expression and active learning.

- Extensive **listening** practice helps students to succeed in their daily lives.

- *Reading* and *Writing* lessons develop essential academic skills and provide real-life models, tasks, and practice.

- *Review and Challenge* helps teachers to assess students' progress and meet the needs of multi-level classrooms.

- Easy-to-follow, **two-page lessons** give students a sense of accomplishment.

Additional Components

- The **Teacher's Edition** includes unit tests, multi-level strategies, learner persistence tips, expansion activities, culture, grammar and language notes, and answer keys.

- A **Teacher's Resource Disk**, in the back of the Teacher's Edition, offers numerous worksheets for supplementary grammar practice, supplementary vocabulary practice, graphic organizers, and learner persistence.

- **Color transparencies** provide an ideal resource for introducing, practicing, and reviewing vocabulary.

- The **Audio Program** contains recordings for all listening activities in the Student Book.

- The *ExamView® Assessment Suite* includes hundreds of test items, providing flexible, comprehensive assessment.

Unit Description

Each of the twenty units centers on a practical theme for the adult learner. A unit consists of 14 pages and is divided into the following lessons: *Vocabulary and Listening, Grammar to Communicate 1, Grammar to Communicate 2, Grammar to Communicate 3, Review and Challenge, Reading,* and *Writing.*

Each lesson is presented on two facing pages and provides clear, self-contained instruction taking approximately 45 to 60 minutes of class time. In some cases, the *Reading* and *Writing* sections may take longer.

Vocabulary and Listening

Each unit opens with an eye-catching illustration that sets the context and presents high frequency, leveled vocabulary that is recycled in the unit and throughout the course. After hearing the new words, students listen to a dialogue related to the unit theme. In the dialogue, students hear the grammar for the unit before it is formally presented. Students listen for meaning and check their comprehension and inference skills in follow-up exercises.

Grammar to Communicate

Each unit has three *Grammar to Communicate* lessons that present target structures in concise charts. Students practice each language point through a variety of exercises that build from controlled to open-ended. Extensive meaningful practice leads students toward mastery.

Look Boxes. *Grammar to Communicate* is often expanded with tips in *Look Boxes*. These tips provide information on usage, common errors, and vocabulary.

Time to Talk. *Grammar to Communicate* culminates with a *Time to Talk* activity. This highly communicative activity gives students the chance to personalize what they have learned.

Review and Challenge

Review and Challenge helps students review the unit material, consolidate their knowledge, and extend their learning with a variety of expansion activities. *Review and Challenge* includes:

Grammar. Students check their understanding of the three grammar lessons of the unit.

Dictation. Students listen to and write five sentences that recycle the language of the unit, giving them the opportunity to check their aural comprehension.

Speaking. Students engage in a speaking activity related to the unit theme. This allows for lively practice as well as reinforcement of instructional material.

Listening. Students listen to realistic material, such as radio interviews and reports. Comprehension exercises check students' understanding of the main idea and details, as well as their ability to make inferences. The listening section ends with a *Time to Talk* activity that calls for students to demonstrate what they have learned as they actively apply the material to their own lives.

Reading

The reading lesson recycles the grammar and vocabulary that have been taught in the unit. In *Getting Ready to Read*, students practice skills such as predicting and skimming before moving on to the reading selection, which is usually a magazine-style article. The selection contains new vocabulary, which is practiced on the facing page in *After You Read*. Following the vocabulary exercise are comprehension questions. A *Reading Skill* box explains the skill being practiced in the unit.

Writing

The writing lesson begins with *Getting Ready to Write*, which features a *Writing Tip* and an exercise. The *Writing Tip* highlights a grammar or an editing point that will be used in the exercise and the *Prewriting* and *Writing* tasks. Following *Getting Ready to Write* is a model paragraph. On the facing page, students will complete a prewriting task, such as filling in an outline or using examples, before they move on to the final writing assignment.

Beyond the Unit

There are a number of supplementary resources in the back of the book.

Grammar Summaries

The grammar summaries are a comprehensive reference for all of the grammar points covered in the units. They provide detailed explanations and helpful examples for students who need more support.

Charts

Information on a variety of usage and grammar points, including spelling, verbs, and pronunciation, is summarized in a series of easy-to-use charts.

Partner Activities

This section includes material students will need to complete several of the *Time to Talk* activities.

Audioscript

The audioscript includes all the recorded material that is not on the student book page.

Standards and Assessment

Standards. Meeting national and state standards is critical to successful adult instruction. *Center Stage 3* clearly integrates material from key grammar and life skills standards. The Scope and Sequence on pages iv–xi links each unit with the corresponding standards.

Assessment. *Center Stage* also includes several assessment tools. Teachers have multiple opportunities for performance-based assessment on productive tasks using the 80 *Time to Talk* communicative activities. In addition, teachers can test student performance in the *Review and Challenge* section. Students have many opportunities for self-assessment in the *Review and Challenge* section.

The testing material for *Center Stage* includes end-of-unit tests found in the *Teacher's Edition*. In addition, the *ExamView® Assessment Suite* includes hundreds of test items for each Student Book.

About the Authors

Lynn Bonesteel has been teaching ESL since 1988. She is currently a full-time senior lecturer at the Center for English Language and Orientation Programs at Boston University Center for English Language and Orientation Programs (CELOP). Ms. Bonesteel is also the author of *Password 3: A Reading and Vocabulary Text*.

Samuela Eckstut-Didier has taught ESL and EFL for over twenty-five years in the United States, Greece, Italy, and England. She currently teaches at Boston University, Center for English Language and Orientation Programs (CELOP). She has authored or co-authored numerous texts for the teaching of English, notably *Strategic Reading 1, 2 and 3*; *What's in a Word? Reading and Vocabulary Building*; *Focus on Grammar Workbook*; *In the Real World*; *First Impressions*; *Beneath the Surface*; *Widely Read*; and *Finishing Touches*.

About the Series Consultants

MaryAnn Florez is the lead ESL Specialist for the Arlington Education and Employment Program (REEP) in Arlington, Virginia where she has program management, curriculum development, and teacher training responsibilities. She has worked with Fairfax County (VA) Adult ESOL and the National Center for ESL Literacy Education (NCLE), and has coordinated a volunteer adult ESL program in Northern Virginia. Ms. Florez has offered workshops throughout the U.S. in areas such as teaching beginning level English language learners, incorporating technology in instruction, strategies for a multi-level classroom, and assessment. Her publications include a variety of research-to-practice briefs and articles on adult ESL education. Ms. Florez holds an M.Ed in Adult Education from George Mason University.

Sharon Seymour is an ESL instructor at City College of San Francisco where she has extensive experience teaching both noncredit adult ESL and credit ESL. She recently completed ten years as chair of the ESL Department at CCSF. She is also currently a co-researcher for a Center for Advancement of Adult Literacy Project on Exemplary Noncredit Community College ESL Programs. Ms. Seymour has been president of CATESOL and a member of the TESOL board of directors and has served both organizations in a variety of capacities. She has served on California Community College Chancellor's Office and California State Department of Education committees relating to ESL curriculum and assessment. Ms. Seymour holds an M.A. in TESOL from San Francisco State University.

Tour of the Program

Welcome to *Center Stage*

Center Stage is a four-level, four-skills course that supports student learning and achievement in everyday work and life situations. Practical language and timely topics motivate adult students to master grammar along with vocabulary, speaking, listening, reading, and writing skills.

Target grammar is clearly defined at the start of the unit.

Students **listen** for general comprehension and details in real-life contexts.

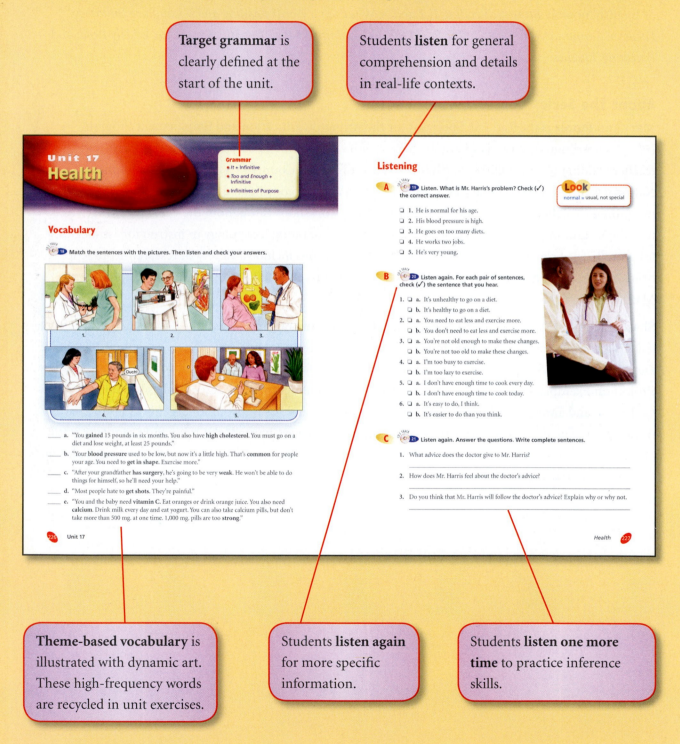

Theme-based vocabulary is illustrated with dynamic art. These high-frequency words are recycled in unit exercises.

Students **listen again** for more specific information.

Students **listen one more time** to practice inference skills.

Each unit has three **Grammar to Communicate** lessons that present the target grammar in a clear and concise chart followed by practice exercises.

Look Boxes expand on the *Grammar to Communicate* charts and include usage information, common errors, and vocabulary notes.

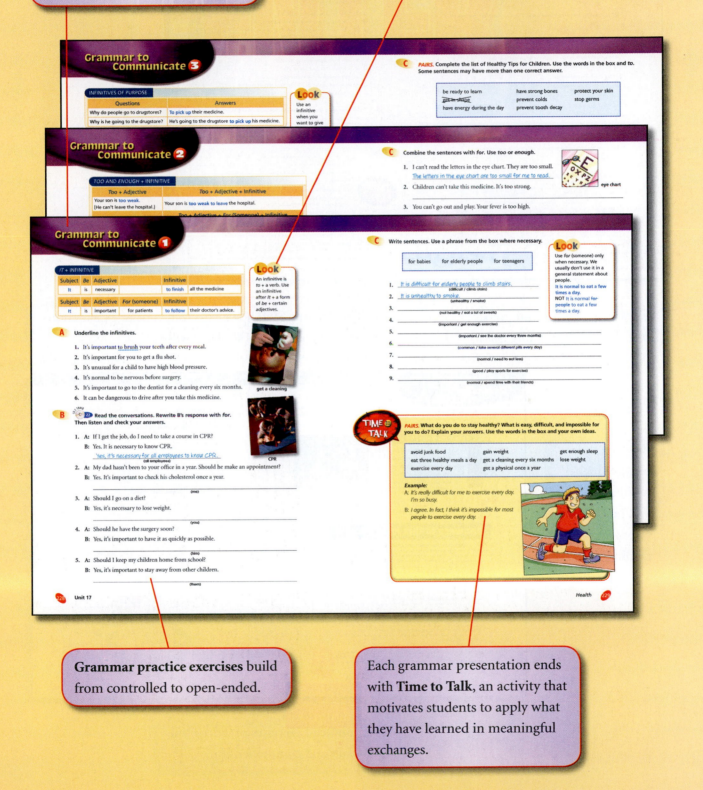

Grammar to Communicate 3

INFINITIVES OF PURPOSE

Questions	Answers
Why do people go to drugstores?	To pick up their medicine.
Why is he going to the drugstore?	He's going to the drugstore to pick up his medicine.

Look
Use an infinitive when you want to give

C *PAIRS.* Complete the list of Healthy Tips for Children. Use the words in the box and *to*. Some sentences may have more than one correct answer.

be ready to learn	have strong bones	protect your skin
get in shape	prevent colds	stop germs
have energy during the day	prevent tooth decay	

Grammar to Communicate 2

TOO AND ENOUGH + INFINITIVE

Too + Adjective	Too + Adjective + Infinitive
Your son is too weak. [He can't leave the hospital.]	Your son is too weak to leave the hospital.

C Combine the sentences with *for*. Use *too* or *enough*.

1. I can't read the letters in the eye chart. They are too small.
   The letters in the eye chart are too small for me to read.

2. Children can't take this medicine. It's too strong.

3. You can't go out and play. Your fever is too high.

eye chart

Grammar to Communicate 1

IT + INFINITIVE

Subject	Be	Adjective		Infinitive	
It	is	necessary		to finish	all the medicine

Subject	Be	Adjective	For (someone)	Infinitive	
It	is	important	for patients	to follow	their doctor's advice.

Look
An infinitive is *to* + a verb. Use an infinitive after *It* + a form of *be* + certain adjectives.

A Underline the infinitives.

1. It's important to brush your teeth after every meal.
2. It's important for you to get a flu shot.
3. It's unusual for a child to have high blood pressure.
4. It's normal to be nervous before surgery.
5. It's important to go to the dentist for a cleaning every six months.
6. It can be dangerous to drive after you take this medicine.

get a cleaning

B Read the conversations. Rewrite B's response with *for*. Then listen and check your answers.

1. A: If I get the job, do I need to take a course in CPR?
   B: Yes. It is necessary to know CPR.
      Yes, it's necessary for all employees to know CPR.
      (all employees)

2. A: My dad hasn't been to your office in a year. Should he make an appointment?
   B: Yes. It's important to check his cholesterol once a year.
      _____
      (me)

3. A: Should I go on a diet?
   B: Yes, it's necessary to lose weight.
      _____
      (you)

4. A: Should he have the surgery soon?
   B: Yes, it's important to have it as quickly as possible.
      _____
      (him)

5. A: Should I keep my children home from school?
   B: Yes, it's important to stay away from other children.
      _____
      (them)

CPR

C Write sentences. Use a phrase from the box where necessary.

| for babies | for elderly people | for teenagers |

1. It is difficult for elderly people to climb stairs.
   (difficult / climb stairs)
2. It is unhealthy to smoke.
   (unhealthy / smoke)
3. _____
   (not healthy / eat a lot of sweets)
4. _____
   (important / get enough exercise)
5. _____
   (important / see the doctor every three months)
6. _____
   (common / take several different pills every day)
7. _____
   (normal / need to eat less)
8. _____
   (good / play sports for exercise)
9. _____
   (normal / spend time with their friends)

Look
Use *for (someone)* only when necessary. We usually don't use it in a general statement about people.
It is normal to eat a few times a day.
NOT It is normal for people to eat a few times a day.

TIME TO TALK
PAIRS. What do you do to stay healthy? What is easy, difficult, and impossible for you to do? Explain your answers. Use the words in the box and your own ideas.

avoid junk food	gain weight	get enough sleep
eat three healthy meals a day	get a cleaning every six months	lose weight
exercise every day	get a physical once a year	

Example:
A: *It's really difficult for me to exercise every day. I'm so busy.*
B: *I agree. In fact, I think it's impossible for most people to exercise every day.*

Unit 17

Health

Grammar practice exercises build from controlled to open-ended.

Each grammar presentation ends with **Time to Talk**, an activity that motivates students to apply what they have learned in meaningful exchanges.

Review and Challenge reviews, consolidates, and extends the *Grammar to Communicate* lessons.

Challenging listening exercises give students practice with more advanced listening skills.

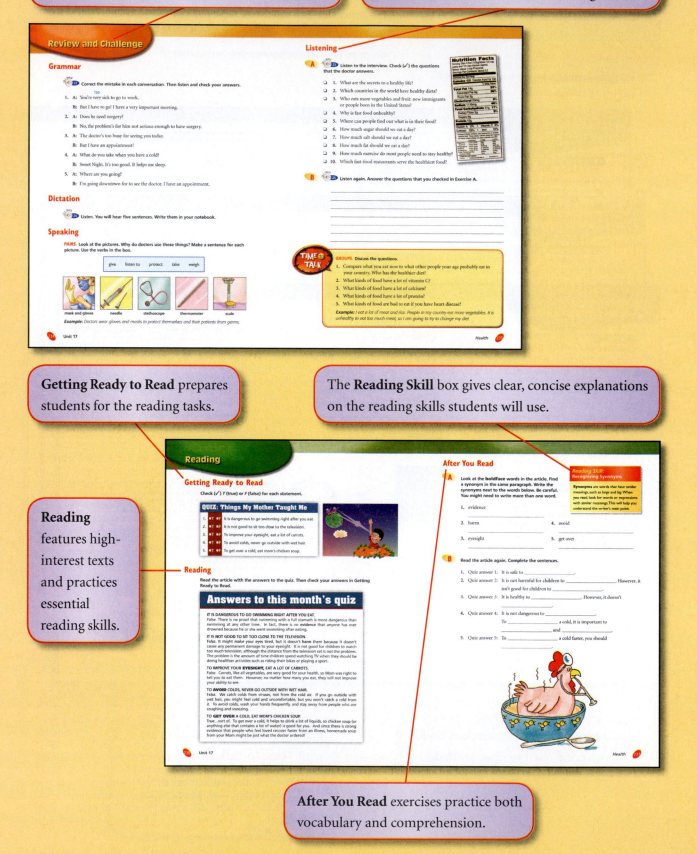

Getting Ready to Read prepares students for the reading tasks.

The **Reading Skill** box gives clear, concise explanations on the reading skills students will use.

Reading features high-interest texts and practices essential reading skills.

After You Read exercises practice both vocabulary and comprehension.

Getting Ready to Write reinforces skills needed to prepare students for the writing tasks.

Writing Tips give editing and grammar guidelines.

Prewriting features charts, outlines, and graphic organizers. In **Writing**, students use what they have learned to write a paragraph successfully.

The **Model Paragraph** gives students a realistic sample to follow.

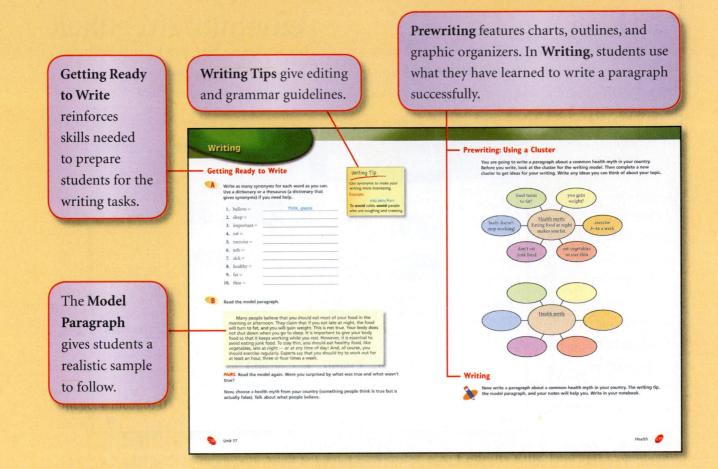

Beyond the Unit

Grammar Summaries review and expand on the *Grammar to Communicate* presentations.

A variety of **Charts** provide additional support.

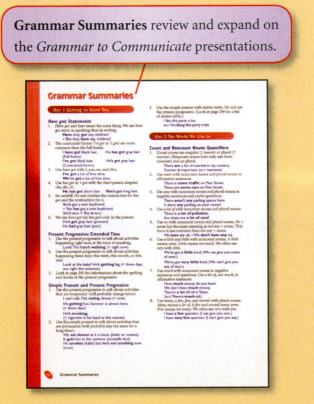

Teaching Support

The *Center Stage Teacher's Edition* features learning goals, learner persistence tips, step-by-step teaching notes, expansion activities, multilevel strategies, unit tests, and answer keys. The accompanying **Teacher's Resource Disk** includes supplementary grammar and vocabulary exercises, learner persistence worksheets, and graphic organizers.

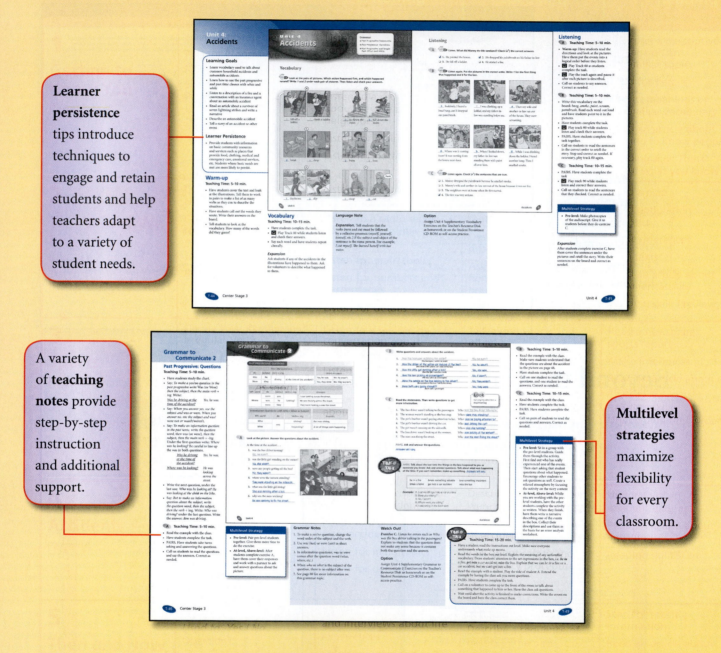

Learner persistence tips introduce techniques to engage and retain students and help teachers adapt to a variety of student needs.

A variety of **teaching notes** provide step-by-step instruction and additional support.

Multilevel strategies maximize flexibility for every classroom.

The complete *Center Stage* program
- Audio program
- *ExamView® Assessment Suite*
- Transparencies
- Companion Website

CENTER STAGE

Express Yourself in English

3

Getting to Know You

Vocabulary

A CD 1 TRACK 2 **Match the numbers with the words. Then listen and check your answers.**

_____ bangs _____ a beard _1_ curly hair _____ a mustache _____ straight hair _____ wavy hair

B CD 1 TRACK 3 **Read about and listen to people at the party. What meaning do the boldface words have? Write + (good), – (bad), or O (not good or bad).**

_+_ 1. "Amy is really funny. I like her **sense of humor**."

_____ 2. "Felicia has **a bad temper**. She's always angry about something."

_____ 3. "Lupe has **a nice personality**. She's friendly and kind. Everybody likes her."

_____ 4. "Ron has a new girlfriend. He **is going out with** Azalee."

_____ 5. "Chris and Lupe moved here Friday. They **are getting to know** everybody."

_____ 6. "I **get along with** all my neighbors. I like them very much."

Listening

A 🔘 CD 1 TRACK 4 **Listen. Marco and Betsy are at a party. What are they talking about? Check (✓) the main topic of their conversation.**

       ❑ old friends   ❑ people at the party   ❑ coworkers   ❑ families

B 🔘 CD 1 TRACK 5 **Read and listen again. Write the missing words. Use the words in the box.**

doesn't	Has	got	~~What's~~
don't	going	she's	works

Marco: ___*What's*___ she like?
          1.

Betsy: I'm just getting to know her, but I think

       she's _____ a nice personality.
               2.

Marco: Is she _____ out with anyone?
                3.

Betsy: Yeah, _____ got a boyfriend.
             4.

Marco: Oh well, too bad. Hey, is that Amy Parsons?

Betsy: No. Amy Parsons _____ look like that.
                    5.

       Amy's got long hair, and she's a lot shorter.

Marco: Oh, yeah, you're right. So who is she?

Betsy: I _____ know her name, but she lives on Elm St., next to the Fosters. She
        6.

       _____ at the mall.
        7.

Marco: _____ she got a boyfriend?
         8.

Betsy: No, but she's got a husband.

Look

What does he look like? =
Is he tall or short? Is his hair long?
What is she like? =
Is she nice? Is she friendly?

C 🔘 CD 1 TRACK 6 **Listen again. Check (✓) the sentences that are true.**

❑ 1. Marco and Betsy see each other every day.

❑ 2. Marco and Betsy live in the same neighborhood.

❑ 3. Marco is a student.

❑ 4. Betsy works at Clark's.

❑ 5. Felicia Banks doesn't have a boyfriend.

❑ 6. Marco is looking for a girlfriend.

Grammar to Communicate 1

HAVE GOT: STATEMENTS

Subject	Have / Has got		Subject	Have / Has not got	
I You We They	**have got**	long hair.	I You We They	**have not got**	long hair.
He She It	**has got**		He She It	**has not got**	

Contractions	Contractions
I**'ve got** long hair.	I **haven't got** long hair.
He**'s got** long hair.	He **hasn't got** long hair.

A Complete the sentences. What do the people at the party on page 2 look like? Write their names. Some sentences have more than one correct answer.

1. ____Chris____ has got a beard.

2. _____ hasn't got a mustache.

3. _____ and _____ have got wavy hair.

4. _____ and _____ haven't got curly hair.

5. _____ has got glasses.

6. _____ and _____ haven't got bangs.

> **Look**
>
> *Have got* and *have* mean the same thing. *Have got* is more informal.
>   Alex **has got** a beard =
>   Alex **has** a beard.
>   I **haven't got** long hair =
>   I **don't have** long hair.

PAIRS. Compare sentences. How many of your sentences are the same?

B Rewrite the sentences. Use *have got, has got, haven't got,* or *hasn't got.*

1. My sister doesn't have bangs. _____My sister hasn't got bangs._____

2. My parents have brown eyes. _____

3. My brother has a mustache. _____

4. My grandparents don't have grey hair. _____

5. My mother and I don't have glasses. _____

Check (✓) the sentences that are true about your family.

C   Read the sentences about Carolina's family. Cross out the contraction(s) in each sentence. Then write the full form of the verb. Which two people does Carolina look like?

1. "My mother's _{is} tall, and she's _{has} got wavy, red hair, and green eyes."

2. "My father's a little heavy, but he's good-looking. He's got blue eyes."

3. "My sister's got blue eyes and a big nose. Her hair's long."

4. "My older brother's got big, brown eyes and brown hair. He's cute."

5. "My younger brother's very tall. He's got a big nose and green eyes."

6. "My son's got my eyes. He's 8 years old."

> **Look**
>
> The third-person singular of *be* and *have* are contracted the same way.
>
> My **mother's** tall = My **mother is** tall
> She's got wavy hair = **She has** got wavy hair

PAIRS. Describe your family. Who do you look like?

D   Look at the picture on page 2. Complete the sentences. Use *have got, has got, haven't got,* or *hasn't got.*

1. <u>Amy</u> ___has got___ long hair.
2. <u>Chris</u> and <u>Lupe</u> _____ glasses.
3. <u>Chris</u> _____ a mustache.
4. <u>Marco</u> _____ a beard.

5. <u>Ron</u> and <u>Lupe</u> _____ straight hair.
6. <u>Betsy</u> _____ long, wavy hair.
7. <u>Felicia</u> and <u>Ron</u> _____ bangs.
8. <u>Lupe</u> and <u>Marco</u> _____ curly hair.

Change the underlined names above. Use the names of your classmates. Then compare sentences with another student. Did you write the same names?

Example: José has got a beard.

PAIRS. Write a description of one of your classmates.

WRAP UP. Read your description to the class. Can they guess the name of the classmate?

Example: This person isn't very tall. He's got short, straight hair. He hasn't got a beard, but he's got a mustache. Who is this person?

Grammar to Communicate 2

PRESENT PROGRESSIVE: EXTENDED TIME

Subject	Be	Verb + -ing		Subject	Be + not	Verb + -ing	
I	am			I	am not		
He	is	working	these days.	He	is not	working	these days.
We	are			We	are not		

Contractions	Contractions
I + am = **I'm**	I + am + not = **I'm not**
He + is = **He's**	He + is + not = **He's not** / **He isn't**
We + are = **We're**	We + are + not = **We're not** / **We aren't**

Yes / No Questions			Short Answers				
Be	Subject	Verb + -ing		Affirmative		Negative	
Am	I			I am.		I 'm not.	
Is	he	working?	Yes,	he **is.**	No,	he 's not. / he isn't.	
Are	we			we are.		we 're not. / we aren't.	

A These people are at a party. Read their conversations. When is the underlined part happening? Write *RN* for right now and *TD* for these days.

1. **Ana:** Are your kids here?
   _RN_ **Lou:** Yes. <u>They're playing</u> a computer game in their room.

2. **Amy:** Hi, Bob. How are things?
   ____ **Bob:** Pretty good. <u>I'm getting ready</u> for a trip to Brazil.

3. **Rosa:** Are you taking classes this semester?
   ____ **Stan:** No, I'm not. <u>I'm working</u> two jobs.

4. **Irina:** Mmm . . . This cake is delicious.
   ____ **Chris:** Thanks. <u>I'm taking</u> a cooking class. We made it there.

5. **Lisa:** Where's Tom?
   ____ **Lucy:** He<u>'s helping</u> Juan with something in the kitchen.

6. **Joe:** Why do you want to work more hours?
   ____ **Ray:** Things <u>are getting</u> so expensive. I need the money.

Look

Use the present progressive for:
- activities right now.
  I can't talk right now. I**'m working.**
- activities these days (this week, this month, this year).
  Are you working these days?
  No, **I'm looking for** a job.

See page 295 for spelling rules with the present progressive.

B **Complete the sentences. Make the first sentence negative and the second sentence affirmative. Use the words in the box and the present progressive.**

cook	eat out	~~go~~	spend	~~take~~	visit
eat	get to know	look	stay	try	work

1. I _____*am not going*_____ to school full time, but I _____*am taking*_____ an English class this year.

2. My parents _____ with me this month. They _____ my sister in Arizona.

3. My brother _____ much time with his high school friends anymore. He _____ a lot of new people at college.

4. My son _____ these days, but he _____ for a job.

5. I _____ a lot of bread these days. I _____ to lose weight.

6. My wife and I _____ a lot these days. We _____ more at home.

C **Write yes / no questions about these days. Use the words in the boxes.**

you	do interesting things
you and your family	get to know new people
you and your friends	have a lot of fun
your boyfriend	make a lot of money
your children	sleep well
your girlfriend	spend a lot of money
your husband	spend time with family
your parents	take a class
your wife	work hard

1. _____*Are you spending a lot of money*_____ _____*these days?*_____

2. _____

3. _____

4. _____

5. _____

6. _____

TIME to TALK

PAIRS. Ask and answer the questions you wrote in Exercise C.

Example:
A: *Are you working hard these days?*   A: *Is your wife taking a class these days?*
B: *Yes, I am.*   B: *No, she isn't.*

Grammar to Communicate 3

SIMPLE PRESENT AND PRESENT PROGRESSIVE

Simple Present: Statements		
Subject	Verb	
I	drive do not drive	to work most of the time.

Present Progressive: Statements		
Subject	*Be*	Verb + *-ing*
I	am am not	driving	to work these days.

Yes / No Questions	Short Answers
Do they drive to work most of the time?	Yes, they do. No, they don't.

Yes / No Questions	Short Answers
Are they driving to work these days?	Yes, they are. No, they aren't.

Information Questions	Answers
Where do you work?	At home.

Information Questions	Answers
Where are you working these days?	At home.

A 🔊 **7** **Read and listen to the conversations. Then read the explanations and circle** *simple present* **or** *present progressive*.

Conversation 1

Ann: Who's that guy in the corner?

Dia: His name's Luke Grava.

Ann: What's he like?

Dia: He's a little shy. He **doesn't talk** much, but he's got a nice personality.

Ann: **Does** he **live** here in the neighborhood?

Dia: He **lives** in Dover with his wife.

Conversation 2

Joe: She's got a good sense of humor. What's her name?

Ken: That's Vera. She**'s visiting** from L.A.

Joe: **Is** she **staying** with you?

Ken: No, she**'s staying** at Dan and Meg's. They're away for the summer. **They're driving** from Texas to Guatemala.

Joe: Wow. That's an adventure!

Ken: Yeah, they're very adventurous.

1. Conversation 1 uses the **simple present / present progressive** for something that is permanent (= probably going to stay the same for a long time).

2. Conversation 2 uses the **simple present / present progressive** for something that is temporary (= probably going to change soon).

B Complete the sentences. Use the simple present or the present progressive of the verbs in the box. Some are affirmative, and some are negative.

| eat out | ~~get along with~~ | go out with | make | tell |

1. My boss has got a bad temper, so she __doesn't get along with__ many people.
2. Juan and Sylvia have got young children, so they _____ a lot.
3. Peter hasn't got a very good sense of humor. He _____ good jokes.
4. Martine's got a new job, so she _____ more money these days.
5. Al's got a new girlfriend every month. This month he _____ Sheila.

C Complete the questions. Write the correct form of the verb.

1. Are you energetic? _____ _Do you do_ _____ a lot of different things every day?
   (you / do)
   _____ _Are you doing_ _____ a lot of different things this month?

2. Are you easygoing? _____ with most people?
   (you / get along)
   _____ with your teacher this semester?

3. Are you sociable? _____ things with people a lot? Who
   (you / do)
   _____ things with these days?

4. Is your mother a worrier? _____
   (she / worry)
   all the time? What _____ about

   these days?

5. Are your friends workaholics?

   _____ every day?
   (they / work late)
   _____ this week?

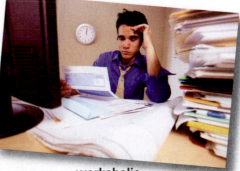

workaholic

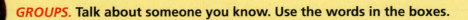

TIME to TALK

GROUPS. Talk about someone you know. Use the words in the boxes.

adventurous	sociable		a bad temper
easygoing	a workaholic		a good personality
energetic	a worrier		a good sense of humor

Example: *My brother is a worrier. These days he's worrying about school.*
My sister is easygoing. She's got a good sense of humor. She enjoys life.

Review and Challenge

Grammar

8 This conversation has seven mistakes. The first mistake is corrected for you. Find and correct the other six mistakes. Then listen and check your answers.

are things going

Stan: Hi, Jack. How ~~things going~~?

Jack: I'm pretty busy. I take five classes this semester.

Stan: Really? That's a lot. I'm just taking three. Do you like your teachers?

Jack: Yes. I get along with all of them. I really like my math teacher. He got a good sense of humor, and he's explaining things really well.

Stan: I like my teachers, too. So, where you go now?

Jack: I'm going home. Peggy's wait for me in the car.

Stan: Oh, are you two going out these days?

Jack: No, we're just friends. She have got a boyfriend.

Dictation

9 Listen. You will hear five sentences. Write them in your notebook.

Speaking

PAIRS. Talk about yourself. Use the words in the box and your own ideas. Answer these questions:

1. What's usually true about you?

2. What's true these days, but not always?

3. What's different these days?

cook a lot	exercise a lot	stay at home on weekends
eat a lot of fast food	play (your idea)	study hard
eat healthy food	sleep very well	watch sports on TV
eat out	spend time with family	work overtime

Example:

A: *I usually exercise a lot, but these days I'm not exercising much. I haven't got time. I'm working a lot of overtime.*

Listening

A **10** Listen to the radio report. What is the reporter trying to find out? Check (✓) the correct answer.

❏ 1. Do people in the city have a lot of neighbors?

❏ 2. Do people in the city get to know their neighbors?

❏ 3. Do people in the city like their neighbors?

B **10** Listen again. Evangeline talks to three people: a young woman, a man, and an older woman. Read the sentences and write *T* (true) or *F* (false).

_____ 1. The young woman is living with her friend.

_____ 2. The man's neighbors have got pets.

_____ 3. The man knows one of his neighbors very well.

_____ 4. The old woman is not very sociable.

ON YOUR OWN. Read the sentences. Check (✓) the sentences that you agree with.

❏ 1. I know most of the people in my neighborhood.

❏ 2. My neighbors don't know very much about me, and that's a good thing.

❏ 3. Most people haven't got time to get to know their neighbors.

❏ 4. A lot of new people are moving into my neighborhood these days.

❏ 5. The people in my neighborhood get along very well.

❏ 6. It is important to have a close relationship with your neighbors.

❏ 7. Most people in my country have close relationships with their neighbors.

❏ 8. People in my country usually live in one place all their lives.

GROUPS. Talk about your answers. Do you agree?

Example: A: *I agree with Number 1. I know most of my neighbors.*
B: *I don't agree. I'm so busy. I haven't got time to meet my neighbors.*

Reading

Getting Ready to Read

How do people in your country meet and get to know new people? List four ways.

1. _____
2. _____
3. _____
4. _____

Reading

Read the article. Does the writer talk about any of the things you wrote about in Getting Ready to Read?

A NEW WAY OF GETTING TO KNOW PEOPLE

These days, people are getting to know other people in lots of different ways. Of course, many people make friends in traditional ways. They talk to **strangers** at parties. They join clubs, play team sports, or take classes. **Old friends** introduce people to new friends. But more and more people these days are making friends on the Internet.

How do people make friends on the Internet? They visit **chat rooms** and **blogs**. In chat rooms, people write messages to each other. Everyone in the chat room can read the messages. There are different chat rooms for people with different interests. For example, English students can go to special chat rooms to learn English.

On blogs, people write about many different topics. Other people read the blogs and write comments about them. You do not have to be important to write a blog, but the writers of some blogs become famous. For example, one woman wrote a blog about cooking dinner every night. She used a recipe from a famous French cookbook every night for a year. People loved it, so she made it into a book.

There are some problems with meeting people on the Internet. The Internet can be a dangerous place. Some Internet users are **criminals**. They want to steal your money or hurt you. For this reason, it's not a good idea to share your **private** information on the Internet.

On the other hand, some people say it is easier to make friends on the Internet. Some shy people are afraid to talk to new people **in person**, but they aren't afraid to write to people. Also on the Internet, it **doesn't matter** where you live. You can make friends with people all over the world.

After You Read

 A   Look at the **boldface** words in the article. Guess their meaning. Then read the sentences, and circle the correct answer.

1. A **stranger**
   a. does not know you.   b. does bad things.

2. An **old friend** is
   a. not young.   b. not new.

3. In a **chat room**, people
   a. can see each other.   b. write to other people.

4. On a **blog**, people
   a. have conversations with other people.   b. write things for other people to read.

5. A **criminal**
   a. does not know you.   b. does bad things.

6. When something is **private**, you
   a. tell a lot of people about it.   b. don't tell a lot of people about it.

7. When you talk to a friend **in person**, you
   a. can see, hear, and touch him or her.   b. can hear him or her, but you can't touch or see him or her.

8. If something **doesn't matter** to you, it is
   a. not safe for you.   b. not important to you.

B   Read the article again. Write *T* (true) or *F* (false) for each statement. Then correct the false statements.

_F_ 1. People ~~aren't~~ *are* making friends in traditional ways these days.

____ 2. A lot of people make friends on the Internet.

____ 3. Writers of blogs are usually famous.

____ 4. In chat rooms, strangers read your messages.

____ 5. On the Internet, it doesn't matter if you are shy.

____ 6. It is easy to meet people on the Internet.

Writing

Getting Ready to Write

 A   Read the sentences. Change the repeated nouns to pronouns.

1. Many teenagers want to meet a lot of people, and ~~teenagers~~ *they* try to make friends on the Internet.

2. It isn't easy to get to know people well. You have to meet people in person.

3. The Internet helps people make friends, but the Internet is also dangerous.

4. Some people send messages to people's friends every day.

5. You can send messages to strangers, but don't meet strangers in person.

6. I like to take classes at night. Classes are a good way to make friends.

B   Read the model paragraph.

>   More and more young people are making friends on the Internet these days. They are also sending messages to other people on their cell phones. They are not really talking. In my opinion, this is not the best way to meet people. You cannot really get to know a person on the Internet. People sometimes tell lies on the Internet. To make real friends, you have to meet people, look at them, and listen to them. For example, you can join a sports team. I met my best friend three years ago on a soccer team. We both love soccer. We play every weekend. After the games, we have dinner and talk about everything. We are real friends, not Internet friends.

PAIRS. Read the model again. According to the writer, what is the best way to make friends?

Do you agree? Discuss.

Prewriting: Answering Questions

You are going to write a paragraph about making friends. Before you write, answer questions about the topic.

1. What do you think about the ways people are getting to know one another these days? Are they good or bad?

2. In your opinion, what is the best way to make new friends?

3. Describe how you met a new friend.

Writing

Now write a paragraph about making friends. The writing tip, the model paragraph, and your notes will help you. Write in your notebook.

Grammar

- Count and Noncount Nouns: Quantifiers
- Count and Noncount Nouns: *Plenty of / Enough / Too much / Too many*
- *Both / Neither / Either*

Vocabulary

🔘 **11** Match the numbers with the words. Then listen and check your answers.

_____ crime
_____ a factory
_____ a farm
_____ a field
_____ parking
_____ a parking space
_____ pollution
_____ public transportation
__1__ a skyscraper
_____ sunshine
_____ a tourist
_____ traffic

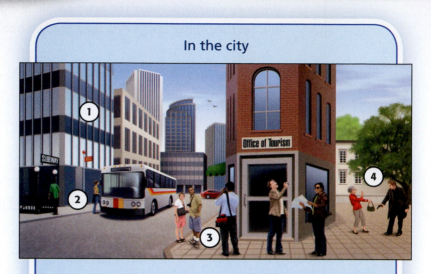

In the city

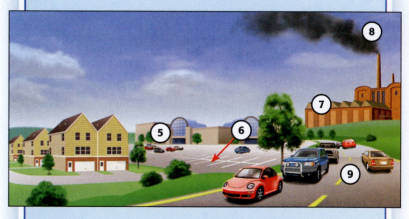

In the suburbs

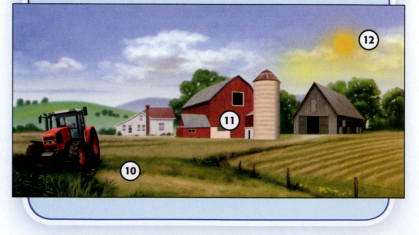

In the country

Listening

 A  Listen. Ben and Rita are talking about life in the city and life in the suburbs. Check (✓) the topics that they mention.

❑ crime

❑ kids

❑ money

❑ open space

❑ parking

❑ pollution

❑ public transportation

❑ schools

❑ time

❑ traffic

> **Look**
>
> open space = land with no buildings on it

B Listen again. Complete the sentences about the conversation. Write *city* or *suburbs*.

1. There are very few good schools in the _____city_____.

2. There is plenty of open space in the _____.

3. Ben and his wife moved to the _____, but neither of them is happy there.

4. A lot of people are moving out of the _____.

5. There aren't enough houses and apartments in the _____.

6. People drive several hours a day when they live in the _____.

7. There are no trains before 7 A.M. in the _____, and there are only a few trains after 5 P.M.

8. There is very little parking in the _____.

C Listen again. Check (✓) the sentences that are true.

❑ 1. Rita is sick.

❑ 2. Rita lives in the city.

❑ 3. Rita wants to move.

❑ 4. Ben has an apartment in the city and a house in the suburbs.

❑ 5. Both Ben and Rita have children.

❑ 6. Ben takes public transportation to work.

❑ 7. Ben wants to move back to the city.

Grammar to Communicate 1

COUNT AND NONCOUNT NOUNS: QUANTIFIERS

	Quantifier	Count Noun		Quantifier	Noncount Noun
There are	a lot of many several some a few	schools.	There's	a lot of some a little	traffic.
There aren't	any many		There isn't	any much	
There are	no (very) few		There's	no (very) little	

Look

We can use quantifiers in other sentences.
The town has **many** schools.
The town doesn't have **any** traffic.

A 🔘 CD 1 TRACK 13 **Read and listen to a student's oral report about his country. Circle the count nouns and underline the noncount nouns.**

Look

several = five or six
a little / a few = some
(very) little = not much
(very) few = not many

I live in a beautiful (country.) The <u>weather</u> is great. There's always a lot of sunshine and very little rain. There are a few big cities, but most people live in small towns and villages. I'm from the capital city. It's an exciting place. There are a lot of great stores and restaurants, but there aren't any skyscrapers. My parents and I live in an apartment near several stores. The apartment is small and doesn't have much space, but we like it. Most people in my country haven't got a lot of money, but we've got many other good things. I miss my country a lot.

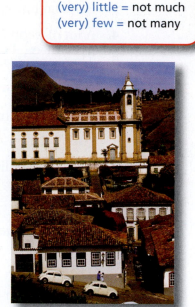
village

B **Complete the sentences about your country. Write *is, isn't, are,* or *aren't*.**

1. The weather _____ good.
2. Our music _____ great.
3. The food _____ wonderful.
4. People _____ friendly.
5. There _____ a lot of skyscrapers.

6. People's homes _____ big.
7. There _____ a lot of villages.
8. There _____ many big cities.
9. There _____ a lot of open space.
10. There _____ a long river.

18   Unit 2

C Complete the sentences with *a little*, *very little*, *a few*, or *very few*.

1. We never eat out because there are ___very few___ good restaurants around here.

2. There are _____ restaurants near my home. Three of them are very good.

3. People need cars in my town because there's _____ public transportation.

4. My street is almost always quiet. There's _____ noise.

5. There are _____ stores. We shop in another town.

6. You see _____ people on the streets during the day. They're at work.

7. There are _____ banks. Two are on my street, and one is around the corner.

8. There's _____ crime, but we feel safe.

D What do people in your country eat? Write sentences with *a few*, *very few*, *a little*, *very little*, *a lot of*, or *no*. Use the words in the box and your own ideas.

beans	bread	corn	fruit	hot peppers	pork	rice
beef	cheese	fish	hot dogs	ice cream	potatoes	spicy food

1. _In my country, we eat a lot of beef, but we eat very little cheese._____

2. _____

3. _____

4. _____

5. _____

6. _____

7. _____

PAIRS. Talk to a student from a different country. Do people from your countries eat the same things?

GROUPS. Talk about the city or town where you live now. What does it have? What doesn't it have? What do people eat? What don't they eat?

Example:
A: *There's a lot of traffic in our city.*
B: *But there isn't a lot of crime.*

COUNT AND NONCOUNT NOUNS: *PLENTY OF / ENOUGH / TOO MUCH / TOO MANY*					
	Quantifier	Count Noun		Quantifier	Noncount Noun
There are	**plenty of** **enough**	houses.	There is	**plenty of** **enough**	space.
There aren't There are	**enough** **too many**	apartments. people.	There isn't There is	**enough** **too much**	sunshine. rain.

A   Match the problems on the left and the information on the right.

  _d_ 1. Houses cost too much money.

      2. There aren't enough police officers.

      3. There are too many factories.

      4. There aren't enough parking spaces.

      5. There is too much rain.

a. There are too many cars.

b. There is too much crime.

c. There isn't enough sunshine.

d. There aren't enough inexpensive houses.

e. There aren't enough parks.

Look

enough = the correct amount
not enough = less than the correct amount
plenty of = a lot, more than enough
too much / too many = more than the correct amount

B   Complete the sentences. Be careful. Some are affirmative, and some are negative.

1. Tom and Linda's apartment has two bedrooms. They have seven children. They
    ___*don't have enough*___ space.
    (have / enough)

2. Ellen's home has two bedrooms. She has one child. She _____*has enough*_____ space.
    (have / enough)

3. There are three bus stops, a train station, and a subway station near my home. There
    _____ public transportation.
    (be / plenty of)

4. There are 1 million people in my city and one hospital. There _____
    hospitals.
    (be / enough)

5. Every night, I drive around for an hour looking for a place to park. There
    _____ parking spaces.
    (be / enough)

6. My wife and I have two phones in the house. We both have cell phones, too. We
    _____ phones.
    (have / enough)

7. There are four markets on my street. There _____ markets.
    (be / plenty of)

C   Write a sentence about each picture. Use the words in the box and *too much* or *too many*.

| buildings | people | rain | traffic |

1. _____

2. _____

3. _____

4. _____

D   Check (✓) the sentences that people probably say. Put an *X* next to the sentences that people probably do not say. In the sentences with an *X*, cross out *too much* or *too many* and write *a lot of*.

  ___X___ 1. There are ~~too many~~ *a lot of* good restaurants in my neighborhood.

  ___✓___ 2. I don't like the area because there are too many dirty streets.

  _____ 3. We don't go out at night. There's too much crime.

  _____ 4. It's a nice neighborhood. There are too many friendly people.

  _____ 5. There is too much sunshine. The weather's always beautiful.

  _____ 6. The traffic is always bad. There are too many cars.

  _____ 7. You'll find a parking space near the school. There are too many parking spaces.

GROUPS. Talk about the problems in big cities, small villages, the country, and the suburbs. Then discuss which place you prefer to live in, and why.

Example:
A: *In cities, there's too much crime.*
B: *There isn't much crime in villages, but there aren't enough activities for teenagers.*

Grammar to Communicate 3

BOTH / NEITHER / EITHER

Both / Neither / Either	Count Noun	Verb	
Both	places	are	fine.
Neither **Either**	place	is	

Both / Neither / Either	of		Count Noun	Verb	
Both	of	the those his	places	are	fine.
Neither **Either**	of	the those his	places	is	

The two places are good.	We	like	**both**	places.	
The two places are bad.	We	like	**neither**	place.	
		don't like	**either**		

We	like	**both**		the those his	places.
We	like	**neither**	of		
	don't like	**either**			

A Read the sentences. Which two cities are the sentences about? Write the names.

1. Both cities have more than 8,000,000 people.

2. Neither city is in South America.

3. Both cities are the capital of their country.

4. Most people don't speak Spanish in either city.

5. It snows in the winter in both cities.

6. There are no beaches because neither city is near the sea.

CITY	POPULATION
Seoul, South Korea	10,231,217
São Paulo, Brazil	10,009,231
Mumbai, India	9,925,891
Jakarta, Indonesia	9,373,900
Karachi, Pakistan	9,339,023
Moscow, Russia	8,297,056
Istanbul, Turkey	8,260,438
Mexico City, Mexico	8,235,744
Shanghai, China	8,214,384
Tokyo, Japan	8,130,408
New York City, United States	8,000,278
Bangkok, Thailand	7,506,700

The cities are _____ and _____.

PAIRS. Take turns saying the sentences. Add *of the*.

Look

We use *both*, *either*, and *neither*, to talk about <u>two</u> people, places, or things.
both = one and the other
either = one or the other
neither = not one and not the other

B Rewrite the sentences. Use *both*, *neither*, or *either* and *of the*. Write in your notebook.

1. São Paulo and Seoul have more than 10 million people.

   <u>Both of the cities have more than 10 million people.</u>

2. New York and Mexico City are not in South America.

   <u>Neither of the cities is in South America.</u>

3. It doesn't snow in Jakarta or Mumbai.

4. There are a lot of skyscrapers in Tokyo and Shanghai.

5. People don't speak Chinese in Karachi or Istanbul.

6. Tokyo and Mumbai are not near the Atlantic Ocean.

PAIRS. Take turns saying the sentences without *of the*.

Example: *Both cities have more than 10 million people.*

C Complete the sentences with *both*, *neither*, or *either*. Add *of* where necessary.

1. **A:** Did you go to San Juan or Arecibo?

   B: We went to _____ both _____ places.

2. **A:** Who is from Mexico, Miguel or Pedro?

   B: _____ Neither of _____ them is from Mexico. They are from Peru.

3. **A:** Who comes from Bangkok, you or Aran?

   B: _____ us come from Bangkok. His home is a mile from mine.

4. **A:** Where do your son and daughter live?

   B: _____ my children live in Toronto. They go to school there.

5. **A:** Who speaks Chinese, you or your wife?

   B: _____ us. We don't know any Chinese.

6. **A:** Do you want to visit Mexico City or São Paulo?

   B: I can't visit _____ city. I haven't got enough money.

7. **A:** Do Jakarta and Mumbai have a lot of cold weather?

   B: No, it isn't cold in _____ them.

> **Look**
>
> You must use *of* with *both*, *either*, and *neither* before the pronouns *us*, *you*, and *them*.
> Do **either of them** come from Peru?

TIME to TALK

GROUPS. Look at the world map on pages 302–303. Write sentences about two places.

WRAP UP. Read your sentences to the class. Can they guess the places?

Example:
Group A: *Both of the countries are in South America. Neither country is very large.*
    Class: *Are the countries Ecuador and Guyana?*
Group A: *No, they aren't. Here's more information. There are no beaches in either country.*

Review and Challenge

Grammar

CD 1 TRACK 14 Complete the note with the words in the box. Then listen and check your answers. Some sentences have more than one correct answer. Be careful. There are extra words.

are	both	a few	isn't	much	no	too many	very few
aren't	enough	is	~~a little~~	neither	plenty of	too much	very little

I'm writing from my new home. The neighborhood is safe, and it's quiet most of the time. There's ___a little___ noise in the morning, but I get up early anyway. The rent is very
1.
cheap, but there is _____ public transportation. Just one bus stops on my street. That's
2.
not great, but I'm lucky because there are _____ inexpensive stores and restaurants.
3.

My apartment's fine, but there are _____ problems. First of all, the rooms are
4.
small, so there _____ a lot of space. Second, there isn't _____ light. There isn't
5.   6.
_____ sunshine around here, and my bedroom has _____ windows, zero! There
7.   8.
are two windows in the living room, but _____ of them are very small. I miss the
9.
sunshine back home!

Dictation

CD 1 TRACK 15 Listen. You will hear five sentences. Write them in your notebook.

Speaking

GROUPS. What are some serious problems in the country where you are living? Use the words in the box and your own ideas.

crime	natural disasters	poverty
health care	pollution	unemployment

Example:
A: *I think there is too much pollution in the big cities.*
B: *I agree. A lot of people have health problems because of the bad air.*

Listening

A **16** Listen to the radio report about the Republic of Cape Verde. Check (✓) the questions that the report answers. Then answer those questions.

❏ 1. Where is Cape Verde?   _____

❏ 2. How many people live in Cape Verde today?   _____

❏ 3. What do people in Cape Verde eat?   _____

❏ 4. How many big cities are there in Cape Verde? _____

❏ 5. How much sunshine is there in Cape Verde?   _____

❏ 6. Are there a lot of mountains in Cape Verde?   _____

PAIRS. Ask and answer the questions that you checked.

B **16** Listen again. Read the sentences and write *T* (true) or *F* (false).

_____ 1. Cape Verdeans don't eat a lot of fish.

_____ 2. Cape Verdeans don't sell much fish to other countries.

_____ 3. Cape Verde does not have enough natural resources.

_____ 4. There is too much rain on the island.

_____ 5. There are too many big farms on the island.

_____ 6. Cape Verdeans buy a lot of food from other countries.

_____ 7. There are no good hotels in Cape Verde.

_____ 8. Many Cape Verdeans work in tourism.

> ## Look
>
> natural resources = things such as land, minerals (for example, silver), or natural energy (for example, oil) that exist in a country

TIME to TALK

GROUPS. Write a report about your country for the class. Use the words in the box or your own ideas.

climate	exports	imports	natural resources
culture and art	geography	major industries	population

WRAP UP. Now choose one person from your group to give the report. Bring in pictures or something else from your country to show the class.

Reading

Getting Ready to Read

Preview the article. Then check (✓) the topic of the article.

❑ housing in Portland

❑ retired people in Portland

❑ a problem in Portland

Reading

Read the article. Was your answer to Getting Ready to Read correct?

WHERE ARE THE CHILDREN?

In many ways, Portland, Oregon is a **success story.** Well-educated people from all over the United States are moving there. In downtown Portland, there are a lot of new homes and businesses, and many new jobs. There are plenty of parks and open space, and there is not much crime. The public transportation system is excellent, so there is not a lot of air pollution or traffic. The weather is **mild**, with very few days of bad weather. But there is a problem in Portland: there are not enough children.

From 1990 to 2003, the population of Portland went up by about 90,000 people. However, very few of the new **residents** were children. In fact, Portland is closing many public schools because there aren't enough students to **fill** them. So who are these new residents? Many are **retired.** Others are single and are not planning to have any children.

Why aren't there more families in downtown Portland? The answer is simple: the high cost of housing. There are plenty of new houses and apartments, but they are very expensive. Young families don't have enough money to live in a city like Portland.

But is the low number of children in Portland really a problem for the retired and single residents of the city? According to Phillip Longman from the New America Foundation, it is a serious problem. ". . . Having fewer children really **diminishes** the quality of life in a city." Children ride their bikes on the streets and play in the parks. Their parents are **active** in the community. They care about **issues** such as public safety. And as children get older, they get jobs, open their own businesses, and begin their own families. All of these things are good for a city.

After You Read

A   Look at the **boldface** words in the article. Guess their meaning. Match the words with the correct definitions.

__f__ **1.** success story

_____ **2.** mild

_____ **3.** residents

_____ **4.** fill

_____ **5.** retired

_____ **6.** diminish

_____ **7.** active

_____ **8.** issues

a. people who live in a place

b. make something worse

c. busy doing things

d. not too cold or hot

e. problems or subjects that people discuss

f. something or someone that does well when others do not do well

g. use all of the space in a place

h. not working, usually because of old age

B   Read the article again. Then answer the questions.

1. What are some good things about the city of Portland?

_____

_____

_____

2. What are some problems in the city of Portland?

_____

_____

_____

Downtown Portland

Writing

Getting Ready to Write

A   Luis has just moved to a small town from a big city. Read his diary. Look at the underlined verbs. Circle the correct verb.

> May 15
>
> I'm having a hard time here. Everything (is)/ are clean and beautiful, and the people is / are friendly, but something is / are wrong. At first I wasn't sure what the problem was, but now I know. There isn't / aren't enough single people. Everyone is / are married. Well, everyone except me. Everybody works / work and has / have children, so nobody has / have any free time. There is / are nothing to do, and nobody to do it with. There are only two restaurants in town, and both of them closes / close at 9:00. No one goes / go out at night. It is / are really strange. In my old city, there was / were plenty of single people, and there was / were fun things to do every night of the week. Where is / are all the single people? Am I really the only one?

B   Read the model paragraph.

> Mexico City is in the south central part of Mexico. There are tall volcanoes and mountains near the city. More than 8.2 million people live in the city. With so many people, Mexico City is a very exciting place. Something is always happening. There are famous museums, excellent nightclubs, and wonderful restaurants. And everything is open until very late. Nobody goes to bed early in Mexico City! But there are also too many cars, too much traffic, and too much air pollution. Everyone in Mexico City complains about the pollution, but there are no easy solutions. People are trying to improve the air quality, but they haven't solved the problem yet.

PAIRS. **Read the model again. According to the writer, what are the good things about Mexico City? What are the problems?**

Now talk about another city. Discuss the good things and the problems.

Prewriting: Taking Notes

You are going to write a paragraph about a city. Before you write, read the notes for the writing model. Then take notes about a city you know.

Writing Model
Mexico City

Location
south central part of Mexico

mountains and volcanoes around the city

Population 8.2 million

Good things large and exciting

museums, nightclubs, restaurants

everything is open late

no one goes to bed early

Problems too many cars

too much traffic

air pollution

City:
Location
Population
Good things
Problems

Writing

Now write a paragraph about a city you know. The writing tip, the model paragraph, and your notes will help you. Write in your notebook.

Grammar
- Simple Past: Regular and Irregular Verbs
- Simple Past: Questions
- Clauses with *Because, Before, After, As soon as*

Vocabulary

CD 1 TRACK 17 **Complete the sentences with the words in the box. Listen and check your answers. Then circle the nouns in the boxes and underline the verbs.**

| cheer   goal   misses   team |

We _____ when a player on our
     1.
_____ scores a _____. We
     2.   3.
also cheer when a player on the other
team _____.
        4.

| beat   lose to   runs   score |

The _____ is 3 to 1. We have
         5.
three _____. We're going to win.
            6.
The Cubs often _____ us, but
                        7.
today they're going to _____ us.
                              8.

| court   is tied   passes   points |

There are two minutes left, and the
score _____ 98 to 98. Kelly misses
          9.
a shot. Now Ruiz gets the ball and
_____ it across the _____
     10.   11.
to Jones. She makes the shot and scores
two _____.
        12.

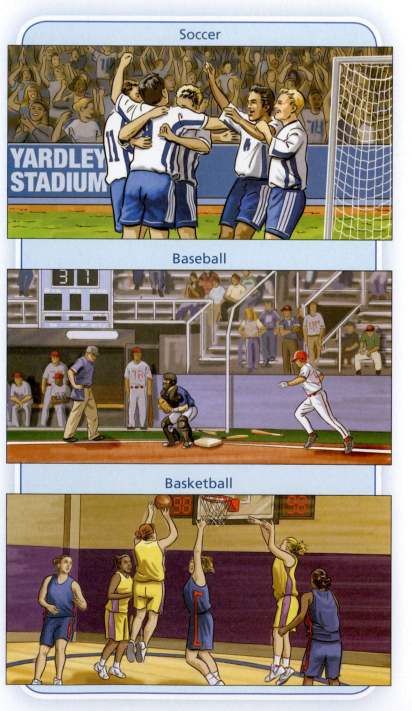

Soccer

YARDLEY STADIUM

Baseball

Basketball

Listening

A 🔘 18 **Listen. Why is Mina angry? Check (✓) the correct answer.**

❏ 1. Tony didn't call her.

❏ 2. Tony went to the match last night with Barney.

❏ 3. Tony forgot about their date.

❏ 4. Tony didn't like the movie.

score a goal

fans

B 🔘 19 **Listen again. Who said it? Write *M* (Mina) or *T* (Tony).**

__T__ 1. What did I promise?

_____ 2. You wanted to see a movie.

_____ 3. And who did I want to see it with?

_____ 4. Did you want to see it with me?

_____ 5. But I didn't know that it was tonight.

_____ 6. Yes, you did. Before I got the tickets, I called you and asked.

_____ 7. You said tonight was fine.

C 🔘 20 **Listen again. Put the sentences in the correct order. Write *1* for the first thing that happened and *6* for the last.**

_____ a. Barney invited Tony to the game.

_____ b. Tony said yes to Mina.

_____ c. Mina got angry with Tony because he forgot about the movies.

__1__ d. Before Mina bought the movie tickets, she called Tony and asked him to go with her.

_____ e. Tony said yes to Barney.

_____ f. After Tony talked to Mina, Barney stopped by.

Grammar to Communicate ❶

SIMPLE PAST : REGULAR AND IRREGULAR VERBS

<table>
<tr><th colspan="2">Regular Verbs</th><th></th><th colspan="2">Irregular Verbs</th><th></th></tr>
<tr><th>Subject</th><th>Verb</th><th></th><th>Subject</th><th>Verb</th><th></th></tr>
<tr><td>I
You</td><td>missed
didn't miss</td><td rowspan="3">the game.</td><td>I
You</td><td>saw
didn't see</td><td rowspan="3">the ball.</td></tr>
<tr><td>He
She</td><td>watched
didn't watch</td><td>He
She</td><td>lost
didn't lose</td></tr>
<tr><td>We
They</td><td>played
didn't play</td><td>We
They</td><td>got
didn't get</td></tr>
</table>

Look

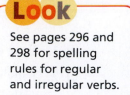

See pages 296 and 298 for spelling rules for regular and irregular verbs.

A Which sports are the sentences about? Write *S* (soccer), *BK* (basketball), or *BB* (baseball). In some sentences, more than one sport is correct.

   _S_   **1.** The player kicked the ball 100 feet.

   _S, BK_ **2.** The player shot the ball.

   _____ **3.** The player hit the ball.

   _____ **4.** The player threw the ball.

   _____ **5.** The player caught the ball.

   _____ **6.** The player scored a goal.

   _____ **7.** The player missed the ball.

   _____ **8.** The player passed the ball.

   _____ **9.** The players jumped.

   _____ **10.** My team beat your team.

   _____ **11.** We won.

   _____ **12.** We all cheered.

catch

hit

jump

kick

shoot

throw

B Write the verbs from Exercise A in the correct column. Then write the base form.

REGULAR VERBS		IRREGULAR VERBS	
Simple Past	Base Form	Simple Past	Base Form
kicked	kick	shot	shoot
_____	_____	_____	_____
_____	_____	_____	_____
_____	_____	_____	_____
_____	_____	_____	_____
_____	_____	_____	_____

C Complete the pairs of sentences. In each pair, the first sentence is affirmative and the second sentence is negative.

1. I won the first game.   I ___didn't win___ the second game.

2. They lost on Monday.   They _____ on Wednesday.

3. She _____ the older player.   She didn't beat the younger player.

4. I bought two tickets for the game.   I _____ three tickets.

5. We _____ good seats.   We didn't have bad seats.

6. He relaxed at the end of the game.   He _____ at the beginning of the game.

7. We wanted to play in the morning.   We _____ to play at night.

8. They _____ yesterday.   They didn't practice the week before the game.

D   **21** Complete the sports report. Use the past tense of the verbs. Be careful. Some are affirmative, and some are negative. Then listen and check your answers.

Last night ___was___ a big night for basketball fans.
      1. (be)

There _____ five big games across the country.
      2. (be)

The most exciting game _____ in Detroit. It was
                        3. (take place)

close all night. In the final seconds, the Peaks and the

Lions _____ 110 to 110. But then Mike Collins
      4. (be tied)

_____ the ball to Aaron Brown. Brown _____
   5. (pass)   6. (shoot)

the ball from the middle of the court and _____
                                            7. (win)

the game for the Peaks. In New York, the Wings

_____ well at all. They _____ to the Stars, and it _____ pretty. The
   8. (play)   9. (lose)   10. (be)

Wings _____ their best player, Darryl Thompson, and their other top player, Sam
      11. (have)

Watson, _____ any points. He _____ every shot. The final score? The Stars
        12. (score)   13. (miss)

_____ the Wings 121 to 78. One thing's for sure: The Wings need help.
   14. (beat)

SPORTS NOW
Daryl Thompson: Broke his leg! Out for five games
No points for Sam Watson: What happened?
Peaks 113 ....Lions 110
Stars 121 .... Wings 78
Jags 96 ....Jets 88
Nets 112.......................Tigers 102
Greens 92 ....Sharks 86

Look

take place = happen

TIME to TALK *PAIRS.* Imagine you are sports broadcasters. Discuss a game in your town or city. Then write a report. Use Exercise D as a model.

Sports **33**

Grammar to Communicate 2

SIMPLE PAST: QUESTIONS

Yes / No Questions

Did	Subject	Verb	
Did	you	play	on the team?

Short Answers

Yes, I did.	No, I didn't.

Information Questions

Wh- word	Did	Subject	Verb	
Where	did	they	play	the game?

Answer

They played in Santiago.

Information Questions with What / Who as Subject

Wh- word	Verb	
Who	played	against Santiago?

Answer

Milan played against Santiago.

Information Questions with How Many

How many	Subject	Verb	
How many	people	watched	the game?

Answer

More than a million people watched it.

A **David is asking Mahtab what she did last night. Match the questions and answers.**

__d__ 1. What did you do last night?

_____ 2. Wow! How did you get tickets?

_____ 3. Who did you go with?

_____ 4. So how was it? Who won?

_____ 5. What? Why did you leave?

_____ 6. Did you say the *movies*?

a. I went with Paul.

b. I don't know. We left before the end.

c. We didn't want to be late for the movies.

d. I went to the Sparks/Tigers game.

e. My boss gave them to me.

f. Yes, I did. We saw *Last Dream*. It was great!

B 🔵 22 **Complete Mahtab and David's conversation. Then listen and check your answers.**

Mahtab: Why are you so upset? ___Did you want___ to go to the game?
  1. (you / want)

David: Sure. The Sparks are great . . . wait a minute . . . you don't even like

  basketball! _____ your boss that?
    2. (you / tell)

Mahtab: No, of course not! I told him I loved basketball.

David: _____ you about the game this morning?
    3. (he / ask)

Mahtab: No, he didn't. Oh, no! Quick, tell me — who _____?
    4. (win)

David: I don't know. _____? I didn't have any tickets.
    5. (you / forget)

C Write questions with *How many*, *Where*, *When*, and *Who*. Then answer the questions.

1. the first World Cup / take place

   When did the first World Cup take place?

     (a.) in 1902   **b.** in 1930   **c.** in 1950

2. the first World Cup / take place

   _____

   a. in China   **b.** in Uruguay   **c.** in the United States

3. people / watch / the World Cup on TV for the first time

   _____

   a. in 1926   **b.** in 1958   **c.** in 1974

4. England / win / the World Cup

   _____

   a. in 1966   **b.** in 1998   **c.** in 1966 and 1998

5. win / the 2002 World Cup

   _____

   a. Brazil   **b.** Japan   **c.** the United States

6. people / see / the 2002 World Cup on TV

   _____

   a. 2 million   **b.** 10 million   **c.** 1.7 billion

PAIRS. Compare your answers. Then check your answers on page 306.

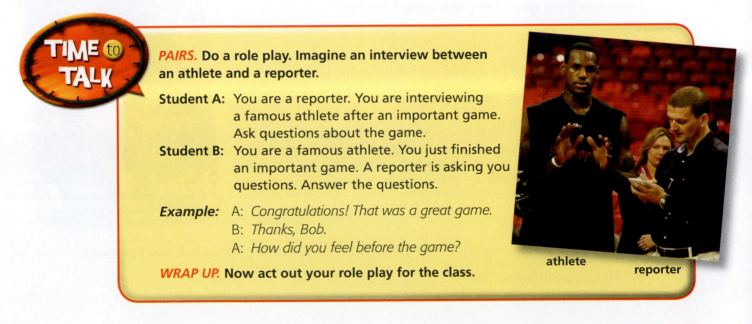

TIME to TALK

PAIRS. Do a role play. Imagine an interview between an athlete and a reporter.

Student A: You are a reporter. You are interviewing a famous athlete after an important game. Ask questions about the game.

Student B: You are a famous athlete. You just finished an important game. A reporter is asking you questions. Answer the questions.

Example: A: *Congratulations! That was a great game.*
B: *Thanks, Bob.*
A: *How did you feel before the game?*

WRAP UP. Now act out your role play for the class.

athlete   reporter

CLAUSES WITH *BECAUSE, BEFORE, AFTER, AS SOON AS*

	Dependent Clause			Independent (Main) Clause		
	Subject	Verb		Subject	Verb	
Because	he	was	a good player,	the team	won	a lot of games.
Before		joined	the Wings,		was not	very good.
After		became	the number one player,		gave	him more money.
As soon as		left	the Wings,		started to lose	again.

A Make sentences about Brazilian soccer player Pelé.
Match the information in the columns.

 1. Because Pelé's father was a soccer player,

2. Before his friends started calling him Pelé,

3. Pelé became famous

4. As soon as Pelé scored his 1,000th goal in 1969,

5. After he retired in Brazil,

a. after people saw him play in the 1958 World Cup.

b. he played soccer in the United States for two years.

c. his nickname was "Dico."

d. Pelé learned to play soccer at a very young age.

e. Brazilians all over the world started to cheer.

Look

You can say:
Before she played basketball, she played soccer. *(comma)*
OR
She played soccer **before** she played basketball. *(no comma)*

B Complete the sentences about American athlete Michael
Jordan. Write *after*, *as soon as*, *because*, or *before*. Some
sentences have more than one correct answer.

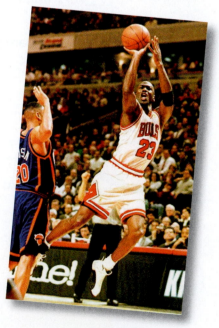

1. Michael Jordan was born in New York. _____After_____ he was born, his family moved to North Carolina.

2. _____ he became the top player in basketball, his family was not rich.

3. _____ he graduated from high school, he played basketball in college.

4. The Chicago Bulls were not a successful team _____ he played for them.

5. _____ he retired from basketball, he played on a professional baseball team.

6. He stopped playing baseball _____ he wasn't very good.

C Combine the sentences, and make new sentences about a famous athlete. Add commas where necessary.

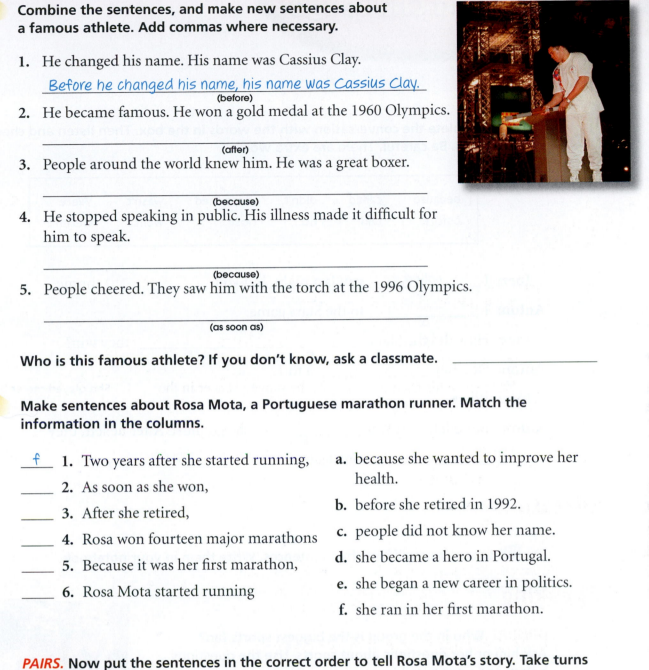

1. He changed his name. His name was Cassius Clay.

   <u>Before he changed his name, his name was Cassius Clay.</u>
   (before)

2. He became famous. He won a gold medal at the 1960 Olympics.

   _____
   (after)

3. People around the world knew him. He was a great boxer.

   _____
   (because)

4. He stopped speaking in public. His illness made it difficult for him to speak.

   _____
   (because)

5. People cheered. They saw him with the torch at the 1996 Olympics.

   _____
   (as soon as)

Who is this famous athlete? If you don't know, ask a classmate. _____

D Make sentences about Rosa Mota, a Portuguese marathon runner. Match the information in the columns.

__f__ 1. Two years after she started running,	**a.** because she wanted to improve her health.
____ 2. As soon as she won,	**b.** before she retired in 1992.
____ 3. After she retired,	**c.** people did not know her name.
____ 4. Rosa won fourteen major marathons	**d.** she became a hero in Portugal.
____ 5. Because it was her first marathon,	**e.** she began a new career in politics.
____ 6. Rosa Mota started running	**f.** she ran in her first marathon.

PAIRS. Now put the sentences in the correct order to tell Rosa Mota's story. Take turns saying the sentences.

Example: _Rosa Mota started running . . ._

GROUPS. Write about a famous athlete. Do not write the athlete's name.

Example: _This tennis player became famous about ten years ago. After she started playing professionally, her sister began to play, too._

WRAP UP. Read your sentences to the class. Ask the class to guess the name of the athlete.

Review and Challenge

Grammar

CD 1 TRACK 23 Complete the conversation with the words in the box. Then listen and check your answers. Be careful. There are extra words.

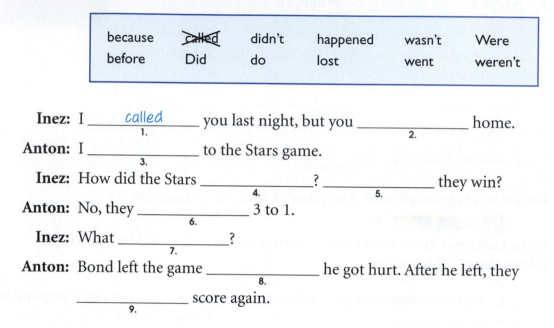

| because | ~~called~~ | didn't | happened | wasn't | Were |
| before | Did | do | lost | went | weren't |

Inez: I _____called_____ you last night, but you _____ home.
                    1.   2.

Anton: I _____ to the Stars game.
                      3.

Inez: How did the Stars _____? _____ they win?
                                        4.   5.

Anton: No, they _____ 3 to 1.
                            6.

Inez: What _____?
                      7.

Anton: Bond left the game _____ he got hurt. After he left, they
                                          8.

_____ score again.
        9.

Dictation

CD 1 TRACK 24 Listen. You will hear five sentences. Write them in your notebook.

Speaking

GROUPS. Who in the group is the biggest sports fan? Ask him or her questions about sports. Use the questions below and your own ideas.

get an autograph

1. When did you first become interested in sports?

2. Why did you get interested in sports?

3. Who were your sports heroes when you were young and why?

4. Did you ever do any of these things when you were young?

   • see a game in person
   • get an autograph from a player
   • talk to a player
   • write to a player

Example:
A: *Did you ever get an autograph from a player?*
B: *Yes! I got an autograph from my favorite tennis player when I was 15 years old. It was so exciting!*

Listening

A CD 1 TRACK 25 Listen. A reporter is talking to Dr. Ramon Perez about the first team sport. Check (✓) the picture that matches Dr. Perez's description.

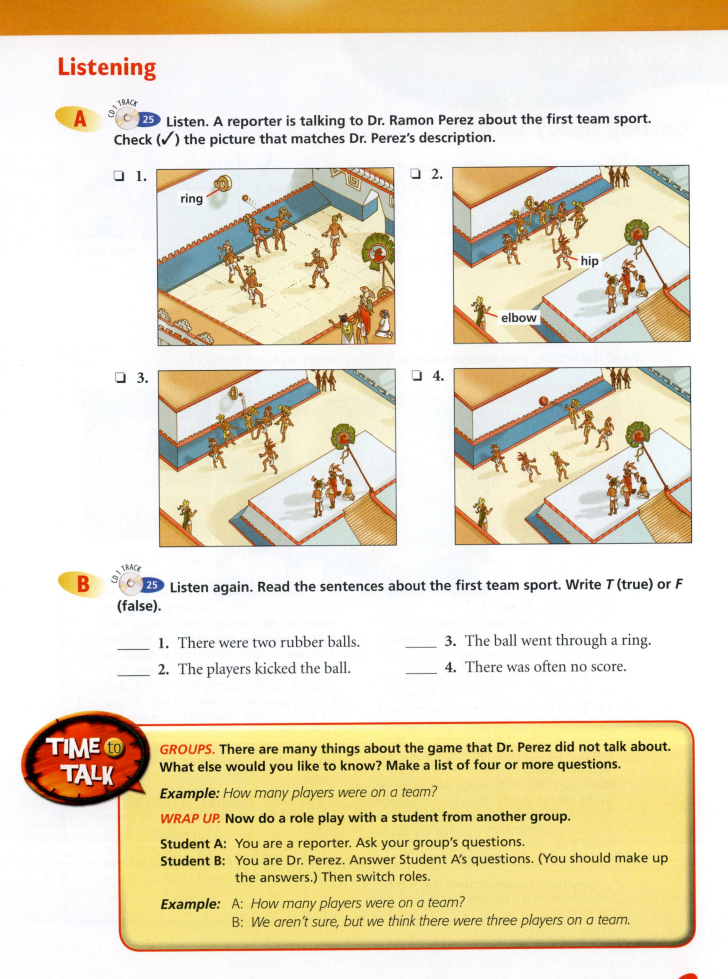

❏ 1.

ring

❏ 2.

hip

elbow

❏ 3.

❏ 4.

B CD 1 TRACK 25 Listen again. Read the sentences about the first team sport. Write *T* (true) or *F* (false).

_____ 1. There were two rubber balls.   _____ 3. The ball went through a ring.

_____ 2. The players kicked the ball.   _____ 4. There was often no score.

TIME to TALK

GROUPS. There are many things about the game that Dr. Perez did not talk about. What else would you like to know? Make a list of four or more questions.

Example: How many players were on a team?

WRAP UP. Now do a role play with a student from another group.

Student A: You are a reporter. Ask your group's questions.
Student B: You are Dr. Perez. Answer Student A's questions. (You should make up the answers.) Then switch roles.

Example: A: *How many players were on a team?*
        B: *We aren't sure, but we think there were three players on a team.*

Reading

Getting Ready to Read

Look at the pictures and the photograph. What do you think the article is going to be about?

_____

_____

crooked straight

back brace

Reading

Read the article. Was your answer to Getting Ready to Read correct?

JAMES BLAKE'S STORY

Andre Agassi and James Blake at the 2005 U.S. Open

At the 2005 U.S. Open, James Blake and Andre Agassi played one of the best tennis matches in history. Blake's **performance** in the match was **impressive**, but his life story is even more impressive.

James Blake began to play tennis when he was very young. But when he was 13, he got a serious illness called scoliosis. Scoliosis makes a person's back crooked. Blake had to wear a back brace eighteen hours a day for the next four years. But that didn't stop him. In a few short years, Blake was the best college tennis player in the United States. Then he left college to become a professional player. Because Blake was handsome and polite, **the media** loved him. _People_ magazine named him "the world's sexiest athlete."

Everything was perfect until May 6, 2004, when Blake had a terrible accident. He fell down during a tennis match and broke his neck. He wasn't **paralyzed**; however, he couldn't play tennis. But that was not the end of Blake's **troubles**. Two months after he had his accident, his father, Thomas, died. Then, a few days after his father's **death**, Blake woke up in terrible pain. He couldn't move his face. At the hospital, the doctors gave him some bad news. He had an illness called shingles. The doctors said that he got sick because he was **upset** about his father's death.

But Blake remembered his father's words: "If there's a problem, you're going to fix it." So as soon as he **recovered**, Blake started to play tennis again. A year after his father died, he played in the U.S. Open against one of the world's best players.

After You Read

A Look at the **boldface** words in the article. Guess their meaning. Match the words with the correct definitions.

_f_	**1.** performance	**a.**	very special and excellent
____	**2.** impressive	**b.**	not able to move
____	**3.** the media	**c.**	got better after an illness
____	**4.** paralyzed	**d.**	very unhappy
____	**5.** troubles	**e.**	the end of a person's life
____	**6.** death	**f.**	the way he played
____	**7.** upset	**g.**	problems
____	**8.** recovered	**h.**	newspapers, television, and magazines

B Put the statements in order from 1 to 9. Write the numbers in the blanks.

> **Reading Skill:**
> **Understanding Time Order**
>
> When you read a story, it is important to understand when things happened. What happened first? Second? Third? Time phrases, such as *in a few years*, and dates tell you the order of events.

____ **a.** Blake broke his neck.

____ **b.** Blake was the best college player in the United States.

____ **c.** Blake left college.

____ **d.** Blake played against Agassi at the U.S. Open.

____ **e.** Blake's father died.

____ **f.** Blake got shingles.

____ **g.** *People* magazine named Blake the world's sexiest athlete.

____ **h.** Blake got scoliosis.

__1__ **i.** Blake learned how to play tennis.

James Blake during a match

Writing

Getting Ready to Write

A Read the sentences. Add commas where necessary.

Almost 1,000 years ago, Christian monks began to play

a ball game called La Soule. Players hit the ball to each

other with their hands or a stick. When ordinary people began to play the game they

played outside with gloves and a racket. Then in the 17th century, "real tennis" became

the favorite game of the French royal family. However, after the French royal family was

killed in the French Revolution tennis became unpopular. It became popular again when

rich English people started to play it on grass in the 19th century. The Wimbledon tennis

championship started in 1877. It is still the world's most famous tennis championship.

> **Writing Tip**
>
> Remember that when a time clause comes first, we use a comma.
>
> **Examples:**
> **As soon as he recovered,** he started to play tennis.
>
> Blake began to play tennis **when he was young.**

B Read the model paragraph.

> People first played golf in Scotland in the 1400s. At first, they played on the beach with sticks and rocks. Then golf moved from the beach to golf courses. When players began to use expensive clubs and balls instead of sticks and rocks, golf became a game for rich people. But after factories started to make cheap golf clubs, ordinary people began to play again. By the early 1900s, both men and women were professional golf players. Now professional golf players such as Tiger Woods are world famous. Some players make millions of dollars every year.

rocks

sticks

club

ball

golf course

PAIRS. Read the model again. Where and when did people first play golf?

What do you know about the history of your favorite sport? Do you know where it began? In what country? Discuss.

Prewriting: Using Facts

You are going to write a paragraph about the history of a sport. Before you write, read the list of facts for the writing model. Then read the list of facts for soccer and ice skating. Choose one of the sports to write about.

Writing Model: Golf

- First played in Scotland in the 1400s
- Played on beach with sticks and rocks
- Later, moved from beach to golf courses. Expensive clubs and balls, a game for rich people
- Factories made cheap golf clubs, ordinary people began to play
- Early 1900s, men and women professional golf players
- Players such as Tiger Woods make millions of dollars every year

Soccer

- First played by Chinese, more than 2,000 years ago
- Japanese, Greeks, and Romans also played
- British—modern soccer about 700 years ago
- 1880s, English Football League—teams of professional players
- Today, world's most popular sport for men and women all over the world

Ice Skating

- 5,000 years ago—ice skates for transportation on ice in winter
- 500 years ago—ice skates in Europe for fun
- 1908 Olympic Winter Games, first competitions in figure skating (dancing on ice) and speed skating (skating fast)
- Today, skating popular in cold countries
- Popular in all countries—professional figure skating on TV

Writing

Now write a paragraph about the history of soccer or ice skating. The writing tip, the model paragraph, and the information above will help you. Write in your notebook.

Vocabulary

CD 1 TRACK **26** Look at the pairs of pictures. Which action happened first, and which happened second? Write *1* and *2* under each pair of pictures. Then listen and check your answers.

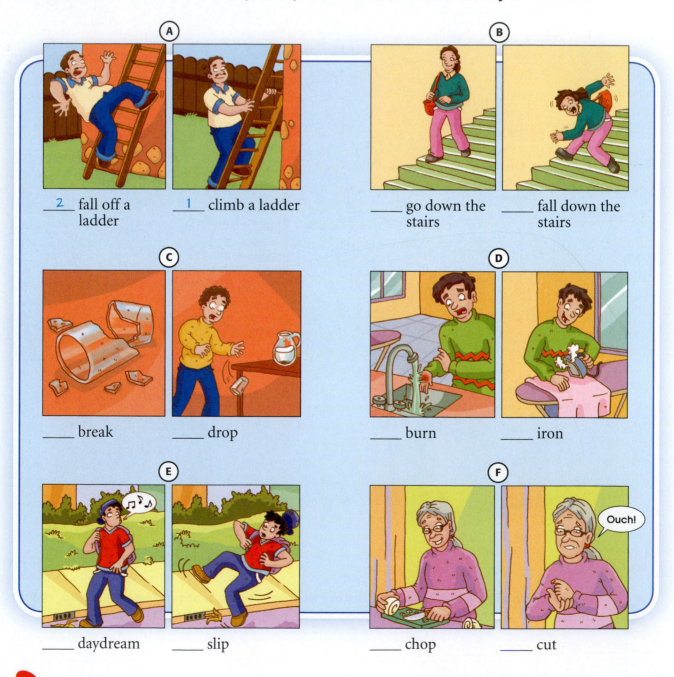

A

__2__ fall off a ladder   __1__ climb a ladder

B

____ go down the stairs   ____ fall down the stairs

C

____ break   ____ drop

D

____ burn   ____ iron

E

____ daydream   ____ slip

F

____ chop   __ __ cut

Ouch!

Listening

A **CD 1 TRACK 27 Listen. What did Manny do this weekend? Check (✓) the correct answers.**

❑ **1.** He painted the house.
❑ **2.** He dropped his paintbrush on his father-in-law.
❑ **3.** He fell off a ladder.
❑ **4.** He started a fire.

B **CD 1 TRACK 27 Listen again. Put the pictures in the correct order. Write *1* for the first thing that happened and *6* for the last.**

_____ Suddenly, I heard a loud bang, and I dropped my paintbrush.

__1__ I was climbing up a ladder, and my father-in-law was standing below me.

_____ Then my wife and mother-in-law ran out of the house. They were screaming.

_____ Where was it coming from? It was coming from the house next door.

_____ When I looked down, my father-in-law was standing there with paint all over him.

_____ While I was climbing down the ladder, I heard another bang. Then I smelled smoke.

C **CD 1 TRACK 27 Listen again. Check (✓) the sentences that are true.**

❑ **1.** Manny dropped the paintbrush because he smelled smoke.
❑ **2.** Manny's wife and mother-in-law ran out of the house because it was on fire.
❑ **3.** The neighbors were at home when the fire started.
❑ **4.** The fire was very serious.

PAST PROGRESSIVE: STATEMENTS

Subject	Be	Verb + -ing		Subject	Be + not	Verb + -ing	
I He She It	was	working	at 5:30.	I He She It	was not wasn't	working	at 5:30.
You We They	were			You We They	were not weren't		

A Look at the picture. There was a fire at 8:00 last night. What were the people doing? Write the correct apartment numbers.

Look

Use the past progressive to talk about activities in progress at a specific time in the past.

1. Mr. Gutierrez in apartment ___1A___ wasn't watching TV. He was having dinner.

2. Mr. and Mrs. Liu in apartment _____ weren't sleeping. They were having dinner.

3. Cindy, Amos, and Al in apartment _____ weren't playing cards. They were watching TV.

4. Annie in apartment _____ wasn't playing computer games. She was sleeping.

5. Deb in apartment _____ wasn't doing the dishes. She was talking on the phone.

6. Johan in apartment _____ wasn't listening to music. He was watching TV.

B Complete the sentences about the people in the apartments. Use the past progressive. Be careful. Some sentences are affirmative, and some are negative.

1. (Apt. 1A) Mr. Gutierrez (have) _____ was having _____ dinner.

    He (watch) _____ wasn't watching _____ TV.

2. (Apt. 2C) Charlie (sleep) _____.

    He (listen) _____ to music.

3. (Apt. 2B) Lucy and her sisters (play) _____ cards.

    They (read) _____.

4. (Apt. 1D) Martha (read) _____ the newspaper.

    She (do) _____ the dishes.

5. (Apt. 3A) Eric and Les (exercise) _____.

    They (play) _____ computer games.

6. (Apt. 2A) Mr. Roberts (wash) _____ the dishes.

    He (dry) _____ them.

C Other people in the apartment building were not at home last night at 8 P.M. Write what they probably said. Use the words in the box and quotation marks.

~~celebrate my wife's birthday~~	talk	walk my dog
go home	wait for the bus	work late

1. "I was at a restaurant with my family."   "We were celebrating my wife's birthday."

2. "I was with my girlfriend at a bus stop."   _____

3. "I was in my car."   _____

4. "I was in the park."   _____

5. "I was at my office."   _____

6. "I was on the phone with a friend."   _____

PAIRS. What about you? Where were you last night at 8 P.M.? What were you doing?

TIME to TALK

PAIRS. **Student A:** Study the picture in Exercise A. Then close your book and try to remember four things that people were doing at the time of the fire.

Student B: Keep your book open and give Student A the correct answers. Then switch roles.

Example: A: *A few people were sleeping.*
B: *No, you're wrong. Only one person was sleeping.*

Grammar to Communicate ❷

PAST PROGRESSIVE: QUESTIONS

Yes / No Questions				Short Answers	
Be	**Subject**	**Verb + -ing**			
Was	he	**driving**	at the time of the accident?	Yes, he was.	No, he wasn't.
Were	they			Yes, they were	No, they weren't.

Information Questions				Answers
Wh- word	**Be**	**Subject**	**Verb + -ing**	
Where	**were**	you	**looking?**	I was looking across the street.
	was	he		He was looking across the street.
	were	they		They were looking across the street.

Information Questions with *Who / What* as Subject			Answers
Wh- word	**Be**	**Verb + -ing**	
Who	**was**	**driving?**	Ben was driving.
What		**happening?**	A lot of things were happening.

A **Look at the picture. Answer the questions about the accident.**

At the time of the accident . . .

1. was the bus driver turning?
   <u>No, he wasn't.</u>

2. was the little girl standing on the corner?
   _____

3. were any people getting off the bus?
   _____

4. where were the women standing?
   _____

5. what was the little girl doing?
   _____

6. why was the man working?
   _____

B **Write questions and answers about the accident.**

1.   <u>Was the teenager watching his sister?</u>   <u>No, he wasn't.</u>
              (the teenager / watch his sister)

2.   _____   _____
         (the driver of the yellow car / look at the bus)

3.   _____   _____
            (the little girl / run after a ball)

4.   _____   _____
            (the bus / pick up passengers)

5.   _____   _____
        (the people on the bus / talk to the driver)

6.   _____   _____
           (both cars / go straight)

Look

not paying attention =
daydreaming

C **Read the statements. Then write questions to get more information.**

1.   The bus driver wasn't talking to the passengers.   Who <u>was the bus driver talking to?</u>

2.   The women weren't standing at the bus stop.   Where _____

3.   The girl's brother wasn't paying attention to her.   What _____

4.   The girl's brother wasn't driving the car.   Who _____

5.   The girl wasn't running on the sidewalk.   Where _____

6.   The bus driver wasn't looking at the women.   Who _____

7.   The man was fixing the street.   Why _____

PAIRS. Ask and answer the questions.

PAIRS. Talk about the last time the things in the box happened to you or someone you know. Ask and answer questions. Talk about what was happening at the time. If you can't remember, make up something.

be in a fire	break something valuable	lose something important
break a bone	get into a car accident	miss the bus

Example: A: *Last month I got into a car accident.*
B: *Were you driving?*
A: *No, I wasn't.*
B: *Where were you sitting?*
A: *I was sitting in the back seat.*

PAST PROGRESSIVE AND SIMPLE PAST: *WHEN* AND *WHILE*

Situations	Timelines	Example Sentences
two actions, one action in progress when another action happens	fell / Now / Past ——×——— Future / was walking fell / Now / Past ——×——— Future / were standing	The woman **fell while** she **was walking** down the street. **When** the woman **fell,** some teenagers **were standing** nearby.
two actions, one happens immediately after the other	Now / Past ×——×— Future / fell hurt Now / Past ×——×— Future / fell ran	**When** the woman **fell,** she **hurt** her leg. The teenagers **ran** to help the woman **when** she **fell**.
two actions happening at the same time	Now / Past ——————— Future / were helping / were calling	**While** the teenagers **were helping** the woman, a store owner **was calling** her family.

A Read the sentences. Circle the action that happened first. If both actions happened at the same time, underline them.

1. I was <u>daydreaming</u> while I was <u>chopping onions</u>.
2. While I was chopping onions, I cut my finger.
3. When I cut my finger, I got a Band-Aid.
4. I was opening the box of Band-Aids when the phone rang.
5. While I was running to get the phone, I slipped and fell on the floor.

B Write sentences. Put the words in the correct order. Use commas where necessary.

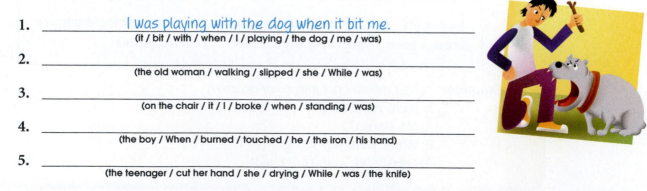

1. _____ I was playing with the dog when it bit me. _____
   (it / bit / with / when / I / playing / the dog / me / was)

2. _____
   (the old woman / walking / slipped / she / While / was)

3. _____
   (on the chair / it / I / broke / when / standing / was)

4. _____
   (the boy / When / burned / touched / he / the iron / his hand)

5. _____
   (the teenager / cut her hand / she / drying / While / was / the knife)

C How did the people have accidents? Write two sentences about each set of pictures.
Use *when* or *while*.

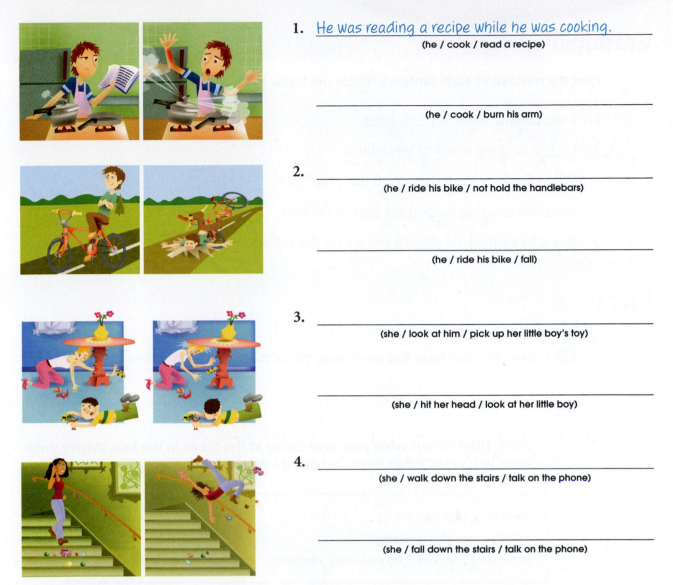

1. He was reading a recipe while he was cooking.
   _____
   (he / cook / read a recipe)

   _____

   _____
   (he / cook / burn his arm)

2. _____
   (he / ride his bike / not hold the handlebars)

   _____

   _____
   (he / ride his bike / fall)

3. _____
   (she / look at him / pick up her little boy's toy)

   _____

   _____
   (she / hit her head / look at her little boy)

4. _____
   (she / walk down the stairs / talk on the phone)

   _____

   _____
   (she / fall down the stairs / talk on the phone)

PAIRS. Now look at the pictures on page 44. Describe what happened in each picture.
Use *when* and *while*. Then tell your sentences to the class.

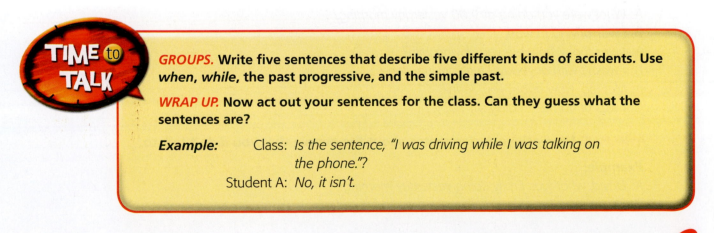

TIME to TALK

GROUPS. Write five sentences that describe five different kinds of accidents. Use *when*, *while*, the past progressive, and the simple past.

WRAP UP. Now act out your sentences for the class. Can they guess what the sentences are?

Example: Class: *Is the sentence, "I was driving while I was talking on the phone."?*
              Student A: *No, it isn't.*

Review and Challenge

Grammar

Find the mistake in each sentence. Circle the letter and correct the mistake.

1. I <u>was</u> <u>talking</u> <u>while</u> she <u>was drove</u>.   *driving*
      A   B   C   (D)

2. He <u>was</u> <u>running</u> when <u>he</u> <u>was falling</u>.
       A   B   C   D

3. <u>When</u> the fire <u>was starting</u>, <u>I</u> <u>left</u> the building.
      A   B   C D

4. <u>Were</u> you <u>and Bob</u> sleep <u>at the time</u> of the fire?
     A   B   C   D

5. <u>While</u> he <u>painted</u>, he <u>slipped</u> and <u>fell</u> off the ladder.
     A   B   C   D

Dictation

🔊 **28** Listen. You will hear five sentences. Write them in your notebook.

Speaking

ON YOUR OWN. Think about what you were doing at the times in the box. Where were you? Who were you with? What were you doing? Write your answers in your notebook.

Sunday at 3:00 P.M.	at 7:00 yesterday evening
at 9:00 yesterday morning	at midnight last night
between 12:00 and 2:00 yesterday afternoon	at 6:00 this morning

CLASS. Then walk around the class and ask your classmates about their activities. Who was doing the same thing at the same time as you? Who was doing something different?

Example:

A: *What were you doing at 9:00 yesterday morning?*
B: *I was driving to work.*
A: *I was too. Who were you driving with?*
B: *I wasn't with anybody. I was driving alone.*
A: *Me, too. How about you, Jean?*
C: *I was at home, feeding my baby.*

WRAP UP. Now ask your classmates about the people that you didn't talk to.

Example:

A: *David, what was Emily doing yesterday morning?*
D: *She was on the subway. She was coming home from work.*

52 Unit 4

Listening

A **29** Listen. Mrs. White was in an accident. She is talking to her insurance agent. Check (✓) the diagram that shows what happened.

→	= Direction
1	= Mrs. White's car
2	= Car that hit Mrs. White
3	= Van
N	= North

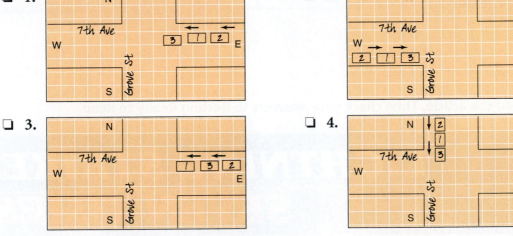

❏ 1.   ❏ 2.

❏ 3.   ❏ 4.

B  **29** Listen again. Which of the vehicles do the sentences describe? Write *1* (Mrs. White's car), *2* (the car that hit Mrs. White's car), or *3* (the van). Be careful. Some sentences have more than one correct answer.

Look

vehicle = something, for example, a car or a bus, that carries people or things

___2___ 1. The driver went to the hospital.

_____ 2. The vehicle was moving fast.

_____ 3. The driver was talking on a cell phone.

_____ 4. The vehicle wasn't moving.

_____ 5. The driver was wearing a seatbelt.

wear a seatbelt

bleed

TIME to TALK

PAIRS. Talk about a car accident.

Student A: Turn to page 301. Imagine that you were in the car accident in the diagram. Describe the accident to Student B.

Student B: Turn to page 304. Listen to Student A and draw a diagram of his or her accident. Switch roles. Student B describes his or her accident to Student A, and Student A draws. Then, check each other's diagrams.

Example:

A: *I got into an accident.*

B: *What happened? Where were you?*

Reading

Getting Ready to Read

Scan the article. In which years did lightning strike Roy Sullivan? Write the years.

_1942,_

Reading Skill:
Scanning

When you **scan** a text, you are looking for specific information. You move your eyes very quickly over the text to find something, like a date or a name.

Reading

Read the article. Then check your answers to Getting Ready to Read.

LIGHTNING STRIKES SEVEN TIMES!

Some people say that lightning never **strikes** twice. But sometimes, it does! Just ask Roy Sullivan. In his lifetime, Sullivan, a park ranger from Virginia, **survived** seven **incredible** lightning strikes.

Six of the strikes hit Sullivan at Shenandoah National Park. The first happened in 1942 when he was standing in a lookout tower. It **took off** one of his toenails. The second strike **occurred** in 1969 while he was driving. It burned off his eyebrows. The third strike came in 1970 as he was walking across his front yard. It burned his shoulders. The fourth, in 1972, hit him when he was standing in a ranger station. That strike burned off all of his hair. The fifth, sixth, and seventh strikes all occurred within just four years.

The fifth strike happened in 1973. Sullivan was at work when he saw that a storm cloud was forming. He got in his truck and tried to go faster than the cloud. As soon as he was sure that he was safe, he got out of his truck. But that was a mistake.

A park ranger in a lookout tower.

"I actually saw the lightning shoot out of the cloud this time," he said. "It was coming straight for me." The strike set his hair on fire and **traveled** down his leg. Then it took off his shoe. The sixth strike came in 1974 as he was checking a campground. Finally, the seventh found him in 1977 while he was fishing.

The lightning strikes **damaged** both Sullivan's health and his relationships. After people heard his story, they were afraid to be around him. "Naturally, people **avoid** me," Sullivan told a reporter. "I was walking with the chief ranger one day, and lightning struck way off, and he said, 'I'll see you later, Roy.'"

After You Read

A   Look at the **boldface** words in the article. Guess their meaning. Match the words with the correct definitions.

___h___ **1.** strikes

_____ **2.** survived

_____ **3.** incredible

_____ **4.** took off

_____ **5.** occurred

_____ **6.** traveled

_____ **7.** damaged

_____ **8.** avoid

a. hurt

b. stay away from

c. went

d. very strange and difficult to believe

e. removed by a strong force

f. happened

g. continued to live after a serious accident

h. hits someone or something

B   What was Roy doing at the time of the lightning strikes? Write full sentences.

Strike 1:   _He was standing in a lookout tower at a national park._

Strike 2:   _____

_____

Strike 3:   _____

_____

Strike 4:   _____

_____

Strike 5:   _____

_____

Strike 6:   _____

_____

Strike 7:   _____

_____

Accidents   **55**

Writing

Getting Ready to Write

Writing Tip

Remember that the past progressive and simple past show when different events happen.

Example:
The second strike **occurred** in 1969 while Roy **was driving**.

A Look at the pictures. Write sentences. Use the word in parentheses and the simple past or past progressive of the verbs. Add commas where necessary.

1. (while) I / swim / I / see a bolt of lightning

   <u>While I was swimming, I saw a bolt of lightning.</u> OR

   <u>I saw a bolt of lightning while I was swimming.</u>

2. (when) my mother / hear the storm / she / ran down to the beach

   _____

   _____

3. (when) I / swim toward the beach / I / see my mother

   _____

   _____

B Read the model paragraph.

> Last Saturday, a lot of people were enjoying the beautiful weather in the park. One woman was walking a big dog. Suddenly the dog saw a duck in the lake. The dog jumped into the lake and pulled the woman into the water! At first it was funny, but then the woman started to scream. I was getting ready to jump in the water when the dog grabbed a tree branch. He swam over to the woman with the branch, and she grabbed it. Then the dog swam back to the shore. When the dog pulled the woman out of the water, everybody started to cheer. It was incredible!

PAIRS. Read the model again. What was incredible about the day in the park?

Then tell your partner about something incredible or surprising that happened to you.

Prewriting: Visualizing

You are going to write a story about the event you described to your partner on page 56. Before you write, draw a series of pictures to show the different things that happened. Visualizing will help you remember the details of your story.

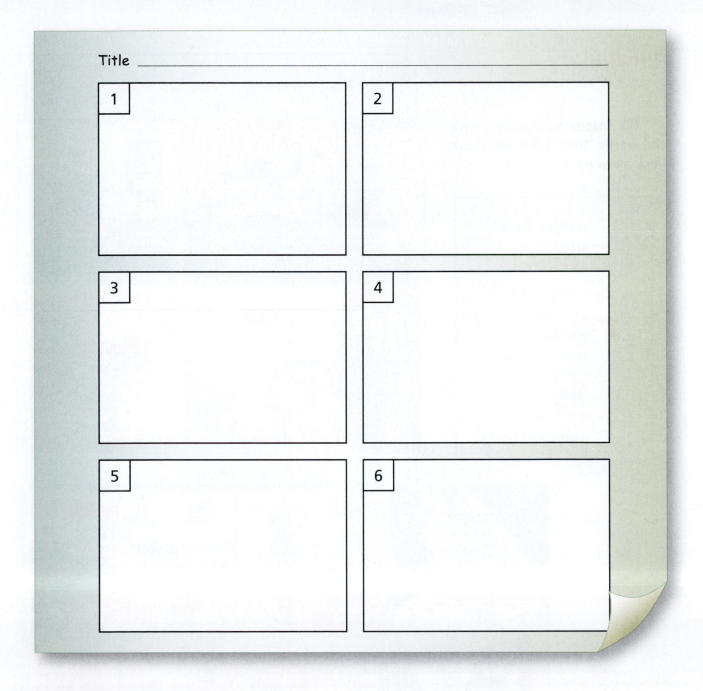

Title _____

1	2
3	4
5	6

Writing

Now write a story about the incredible or surprising event. The writing tip, the model paragraph, and your pictures will help you. Write in your notebook.

Unit 5
Then and Now

Grammar
- *Used to:* Statements
- *Used to:* Yes / No Questions
- *Used to:* Information Questions

Vocabulary

CD 1 TRACK 30 Match the numbers with the words. Then listen and check your answers.

_____ change a diaper

_____ dress

_____ feed

_____ get dressed up

_____ give a bath

__1__ give birth

_____ make one's own clothes

_____ repair

_____ throw away

_____ wear casual clothes

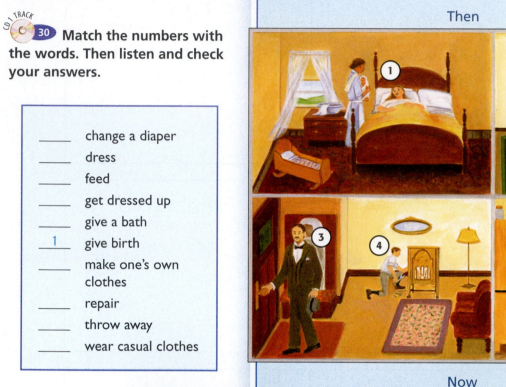

Then

Now

Listening

 A  Listen. Tina is talking to her grandmother. What are they talking about? Check (✓) the main topic of their conversation.

❏ when Tina's grandmother was a little girl

❏ how Tina's grandmother and grandfather met

❏ dating in the past

ask someone out

Would you like to go to the school dance with me?

go on a date

B Listen again. Who said it? Write *T* (Tina) or *G* (her grandmother).

___T___ 1. Did you use to go on dates?

_____ 2. Yes, of course we did.

_____ 3. What did you use to do?

_____ 4. We used to go bowling.

_____ 5. In fact, there didn't use to be any malls.

_____ 6. Did you go on dates every Saturday night?

_____ 7. No, I didn't.

 C Listen again. Check (✓) the things that were true about dating when Tina's grandmother was a teenager.

❏ 1. Young people didn't use to go to the movies on dates.

❏ 2. The girl used to pay.

❏ 3. The guys used to pick the girls up.

❏ 4. The guys used to meet the girls' parents.

❏ 5. The girls used to meet the guys' parents.

❏ 6. Boys and girls used to meet at the mall.

Grammar to Communicate ❶

USED TO: STATEMENTS

Subject	Used to	Verb		Time Expression	Subject	Didn't use to	Verb		Time Expression
I	used to	live	in Miami,	but I don't **anymore**.	I	**didn't use to**	**have**	a pet,	but I do **now**.
You					You				
He	used to	live	in Miami.		He	**didn't use to**	**have**	a pet.	
We					We				
They					They				

A   Mrs. Stein is 85 years old. She is giving her opinion about the lives of men and women when she was a child. Complete her sentences. Write *men* or *women*.

1. "___Women___ used to wear skirts and dresses to work, but now they don't."

2. "_____ used to make their own clothes, but they don't anymore."

3. "_____ didn't use to feed babies, but they often do now."

4. "_____ didn't use to keep their last name after marriage, but they do now."

5. "_____ didn't use to change diapers, but they do now."

6. "_____ used to be good at repairing things, but they aren't anymore."

> ## Look
>
> *Used to + verb =* happened in the past but doesn't happen often now.
> People **used to build** their own houses.
>
> *Didn't use to + verb =* didn't happen often in the past but happens often now.
> Women **didn't use to be** police officers.

B   Write sentences with the words in the boxes. Write in your notebook.

Men	used to / didn't use to	be in the room at the birth of their children.
		give babies baths.
		make all the money for the family.
		stay at home with their children.
		ask men out on dates.
Women	used to / didn't use to	get married at a very young age.
		have their own credit card.
		live alone before marriage.

Example:

Men didn't use to be in the room at the birth of their children.

 60   Unit 5

C Write two sentences about each picture with *used to* and *didn't use to*. Use the words in the box.

~~wash clothes by hand~~	make their own bread	make furniture by hand	grow their own vegetables
~~have washing machines~~	buy bread	make furniture in a factory	buy frozen vegetables

1.

People used to wash clothes by hand.

They didn't use to have washing machines.

2.
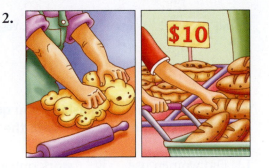

_____

_____

3.

_____

_____

4.

_____

_____

PAIRS. What did people in your country use to make by hand but not anymore? What do they still make by hand today?

PAIRS. Talk about five or more ways your life has changed. Use the words in the box or your own ideas.

> be single / be married
>
> not have children / have a child
>
> live in the country / live in the city
>
> live with your parents / have your own place
>
> live in your country / live in a new country

Example: *I used to be single. I got married last year. Now I cook dinner every night. I didn't use to cook. I used to eat fast food.*

Grammar to Communicate 2

USED TO: YES / NO QUESTIONS										
Did	Subject	Use to	Verb	Affirmative			Negative			
Did	you he we they	**use to**	**work?**	**Yes,**	I he we they	**did.**	**No,**	I he we they	**didn't.**

A Imagine that someone is asking you questions about work life in your country fifty years ago. Complete the questions with the missing words. Then answer the questions.

1. Did women use ___to___ work outside the home?   <u>Yes, they did.</u> OR <u>No, they didn't.</u>

2. _____ women use to go to college?   _____

3. Did women _____ to be in the military?   _____

4. _____ parents use to put their children in daycare?   _____

5. Did fathers use _____ stay home with a sick child?   _____

6. Did men _____ to take time off for a child's birth?   _____

PAIRS. Ask and answer the questions about your countries.

Example:
A: *Did women use to go to college in your country?*
B: *No, they didn't, but they do today.*

B Complete the questions with the correct form of *used to.*

1. **A:** Men are kindergarten teachers these days.

   B: <u>Did they use to be kindergarten teachers</u>_____ years ago?

2. **A:** Women are directors of big companies.

   B: _____ years ago?

3. **A:** Women drive buses and trucks these days.

   B: _____ years ago?

4. **A:** Women are college professors nowadays.

   B: _____ years ago?

5. **A:** Men work as nurses nowadays.

   B: _____ years ago?

6. **A:** Men often wear jeans and T-shirts to work nowadays.

   B: _____ years ago?

C CD 1 TRACK 32 **Complete the conversation between Lucy and her grandmother. Use the correct form of *used to* or *didn't use to*. Then listen and check your answers.**

Lucy: What a terrible day! I hate my job. I'm so happy that it's Friday!

Gram: Why? You're lucky. Life for working women _____*used to be*_____ much more
1. (be)

difficult.

Lucy: What do you mean?

Gram: Well, first of all, look at your sneakers. Women _____ sneakers to work.
2. (wear)

They _____ dressed up.
3. (get)

Lucy: And how about men? _____ dressed up, too?
4. (get)

Gram: Of course. Businessmen _____ hats, suits, and ties to work. And
5. (wear)

everybody _____ from 9:00 to 5:00, Monday to Friday. Oh, and one
6. (work)

more thing . . . do you ever make your boss coffee?

Lucy: Of course not!

Gram: Well, women _____ coffee for their bosses. And they did it for years
7. (make)

because people _____ jobs. They _____ at the same job for
8. (change)   9. (stay)

their whole lives.

TIME to TALK

PAIRS. Do a role play. Imagine a grandparent talking to a grandchild about his or her life as a teenager. Use the conversation in Exercise C as a model.

Student A: You are the grandparent.
Student B: You are the grandchild.

Example:
A: *Your life is a lot easier than mine was when I was your age.*
B: *Easier? In what way?*
A: *Well, teenagers didn't use to have their own cars, for one thing.*
B: *Really? Did you use to walk everywhere?*

WRAP UP. Now act out your role play for the class.

Then and Now 63

Grammar to Communicate 3

USED TO: INFORMATION QUESTIONS

Wh- word	Did	Subject	Use to	Verb	Answers
How often		she		go out?	She **used to go out** every weekend.
Where	did	you	use to	meet?	We **used to meet** at my home.
When		they		go?	They **used to go** on Sundays.
Who		he		date?	He **used to date** Mary.

Wh- word (Subject)	Used to	Verb		Answers
What	used to	**happen**	every Friday?	We **used to go bowling**.
Who		**go?**		Everyone on the team went.

A   Answer the questions about what men and women do these days and what they used to do in many parts of the world. If you are not sure, guess.

1. A man and a woman are standing near a door.

   Who opens the door these days?   *Who used to open the door?*

   a. The man opens the door.   **a.** The man used to open the door.

   b. The woman opens the door.   **b.** The woman used to open the door.

   c. It isn't important.   **c.** It wasn't important.

2. A woman comes into a room. Two men are sitting in the room.

   What do men do these days?   *What did men use to do?*

   a. They say hello.   **a.** They used to say hello.

   b. They stand up and say hello.   **b.** They used to stand up and say hello.

   c. They do nothing.   **c.** They used to do nothing.

3. A man and a woman are standing near a table.

   When does the man sit down these days?   *When did the man use to sit down?*

   a. before the woman   **a.** before the woman

   b. after the woman   **b.** after the woman

   c. at the same time as the woman   **c.** at the same time as the woman

B Write questions about dating fifty years ago. Put the words in the correct order.

1. <u>What did girls use to wear on dates?</u>
   (wear on dates / to / use / girls / did / what)
2. _____
   (used / pay for / who / the date / to)
3. _____
   (where / the man / pick up the woman / did / to / use)
4. _____
   (young people / what / did / to / use / on dates / do)
5. _____
   (did / at what age / girls / start dating / to / use)

PAIRS. Ask and answer the questions about your country.

C Read the statements about family life in some parts of the world today. Write questions about life fifty years ago. Use the correct form of *used to*.

1. Today families rarely have dinner together.

   How often _____<u>did families use to have</u>_____ dinner together?
                          (have)
2. Today people eat fast food three or four times a week.

   How often _____?
                    (eat out)
3. Today many women have their first child after age thirty.

   At what age _____?
                       (have)
4. Many children's parents drive them to school.

   How _____ to school?
            (get)
5. Day care workers often take care of very young children today.

   Who _____ very young children?
            (take care of)

PAIRS. Ask and answer the questions. Do you and your partner agree on the answers?

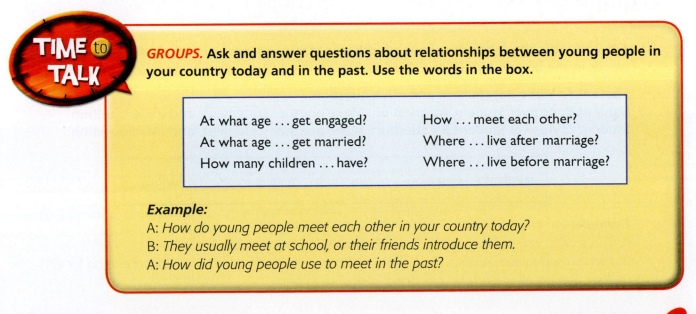

TIME to TALK

GROUPS. Ask and answer questions about relationships between young people in your country today and in the past. Use the words in the box.

At what age . . . get engaged?	How . . . meet each other?
At what age . . . get married?	Where . . . live after marriage?
How many children . . . have?	Where . . . live before marriage?

Example:
A: *How do young people meet each other in your country today?*
B: *They usually meet at school, or their friends introduce them.*
A: *How did young people use to meet in the past?*

Review and Challenge

Grammar

33 This conversation has seven mistakes. The first mistake is corrected for you. Find and correct the other six mistakes. Then listen and check your answers.

Rob: Do you always take your son to school?

Dan: Always.

Rob: ~~Your father use~~ *Did your father use* to take you to school?

Dan: No, never.

Rob: Did your father use to did help around the house?

Dan: My father usen't to do a thing. He used come home, have dinner, and watch TV.

Rob: Who did use to take care of the house?

Dan: My mother, of course.

Rob: You used to help her?

Dan: No, I didn't. My brothers and sisters and I were used to be the same as my father.

Dictation

34 Listen. You will hear five sentences. Write them in your notebook.

Speaking

GROUPS. **Talk about how our lives are different today because of technology. Use the words in the box and your own ideas.**

Student A: Make a statement and ask a question.
Student B: Answer Student A's question. Make another statement, and ask a question.
Student C: Answer Student B's question. Make another statement, and ask a question.

airplanes	electricity	refrigerators	running water	televisions

Example:

A: *There didn't use to be electricity. How did people use to read after dark?*
B: *People used to use candles. There didn't use to be televisions. What did people use to do for fun?*
C: *They used to sit around and talk. There didn't use to be . . .*

Listening

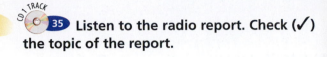

A 🅲🅳 TRACK 35 **Listen to the radio report. Check (✓) the topic of the report.**

❏ changes in women's lives

❏ mothers and fathers in the past

❏ women's lives today

B 🅲🅳 TRACK 35 **Listen again. Complete the sentences with the correct information.**

1. Lynn and Alice Thomas are twins. They are _____ years old.

2. Women used to do all of the _____.

3. There didn't use to be any _____, so women used to wash the family's clothes by _____.

4. Alice and Lynn used to do the laundry _____.

5. They used to get up at _____ in the morning on Mondays, and they didn't finish until _____ at night.

6. Men used to have _____ off.

7. The women used to work _____ days a week.

TIME to TALK

GROUPS. Talk about changes in society in the past 100 years. Which changes are positive? Which changes are negative? Write five sentences for each category.

Examples:

Positive Changes
Housework today is easy. It used to be hard because there didn't use to be any machines.

Negative Changes
People eat a lot of fast food. They used to eat home cooking.

WRAP UP. Share your list with the class. Discuss any differences of opinion.

Reading

Getting Ready to Read

Look at the pictures. Check (✓) which kind of transportation came first.

❑ electric trolley

rails
❑ horsecar

❑ Model T car

❑ omnibus

Reading

Read the article. Was your answer to Getting Ready to Read correct?

Public Transportation
IN AMERICAN CITIES

1 How did people use to get from place to place in American cities? Before the early 1800s, some people rode horses. But most people used to walk.

2 In the 1830s the first kind of public transportation, the omnibus, appeared in American cities. Horses pulled the omnibuses, and they were slow. Then, in the 1840s, someone had the idea to put the omnibus on iron rails. This new vehicle, the horsecar, was faster and more comfortable than the omnibus. But the car didn't stay on the rails very well. When it went off the rails, the passengers had to get out and put it back on. Also, as with the omnibus, the horses used to make the streets very dirty.

3 The horsecar was popular until the invention of the electric trolley in the 1880s. Because trolleys used electricity, the streets were cleaner. Trolleys were also faster than horsecars. However, with so many vehicles on the city streets, there used to be terrible traffic jams. So engineers started to build public transportation above and below the streets. First they built trains that traveled above the streets. These trains were noisy, ugly, and dirty. Then engineers built underground trains below the streets called subways. New York City's subway opened in 1904.

4 The public transportation system of the United States used to be very good. But things began to change in 1908 when Henry Ford invented the Model T car. Americans began to buy their own cars, and they stopped using public transportation. The government spent a lot of money on new highways for the cars, but it spent very little money on buses, trains, and trolleys. As a result, by 1991 the United States had the world's best road system but a very bad public transportation system.

After You Read

A   Check (✓) the features the article mentions for each type of transportation.

	OMNIBUS	HORSECAR	ELECTRIC TROLLEY
clean			
dirty			
comfortable			
uncomfortable	✓		
fast			
slow			
with horses			
without horses			

B   Read the article again. What is the main topic of the article?

_____

_____

What is the topic of each paragraph? Write the paragraph number next to its topic.

_____ electric transportation

_____ the earliest public transportation

_____ transportation before the 1800s

_____ the car's effect on transportation

BOOTH.

Writing

Getting Ready to Write

 A   Combine the two sentences. Use *and* or *or*.

1. My sister and I used to ride our bikes in nice weather. We used to walk in bad weather.

   <u>My sister and I used to ride our bikes in nice</u>
   <u>weather and walk in bad weather.</u>

2. We didn't use to take the bus. We didn't use to drive.

   _____

   _____

3. Parents didn't use to drop their kids off at school. Parents didn't use to pick them up after school.

   _____

   _____

4. Most families used to live close to their workplaces. Most families used to share one car.

   _____

5. People used to buy one car. People used to keep it for years.

   _____

> **Writing Tip**
>
> If you have one subject with two verbs with *used to*, write *used to* only one time. For affirmative sentences, join the two verbs with *and*. For negative sentences, use *or*.
>
> **Examples:**
> **Americans used to walk or ride** in carriages.
>
> **Poor people didn't use to own horses or ride** in carriages.

B   Read the model paragraph.

> In the United States, cars were much less common in the past than they are today. Fifty years ago, families used to have only one car. In most families, the father used to drive the car to work. The mother used to stay at home and do housework. Teenagers didn't use to have their own cars. They used to walk or ride their bikes everywhere. Things are different now. Families often have several cars. Often, all the people in the family have their own cars. It's more convenient now, but because so many people have cars, there's a lot more traffic and pollution than there used to be. Maybe things were better before when people used to ride bikes!

PAIRS. Read the model again. How many cars did Americans use to have, and how many do they have now? Is this true in your country?

Now talk about the way something used to be and the way it is now. You can talk about transportation, roles of men and women, free time activities, food, school life, work life, or your own idea.

Prewriting: Using an Outline

You are going to write a paragraph about the way something used to be and the way it is now. Before you write, choose a main topic from the list, or choose your own main topic.

- Transportation
- Roles of men and women
- Free time activities

- Food
- School life
- Work life

Read the outline for the writing model. Then complete your outline with notes about your topic.

Writing Model
Main Topic: Cars Then and Now

1. How things used to be:
   - families have only one car
   - father drove to work
   - mother stayed home
   - teenagers walked, rode bikes

2. How things are now:
   - families have several cars
   - all the people in the family have own cars
   - more traffic
   - more pollution

Main Topic:

1. How things used to be
   -
   -
   -
   -

2. How things are now
   -
   -
   -
   -

Writing

Now write a paragraph about the way something used to be and the way it is now. The writing tip, the model paragraph, and your notes will help you. Write in your notebook.

Unit 6
Busy Lives

Grammar
- Future: *Will* for Decisions and Promises
- Future: *Be going to* and *Will*
- Future: Present Progressive for Future Arrangements

Vocabulary

36 Match the numbers with the words. Then listen and check your answers.

_____ attend (a meeting)

_____ babysit

_____ be free

__1__ drop off

_____ get the door / answer the door

_____ get the phone / answer the phone

_____ get something to go

_____ give someone a ride

_____ help someone do something

_____ pick up

_____ try out for

At school

At home

I want my mommy.

On Main Street

I'll take you home.

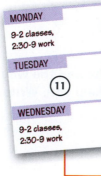

MONDAY
9-2 classes,
2:30-9 work

TUESDAY
(11)

WEDNESDAY
9-2 classes,
2:30-9 work

Listening

A CD 1 TRACK 37 **Listen. Who is talking? Check (✓) the correct answer.**

❑ Billy is talking to his mother and to his friend Tad.

❑ Billy is talking to his mother and to his friend Luz.

❑ Billy is talking to his mother, his friend Luz, and his friend Tad.

❑ Billy's mother is talking to Billy and Luz.

B CD 1 TRACK 38 **Read and listen again. Write the missing words. Use the words in the box.**

are	going to	He'll	~~I'll~~	I'm	to take	trying	you

Mom: _____I'll_____ drop you off at the bus stop.
1.

Billy: That's okay. I'll call Tad. _____ give us a ride.
2.

Mom: Forget it! It's already 7:30. Now say good-bye to Luz and get in the car.

Billy: Luz? My mother can't give us a ride. I'm going _____ the bus. I'll see you at school.
3.

Mom: What time are _____ going to be home tonight?
4.

Billy: Pretty late. I'm _____ out for the soccer team after school.
5.

Mom: Oh, that's right. Good luck.

Billy: Thanks . . . What _____ we having for dinner?
6.

Mom: I don't know. I need to run some errands after work. _____ not going to have time to cook, and your father's not _____ be home.
7.   8.

THINGS TO DO TODAY

go to the bank

dry cleaners—
   drop off shirts

pharmacy—
   pick up prescription

go to the supermarket

run errands

C CD 1 TRACK 39 **Listen again. Check (✓) the sentences that are true.**

❑ 1. Billy is going to drive to school.

❑ 2. Billy is going to get a ride from Luz.

❑ 3. Billy's mother is going to give him a ride to the bus stop.

❑ 4. Billy wants to play on the school soccer team.

❑ 5. Billy is going to be late for school.

Grammar to Communicate 1

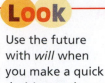

FUTURE: *WILL* FOR DECISIONS AND PROMISES							
Subject	*Will*	Verb		Subject	*Will not*	Verb	
I	**will**	help	you.	I	**will not**	help	you.
They		visit	tomorrow.	They		visit	tomorrow.

Contractions	
I + will → **I'll**	They + will + not → **They won't**

Look

Use the future with *will* when you make a quick decision at the time of speaking.
A: I'm hot.
B: I'll open the window.

A **Match the statements with the responses.**

___c___ 1. **A:** We can't leave the kids alone.   **a.** **B:** I'll get something to go.

_____ 2. **A:** My new phone isn't working.   **b.** **B:** I'll get some at the store.

_____ 3. **A:** I haven't got time to cook.   **c.** **B:** I'll call my sister. She'll babysit.

_____ 4. **A:** There's a problem with the car.   **d.** **B:** No, my secretary will get it.

_____ 5. **A:** We don't have any milk.   **e.** **B:** I'll take it to the garage later.

_____ 6. **A:** Do you need to answer that call?   **f.** **B:** Give it to my son. He'll fix it.

B CD 1 TRACK 40 **Listen to the conversations and complete the sentences with the missing words.**

1. **A:** What's fresh today?

   B: Everything's fresh. These muffins are hot out of the oven.

   A: Mmmm. _____ six.

2. **A:** Mr. Roberts, Charlie Parker is on the line.

   B: Tell him I'm busy. _____ him back later.

   A: But he said it was important.

3. **A:** Hello? Jimmy, it's Mom. I'm working late again tonight.

   B: But what about the movie? You promised.

   A: I'm sorry. Dad isn't busy. Maybe _____ you.

4. **A:** Are you dropping off or picking up?

   B: Dropping off. Wow, you're busy. I'll run some errands and come back at noon.

   A: OK. _____ your prescription ready for you then.

5. **A:** A table for two, please.

   B: And your name, please?

   A: Oh, is there a wait? We're in a hurry. _____ something to go.

C   **What promises do these people make? Use *won't* or *will* and the words in the box.**

> **Look**
>
> Use the future with *will* or *won't* when you make a promise.
> **I'll do** it tomorrow. I promise.

answer	babysit	be	forget	give	open	~~wash~~

1.   The dishes are in the sink. Paul is busy right now. What does he promise his wife?

   "I _____*will wash*_____ them later."

2.   Sara has to work on Saturday, but she doesn't want to leave her kids alone. What do her parents promise?

   "We _____."

3.   Lori's boss wants her to work late on Mondays, but she is worried about taking the bus late at night. What does her boss promise?

   "I _____ you a ride home."

4.   It's Carl's lunch hour, and he's getting something to go. What does the server promise?

   "Your food _____ ready in ten minutes."

5.   Dan forgot to pick his brother up after class last week. What does Dan promise?

   "I _____ this time."

6.   Vera's working late. Her kids are alone at home. What do they promise?

   "Don't worry. We _____ the door for anyone."

7.   Ed's boss always call him during dinner. His wife is angry. What does Ed promise?

   "I _____ the phone during dinner anymore."

TIME to TALK

PAIRS. Write three short conversations. Use a different sentence in the box in each conversation. Use the conversations in Exercise B as models.

"Don't worry. I'll help you do it."	"Thanks! I'll remember this!"
"We'll help you find an apartment."	"He'll pick them up for you."
"My husband will give you a ride."	"I'll get something to go."

Example:
A: *I don't want to paint my apartment. It's so much work.*
B: *Don't worry. I'll help you do it.*
A: *Really? That's great!*

WRAP UP. Now act out one of your conversations for the class.

Grammar to Communicate ❷

FUTURE: *BE GOING TO* AND *WILL*	
Rule	**Example**
Use *be going to* for future actions that you plan before the time of speaking.	**A:** Why are the eggs, sugar, and flour on the kitchen table? **B:** **I'm going to make** a cake. It's Ed's birthday tomorrow.
Use *will* for future actions that you decide at the time of speaking.	**A:** It's Ed's birthday tomorrow. **B:** Really? **I'll make** him a cake. He likes chocolate, right?
Use *will* for promises about the future.	**A:** Can we go to Ed's birthday party? **B:** I'm sorry, but I have to work this weekend. We**'ll visit** him next weekend. I promise.

 A What is the meaning of the **boldface** words? What is the speaker talking about? Write *PL* (a plan before the time of speaking), *D* (a decision at the time of speaking), or *P* (a promise).

__D__ 1. **A:** We need to get some gas.

         B: Okay. I'll **stop** at the next station.

____ 2. **A:** Who's picking up the kids tomorrow?

         B: Betty. She**'s going to be** here at 3:00.

____ 3. **A:** I need a ride home.

         B: Amy's got a car. She**'ll take** you.

____ 4. **A:** **Are you going to try out** for the play?

         B: No, I haven't got time this year.

____ 5. **A:** But you said we could go to the zoo.

         B: **I'll take** you next week. I promise.

____ 6. **A:** Do you need help with the kids?

         B: No, my Mom**'s going to babysit**.

B 🎵 CD 1 TRACK 41 **Complete the conversations. Circle the correct answer. Then listen and check your answers.**

1. **Joe:** Why are you putting on your sneakers?

    Tim: **I'm going to / I'll** play soccer.

2. **Amy:** Are you free this evening?

    Ann: No, **I'm going to / I'll** babysit for the Miller kids.

3. **Paul:** I'm tired.

    Tina: Then give me the keys. **I'm going to / I'll** drive.

4. **Lisa:** Mom's busy tonight and can't take me to the party.

    Dad: I told you yesterday. **I'm going to / I'll** take you to the party.

5. **Fran:** You have a new schedule at work, right?

    Adam: Yes. **I'm not going to / I won't** work on weekends anymore.

C 🔊 **CD 1 TRACK 42** **Complete the conversations. Use *will* or the correct form of *be going to*. Then listen and check your answers.**

1. **Rao:** Could you get sandwiches for the party?

    Ada: I talked to Charlie yesterday. He's going to get _____ the sandwiches.
    (get)

    But I 'll get _____ the drinks.
    (get)

2. **Clara:** Why is the soap and water outside?

    Felix: I _____ the car.
    (wash)

3. **Solana:** Is this your plane ticket?

    Renée: No, it's Javier's. He _____ his parents next month.
    (visit)

4. **Sarita:** Please hurry. My train leaves at 6:00.

    Cab driver: Don't worry. I _____ you there on time.
    (get)

5. **Sergei:** Why do you need the car?

    Barbara: We _____ some errands.
    (run)

6. **Matt:** Did you make an appointment for Tammy?

    Juan: Yes, the doctor _____ her tomorrow at 2:00.
    (see)

7. **Rita:** Mr. Miller called.

    Ming: Oh, good, thanks. I _____ him back right away.
    (call)

8. **Max:** Are you going to pick up Andy after school?

    Sheila: No, he _____ a ride from Sue. She drives on Mondays.
    (get)

9. **Robert:** I'm late for work.

    Irene: I've got the car today. I _____ you a ride.
    (give)

TIME to TALK

PAIRS. Do a role play. Sam and Stella are 17 years old. Sam is picking Stella up for their first date. Stella's father has a lot of questions for Sam. Write a conversation between Stella's father and Sam.

Student A: You are Stella's father. This is Stella's first date. You want to know exactly what she and Sam are going to do. Ask Sam questions.

Student B: You are Sam. Answer Stella's father's questions politely. Use *be going to* to talk about your plans. Try to get him to trust you. Make promises.

Example:

A: *Is that the doorbell? I'll get it.*

B: *Good evening, Mr. Davis. I'm Sam. It's very nice to meet you.*

A: *It's nice to meet you, too. Please come in. . . . So, Sam, where are you going to take my daughter tonight?*

WRAP UP. Now act out your role play for the class.

FUTURE: PRESENT PROGRESSIVE FOR FUTURE ARRANGEMENTS

Statements	
Lynn **is babysitting** tomorrow night.	She **isn't babysitting** tomorrow morning.

Yes / No Question	Short Answers	
Are you **babysitting** tomorrow night?	Yes, I am.	No, I'm not.

Information Questions	Answers
What **is** Lynn **doing** tomorrow night?	She's babysitting.
Where **are** you **babysitting** tomorrow night?	At the Petrov's.

A Look at the October calendar of Jimena and Mike Romero and their children, Annie and Paul. Circle the correct answers.

SUNDAY	MONDAY	TUESDAY	WEDNESDAY	THURSDAY	FRIDAY	SATURDAY
1 M-help Oscar move	2	3 J & M- neighborhood meeting 8 P.M.	4	5 J & M look at new apartment 5:30 P.M.	6 A-babysit 7 P.M.	7 P-baseball game J & M-salsa night
8 P's birthday party	9 A-try out for school play	10 A-dentist appointment 2 P.M.	11	12 J & M- parent/ teacher night 6:15	13	14 P-try out for soccer team

1. Annie **is** / isn't trying out for the school play on October 9th.

2. Jimena and Mike **are** / **aren't** meeting their children's teachers on October 5th.

3. Jimena **is** / **isn't** taking Annie to the dentist on October 10th.

4. Jimena and Mike **are** / **aren't** looking at a new apartment on October 3rd.

5. Jimena and Mike **are** / **aren't** going dancing on October 7th.

B Complete the sentences about the Romero family's busy schedule. Use the correct forms of the verbs from the box. (Today is Saturday, September 30th.)

attend	take
have	try out for
~~help~~	

1. Mike ____is helping____ Oscar move tomorrow.

2. Paul _____ the soccer team in two weeks.

3. Jimena says, "I _____ Paul to his baseball game next Saturday."

4. Mike says, "We _____ a birthday party for Paul next week."

5. Jimena and Mike _____ a neighborhood meeting in a few days.

C Complete the questions about next week.

1. Jim usually works on Tuesday night. _____Is he working_____ next Tuesday night?
2. Cindy usually visits relatives on Sunday. _____ next Sunday?
3. Chris usually cleans on Saturday. _____ next Saturday?
4. Javier and Luisa usually go dancing on Saturday night. _____ next Saturday?
5. Mia and Luis usually go food shopping on Monday night. _____ next Monday?
6. Jenny usually gets a ride to work on Fridays. _____ this Friday?

PAIRS. **Find out about your partner's schedule next week. Ask and answer the questions above.**

Example: A: *Are you working next Tuesday night?*
B: *Yes, I am.* OR *No, I'm not.*

D 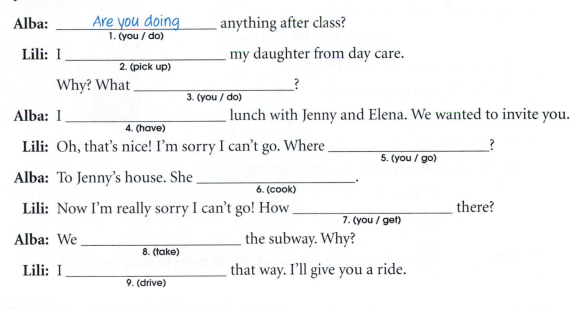 **43 Complete the conversation. Use the present progressive. Then listen and check your answers.**

Alba: _____Are you doing_____ anything after class?
       1. (you / do)

Lili: I _____ my daughter from day care.
          2. (pick up)

       Why? What _____?
                  3. (you / do)

Alba: I _____ lunch with Jenny and Elena. We wanted to invite you.
         4. (have)

Lili: Oh, that's nice! I'm sorry I can't go. Where _____?
                                                      5. (you / go)

Alba: To Jenny's house. She _____.
                              6. (cook)

Lili: Now I'm really sorry I can't go! How _____ there?
                                              7. (you / get)

Alba: We _____ the subway. Why?
            8. (take)

Lili: I _____ that way. I'll give you a ride.
          9. (drive)

GROUPS. Plan a time to get together for a party. When is everyone in the group free? Ask and answer questions about your schedules.

Example:

A: *I'm free on Tuesday evening. What are you doing on Tuesday?*
B: *Tuesday's not good for me. I'm working late. How about Thursday night? I'm not working on Thursday.*

Grammar

44 Complete the conversations. Write the correct future form of the verbs in the box. Some are affirmative, and some are negative. Then listen and check your answers.

| be | ~~call~~ | go | have | pay | work |

1. **A:** Bye, darling. Have a good day.

   B: Bye-bye. I'll call _____ you later.

2. **A:** Oh, no! I haven't got my wallet with me!

   B: That's OK. I _____. You can pay next time.

3. **A:** Is Linda pregnant?

   B: Yes, she _____ a baby in three months.

4. **A:** So, what did you decide? _____ you
   _____ to New York this weekend?

   B: No, we haven't got the money.

5. **A:** Don't forget about tonight.

   B: Don't worry. We _____ late.

6. **A:** Which days _____ you _____ this week?

   B: Monday to Saturday. I'm off on Sunday.

Dictation

45 Listen. You will hear five sentences. Write them in your notebook.

Speaking

PAIRS. Look at the pictures on page 72. What are the people in the pictures saying? Use *will*, *be going to*, or the present progressive.

Example:
A: *Oh, honey. Please don't cry. Your mommy will be home very soon. I promise.*

Say your sentences to the class. Can they guess who is talking?

Example:
B: *The babysitter is talking to the little girl.*
A: *You're right.*

Listening

 **A** Listen. Who is talking in each conversation? Check (✓) the correct column.

	CONVERSATION				
	1	**2**	**3**	**4**	**5**
cab driver and customer					
classmates					
friends	✓				
restaurant cashier and customer					
mother and son					

 B Listen again. Answer the questions. Write complete sentences.

1. **Conversation 1:** What did the man just tell the woman?

    He lost his job.

2. **Conversation 2:** What are the people going to do?

    _____

3. **Conversation 3:** Why is the woman upset?

    _____

4. **Conversation 4:** What are the people doing?

    _____

5. **Conversation 5:** What is the woman going to do?

    _____

GROUPS. Choose a topic. Ask and answer the questions.

Busy Lives	Promises	Making Plans
Is your life very busy? What are you doing in the next few days?	Do you make a lot of promises? What will you probably do for someone this week?	Do you usually plan things in advance? What are you going to do this month? This year?

Example:
A: *I choose Busy Lives.*
B: *Is your life very busy?*
A: *Yes, it is. Today, I'm working until 9:00. I'm going to get home late, so I'll study Monday.*

Reading

Getting Ready to Read

The article talks about the job of a personal assistant. What kind of things do you think personal assistants do? List three things.

1. _____
2. _____
3. _____

Reading

Read the article. Does the writer talk about any of the things you wrote about in Getting Ready to Read?

HIRING A WIFE

It's 7:00 A.M., and personal assistant Diana Cid is checking her schedule. She has a busy morning. At 7:30, she's dropping off Mrs. Harlow's children at school. Then she's picking up Mrs. Dawson's dog and taking it to the **vet**. While the dog is seeing the vet, she's going to answer Mrs. Lopez's e-mail. Then she's picking up Mrs. Dawson's son from kindergarten and taking him and the dog back home to the babysitter. If she has time before lunch, she's going to buy a birthday gift for Mrs. Lopez's husband.

Personal assistants, or **lifestyle managers**, like Cid are becoming more and more common these days. Their **clients** are usually working mothers with extra money, but no time to run errands. As Cid says, "My clients need a wife. They need someone who will do the things that wives used to do: pick up the dry cleaning, go grocery shopping, take the kids to school, walk the dog . . . You name it, I'll do it." Personal assistants like Cid usually **charge** $15 to $21 an hour. Some clients hire them for just an hour or two a week, while others need someone every day.

Cid has her own small business and works alone. However, the services she provides are becoming **big business**. New businesses like Cid's are starting up all over the country. They are even **spreading** from the United States to Europe. Their services are especially popular with large companies. The companies pay a monthly **fee** for the service, and give it to their best customers free-of-charge. These personal assistants will do much more than just run errands. In big cities like New York and Los Angeles, they will find their clients tickets to popular **shows**, get them **reservations** at the best restaurants in town, or even do their clothes shopping for them.

After You Read

A   Look at the **boldface** words in the article. Guess their meaning. Then read the sentences and circle the correct answer.

1. A **vet** is a
   - **a.** doctor for animals. *(circled)*
   - **b.** hairdresser for dogs.

2. A **lifestyle manager** is another name for a
   - **a.** large company.
   - **b.** personal assistant.

3. When you have **clients**,
   - **a.** they pay you.
   - **b.** you pay them.

4. If someone **charges** you $16 an hour,
   - **a.** you pay him or her.
   - **b.** you pay the credit card company.

5. If something is **big business**, it is
   - **a.** successful.
   - **b.** unsuccessful.

6. When something **spreads**, it
   - **a.** costs more money.
   - **b.** becomes more common.

7. A **fee** is money that you
   - **a.** pay for a service.
   - **b.** put in the bank.

8. A **show** has
   - **a.** waiters and waitresses.
   - **b.** actors and actresses.

9. When you make a **reservation** at a restaurant, you want to
   - **a.** eat at a particular time.
   - **b.** get your food to go.

B   Read the article again. Then find the pronouns. What do they refer to? Write the noun.

1. it (line 5)   _Mrs. Dawson's dog_
2. him (line 7)   _____
3. They (line 12)   _____
4. them (line 15)   _____
5. she (line 17)   _____
6. them (line 23)   _____

> **Reading Skill:**
> **Understanding Pronouns**
>
> **Pronouns** replace nouns. To understand a text, you need to know which nouns the pronouns refer to.

Writing

Getting Ready to Write

 A **Combine the sentences with *and*.**

1. I am going to go to college. I am going to study business.

    <u>I am going to go to college and study business.</u>

2. I am retiring in two years. I am moving to Florida.

    _____

    _____

3. I am selling my apartment. I am buying a house.

    _____

4. I will borrow some money. I will start my own business.

    _____

5. I am going to quit this job. I am going to open a restaurant.

    _____

> ### Writing Tip
>
> If you have one subject with two verbs with *be going to* or *will*, write *be going to* or *will* one time. For affirmative sentences, join the two verbs with *and*.
>
> **Example:**
> **She is going to expand** her business **and hire** more employees.

 B **Read the model paragraph.**

> Next month, I am quitting my job and opening a restaurant in Chelsea. I am getting a loan from the bank and a lot of help from my family. It is going to be a family restaurant, and it will serve traditional Haitian food. My mother will cook, my father will take care of the bills, my sisters will wait on tables, and my little brother will wash dishes. I will be responsible for everything else. I owned a successful restaurant in my country, and that experience will help me. Things are a little different here, but my mother is a fantastic cook, and people everywhere like good food. I think that my restaurant will be a success.

PAIRS. **Read the model again. Why does the writer think his restaurant will be a success?**

Do you have any interesting future plans? Discuss.

Prewriting: Answering Information Questions

You are going to write a paragraph about your future plans. Before you write, read the notes for the writing model. Then answer the information questions about your future plans.

Writing Model
<u>Plans to open a restaurant</u>

What?
    restaurant
    traditional Haitian food

Where?   Chelsea

When?   next month

How?
    bank loan
    family help

Who?
    Mom: cook
    Dad: bills
    Rose: waitress
    Mark: dishes
    me: manager, owner

Why will the plans succeed?
    past experience
    mother good cook
    good food

My plans:
What?
Where?
When?
How?
Who?
Why will the plans succeed?

Writing

Now write a paragraph about your future plans. The writing tip, the model paragraph, and your notes will help you. Write in your notebook.

Vocabulary

CD 1 TRACK 47 Match the numbers with the words. Then listen and check your answers.

_1_ apply for	____ get a scholarship	____ take a final
____ cheat	____ improve	____ take an exam
____ fail a class/course	____ major in	____ take five courses
____ get good grades	____ pass a class/course	____ transfer

1.

2.

BC Scholarship Application

Full Legal Name	Last Name **Diaz**	First Name **Maria**	Middle Name
Address	Number/Street **00 S.W. 2nd**	City/Count **Miami**	State **FL** Zip **33130**

APPROVED

E-mail address **mariadiaz@mail.com**

U.S. Social Security Number **999-99-9999**

Home phone number **(222)555-1234**

☐ Male ☒ Female Date of Birth (Mo./Day/Yr.) ___/___/___

APPLY NOW!

3.

BC Course Registration

FALL SEMESTER

TITLE	DAYS	TIME	LOCATION	CREDITS
English 101	Monday, Friday	8:00–8:50	Feldman Hall	3.00
Math 2	Tuesday, Thursday	9:00–10:40	Williams Hall	3.00
Art 101	Monday	12:00–2:30	Arts Building	3.00
Economics 1	Wednesday, Friday	9:00–10:40	Dickson Hall	3.00
Business 101	Monday, Friday	3:00–4:40	Dickson Hall	3.00

4.

College Transcript 2007

Course	Semester	Grade	Credits
English 101	Fall	A	3
Math 2	Fall	B+	3
Art 101	Fall	A-	3
Economics 1	Fall	B+	3
Business 101	Fall	A	3

5.

6.

BC Course Registratic

SPRING SEMESTER

TITLE	DAYS	TIME	LOCATION	CREDI
Business English	Monday, Friday	10:00–10:50	Dickson Hall	3.00
Business Writing	Tuesday, Thursday	9:00–10:40	Dickson Hall	3.00
Business Management	Tuesday, Thursday	11:00–12:40	Student Building	3.00

7.

Exam Have a great summer! **Ben Lee June 10 2007** 88

8.

BC Request to Transfer

for office use only:
Application # 1913

APPROVED

Date May 01 2007

1. Name:
last **Lee** first **Ben** middle   ID number (or SSN) **999-99-9999**

2. Transfer from **Bart College** Last Day **June 16, 2007**

3. Transfer to **Char College** First Day **Sept. 4, 2008**

9.

10.

College Transcript 2007

Course	Semester	Grade	Credits
Math 1	Fall	F	3
English 101	Fall	B	3
Chemistry	Fall	B-	3

11.

College Transcript 2008

Course	Semester	Grade	Credits
Math 1	Spring	C	3
English 101	Spring	B	3
Chemistry	Spring	B-	3

12.

Exam 70 **Lou Miles Feb. 18 2008**

Exam 88 **Lou Miles March 20 2008**

Listening

A CD 1 TRACK 48 **Listen. Why did Mrs. Parker call Mrs. Martin? Check (✓) the correct answer.**

❏ 1. Mrs. Parker is going to be Tommy Martin's teacher next year.

❏ 2. Mrs. Martin sent Mrs. Parker an e-mail.

❏ 3. Mrs. Martin is worried about her son, Tommy.

❏ 4. Tommy Martin is not doing well in school.

❏ 5. The principal tried to contact Mrs. Martin.

> **Look**
>
> principal = the person responsible for a school, the students, and the teachers

B CD 1 TRACK 49 **Listen again. For each pair of sentences, check (✓) the sentence that you hear.**

1. ☑ a. He might not be ready for high school next year.

   ❏ b. He might be ready for high school next year.

2. ❏ a. As soon as I get home tonight, I'll take Tommy out of the house.

   ❏ b. As soon as I get home tonight, I'll take care of this.

3. ❏ a. If he tries harder, he'll be fine.

   ❏ b. If he doesn't try harder, he'll fail.

4. ❏ a. We want to know exactly, so we'll test him.

   ❏ b. We won't know exactly until we test him.

5. ❏ a. I'll call you when we finish.

   ❏ b. I'll call you when it finishes.

C CD 1 TRACK 50 **Listen again. Answer the questions. Write complete sentences.**

1. Where is Mrs. Martin when Mrs. Parker calls?

   _____

2. What will Tommy have to do this summer?

   _____

3. Why didn't Mrs. Martin answer Mrs. Parker's calls or e-mails?

   _____

4. What does Mrs. Parker think Tommy's problem is?

   _____

5. What is going to happen in an hour?

   _____

Grammar to Communicate 1

FUTURE: *IF* CLAUSES FOR POSSIBILITY

If	If Clause (Possible Situation) Subject	Verb		Main Clause (Result) Subject	Verb
	you	do		you	will pass. / are going to pass.
If	he	does	the homework,	he	won't fail. / isn't going to fail.
	I	don't do		I	will fail. / am going to fail.
	she	doesn't do		she	won't pass. / isn't going to pass.

Look

Use the present in the *if* clause.
Use the future in the main clause.
The *if* clause can be before or after the main clause.
If I move, I'll transfer.
OR
I'll transfer if I move.

A Who is saying each sentence? Write *K* for a kindergarten teacher (teacher of 5-year-olds) or *HS* for a high school teacher (teacher of 15–18-year olds).

__K__ 1. If you're nice to the other children, they'll be nice to you.

_____ 2. If you don't take the exam, you're going to fail.

_____ 3. You'll get a cookie if you take a nap.

_____ 4. I'll call your mommy if you're sick.

_____ 5. If you have any questions about the exam, I'll help you after class.

_____ 6. You aren't going to graduate if you are absent a lot.

B Match the possible situations on the left and the results on the right. Then write sentences with *if*.

__e__ 1. I get a scholarship

_____ 2. it rains

_____ 3. you miss the bus

_____ 4. she fails another class

_____ 5. he doesn't finish his homework tonight

_____ 6. they pass their finals

a. graduate

b. finish it before school tomorrow

c. be late for school

d. the graduation ceremony be in the gym

e. go to college

f. not get a diploma

get a diploma

get a degree

1. __If I get a scholarship, I'll go to college.__

2. _____

3. _____

4. _____

5. _____

6. _____

C Complete the sentences with the correct form of the verbs. Use *will* or *be going to*.

1. If you _____read_____ quietly, I _____ you homework.
   (read)   (not give)

2. If your grades _____, we _____ you help.
   (not improve)   (get)

3. If you _____ quiet, all of you _____ after class.
   (not be)   (stay)

4. I _____ you extra homework if you _____ well on the test.
   (give)   (not do)

5. If you _____, you _____ stay after school.
   (not pay attention)   (have to)

6. I _____ you with the book if it _____ hard for you.
   (help)   (be)

7. We _____ a game on Friday if you _____ good
   (play)   (be)
   tomorrow.

D Complete the sentences with your own ideas.

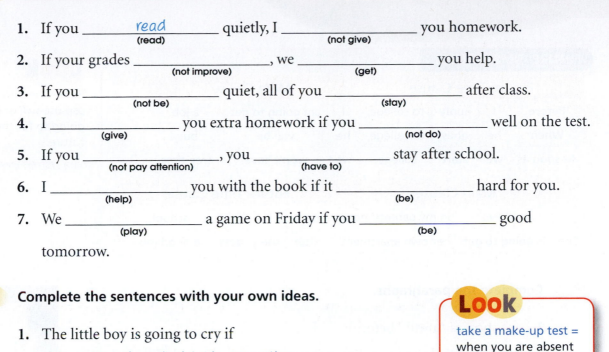

1. The little boy is going to cry if

   his mother doesn't pick him up on time.

2. The teacher will give you a make-up test if _____

   _____

3. You won't get your diploma if _____

4. The teacher will get angry if _____

5. Parents will complain if _____

6. The students will pay attention if _____

Look

take a make-up test =
when you are absent
the day of the test,
you take a **make-up
test** on another day

TIME to TALK

GROUPS. Sit in a circle. Tell a chain story. Start your story with one of the ideas in the box. Student A starts the story. Student B, to the right, continues the story. Continue until each student has had two turns. Then write your story.

do well in school	miss the bus
drop out of school	not pay attention in class

Example:
A: *You will miss the bus if you don't hurry.*
B: *If you miss the bus . . .*

WRAP UP. Now read your story to the class.

Grammar to Communicate ❷

FUTURE: TIME CLAUSES

Future Time Clause				Main Clause		
Before	I	**apply**	to college,	I	**am going to get**	a job.
When	he	**goes**	to college,	he	**will be**	busy.
As soon as	we	**start**	college,	we	**won't have**	free time.

Main Clause			Future Time Clause			
I	**will live**	in my parents' home	**until**	I	**finish**	school.
She	**is going to get**	her own apartment	**after**	she	**gets**	a good job.

Look

Remember: We can use *will* or *be going to* for the future.

A Complete the paragraphs.

1. (as soon as / until / before)

    ___As soon as___ I graduate, I'm going to get a full-time job. I'll work

    _____ I get married. Then I'm going to stop working and have a

    baby. _____ I have a baby, I'm going to buy a house.

2. (after / before / when)

    _____ I graduate, I'm going to start college. I'm going to visit

    my family in Guatemala _____ classes start in September. I'll

    take a lot of different courses _____ I'm in college, but I think I

    will major in biology.

B Two other students are writing about their plans after high school.
Complete the sentences with the correct form of the verbs. Use *be going to* or *will*.

1. (graduate / help / work / save / go / major in)

    When I ____graduate____, I _'m going to help_ OR _I will help_____ my parents in their

    store. I _____ there until I _____ enough money for college. When I

    _____ to college, I _____ business.

2. (end / find / take / start / get / transfer)

    Before high school _____, I _____ a part-time job. I

    _____ some evening classes at a community college as soon as the new semester

    _____. After I _____ my associate's degree, I _____ to a

    four-year college.

C Complete the sentences about the people's dreams for the future. Use *when*, *as soon as*, *before*, or *after*. Some sentences have more than one correct answer.

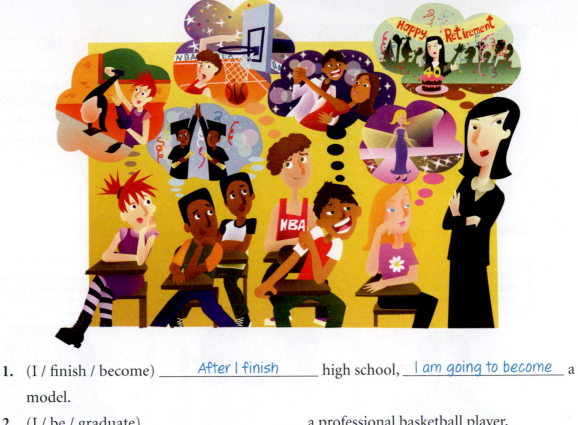

1. (I / finish / become) _____*After I finish*_____ high school, _____*I am going to become*_____ a model.

2. (I / be / graduate) _____ a professional basketball player, _____.

3. (he / go / ask) _____ away to college, _____ her to marry him.

4. (she / retire / be) _____, _____ 40.

5. (she / graduate / apply) _____, _____ to beauty school.

6. (they / get / celebrate) _____ their diplomas, _____.

PAIRS. Look at page 301. It is Tommy's junior year of high school, and he is thinking about college. Read the checklist. Talk about the things that he is going to do and when he is going to do them.

Example:
In the spring, Tommy is going to make an appointment with the school guidance counselor. When she meets with him, she'll discuss several different colleges with him. After he chooses colleges. . . .

Grammar to Communicate 3

FUTURE: *MAY* AND *MIGHT* FOR POSSIBILITY			
Subject	Modal	Verb	
I He She We You They	**may** **might** **may not** **might not**	**take**	another English course.

Look

Use *maybe* or *perhaps* when something may be true or may happen, but you are not sure.

A Who is sure about the future? Circle the person's name.

I might take some evening classes in the fall, or I might wait until next year.

Tom

I may go to cooking school, but I may not have the money for a couple of years.

Joe

Next month I'm going to go back to school. I'm going to study to be a nurse.

Yolanda

B Rewrite the sentences with *may*. Do not change the meaning.

1. Maybe I'll learn to use a computer.   <u>I may learn to use a computer.</u>
2. Perhaps he'll take a class in car mechanics.   _____
3. Maybe she won't have money to take a class.   _____
4. Perhaps they're going to apply to college.   _____

Rewrite these sentences with *might*. Do not change the meaning.

5. Perhaps I'll go to the community college.   _____
6. Maybe she's not going to study full time.   _____
7. Maybe he's going to become a plumber.   _____
8. Perhaps I won't transfer to a new school.   _____

C Read about what the students are doing now. Then complete the sentences about their future. Use *might* or a form of *be going to* and the words in the box.

| get | graduate | improve | major in | pass | ~~take~~ |

1. Lyn is looking at brochures for an art class, but she is not sure about the class.

   She might take an art class.

2. Henry is writing a check for a car mechanics class.

   He is going to take a car mechanics class.

3. Ricky is applying for a scholarship, but a lot of other people are also applying.

   _____

4. Rosa knows that she wants be a math teacher. She loves math and teaching.

   _____

5. Fatima's English isn't very good, but she's studying a lot in her English class.

   _____

6. Marsha and Jane are in their last year at college. They have very good grades.

   _____

7. Joe and Ann's grades aren't good, but it's the end of the semester, and they're trying.

   _____
   _____

PAIRS. Compare your answers.

TIME to TALK

CLASS. Play this game.

STEP 1: Write four sentences about the future. Write about one thing that you are definitely going to do, two things that you might do, and one thing that you might not do. Use *be going to*, *may*, *might*, and *might not*.

STEP 2: Your teacher will collect the papers and put them in a box.

STEP 3: Each student will take a paper from the box and read the sentences out loud.

STEP 4: The other students will guess who wrote the sentences.

Example:
I am going to go to nursing school. I may go home to visit my family first. . . .

Grammar

Find the mistake in each sentence. Circle the letter and correct the mistake.

as soon as

1. I'm going to transfer to Center College as soon the semester ends.
   A   B   Ⓒ   D

2. I might to major in music, or I may study Spanish.
     A B   C   D

3. If you will study for the next test, you will get a good grade.
        A   B   C D

4. Until she is going to go to college, she is going to work full time.
    A   B   C   D

5. I take a makeup exam next month if I don't take the final exam Friday.
    A   B   C   D

Dictation

🔊 **51** **Listen. You will hear five sentences. Write them in your notebook.**

Speaking

PAIRS. **Choose a situation and write a conversation. Then act it out for the class.**

Situation 1

Student A: You are a new student in an evening course that started last week. Ask the teacher about information you missed. Ask about things such as absences and tests.

Student B: You teach an evening course that started last week. Answer the questions of a student who missed the first week of class.

Situation 2

Student A: You are a parent of a 12-year-old. Your son didn't get good grades on his report card. You go to parent-teacher's night to talk to the teacher about your son.

Student B: You are a teacher. Your students are 12 years old. It is parent-teacher's night, and you are talking to the parent of one of your students.

Example: (Situation 1)

A: *Excuse me. I have some questions about the course. I might need to stay home with my son sometimes. Will there be a problem if I miss class?*

B: *Well, if you are absent too much, you will not get a certificate at the end of the course.*

Listening

A 🔘 **52** **Listen to the radio show. A reporter is talking to two people who want to become the mayor. They are talking about the problems with the city's schools. Check (✓) the problems that they mention.**

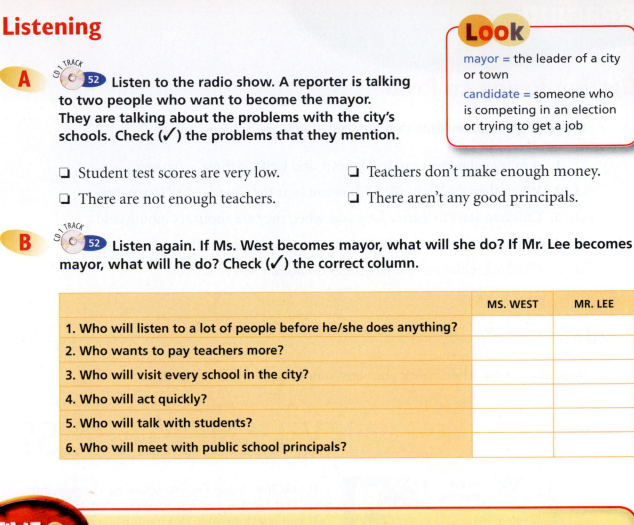

> **Look**
>
> mayor = the leader of a city or town
>
> candidate = someone who is competing in an election or trying to get a job

❏ Student test scores are very low.　　❏ Teachers don't make enough money.

❏ There are not enough teachers.　　❏ There aren't any good principals.

B 🔘 **52** **Listen again. If Ms. West becomes mayor, what will she do? If Mr. Lee becomes mayor, what will he do? Check (✓) the correct column.**

	MS. WEST	MR. LEE
1. Who will listen to a lot of people before he/she does anything?		
2. Who wants to pay teachers more?		
3. Who will visit every school in the city?		
4. Who will act quickly?		
5. Who will talk with students?		
6. Who will meet with public school principals?		

TIME to TALK

GROUPS. Talk about the public schools in your city or town. Answer the questions and take notes as you listen to the discussion.

1. Talk about the good and bad things about the public schools in your area. Which schools are the best? Which are the worst? What are the problems?

2. Should there be changes in the public schools in your area? Why or why not? Which changes might happen? Which changes might not happen? Which changes won't happen?

3. Do you think that the public schools in your area will stay the same, improve, or get worse in the future?

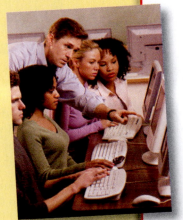

Example:
A: *Our principal is going to meet with the mayor to ask for money to buy new computers.*
B: *That's great. Our principal may do the same thing.*

WRAP UP. Now compare notes with other groups.

Getting Ready to Read

Check (✓) the statements that are true. If you are not sure, guess.

❏ 1. A bilingual person can speak, read, and write in three languages.

❏ 2. When they are born, all children can hear the sounds of all languages.

❏ 3. Children start to learn a language when they are about six months old.

❏ 4. Children with two first languages sometimes confuse the two languages.

❏ 5. Children with two first languages do not do well in school.

Reading

Read the article. Then check your answers to Getting Ready to Read.

HOW MANY LANGUAGES?

If you live in an English-speaking country but your first language is not English, what language will you speak to your children at home? What if you and your **spouse** speak different languages? Which language will you use with your children? If your children hear both languages at home, will they have problems when they get to school? Here is some information that might help to answer these questions.

First, which language should you use with your children at home? At birth, all children can hear the sounds of all languages. However, if you speak to children in just one language, after about six to nine months, they will hear only the sounds of that language. If you want children to have two first languages, they will need to hear each of them at least 30 percent of the time when they are babies. If you and your spouse speak two different languages, you may each decide to talk to your baby in your first language, or you might choose the language that the child will not hear in school. In either case, your child will **benefit**.

Second, how well do bilingual children do in school? When children grow up with two first languages, they will sometimes confuse them. If they can't think of a word in one language, they might use a word from the other language. However, this will stop as soon as the child learns enough vocabulary. It is also true that bilingual children might learn to read later than **monolingual** children. However, they will soon **catch up**. Then they will be able to read, write, and speak two languages for the rest of their lives. And that is a wonderful gift to give any child.

After You Read

 A   Look at the **boldface** words in the article. Try to guess the meaning from the context. Write a definition or description.

Reading Skill:
Guessing Meaning
From Context

Often, you do not need to use a dictionary to understand the meaning of a new word in a text. You can guess the meaning from the **context** (the words and sentences before and after the new word).

1. spouse: _____

2. benefit: _____

3. monolingual: _____

4. catch up: _____

Now look up the words in the dictionary. Were your definitions close to the dictionary definitions?

B   Read the article again. Then answer the questions.

1. At what age do babies lose their ability to hear the sounds of all languages?

    _____

    _____

2. How much time should a baby listen to a language every day?

    _____

    _____

3. If you and your spouse speak two different languages and you want your child to speak both, what can you do?

    _____

    _____

4. In what ways might school be more difficult at first for a bilingual child than for a monolingual child?

    _____

    _____

Writing

Getting Ready to Write

A   Complete the sentences with the correct form of the verbs.

> **Writing Tip**
>
> Remember: When you use a time clause to talk about the future, you use the present tense in the time clause.
>
> **Example:**
> I will send my son to a bilingual school **when he is five**.

I just moved to Boston from Brazil. My daughter is five. She ___will start___

                                                             1. (start)

school as soon as she _____ six. Of course, when her teachers _____ to her
                        2. (be)   3. (speak)

in English, she _____ in English. My husband and I will continue to speak to her
                4. (answer)

in Portugese. My son is four, and he speaks Portuguese. After he _____ school, he
                                                  5. (start)

_____ English too. I want all of us to know both languages. I _____ an English
6. (speak)   7. (take)

class as soon as I _____ unpacking!
                  8. (finish)

B   Read the model paragraph.

> My husband and I are Russian. We live in the United States, but we speak Russian at home. Our four-year-old son, Sergei, understands Russian very well, but he almost never speaks it. I am worried that after he starts school, he will not understand Russian anymore, and he will never learn to speak it. My mother might come to live with us next year. She does not speak any English. If Sergei wants to speak to her, he will need to use Russian. If she does not come, we are going to send Sergei to a private bilingual school. It is expensive, but we want our son to understand our language and culture.

PAIRS. Read the model again. How is the writer going to help her child to be bilingual?

Talk about things you are doing to learn English. What are you doing now? What will you do in the future?

Prewriting: Taking Notes

You are going to write a paragraph about learning a new language. Before you write, read the notes for the writing model. Then complete the chart with notes about your ideas.

Writing Model
Helping our son learn a new language

Now
Living in U.S.
Russian at home
Sergei: Understands Russian/Eng
        Speaks only Eng
Problem—future?

Future
Grandmother?
Bilingual school?

Goal: Sergei will be bilingual.

Learning a new language
Now
Future

Writing

Now write a paragraph about learning a new language. The writing tip, the model paragraph, and your notes will help you. Write in your notebook.

Unit 8
Getting a Job

Vocabulary

CD 2 TRACK **2** Read the story, and look at the pictures. The pictures are not in the correct order. Write the number of each picture in the correct place in the story. Then listen and check your answers.

___4___ Adam **searched** for a job in the newspaper and online. _____ He **contacted** Sam Alvarez on Monday. Mr. Alvarez **owned** a 24-hour convenience store. He needed a cashier.

_____ Adam **heard from** Mr. Alvarez on Tuesday. _____ Adam went to see Mr. Alvarez. Adam told him he didn't know how to use a **cash register**. But Mr. Alvarez liked Adam and **hired** him as the new cashier. _____ Adam learned how to use the cash register. Mr. Alvarez **trained** him.

_____ The first month, Adam worked **the day shift**. But the second month, he worked **the night shift**. _____ All the cashiers **handled** a lot of money. One cashier made many mistakes, so Mr. Alvarez **fired** her. _____ After that, Adam worked **overtime**. He often worked sixty hours a week. He was very tired. After six months, Adam **quit** his job. Now he's searching for a new job.

Listening

A **Listen. What is the relationship between the two speakers? Check (✓) the correct answer.**

❑ boss and employee   ❑ classmates   ❑ father and daughter   ❑ husband and wife

B **Read and listen again. Write the missing words. Use the words in the box.**

already	~~ever~~	gotten	has	Have	haven't	I've	started

Ignacio: Have you ____*ever*____ handled money?
                                     1.

Natalia: Just when I sold vegetables at a farm last summer. But _____ never used
                                                           2.
a cash register.

Ignacio: Oh, it's easy.

Natalia: Really? _____ you ever used one?
                           3.

Ignacio: Uh, no, I _____. But a lot of my friends have. Just go in and apply.
                             4.

Natalia: Hmmm . . . maybe I will. Thanks for the information. So, how about Tracy?
Has she _____ her new job?
                     5.

Ignacio: Yes, she _____.
                     6.

Natalia: And how does she like it?

Ignacio: She loves it.

Natalia: Has she _____ her first paycheck yet?
                     7.

Ignacio: No, she hasn't, but I think she's _____ spent more than she's made!
                                                           8.

C **Listen again. Check (✓) the sentences that are true.**

❑ 1. Ignacio has a job as a cashier.

❑ 2. Natalia might apply for a job at Danny's.

❑ 3. Ignacio's friends are going to teach Natalia how to use a cash register.

❑ 4. Tracy is working.

❑ 5. Tracy has two jobs.

❑ 6. Natalia is nervous about looking for a job.

Getting a Job   **101**

PRESENT PERFECT: REGULAR VERBS

Subject	Have / Has	Past Participle	Subject	Have not / Has not	Past Participle
I We You They	have	called.	I We You They	have not	called.
He She	has		He She	has not	

Contractions

I + have = **I've**	I + have not = **I haven't**
He + has = **He's**	He + has not = **He hasn't**

Look

Use the present perfect to talk about indefinite times in the past.
I **have started** a new job.

Use the simple past to talk about definite times in the past.
I **started** a new job **yesterday**.

A The people in the chart are looking for jobs. Complete the sentences. Use *has*, *hasn't*, *have*, or *haven't*.

	CARLOS	JENNIFER	MIKE	SANDRA
apply for a job	yes	yes	no	no
look in the newspaper	yes	no	yes	yes
attend a job fair	no	no	yes	yes
contact an employment agency	no	no	no	yes
talk to a job counselor	no	yes	yes	yes
search for jobs online	yes	no	no	no

Look

employment agency = a company that helps people find jobs

job counselor = a person who gives people advice about jobs to apply for

online = on the Internet

job fair = a place where companies look for workers, and workers look for jobs

1. Jennifer ____has____ applied for a job.
2. Mike and Sandra ____haven't____ applied for a job.
3. Sandra, Mike, and Carlos _____ looked in the newspaper.
4. Jennifer _____ looked in the newspaper.
5. Carlos and Jennifer _____ attended a job fair.
6. Sandra _____ attended a job fair.

attend a job fair

B Write new sentences about the people in Exercise A. Write an affirmative sentence and a negative sentence. Use the present perfect.

1. apply for a job

   Mike hasn't applied for a job.

   Jennifer and Carlos have applied for a job.

2. contact an employment agency

   _____

   _____

3. talk to a job counselor

   _____

   _____

4. search for jobs online

   _____

   _____

PAIRS. Talk about yourself. Use the verbs in the chart in Exercise A.

C Write sentences with *ever* and *never*. Some are affirmative, and some are negative.

1. _I haven't ever applied for a job._
   (I / ever / apply / for a job)

2. _____
   (My mother / never / work / full-time)

3. _____
   (My father / ever / own / a business)

4. _____
   (I / never / handle / a lot of money)

5. _____
   (My friends / ever / help / me find a job)

6. _____
   (I / ever / train / people)

Look

Use *ever* with a negative verb.
I haven't ever worked.
Use *never* with an affirmative verb.
I have never worked.

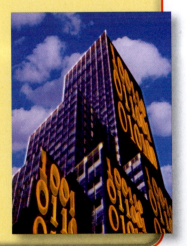

TIME to TALK

GROUPS. Talk about the things that you have never done in your work life. Would you like to do those things someday? Use the ideas in the box.

fire a worker	work for a relative
hire a worker	work outdoors
manage a department	work overtime
start your own business	work the day shift
work for a large corporation	work the night shift

Example:
A: *I have never worked for a large corporation.*
B: *I haven't ever worked for a large corporation either, but I would like to. They give good benefits.*

Grammar to Communicate ②

PRESENT PERFECT: IRREGULAR VERBS							
Subject	Has / Have	Past Participle		Subject	Has not / Have not	Past Participle	
I You We They	have	been	there.	I You We They	have not	been	there.
He She	has			He She	has not		

 A Match the parts of sentences.

__g__ 1. She's <u>quit</u> her job, but

_____ 2. They've <u>made</u> many phone calls, but

_____ 3. She's <u>taken</u> the test, but

_____ 4. I've <u>done</u> the report, but

_____ 5. They've <u>met</u> two people from the company, but

_____ 6. I've <u>sent</u> two e-mails, but

_____ 7. I've <u>gone</u> to several job fairs, but

a. I haven't <u>heard</u> from anyone.

b. they haven't <u>seen</u> the boss.

c. they haven't <u>spoken</u> to anyone.

d. she hasn't <u>gotten</u> her score.

e. I haven't <u>given</u> it to my boss.

f. I haven't <u>had</u> any interviews.

g. she hasn't <u>found</u> a new job.

B Complete the table. Look at the chart and the underlined words in Exercise A for help.

BASE FORM OF VERB	SIMPLE PAST	PAST PARTICIPLE
1. be	was / were	been
2. do	did	
3. find		found
4.	got	gotten
5. give	gave	
6. go		gone
7.	had	had
8. hear	heard	

BASE FORM OF VERB	SIMPLE PAST	PAST PARTICIPLE
9. make	made	
10. meet		met
11.	quit	quit
12. see		seen
13. send	sent	
14.	spoke	spoken
15. take	took	

C Complete the sentences. Write the present perfect of the verbs.

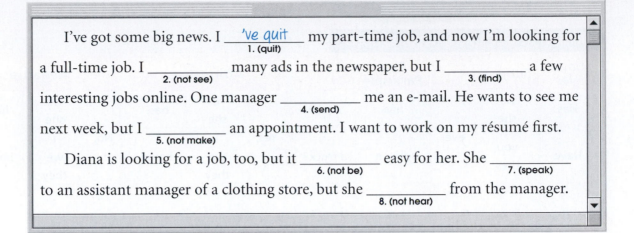

I've got some big news. I ___'ve quit___ my part-time job, and now I'm looking for
1. (quit)

a full-time job. I _____ many ads in the newspaper, but I _____ a few
2. (not see)   3. (find)

interesting jobs online. One manager _____ me an e-mail. He wants to see me
4. (send)

next week, but I _____ an appointment. I want to work on my résumé first.
5. (not make)

Diana is looking for a job, too, but it _____ easy for her. She _____
6. (not be)   7. (speak)

to an assistant manager of a clothing store, but she _____ from the manager.
8. (not hear)

D Complete the sentences. Use the present perfect of the words in the box. Add *already* to the affirmative sentences and *yet* to the negative sentences.

| do | ~~get~~ | have | meet | take |

> **Look**
>
> Use *already* in affirmative sentences for something finished.
> **I've already** quit my job. I'm not working there now.
>
> Use *yet* in negative sentences for something not finished.
> **I haven't** quit my job **yet**. I'm still working there.

1. This is my third day at work. I ___haven't___ ___gotten___
    my first paycheck ___yet___.

2. About twenty people work in my new office. I _____
    _____ _____ fifteen of them.

3. Can I leave early? I _____ _____ _____
    all my work.

4. My coworkers are always busy. I _____ _____ lunch with any of them
    _____.

5. This is Ben's first month in the office, and he's busy all the time. He _____
    _____ a day off _____.

GROUPS. Discuss what you have already accomplished in your life and what you have not accomplished yet. Talk about work, education, family, friends, health, money, travel, or any other topic.

Example:
A: I've already graduated from high school, but I haven't started college yet.
B: I've already graduated from college, but I haven't found a good job yet.

WRAP UP. Now tell the class about the accomplishments of your group.

Grammar to Communicate 3

PRESENT PERFECT: YES / NO QUESTIONS

Have/ Has	Subject		Past Participle		Affirmative				Negative		
Has	he she	ever	had	a job?	Yes,	he she	has.	No,	he she	hasn't.
Have	you they		driven	a truck?		I we they	have.		I we they	haven't.

 A Answer the questions. Use short answers.

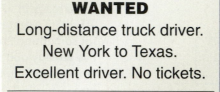

WANTED

Long-distance truck driver.
New York to Texas.
Excellent driver. No tickets.

> Yes, I have experience as a truck driver. I've never gotten a ticket. And an old friend lives in Texas and I drive there from New York every year.

1. Has the man ever been to Texas? _____

2. Has he ever driven 1,500 miles? _____

3. Has he ever worked as a driver? _____

4. Has he ever gotten a ticket? _____

B Write questions. Use *ever* and the present perfect.

1. _Have you ever owned a business?_____
    (you / own / a business)

2. _____
    (you / do / this kind of work)

3. _____
    (your co-workers / complain / about you)

4. _____
    (you / work / the night shift)

5. _____
    (you / miss / a day of work)

6. _____
    (you / train / a co-worker)

7. _____
    (a co-worker / make / you angry)

Which questions would an interviewer probably <u>not</u> ask at an interview?

C Three people have applied for a job as manager of a supermarket. Look at the information about them. Write questions with *ever*. Then answer the questions.

	BE A MANAGER	TRAIN WORKERS	HAVE A PROBLEM WITH A CO-WORKER	FIRE PEOPLE	HANDLE A LOT OF CASH	HIRE PEOPLE
Lenore Johnson	yes	no	yes	yes	yes	yes
Christine Huggins	no	no	yes	no	no	yes
Roger Mendoza	no	yes	no	yes	yes	yes

1. _Has Ms. Johnson ever been a manager?_   _Yes, she has._
   (Ms. Johnson / be a manager)

2. _Have Ms. Huggins and Mr. Mendoza ever been managers?_   _No, they haven't._
   (Ms. Huggins and Mr. Mendoza / be managers)

3. _____   _____
   (Ms. Huggins / train workers)

4. _____   _____
   (Ms. Johnson and Ms. Huggins / have problems with a coworker)

5. _____   _____
   (Ms. Johnson and Mr. Mendoza / fire people)

6. _____   _____
   (Ms. Huggins / handle a lot of cash)

7. _____   _____
   (Mr. Mendoza / hire people)

PAIRS. Ask and answer other questions about the job candidates. Who do you think should get the job?

TIME to TALK

GROUPS. What kinds of jobs do the people in your group want in the future? What questions might an interviewer ask for each job? Write two or more questions for each person in your group.

STUDENT	JOB	QUESTIONS
Marcella	hairdresser	Have you ever been to beauty school? Have you ever worked in a hair salon?

WRAP UP. Now tell the class about the jobs the people in your group want. Does a student in another group want the same job? If so, compare the questions.

Review and Challenge

Grammar

6 This conversation has seven mistakes. The first mistake is corrected for you. Find and correct the other six mistakes. Then listen and check your answers.

Raj: Hi, Liz. How are you and the family? ~~Have~~ *Has* Annie found a job?

Liz: No, she doesn't. It's ever been easy for her to find a job.

Raj: Is she ever searched for a job online? I've found lots of jobs that way.

Liz: I'm not sure. But she's go to several employment agencies. How about your new job? You have started yet?

Raj: Yes, I've. It's a little hard because I have to work the night shift.

Liz: Oh, that is hard. I guess I'm lucky. I've always had the day shift.

work the night shift

Dictation

7 Listen. You will hear five sentences. Write them in your notebook.

Speaking

ON YOUR OWN. Look at the experiences in the chart. Make questions with *ever*. Then walk around the classroom and ask the questions. Write your classmates' names in the chart.

Example:
You: *Raul, have you ever had a job?*
Raul: *No, I haven't had a job yet.*

EXPERIENCES	CLASSMATES
never had a job	Raul
never spoken English at work	
never worn a uniform at work	
never had a bad boss	
never disliked a co-worker	
never been late to work	
never quit a job	
never worked overtime	
never worked the night shift	

Listening

A **Listen to the interview. Why has Ms. Yu applied for the management training program? Check (✓) the reasons that she mentions.**

❏ 1. She wants to own her own business.

❏ 2. She's been a very successful manager.

❏ 3. She wants to work for a large company.

❏ 4. She doesn't like working alone.

❏ 5. She doesn't want to clean houses her whole life.

Look

Big companies, for example hotels, often have management training programs. The company chooses people for the program and trains them to be managers.

B **Listen again. Make a list of the things that Ms. Yu has and hasn't done. Use the words in the box. Change the verbs to past participles.**

have an easy life	manage a business	take care of her family	work alone
~~have children~~	manage people	train workers	work for a large company
hire workers	own a business		

Ms. Yu has 1. ___had children___. Ms. Yu hasn't 6. _____.

2. _____. 7. _____.

3. _____. 8. _____.

4. _____. 9. _____.

5. _____. 10. _____.

PAIRS. Do you think Ms. Yu will get into the management training program? Explain.

PAIRS. **Do a role play.**

Student A: You are the human resource manager at an employment agency. You have openings for the jobs in the box. Interview Student B.

Student B: You have applied for one of the jobs in the box. You have an interview with the human resource manager. Then change roles.

bus driver	cashier	construction worker	cook	salesperson

Example:

A: *Have you ever worked as a cook?*

B: *No, I haven't. But I am taking classes at the cooking school.*

WRAP UP. **Now act out one of your role plays for the class.**

Reading

Getting Ready to Read

Read the first paragraph of the article. What is the main topic of the article?

_____

Reading

Read the article. Was your answer to Getting Ready to Read correct?

MYSTERY SHOPPERS

Mary Beth has been at the mall all day. She has bought some shoes, gotten a haircut, and had a nice lunch, but she has not spent one penny of her own money. In fact, she's made $40. How? Mary Beth is a mystery shopper.

Mystery shoppers have been around for years, but most people have never heard of them. That is because mystery shoppers look like regular customers. Businesses hire mystery shoppers because they want information that is difficult to get. For example, imagine that a restaurant owner has received several complaints about poor service. However, when he is at the restaurant, there are no problems. That is not surprising, since most employees work harder when the boss is around. To find out the truth about the complaints, he might decide to use a mystery shopper. If he does, he will contact an agency. That agency will e-mail the mystery shopper and ask him or her to go to the restaurant. The shopper will look and act like a regular customer. Afterwards, he or she will answer detailed questions about the experience. In some cases, the shopper will also be paid, usually from $10 to $20.

To become a mystery shopper, you need to take a training course. Sometimes the course is free, but sometimes you have to pay. You also need to have a computer and an e-mail address. You might not make any money at first, but you will get a free meal or a store discount. Mystery shoppers who have had a lot of experience get paid, but even they rarely do it full time. For most mystery shoppers, it is not really a job. It is a good way to get free meals and store discounts by doing what they love to do: Eat out and shop.

After You Read

 A   **Read the article again. Put the following statements in order from 1 to 8. Write the numbers on the blanks.**

_____ **a.** The mystery shopper answers the list of questions about the service at the store.

_____ **b.** The store owner visits the store, but he doesn't see any service problems.

_____ **c.** The mystery shopper gets paid.

_____ **d.** The mystery shopper gets an e-mail from the agency about the job, along with a list of questions.

_____ **e.** The mystery shopper visits the store and acts like a regular customer.

__1__ **f.** The store owner gets several complaints about the service at his store.

_____ **g.** The mystery shopper e-mails the answers back to the mystery shopping agency.

_____ **h.** The store owner contacts an agency.

B   **Read the article again. Answer the questions.**

1. What kinds of businesses use mystery shoppers?

_____

_____

2. Do most people notice mystery shoppers? Why or why not?

_____

_____

3. Why do business owners need to hire mystery shoppers?

_____

_____

4. How do mystery shoppers find out about available jobs?

_____

_____

5. What do mystery shoppers get for their services?

_____

_____

Writing

Writing Tip

When you write a formal letter, put your address and the date on the right side and the name and address of the person you are writing to (the recipient) on the left side.

Getting Ready to Write

A Read the beginning of the formal letter. Circle the address of the person who the letter is for.

443 11th Street
Mountain View, CA 94040
July 21, 2007

Store Manager
Waterman's Book Store
4111 15th St.
Mountain View, CA 94040

B Read the model letter.

5 Walker Lane
West Roxbury, MA 02131
July 21, 2007

Dolores Frankel
Store Manager
Bellman's Department Store
105 Park Rd.
Centerville, MA 02130

Dear Ms. Frankel,

I am writing to complain about one of the cashiers in your store. I was in your store yesterday to buy a dress. The cashier was a young woman in a green shirt, and she was talking on the phone with her friend. I waited for several minutes to pay for the dress, but she didn't stop talking. Then, when I tried to get her attention, she turned her back! Finally, I left.

I wanted to tell you about this because I have never had an experience like this in your store before. The service has always been great, and your cashiers have always been very polite. I'm very disappointed that you have hired such a rude cashier. Do you know what is really going on in your store? If you don't, why don't you find out?

Sincerely,

Antonia DeGrandi
Antonia DeGrandi

PAIRS. Read the model again. What happened to the writer?

Has anything similar ever happened to you? Tell your partner about it.

112 Unit 8

Prewriting: Answering Questions

You are going to write a formal letter to complain about something bad that happened to you. Before you write, answer the questions.

1. What is your address?
2. What is today's date?
3. What is the address of the person you are writing to?
4. What happened to you?
5. Has anything like this ever happened to you before?
6. What do you want the recipient to do?

Writing

Now write a formal letter to complain about something bad that happened to you. The writing tip, the model letter, and your notes will help you. Write in your notebook.

Unit 9
Relationships

Vocabulary

CD 2 TRACK
9 Complete the sentences with the words in the box. Listen and check your answers. Then circle the nouns in the boxes and underline the verbs.

birth	honeymoon	newlyweds

Mira and Andy got married in May. Like many _____, they went to Hawaii on
1.
their _____. Now they are waiting for
2.
the _____ of their first child.
3.

marriage	remarried	widow	widower

Liz and her husband, Joe, had a happy
_____. Joe died last year, and Liz
4.
became a _____. Last week, Liz was
5.
_____. Her new husband, Al, was a
6.
_____. It's his second marriage too.
7.

argued	broke up	fight

Ana and Ed went out for a year, but they did not get along very well. They _____
8.
a lot. They had a _____ almost every
9.
day, so they _____. Now, Ana has a
10.
new boyfriend.

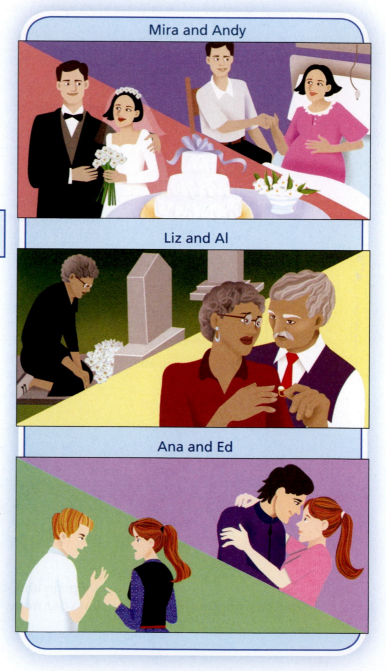

Mira and Andy

Liz and Al

Ana and Ed

Listening

A CD 2 TRACK **10** **Listen. What is the relationship between Lauren and Rachel? Check (✓) the correct answer.**

❏ an aunt and a niece   ❏ best friends   ❏ neighbors   ❏ sisters   ❏ sisters-in-law

B CD 2 TRACK **11** **Listen again. For each pair of sentences, check (✓) the sentence that you hear.**

1. ☑ **a.** We've been getting along great.
   ❏ **b.** We're getting along great.

2. ❏ **a.** We've been busy with the new house, and I've been making friends in the neighborhood.
   ❏ **b.** We're very busy with the new house, and I'm making friends in the neighborhood.

3. ❏ **a.** And have you be running much?
   ❏ **b.** And have you been running much?

4. ❏ **a.** It's going to rain for weeks.
   ❏ **b.** It's been raining for weeks.

5. ❏ **a.** We've been wearing summer clothes since the beginning of June.
   ❏ **b.** We've worn summer clothes since the beginning of June.

6. ❏ **a.** But you're only getting married in February.
   ❏ **b.** But you've only been married since February.

Look

make friends = start to know and like people you meet

C CD 2 TRACK **12** **Listen again. Check (✓) the sentences that are true.**

❏ **1.** Rachel and Lauren talked on the phone yesterday.
❏ **2.** Rachel didn't use to cook a lot.
❏ **3.** Rachel and Lauren live near each other.
❏ **4.** Rachel's husband doesn't like children.
❏ **5.** Rachel doesn't see her nephews often.
❏ **6.** Rachel has children.

Grammar to Communicate 1

Subject	*Have / Has*	Past Participle		*For / Since*	Time Expression
I	have			for	a long time.
		known	Jim		ten years.
She	has			since	2002.
					college.

A Read the situations. Circle the correct explanation of each situation.

1. Loretta hasn't remarried since her divorce.
   a. Loretta is married now.
   b. Loretta isn't married now. *(circled)*

Look

Use *for* and *since* with the present perfect to show that something began in the past and is also true now.

2. Mrs. Norton has been a widow for five months.
   a. Mrs. Norton is married now.
   b. Mrs. Norton's husband died five months ago.

3. Roger hasn't had a girlfriend since last year.
   a. Roger and his girlfriend broke up last year.
   b. Roger didn't have a girlfriend last year.

4. Mike and Sara have been angry with each other for a couple of days.
   a. Mike and Sara are angry now.
   b. Mike and Sara aren't angry now.

5. Nick has wanted to go out with his classmate Angela since May.
   a. Nick wants to go out with Angela now.
   b. Nick wanted to go out with Angela in May. He doesn't want to go out with her now.

B Underline the time expressions with *for* and *since* in Exercise A. Then write them in the correct row.

FOR	five months,
SINCE	her divorce,

Complete the statements. Circle the correct answer.

1. Use *for* before
   a. a specific time (for example, *yesterday*)
   b. a period of time (for example, *five minutes*)

2. Use *since* before
   a. a specific time (for example, *yesterday*)
   b. a period of time (for example, *five minutes*)

Complete the letter with _for_ or _since_.

Dear Love's Helper,

I've had the same boyfriend _____ six years. I've known him
               1.

_____ college. I've wanted to get married _____ last year, but he
2.   3.

hasn't asked me yet. He says he's not ready. His parents have been divorced

_____ ten years, so I think he's afraid. I've loved him _____ our
4.   5.

first date, but I don't want to be single forever. What should I do?

Forever Single

D

**Rewrite the sentences. Use the present perfect and _for_. Use the words in the box.
Write in your notebook.**

be divorced	be separated	have the same girlfriend
be married	be a widower	~~know each other~~

1. Chris and Al met each other six months ago.

   They've known each other for six months.

2. David and Cindy are newlyweds. They got married two months ago.

3. Petra got divorced two years ago.

4. Michael's wife died last year. He has not remarried.

5. Carlos and his wife separated after they had a fight last year.

6. Sam started going out with his girlfriend last month. They haven't broken up.

Rewrite the sentences with _since_. (It's November now.)

Example: _They've known each other since May._

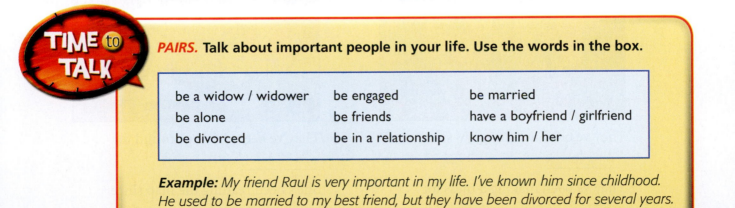

PAIRS. Talk about important people in your life. Use the words in the box.

be a widow / widower	be engaged	be married
be alone	be friends	have a boyfriend / girlfriend
be divorced	be in a relationship	know him / her

Example: _My friend Raul is very important in my life. I've known him since childhood.
He used to be married to my best friend, but they have been divorced for several years._

Grammar to Communicate 2

PRESENT PERFECT PROGRESSIVE: *FOR* AND *SINCE*

Subject	Have / Has	Been + Present Participle	For / Since	Time Expression	Subject	Have not / Has not	Been + Present Participle	For / Since	Time Expression
I We You They	have	been talking	for	10 minutes.	I We You They	have not	been talking	for	25 minutes.
He She	has		since	11:00.	He She	has not		since	11:00.

A Complete the sentences with the missing time expressions.

Look

Use the present perfect progressive to show that something began in the past and is also true now.

1.

She's been waiting for <u>15 minutes</u>.

It's been raining since <u>6:00</u>.

2.

She's been talking since _____.

He's been waiting for _____.

3.

They've been watching TV since _____.

They've been making a mess for _____.

4.

They've been driving around for _____.

She's been reading the map since _____.

B   The people in the pictures in Exercise A are talking. Complete their conversations. Use the present perfect progressive.

1. **A:** I _____ for a half hour.
   (wait)

   B: You _____ for a half hour. I'm only 15 minutes late.
   (not wait)

2. **A:** You _____ for an hour.
   (talk)

   B: I _____ for an hour. It's 11:30 and Lynn called at 11:00.
   (not talk)

3. **A:** You and your friends _____ TV all day.
   (watch)

   B: We _____ all day. It's 3:30 and the game started at 2:00.
   (not watch)

4. **A:** You _____ around for hours.
   (drive)

   B: I _____ for hours. We left the house 45 minutes ago.
   (not drive)

C   Complete the sentences with the correct form of the verb. Use the present perfect or present perfect progressive.

1. We _____*have been*_____ friends since we were kids. Our children
   (be)

   ____*have been playing*____ together since kindergarten.
   (play)

2. Rita and Jane _____ each other for
   (know)

   many years, but they _____ more
   (spend)

   time together since the birth of their children.

3. Chris and Joe _____ a lot since his
   (argue)

   birthday party. They _____ any
   (not have)

   parties since then.

4. I know you _____ for my call since
   (wait)

   Monday, but I _____ any free time.
   (not have)

> **Look**
>
> Use the present perfect progressive for action verbs that began in the past and continue now.
> We **have been dating** for years.
> Use the present perfect with nonaction verbs.
> I **have known** her for two years.

TIME to TALK

PAIRS. **Student A:** Look at page 301. Read your first sentence to Student B.
Student B: Look at page 304. Check the sentence that Student A says.

Then switch roles. Student B, read your first sentence and Student A checks the correct sentence. Take turns reading your sentences.

Grammar to Communicate 3

PRESENT PERFECT PROGRESSIVE: QUESTIONS

Have / Has	Subject	Been + Present Participle	Affirmative			Negative		
Has	he she	**been dating?**	**Yes,**	he she	**has.**	**No,**	he she	**hasn't.**
Have	you they			I they	**have.**		I they	**haven't.**

Information Questions with *How long*				Answers
How long	**has**	he	**been going out** with her?	For a month. Since June.
	have	you		

A Deb is talking to Carla about her relationship with Jim. Answer the questions.

1. **Carla:** Have you and Jim been arguing a lot? **Deb:** Yes, _____.
2. **Carla:** Have you been going out with other guys? **Deb:** No, _____.
3. **Carla:** Has Jim been talking to other girls? **Deb:** Yes, _____.
4. **Carla:** Has Jim been spending all his free time with you? **Deb:** No, _____.
5. **Carla:** Has Jim been going to your house on weekends? **Deb:** No, _____.

B Tony is unhappy because he doesn't know many people. Ask questions with *how long* and the present perfect progressive of the underlined words.

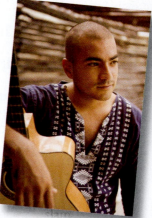

1. <u>I'm living in the United States</u>, but I don't know any Americans.

   How long have you been living in the United States?

2. <u>I'm staying at my relatives' house</u>. They work all the time.

   _____

3. <u>I'm trying to find a nice person to date</u>, but it isn't easy.

   _____

4. <u>I'm working here</u>. I have a lot of co-workers, but I'm not friends with any of them.

   _____

5. <u>I'm taking an English class</u>, but my classmates are always busy after class.

   _____

PAIRS. Check (✓) the sentences that are true for you. Then ask and answer the questions.

C What has been happening? Write questions with the present perfect progressive and *lately* or *recently*.

1. <u>Have you been feeling homesick lately?</u>
   (feel homesick / lately)

2. _____
   (spend a lot of time alone / recently)

3. _____
   (work a lot / lately)

4. _____
   (go to a lot of parties / recently)

5. _____
   (go out a lot with your friends / lately)

6. _____
   (speak a lot of English / recently)

7. _____
   (date anyone / lately)

> **Look**
>
> Use *recently* and *lately* to talk about something that began a short time ago and is continuing now.
> Last year, my wife and I had a lot of fights, but **lately** we've been getting along very well.

***PAIRS.* Ask and answer the questions.**

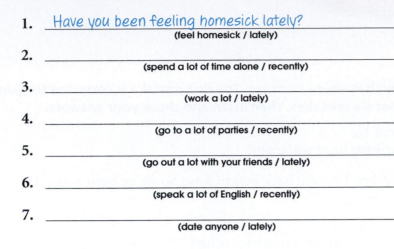

> Have you made a lot of money this year?
>
> I'd rather not say.
>
> If you don't want to answer a personal question, you can say, "I'd rather not say."

CLASS. Walk around the class and talk to your classmates. For each question, find one person who answers "yes." Then ask a question with *How long* and write the person's name and answer. If someone answers "no," ask another classmate.

Example:
You: *Are you married?*
Homero: *Yes, I am.*
You: *How long have you been married?*
Homero: *I've been married since 1999. How about you?*

QUESTION	NAME	HOW LONG . . .
Are you married?	Homero	**(be)** since 1999
Are you a parent?		**(be)**
Do you live alone?		**(live)**
Do you have a roommate?		**(have)**
Do you have a best friend?		**(have)**
Do you have a pet?		**(have)**
Do you play a musical instrument?		**(play)**
Do you play on a sports team?		**(play)**

***WRAP UP.* Now tell the class about a few of your classmates.**

Review and Challenge

Grammar

13 This conversation has seven mistakes. The first mistake is corrected for you. Find and correct the other six mistakes. Then listen and check your answers.

Kate: John, how long ~~we have~~ *have we* been going out?

John: Let's see. It's December. I moved back here in June. So we've been going out since six months.

Kate: And how long have we been knowing each other?

John: For a year.

Kate: And have we any conversations since last year?

John: Sure. Every day. We're having a conversation right now.

Kate: No. I mean a real conversation, a conversation about our relationship.

John: About our relationship?

Kate: Yeah. This is probably a surprise to you, but I'm not happy for about a month.

John: Really? Why not?

Kate: You've been work a lot and you have been not paying attention to me.

John: Oh, come on, Katie. You know I love you.

Dictation

14 Listen. You will hear five sentences. Write them in your notebook.

Speaking

PAIRS. Look at the sentences and illustrations on page 118. Choose one of the situations and do a role play. Then act out your role play for the class.

Example:

A: *I can't believe it! I've been waiting for 15 minutes! We're going to be late for the party. You've known about this party for two weeks!*

B: *I'm sorry, but you know I've been working late every night. I've told you how busy I am at work, but you haven't been listening.*

A: *I've been listening. I think you haven't been trying!*

122 Unit 9

Listening

A **15** **Listen to the radio show. What is the major problem in Mary's relationship? Check (✓) the correct answer.**

❏ her children ❏ her house ❏ her husband's job ❏ money ❏ music

B **15** **Listen again. Check (✓) the correct answers.**

1. What is true about Mary and her husband?

   ❏ **a.** She has never worked.

   ❏ **b.** They've been married a long time.

   ❏ **c.** He has been working since he was a teenager.

   ❏ **d.** They've bought a new house.

   ❏ **e.** They haven't had any children yet.

2. What is Mary worried about?

   ❏ **a.** She and her husband have been arguing a lot recently.

   ❏ **b.** Her husband has been spending a lot of money lately.

   ❏ **c.** Her husband has never saved any money.

   ❏ **d.** Her husband hasn't found a job.

   ❏ **e.** They won't have the money to buy a house.

TIME to TALK

GROUPS. Discuss the questions.

1. Have you ever had a fight with someone over money?

2. In your opinion, what are the most common things that couples argue about?

3. Divorce has become more and more common in the U.S. in the past fifty years. Why do you think it has become so common? In your opinion, is that a good thing or a bad thing?

4. What has been happening with the number of divorces in your country recently? Has it been going up or down, or has it stayed the same?

WRAP UP. Share your answers with the class.

Example: The number of divorces has been going down in my country. I think it is because fewer people are getting married.

Reading

Getting Ready to Read

Read the questions. Then scan the article to find the answers.

Reading Skill:
Scanning for Specific Information

When you need to find information quickly in a reading, look for specific information like numbers or dates. You will find them more quickly than words.

1. When did the One-Child Policy begin? _____

2. How many only children have been born in China since the One-Child Policy began? _____

3. What is "4-2-1"? _____

Reading

Read the article. Were your answers in Getting Ready to Read correct?

THE ONE-CHILD POLICY

In 1979, the Chinese government introduced the One-Child Policy to slow down **population growth**. Families in the city could have only one child. Families in the countryside could have two, but only if the first child was a girl. The policy has been very successful. It has slowed population growth to about 10 million people a year. Now the first **generation** of children born under the policy are becoming adults. It is clear that the policy has changed Chinese family life.

Eighty million children with no brothers or sisters ("only children") have been born in China since 1979. This has resulted in what the Chinese call "4-2-1": four grandparents and two parents **focus** all of their attention **on** one child. But some young Chinese are not happy. Many say that they have always felt lonely because they have no brothers or sisters. They also feel a lot of **pressure** from their parents to be successful. Some people, on the other hand, complain that parents and grandparents have been **spoiling** their children. They believe that the new generation has become too **dependent** on their parents.

In the future, China could have a serious problem. Many Chinese do not have **pensions**, so they depend on their children to take care of them when they retire. In the past, brothers and sisters shared the responsibility for their parents. But only children do not have anyone to share the responsibility with. As Wan Bo, a young Chinese woman says, "My boyfriend and I often talk about how, after marriage, we will need to take care of four old people. Both of us are so busy trying to make money."

The Chinese government has been studying the situation for some time and has decided to allow only children to have two children. That is probably good news to Wan Bo and the 80 million other only children like her.

After You Read

 A   Look at the **boldface** words in the article. Guess their meaning. Then read the sentences, and circle the correct answer.

1. When there is **population growth**, the number of people gets _____.
   - **(a.)** larger   **b.** smaller

2. When a child, her parents, and her grandparents all live in one house, _____ **generations** are living together.
   - **a.** two   **b.** three

3. When you **focus on** something, you _____.
   - **a.** forget about it   **b.** think about it a lot

4. When someone puts **pressure** on you, you feel _____.
   - **a.** comfortable   **b.** uncomfortable

5. When you **spoil** a child, you _____.
   - **a.** give the child too many things   **b.** don't give the child enough things

6. **Dependent** children can _____ take care of themselves.
   - **a.** usually   **b.** rarely

7. A **pension** is _____.
   - **a.** money that you give to your children   **b.** money that you get after you retire

B   Read the article again. Answer the questions.

1. Why did the Chinese government introduce the One-Child Policy?

   _____

2. Has the One-Child Policy been successful?

   _____

3. What do Chinese parents want their children to do?

   _____

4. What do some Chinese people think about the new generation of young Chinese?

   _____

5. What will Chinese children have to do for their parents after they retire?

   _____

6. What has the Chinese government decided to allow only children to do?

   _____

Writing

Getting Ready to Write

 A   Rewrite each sentence. Use *because* or *so*.

> **Writing Tip**
>
> Use linking words to connect one idea to another. Both *because* and *so* show a cause and effect relationship.
>
> Examples:
> **Because** the cost of raising a child has been going up, the birth rate has been going down.
>
> The cost of raising a child has been going up, **so** the birth rate has been going down.

1. Families have been getting smaller, so children are getting a lot of attention.

    Because families have been getting smaller,

    children are getting a lot of attention.

2. Both parents have to work, so they don't have time to take care of more than one child.

    _____

    _____

3. Because some people get married when they are older, they save money before marriage.

    _____

    _____

4. Travel has been getting easier, so a lot of families take trips together.

    _____

    _____

5. Many older people are active these days, so they can do more with their grandchildren.

    _____

    _____

B   Read the model paragraph.

> In many parts of the world, families have been getting smaller recently. There are many reasons for this change. The cost of raising a child has gone up in many parts of the world, so people cannot afford to have large families. Also, in many families both parents work, so they do not have enough time to take care of more than one child. The divorce rate has also been going up. Some couples get divorced before they have children. Finally, in many parts of the world women have careers, so they have been waiting longer to have children. If a woman has her first child when she is 35, she may not have many more children.

PAIRS. Read the model again. Is the information true about your country?

Now talk about another recent change in lifestyles in your country. Discuss the reasons why this change is happening. You can talk about relationships, money, health, education, or your own idea.

Prewriting: Listing Reasons

You are going to write a paragraph about a recent change in people's lifestyles in your country. Before you write, choose a main topic from the list or use your own idea.

- education
- health

- money
- relationships

Read the notes for the writing model. Then complete the chart with notes about your topic.

Writing Model

Change: Families have been getting smaller.

Reasons
1. Cost of raising a child going up → people cannot afford to have large families
2. Both parents have to work → no time to take care of more than one child
3. Divorce rate going up → people divorce before they have children
4. Women have careers → they are waiting to have children

Change:
Reasons 1.
2.
3.
4.

Writing

Now write a paragraph about a recent change in people's lifestyles in your country. The writing tip, the model paragraph, and your notes will help you. Write in your notebook.

Vocabulary

CD 2 TRACK **16** **Complete the sentences with the words in the box. Then listen and check your answers.**

| fashionable | romantic | secret | stars |

The young man and woman are movie

_____. Their clothes are very
   1.

_____. They just got married
   2.

in a _____ ceremony. It was a
   3.

_____ way to get married.
   4.

| attractive | calm | clear | nervous |

Both the man and woman are

_____. The woman is
   5.

_____. The man is _____.
   6.   7.

His speech is not very _____.
             8.

| awful | strange | successful | terrific |

Many people watch *Cook with the Chefs.*

It is a _____ show. Today, Chef
   9.

Chick is wearing a _____ hat.
          10.

His food tastes _____. Chef Bob's
          11.

food tastes _____.
       12.

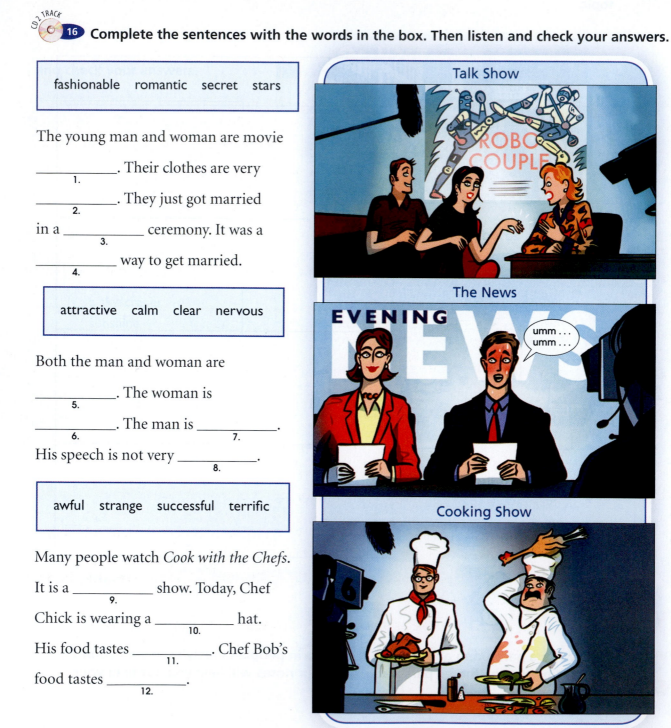

Talk Show

ROBO COUPLE

The News

EVENING NEWS

umm . . .
umm . . .

Cooking Show

Listening

A **17** **Listen to the conversation from a TV soap opera. Where are the man and the woman, and what are they doing? Check (✓) the correct answer.**

❏ 1. They are hiking in the mountains.

❏ 2. They are having a romantic picnic on the beach.

❏ 3. They are having a family barbecue near a lake.

❏ 4. They are having dinner at an expensive outdoor café.

> **Look**
>
> soap opera = a story on television about the lives and problems of a group of people

B **18** **Read and listen again. Write the missing words. Use the words in the box.**

| carefully | perfect | really | ~~romantic~~ | strange | terrific | very |

Lisa: Oh Brad, this is really ___romantic___ . The food looks delicious, and the flowers are
  1.
wonderful. And look at the sky. It's _____ beautiful tonight. Everything is
  2.
just _____ .
  3.

Brad: And you look beautiful. Mmm . . . and you smell pretty _____ , too.
  4.

Lisa: Oh Brad . . . What was that?

Brad: What? Come here . . .

Lisa: No, I'm serious. I heard a _____ noise. Listen . . . There it is again!
  5.

Brad: Relax, Lisa. It's _____ safe out here. Now, where were we?
  6.

Lisa: No, Brad, I'm really serious. Be quiet and listen _____ .
  7.

C **19** **Listen again. Check (✓) the correct description of the soap opera scene.**

❏ 1. Brad and Lisa meet secretly at the beach. The evening starts quite romantically, but then something terrible happens.

❏ 2. Brad and Lisa are walking on the beach. Lisa decides that it is time to tell Brad her secret, but is Brad ready to hear it?

❏ 3. Brad and Lisa are having a romantic evening on the beach. Everything is going perfectly, but then Brad says something really strange.

Grammar to Communicate 1

ADVERBS AND ADJECTIVES

Regular Adjectives					Regular Adverbs		
Subject	Verb	Article	Adjective	Noun	Subject	Verb	Adverb
I	am	a	**slow**	eater.	I	**eat**	slowly.
She	is		**careful**	driver.	She	**drives**	carefully.
They	are		**bad**	dressers.	They	**dress**	badly.

Look

Some adverbs are irregular and do not take *-ly*.

ADJECTIVE	ADVERB
fast	**fast**
good	**well**
hard	**hard**

 A   Underline the adjectives. Circle the adverbs.

WHERE IS DARREN McDOUGAL NOW?

McDougal, the star of the <u>popular</u> soap opera *You and Me* lives (quietly) with his beautiful family in Los Angeles.

Last year he was busy all the time. He worked hard on *You and Me*, and the show did well. But now he's doing things differently.

This year he is happy at home with his young children, Tara, 5, and Ben, 4. His wife, the actress Sara Miller, has a successful show.

She is the smart, attractive police officer in *Life on the Street*. She lives dangerously in the show, but her life with Darren and the children is quiet.

B   Complete the sentences. Use the correct word.

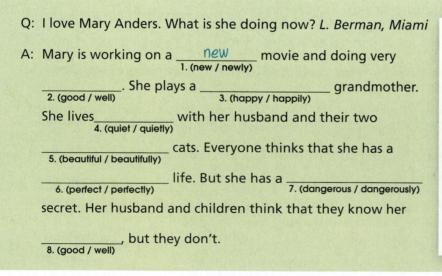

Q: I love Mary Anders. What is she doing now? *L. Berman, Miami*

A: Mary is working on a ____new____ movie and doing very
                     1. (new / newly)

_____. She plays a _____ grandmother.
2. (good / well)   3. (happy / happily)

She lives_____ with her husband and their two
           4. (quiet / quietly)

_____ cats. Everyone thinks that she has a
5. (beautiful / beautifully)

_____ life. But she has a _____
6. (perfect / perfectly)   7. (dangerous / dangerously)

secret. Her husband and children think that they know her

_____, but they don't.
8. (good / well)

C   **Circle the three words that the speaker probably says.**

> **Look**
>
> Some verbs describe our senses. We use adjectives, not adverbs, after these verbs:
> feel   smell   taste
> look   sound
> These flowers **smell beautiful**.
> NOT These flowers smell ~~beautifully~~.

1. On a cooking show:

   A: This tastes _____.

   B: Thank you.

   (**a.** delicious)   (**b.** good)   (**c.** great)   **d.** terrible

2. On a sports show before the game:

   A: Are you ready for the game?

   B: Oh, yeah. I feel _____.

   a. great   **b.** ready   **c.** terrific   **d.** tired

3. On a soap opera:

   A: You smell _____. I love your perfume.

   B: Thank you.

   a. wonderful   **b.** strange   **c.** terrific   **d.** nice

   a bottle of perfume

4. On a talk show:

   A: Your new song sounds _____.

   B: I'm glad you like it.

   a. bad   **b.** beautiful   **c.** interesting   **d.** sweet

5. On a police show:

   A: That guy looks _____.

   B: I know. Something is wrong.

   a. awful   **b.** strange   **c.** handsome   **d.** nervous

TIME to TALK

GROUPS. Talk about the television shows in the box. Which kind of shows do you like? Which kind don't you like? Explain your answers. Use adjectives and adverbs.

cartoons	nature and science shows	sitcoms
cooking shows	the news	soap operas
the home shopping network	police shows	sports
music videos	reality shows	talk shows

Example:
A: *I like to watch talk shows. They are interesting, and the people speak clearly.*
B: *Really? I don't like talk shows. The people speak fast. I can't understand anything!*

Grammar to Communicate 2

ADVERBS OF MANNER

Subject	Verb	Adverb	Forming adverbs from adjectives
The children	sat	**silently.**	Most adjectives → + *ly* (silent / silent**ly**)
They	won	**easily.**	Adjectives with two or more syllables ending in consonants and *y* → change *y* to *i* and add *ly* (easy / eas**ily**)
The actors	dressed	**fashionably.**	Adjectives ending in –*le* → change e to y (fashionable / fashionab**ly**)
The couple	spoke	**romantically.**	Adjectives ending in –*ic* → + *ally* (romantic / romantic**ally**)

Look
Adverbs of manner answer the question *how*.
How do they speak?
They speak **clearly**.

A 🔊 CD 2 TRACK 20 **Listen. How are the people speaking?**

angrily	nervously	romantically	slowly	softly

Look
softly = quietly

The person is speaking . . .

1. _____.   2. _____.   3. _____.   4. _____.   5. _____.

B **Underline the adverbs. Then write the adverb and its adjective form.**

	ADVERB	ADJECTIVE
The Happy Kitchen Learn how to make dinner <u>successfully</u>. With Chef Peter's help, you won't work hard in the kitchen. And all your dinner guests will think you cook terrifically.	successfully _____ _____ _____	successful _____ _____ _____
Doctors' Hospital Dr. Black meets secretly with Charlotte. The student nurses do badly on their exam. Ten patients complain angrily about Dr. Lee.	_____ _____ _____	_____ _____ _____
The Apartment Last week Ruth and Ed were getting along well and living together happily. But things change this week. Do they change temporarily? Or do they change permanently?	_____ _____ _____ _____	_____ _____ _____ _____

C A director of a soap opera is telling the actors and actresses how to act. Complete the directions with adverbs.

1. "You need to be careful. You don't want the police to stop you. Drive ____carefully____."

2. "You're angry. You saw your boyfriend with another woman. Look at him _____."

3. "You need to be romantic. You're in love. Talk to her _____."

4. "You're sad. Your friend is very sick. Look at her _____."

5. "Everyone in the room is very quiet. Don't make a lot of noise. Come in _____."

6. "You haven't seen your friend in a long time, and you're very happy to see her. Enter the room _____."

7. "You're nervous when you make the call. Speak _____."

TIME to TALK

PAIRS. Talk about famous television shows or movies and the people in them. Make sentences with the words in the boxes. Use one word from each box for every sentence.

cartoon	the news	sitcom
cooking show	police show	soap opera
music	reality show	talk show

Verbs	**Adverbs**
act	badly
behave	beautifully
dance	fashionably
dress	fast
laugh	realistically
sing	strangely
speak	terribly
walk	terrifically

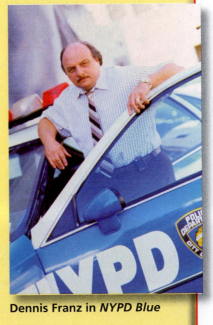

Dennis Franz in *NYPD Blue*

Example:
In my favorite police show, the star of the show dresses badly.

Grammar to Communicate 3

ADVERBS OF DEGREE

Subject	Verb	Article	Adverb	Adjective	Noun
He		an	extremely		
	is		really	good	dancer.
She		a	very		
			pretty		

Subject	Verb	Adverb	Adverb
He		extremely	
	dances	really	well.
She		very	
		pretty	

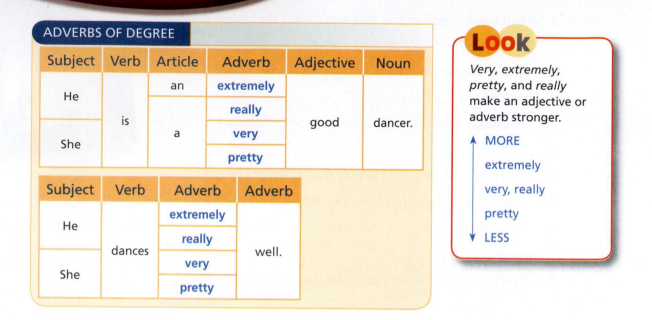

Look

Very, extremely, pretty, and *really* make an adjective or adverb stronger.

↑ MORE

extremely

very, really

pretty

↓ LESS

A   Read the situations, and complete the sentences. Write the correct word.

1. There was a new show on TV last night. You liked it a lot. What do you say?

    "The show was _____ really _____ good."
    (pretty / really)

2. You are talking about an actress on TV. You like her looks, but you don't think she's beautiful. What do you say?

    "She is _____ attractive."
    (extremely / pretty)

3. Your neighbor's daughter wants to be a dancer and lives in Hollywood. You don't think she dances badly, but you don't think she's ready for music videos. What do you say?

    "She dances _____ well."
    (pretty / very)

4. The baseball game started at 8:00 P.M. last night and finished after midnight, and it was very boring. What do you say?

    "The game was _____ long."
    (extremely / pretty)

5. You like the newscaster on Channel 2. She speaks clearly. But you can't understand the newscaster on Channel 10. What do you say?

    "He talks _____ fast."
    (pretty / really)

6. Your friend wants you to watch a show on TV with her, but it starts at 11:00 P.M. and you have to be in work at 6:00 A.M. What do you say?

    "It's _____ late. I can't watch the show with you."
    (pretty / very)

 134   Unit 10

B   Write *very* where possible. If *very* is not possible, write *really*.

1. Talk shows are ____very____ interesting.
2. Some TV shows are ____really____ excellent.
3. Some newscasters talk _____ quickly.
4. Some actors on TV are _____ terrible.
5. A lot of actors in soap operas act _____ well.
6. TV actors get jobs _____ easily.
7. Singers in music videos sing _____ perfectly.
8. Most actresses and actors are _____ gorgeous.

Look

These words have a strong meaning.
great, wonderful, excellent, perfect = very good
terrible, awful = very bad
gorgeous = very beautiful or very handsome

Do not use *very* or *extremely* with these words. Use *really* or *pretty*.

He is really great.
NOT He is ~~very~~ great.

C   Look at the pictures on page 128. Write five new sentences about the people in the pictures. Use *extremely*, *pretty*, *really*, or *very*. Then read your sentences to a partner.

1. The woman in the first picture is really gorgeous.
2. _____
3. _____
4. _____
5. _____
6. _____

ON YOUR OWN. Complete the statements with *pretty*, *very*, *really*, or *extremely*. If you don't agree with the statement, make the verb negative.

1. Television is _____ bad for children.
2. Television is _____ educational.
3. Sitcoms are _____ funny.
4. Police shows are _____ violent.
5. Television commercials are _____ annoying.
6. People in reality shows behave _____ stupidly.
7. Actors and actresses have to work _____ hard.

Example:
A: *I think that television is really bad for children.*
B: *I don't agree. Television isn't always bad for children. Some shows are very good.*

GROUPS. Talk about your opinions.

Review and Challenge

Grammar

Find the mistake in each sentence. Circle the letter and correct the mistake.

1. TV actresses <u>always</u> <u>look</u> <u>really</u> <u>perfectly</u>.
                 A   B   C   D

2. It <u>doesn't sound</u> <u>very</u> <u>good</u>, but it isn't <u>very awful</u>.
             A   B   C   D

3. Some <u>very</u> <u>famously</u> people behave <u>pretty</u> <u>stupidly</u>.
             A   B   C   D

4. Chef Bob's food <u>looks</u> <u>great</u>, but does it <u>taste</u> <u>well</u>?
                     A   B   C   D

5. He's <u>pretty</u> <u>attractive</u>, but he dresses <u>very</u> <u>bad</u>.
         A   B   C   D

Dictation

CD 2 TRACK 21 Listen. You will hear five sentences. Write them in your notebook.

Speaking

PAIRS. Student A: Choose one word from each box and think of a sentence. Then act it out. Do not tell your partner your sentence.

Student B: Guess what Student A's sentence is. Then switch roles. Each student should act out five sentences.

Example: B: *Are you speaking nervously?*
              A: *No, I'm not.*
              B: *Are you speaking fast?*
              A: *Yes, I am.*

Verbs	
behave	smile
eat	speak
laugh	study
read	work

Adverbs	
carefully	nervously
fast	noisily
hard	softly
impolitely	strangely

 136 Unit 10

Listening

A **CD 2 TRACK 22** Listen to scenes from television shows. Write the correct scene number next to the show. Be careful. There is one extra show.

1. cooking show _____
2. police show _____
3. nature show _____
4. soap opera _____
5. newscast _____
6. talk show _____

B **CD 2 TRACK 22** Listen again. Complete the sentences. Use the words in the box.

badly	calmly	hard	nervous	serious
calm	excited	impatient	romantic	softly

Scene 1: The man is trying to sound _____, but he is really _____.

Scene 2: They are both speaking _____. This is a _____ scene.

Scene 3: The man cooks _____. The woman sounds _____.

Scene 4: The situation is very _____, but they are speaking pretty _____.

Scene 5: They are extremely _____, but they are trying _____ to be quiet.

TIME to TALK

PAIRS. Choose one of the situations below, and write a short scene for a television show. Read it like an actor.

A Game Show:
Student A: You are the host. Speak enthusiastically.
Student B: You are a contestant. You are really excited.

A Police Show:
Student A: You are a police officer. You stop a car because it is going very fast. The driver is behaving strangely. You are suspicious.
Student B: You are the driver, but the car is not yours. You stole it. You are nervous, but try to look and sound relaxed.

WRAP UP. Now, act out your scene for the class.

Reading

Getting Ready to Read

Look at the picture and the title of the article, and read the first and last sentence of each paragraph. Check (✓) the questions that you think the article will answer.

❏ **1.** Which countries make the best soap operas?

❏ **2.** What are the differences between soap operas and telenovelas?

❏ **3.** How much money do the directors of telenovelas make?

❏ **4.** Are telenovelas from different countries the same?

❏ **5.** Which topics do telenovelas focus on?

❏ **6.** How are actors in telenovelas different from actors in soap operas?

Reading

Read the article. Were your predictions in Getting Ready to Read correct? Answer as many of the questions as you can in your notebook.

TELENOVELAS

Today almost every country has television soap operas. In Latin America, soap operas are called *telenovelas*. Telenovelas and English-language soap operas are similar in many ways. However, there are some important differences. For example, soap operas are on during the daytime. Telenovelas, on the other hand, are usually on in the evening, during prime time (the most popular time for television viewing). Men and women of all ages and social classes, from the very poor to the very rich, watch telenovelas. In contrast, women between the ages of 18 and 49 usually watch English-language soap operas. Popular soap operas commonly continue for years, but telenovelas usually end **dramatically**, with an exciting surprise, after about six months.

There are also differences between the actors. The actors in telenovelas often become extremely famous in Latin America. They sometimes act in both telenovelas and movies at the same time. The stars of English-language soap operas, in contrast, are popular with their viewers, but they are not as famous as movie stars. The few soap opera actors who **go on to** become movie stars **rarely** continue to appear in soap operas.

Finally, soap operas and telenovelas **deal with** very different topics. Like English-language soap operas today, most telenovelas used to be about romantic relationships. However, telenovelas **increasingly** focus on serious social topics. The topics differ from country to country. For example, telenovelas in Brazil have dealt with single motherhood, government **dishonesty**, and **environmental** problems such as water and air pollution. Mexican telenovelas, on the other hand, are often about differences in social class. In Colombia telenovelas have dealt with crime and **violence**. Telenovelas, therefore, give people an opportunity to talk about the serious problems their countries **face** today.

After You Read

 A Look at the **boldface** words in the article. Guess the meaning. Then match the words with their definitions.

<u> c </u> 1. dramatically   **a.** relating to the air, land, or water on earth

____ 2. go on to   **b.** more and more

____ 3. rarely   **c.** in an exciting way

____ 4. deal with   **d.** lying

____ 5. increasingly   **e.** accept that a difficult situation or problem exists

____ 6. dishonesty   **f.** do something new when you have finished something else

____ 7. environmental   **g.** the act of hurting people on purpose

____ 8. violence   **h.** discuss or be about a particular subject

____ 9. face   **i.** not often

B Read the article again. Match each main point with the example that goes with it.

MAIN POINT

<u> d </u> 1. Today almost every country has television soap operas.

____ 2. Telenovelas and English-language soap operas are similar in many ways. However, there are some important differences.

____ 3. There are also differences between the actors.

____ 4. The topics differ from country to country.

EXAMPLE

a. Telenovelas in Brazil have dealt with single motherhood.

b. The actors in telenovelas often become extremely famous.

c. Soap operas are on during the daytime. Telenovelas are usually on in the evening.

d. In Latin America, soap operas are called *telenovelas*.

> **Reading Skill:**
> **Understanding Examples**
>
> Writers often use **examples** to explain their ideas. When you read, pay close attention to the examples. They will help you to understand the main points.

Actors and television crew working on a telenovela

Writing

Getting Ready to Write

A Rewrite the sentences using *for example*.

1. Television has some positive effects. It entertains people.

   <u>Television has some positive effects. For example,</u>
   <u>it entertains people.</u>

2. There are some serious negative effects of TV. Children watch too much TV and don't exercise enough.

   _____

   _____

3. I think television is a good thing. It teaches people a lot about the world.

   _____

   _____

4. TV has negative effects on people. People become more violent when they watch violent TV shows.

   _____

   _____

> ### Writing Tip
>
> Include examples to explain your main points. Use the expression *for example* to introduce an example.
>
> **Example:**
> The topics differ from country to country. **For example**, telenovelas in Brazil have dealt with single motherhood.

B Read the model paragraph.

> Television can improve your language skills. For example, it can teach you vocabulary. To learn vocabulary from your TV, simply turn on the captions. When you see a new word on the screen, copy it quickly and guess the meaning. Then check it later in your dictionary. Another example of something television can help you with is improving your listening comprehension. To work on your listening comprehension, watch TV with the captions off. Choose one show, and watch it regularly. Listen carefully, but don't worry if you don't always understand. After a few shows, you will become more familiar with the actors' voices. You will also understand the words and expressions that they usually use.

Read the model again. According to the writer, how can you improve your vocabulary by watching TV? How can you improve your listening?

Now talk about your personal experience. Has television helped you to improve your English? Explain.

Prewriting: Using Examples

You are going to write a paragraph about a positive or negative effect of television. Before you write, read the notes for the writing model. Then write examples that explain your ideas.

Writing Model

Positive Effect of TV:
TV can improve language skills

Example 1
improve vocabulary when captions on

Example 2
improve listening comprehension when captions off

_____ Effect of TV:

_____

Example 1

Example 2

Writing

Now write a paragraph about a positive or negative effect of television. The writing tip, the model paragraph, and your notes will help you. Write in your notebook.

Unit 11
The Animal Kingdom

Grammar

- Comparative and Superlative of Adjectives and Adverbs
- Comparative and Superlative of Nouns
- Equatives

Vocabulary

CD 2 TRACK **23** Match the numbers with the words. Then listen and check your answers.

_____ bear _____ chimpanzee _____ donkey _____ lion _____ rabbit _____ bat

_____ camel _____ dolphin _____ elephant _____ penguin 1 rat _____ whale

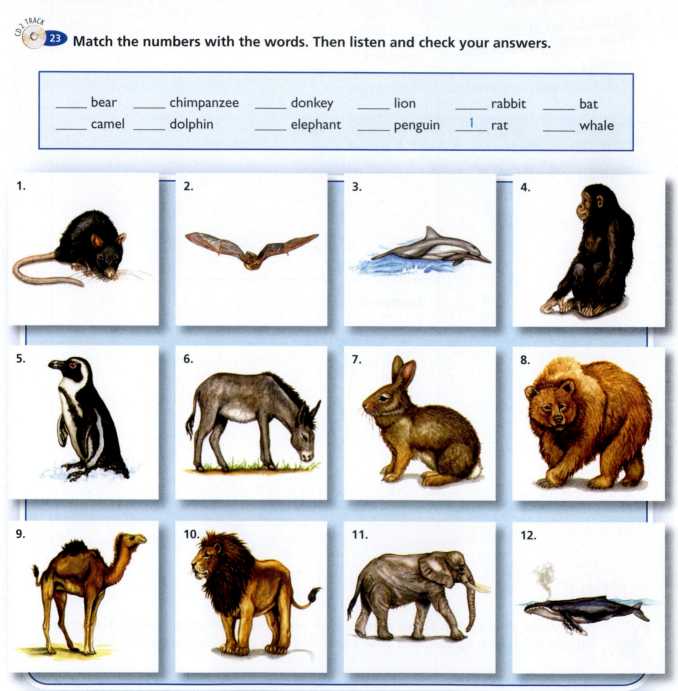

1.

2.

3.

4.

5.

6.

7.

8.

9.

10.

11.

12.

Listening

 A **24** **Listen. Ahmed and May mention one of the animals in the pictures. Check (✓) the animal that they mention.**

❏ 1. a mouse / mice

❏ 2. a snake

❏ 3. a pig

❏ 4. a cheetah

❏ 5. a falcon

❏ 6. a parrot

B **24** **Listen again. Who said it? Write M (May) or A (Ahmed).**

__M__ 1. A lot more people own cats than dogs.

_____ 2. There are as many dogs as children.

_____ 3. Pets aren't as popular as they are in the United States.

_____ 4. In fact, dogs are the least popular pets.

_____ 5. We don't have as much space as Americans do.

_____ 6. What is the most common pet?

_____ 7. It's one of the oldest sports in Asia.

C **24** **Listen again. Who probably agrees with each statement? Check (✓) Ahmed, May, or both Ahmed and May.**

	Ahmed	May
1. "Dogs make good pets."	❏	✓
2. "Birds are cleaner than dogs."	❏	❏
3. "Small dogs or cats are the best pets for people in my country."	❏	❏
4. "Big dogs are not common pets in my country."	❏	❏
5. "Falcons are popular in my country today."	❏	❏

Grammar to Communicate ❶

COMPARATIVE OF ADJECTIVES AND ADVERBS

Regular Adjectives	Comparative	Regular Adverbs	Comparative
One syllable		One syllable	
old	old**er (than)**	fast	fast**er (than)**
nice	nic**er (than)**	late	lat**er (than)**
Two syllables		Two syllables	
easy	eas**ier (than)**	quickly	**more** quickly **than**
Three or more syllables		Three or more syllables	
beautiful	**more** beautiful **(than)**	beautifully	**more** beautiful **than**

Irregular Adjectives		Irregular Adverbs	
good	**better (than)**	well	**better**
bad	**worse (than)**	badly	**worse**
far	**farther (than)**	far	**farther**

A Complete the sentences.

1. _____Lions_____ are more frightening than ___rabbits___.   (rabbits, lions)

2. _____ are prettier than _____.   (pigs, parrots)

3. _____ move more quietly than _____.   (snakes, elephants)

4. _____ are more stubborn than _____.   (donkeys, dogs)

5. _____ are more independent than _____.   (cats, dogs)

6. _____ are more obedient than _____.   (dogs, parrots)

independent   obedient   stubborn   frightening

B Compare the animals. Write sentences in your notebook.

1. dogs / parrots   (live / long)   4. mice / rats   (be / frightening)

2. elephants / pigs   (be / heavy)   5. lions / mice   (move / slowly)

3. cats / chimpanzees   (be / intelligent)   6. dogs / cats   (swim / good)

Example: _Parrots live longer than dogs._

SUPERLATIVE OF ADJECTIVES AND ADVERBS

Regular Adjectives	Superlative	Regular Adverbs	Superlative
One syllable		One syllable	
old	the oldest	fast	the fastest
nice	the nicest	late	the latest
Two syllables		Two syllables	
easy	the easiest	quickly	the most quickly
Three or more syllables		Three or more syllables	
beautiful	the most beautiful	beautifully	the most beautifully

Irregular Adjectives		Irregular Adverbs	
good	the best	well	the best
bad	the worst	badly	the worst
far	the farthest	far	the farthest

C Write sentences about four animals: elephants, penguins, bears, and whales. Use the superlative. Add *not* where necessary. Write in your notebook.

1. elephants / heavy / animal
2. penguins / cute / animal
3. bears / sleep / long
4. whales / swim / far

Example: _Elephants are not the heaviest animals. (Whales are.)_

D Complete the sentences with the comparative or superlative of the words. Then write *T* (true) or *F* (false). Check your answers on page 306.

__T__ 1. Whales are ___the largest___ animals in the animal kingdom. (large)

____ 2. Dolphins hear _____ of all animals. (good)

____ 3. _____ snake weighs 500 pounds (227 kilos). (heavy)

____ 4. Camels can live _____ without water. (long)

____ 5. Snails move _____ of all animals. (slowly)

____ 6. Gorillas live _____ than chimpanzees. (long)

____ 7. Lions run _____ than rabbits. (quickly)

____ 8. Bats see _____ at night than humans do. (well)

GROUPS. Write sentences about animals. Then ask other groups if your statements are true or false. Use Exercise D as a model.

Example: *Cats live longer than dogs.*

The Animal Kingdom 145

COMPARATIVE AND SUPERLATIVE OF NOUNS

	Comparative	Count Nouns		Comparative	Noncount Nouns
Lions have	more visitors than	birds.	Birds make	more noise than	bears.
Birds have	fewer visitors than	lions.	Bears make	less noise than	birds.

	Superlative	Count Nouns		Superlative	Noncount Nouns
Chimpanzees have	the most	visitors.	Lions cost	the most	money.
Snakes have	the fewest	visitors.	Mice need	the least	space.

A Complete the sentences. Write *Zoo A*, *Zoo B*, or *Zoo C*.

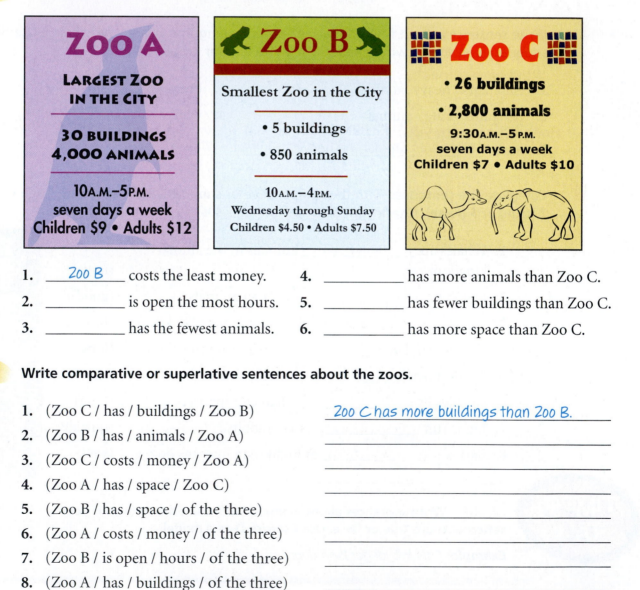

ZOO A

LARGEST ZOO IN THE CITY

30 BUILDINGS 4,000 ANIMALS

10 A.M.–5 P.M.
seven days a week
Children $9 • Adults $12

Zoo B

Smallest Zoo in the City

• 5 buildings
• 850 animals

10 A.M.–4 P.M.
Wednesday through Sunday
Children $4.50 • Adults $7.50

Zoo C

• 26 buildings
• 2,800 animals

9:30 A.M.–5 P.M.
seven days a week
Children $7 • Adults $10

1. ___Zoo B___ costs the least money.

2. _____ is open the most hours.

3. _____ has the fewest animals.

4. _____ has more animals than Zoo C.

5. _____ has fewer buildings than Zoo C.

6. _____ has more space than Zoo C.

B Write comparative or superlative sentences about the zoos.

1. (Zoo C / has / buildings / Zoo B) ___Zoo C has more buildings than Zoo B.___

2. (Zoo B / has / animals / Zoo A) _____

3. (Zoo C / costs / money / Zoo A) _____

4. (Zoo A / has / space / Zoo C) _____

5. (Zoo B / has / space / of the three) _____

6. (Zoo A / costs / money / of the three) _____

7. (Zoo B / is open / hours / of the three) _____

8. (Zoo A / has / buildings / of the three) _____

C CD 2 TRACK 25 **Ten-year-old Stephanie is writing a report about animals. Complete her conversation with a zookeeper. Then listen and check your answers.**

Stephanie: Which animals make _____*more*_____ noise, elephants or lions?
1. (more / the most)

Zookeeper: Hmm. That's a good question. Here at the zoo, probably the lions.

Stephanie: And which animals make _____ noise?
2. (the fewest / the least)

Zookeeper: Oh, that's easy—the snakes.

Stephanie: Which animals cause _____ problems?
3. (the fewest / the least)

Zookeeper: The snakes again!

Stephanie: And which animals cause _____ problems? The
4. (more / the most)

chimpanzees?

Zookeeper: Yes, probably. But they also make _____ money for the
5. (more / the most)

zoo because they get _____ visitors than all of the other
6. (more / the most)

animals.

Stephanie: Really? Even more than the lions?

Zookeeper: Oh yes. The lions definitely get _____ visitors. And the
7. (less / fewer)

poor snakes get _____ visitors of all.
8. (fewer / the fewest)

TIME to TALK

GROUPS. Ask and answer the questions about animals. Use the information in the box and *more, less, fewer, the most, the least,* and *the fewest.*

> eat / fruit (a bat, a chimpanzee, a parrot)
> eat / meat (a shark, a lion, a chimpanzee)
> have / babies in a lifetime (a rat, a chimpanzee, a whale)
> have / mates in a lifetime (a lion, a dolphin)
> have / teeth (a shark, a dolphin)
> make / noise (a whale, an elephant)
> sleep / hours a day (a lion, a horse, a bat)
> travel / miles in a day (an eagle, a rabbit)

Examples: *Which animal has fewer teeth: a shark or a dolphin?*
Which animal has the most babies in a lifetime: a rat, a chimpanzee, or a whale?

WRAP UP. Now ask your questions to the class. [The answers are on page 304.]

Grammar to Communicate 3

EQUATIVES

	as . . . as (= the same)	*not as . . . as* (not the same)
ADJECTIVES	A dog **is as cute as** a cat is.	A rat **isn't as cute as** a dog is.
ADVERBS	Fish **swim as well as** whales do.	Dogs **don't swim as well as** whales do.
COUNT NOUNS	There **are as many cat toys as** dog toys.	There **aren't as many rabbit toys as** cat toys.
NONCOUNT NOUNS	Horses **need as much exercise as** big dogs do.	Small dogs **don't need as much exercise as** big dogs do.

A Complete the sentences. Write *Max* or *Gypsy*.

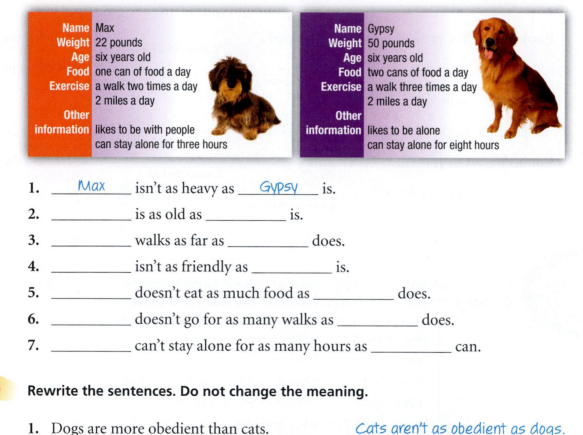

Name	Max
Weight	22 pounds
Age	six years old
Food	one can of food a day
Exercise	a walk two times a day 2 miles a day
Other information	likes to be with people can stay alone for three hours

Name	Gypsy
Weight	50 pounds
Age	six years old
Food	two cans of food a day
Exercise	a walk three times a day 2 miles a day
Other information	likes to be alone can stay alone for eight hours

1. ____Max____ isn't as heavy as ___Gypsy___ is.

2. _____ is as old as _____ is.

3. _____ walks as far as _____ does.

4. _____ isn't as friendly as _____ is.

5. _____ doesn't eat as much food as _____ does.

6. _____ doesn't go for as many walks as _____ does.

7. _____ can't stay alone for as many hours as _____ can.

B Rewrite the sentences. Do not change the meaning.

1. Dogs are more obedient than cats.   ___Cats aren't as obedient as dogs.___

2. Dogs understand people better than cats.   _____

3. Dogs are friendlier than cats.   _____

4. Cats are more independent than dogs.   _____

5. Dogs learn more easily than cats.   _____

6. Cats live longer than dogs.   _____

C A woman is talking about her pets. Complete the sentences with *as . . .* or *as . . . as.*

1. Pets can be _____as helpful as_____ people.
   (helpful)

2. My pets are _____ to me as my friends are.
   (important)

3. A pet can make you smile _____ people.
   (often)

4. Animals are _____ people are.
   (smart)

5. My pets know me _____ my friends do.
   (well)

6. I can communicate _____ with animals as I can with my friends.
   (easily)

Look

Cats aren't as obedient as dogs are.

OR

Cats aren't as obedient as dogs.

Do you have a pet? If so, do you agree with the statements?

D Write sentences. How are the pets similar? How are they different? Use *(not) as . . . as* and the words in the boxes. Then compare sentences with other students.

Popular pets	Verbs		Count Nouns	Noncount Nouns
cats	be	make	hours	food
dogs	cause	need	mice	fun
fish	eat	sleep	problems	mess
parrots	live	understand	words	noise
rabbits			years	space

1. _Cats are as much fun as dogs. Cats don't cause as many problems as dogs._

2. _____

3. _____

4. _____

5. _____

PAIRS. Look at the pictures of the animals in this unit. Choose two animals and compare them. Find five similarities and five differences. Use *as . . . as.*

Example: chimpanzees and rabbits

Rabbits don't need as much love as chimpanzees do.
Rabbits are as cute as chimpanzees.

WRAP UP. Now say your sentences to the class. Are any of your comparisons the same?

Review and Challenge

Grammar

CD 2 TRACK 26 **This paragraph has seven mistakes. The first mistake is corrected for you. Find and correct the other six mistakes. Then listen and check your answers.**

I have two parrots, Gertie and Peter. Gertie is ~~the oldest~~ *older*. She's 25 years old. Peter's only 10. He is gray. Gertie is more colorful as Peter. She's green, blue, and yellow. Both parrots talk a lot. Gertie is talkative as Peter. Gertie knows less words than Peter, but Peter doesn't know as many big words as Gertie does. And they both say the most funny things. Parrots are always messy, but Gertie isn't as messier as Peter. He always makes a big mess. I love both my parrots. They cause the least problems of any pet, and they are the most fun.

Dictation

CD 2 TRACK 27 **Listen. You will hear five sentences. Write them in your notebook.**

Speaking

PAIRS. **Complete the sentences to make common expressions. Use the words in the box.**

a bee	a fox	a mule
a bird	a mouse	an ox

1. She is as busy as _____.
2. You are as strong as _____.
3. He is as quiet as _____.
4. He is as stubborn as _____.
5. I am as free as _____.
6. She is as clever as _____.

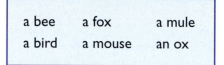

a bee

an ox

a fox

a mule

CLASS. **Check your answers with your teacher. Do you have similar expressions in your language? Which animals do you use in the expressions? What other expressions do you have with animals? Tell the class.**

Listening

A 🔘 *CD 2 TRACK 28* **Listen. Check (✓) the animals that Dr. Downey talks about.**

❏ bears   ❏ cats   ❏ dogs   ❏ giraffes   ❏ mosquitoes   ❏ rats

❏ brown bats   ❏ chimps   ❏ elephants   ❏ lions   ❏ pigs   ❏ whales

B 🔘 *CD 2 TRACK 28* **Listen again. What does Dr. Downey say about the animals in Exercise A? Complete the sentences with the correct animals.**

1. _____ aren't the dirtiest animals.

2. Pigs are almost as intelligent as _____.

3. Some of the smartest animals are _____,

   _____, and _____.

4. _____ sleep more hours than _____.

5. _____ sleep the most hours.

6. _____ sleep the fewest hours.

7. _____ kill the most people every year.

roll

mud

sweat

mosquito

TIME to TALK

GROUPS. Discuss your opinions about animals.

Which animals are:

the best pets?   the most important in your culture?
the cutest?   the most intelligent?
the friendliest?   the most interesting?
the most disgusting?   the most useful to humans?
the most frightening?   the strangest?

Example: *I think dogs are the best pets. They are smart and fun.*

WRAP UP. **Share your opinions with the class.**

Reading

Getting Ready to Read

How are dogs and wolves similar? How are they different? If you are not sure, guess.

Similarities

1. _____ .
2. _____ .

Differences

1. _____ .
2. _____ .

Reading

Read the article. Can you find the similarities and differences you wrote in Getting Ready to Read?

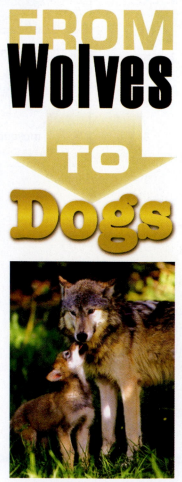

a wolf and her cub

FROM Wolves TO Dogs

Most people know that dogs **evolved from** wolves. But how? Scientists believe that between 20,000 and 100,000 years ago, wolves and humans came into contact for the first time. Some wolves lived near the camps of humans. As they became more **familiar with** people, they moved closer to human camps to find food. That is how the two **species** began to **interact with** each other.

Humans also hunted wolves for meat, so sometimes they killed adult wolves with cubs. Humans **took in** the cubs, probably because young wolves are cute, sociable, and playful. In other words, they are very similar to modern dogs. And like dogs, they are easy to train because they will **obey** the strongest member of the group — in this case, humans.

As young wolves become adults, however, they become more **aggressive** and much more difficult to control than wolf cubs. Humans probably killed most of the wolves as soon as they grew up and became aggressive and dangerous. However, the calmest, least aggressive wolves lived **side by side** with humans. These wolves had cubs, and often their cubs were also calm and lived easily with humans. Finally, after many generations, the wolves that lived with humans were a new species — the dog.

Dogs were as cute and as easy to train as wolf cubs, but their personalities and behavior did not change as they got older. In contrast to the wolf cubs, they continued to see humans as their leaders. For this reason, adult dogs did not become as aggressive or as dangerous as adult wolves. That is how wolves became dogs, and dogs became "man's best friend."

After You Read

A   Look at the **boldface** words in the article. Guess their meaning. Then read the sentences and circle the correct answer.

1. When one animal **evolves from** another animal, it _____.
   a. stays the same as that animal   **b.** becomes a new kind of animal

2. When you become **familiar with** someone, you _____.
   a. get to know the person   b. feel uncomfortable with the person

3. A new **species** is a new _____.
   a. type of plant or animal   b. type of idea

4. When you **interact with** someone, you _____.
   a. have no contact with each other   b. have contact with each other

5. When you **take in** an animal, _____.
   a. you kill it   b. the animal lives with you

6. When you **obey** someone, you _____.
   a. do what the person says   b. don't do what the person says

7. When an animal is **aggressive**, it might _____.
   a. bite you   b. play with you

8. An example of an animal that lives **side by side** with humans is a _____.
   a. shark   b. horse

B   Put the statements in order from 1 to 9. Write the numbers in the blanks.

_____ **a.** Humans took the wolf cubs in and took care of them.

_____ **b.** The least aggressive young wolves continued to live with humans.

_____ **c.** After many generations, a new species, the dog, evolved.

__1__ **d.** Wolves started to live near human camps.

_____ **e.** The wolf cubs became adults and most became aggressive and dangerous.

_____ **f.** Wolves got familiar with humans.

_____ **g.** Humans killed most of the adult wolves.

_____ **h.** The least aggressive young wolves had cubs.

_____ **i.** Humans sometimes killed the parents of wolf cubs.

Writing

Getting Ready to Write

A   Write new sentences. Use the words in parentheses.

1. Like dogs, cows live side by side with humans.
   <u>Unlike dogs, cows are not pets.</u>
          (unlike / are not pets)

2. In contrast to dogs, fish live under water.
   _____
          (both / can swim)

3. Both wolves and lions have fur.
   _____
          (like / eat meat)

4. Like wolves, bears live in forests.
   _____
       (in contrast to / can weigh 500 pounds)

5. Both cats and dogs are trainable.
   _____
         (unlike / easy to train)

> ## Writing Tip
>
> Use *like* and *both* to compare two things:
>
> **Example:**
>
> **Like** wolves, dogs are good at hunting.
>
> **Both** wolves and dogs are good at hunting.
>
> Use *unlike* and *in contrast to* to contrast two things:
>
> **Example:**
>
> **Unlike** wolves, dogs are trainable.
>
> **In contrast to** wolves, dogs are easy to train.

B   Read the model paragraph.

> Sharks and dolphins are similar in many ways. Both animals have fins on their back and sides, and their bodies have a similar shape. Like sharks, dolphins are some of the fastest swimmers in the ocean. However, in contrast to sharks, dolphins are warm-blooded, and they breathe air. Dolphins have much better eyesight and hearing than sharks do. But unlike dolphins, sharks have a very good sense of smell. Some people think that sharks are as intelligent as dolphins, but dolphins are easier to train. They are also much friendlier toward humans.

fin

PAIRS. Read the model again. According to the writer, what are the similarities and differences between sharks and dolphins?

Now talk about two other animals. Discuss the similarities and differences between them.

Prewriting: Using a Venn Diagram

You are going to write a paragraph comparing and contrasting two animals. Before you write, look at the Venn diagram for the writing model.

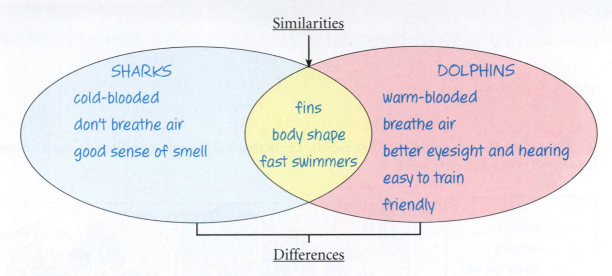

Similarities

SHARKS

cold-blooded

don't breathe air

good sense of smell

fins
body shape
fast swimmers

DOLPHINS

warm-blooded

breathe air

better eyesight and hearing

easy to train

friendly

Differences

Choose two animals and complete the Venn diagram. Choose one of the animal pairs in the box or use your own ideas.

> dogs / cats   lions / tigers   cows / horses   monkeys / gorillas

If you need more information, look in the library or on the Internet. To search the Internet:

- Go to an Internet search engine such as www.google.com.

- Choose two animals that you want to write about. For example, type in "sharks and dolphins."

- Choose a site and click on its Web address.

- Read some of the information on the site. Write notes in your Venn diagram.

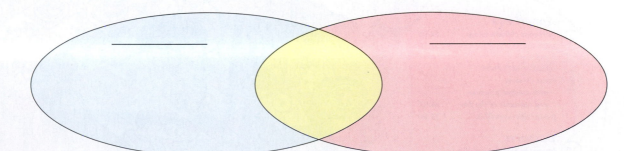

Writing

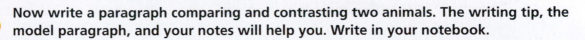

Now write a paragraph comparing and contrasting two animals. The writing tip, the model paragraph, and your notes will help you. Write in your notebook.

Vocabulary

29 Match the numbers with the words. Circle the nouns and underline the verbs. Then listen and check your answers.

_____ appetizer
_____ dessert
__1__ enjoy herself
_____ help herself
_____ main dish
_____ napkin
_____ order
_____ salad bar
_____ seat
_____ serve
_____ specials
_____ stuff herself
_____ treat

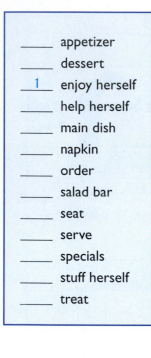

Listening

A CD 2 TRACK **30** Listen. A man goes out to lunch with his wife. Write *W* for the words that describe the woman. Write *M* for the words that describe the man. Be careful. There are two extra answers.

_____ 1. bored _____ 3. impatient _____ 5. rude

_____ 2. friendly _____ 4. polite _____ 6. smart

B CD 2 TRACK **31** Listen again. Put the sentences in each group in order from 1 to 4.

Group 1

_____ By the window?

_____ One of them is, but the others are free.

__1__ The one in the corner? It's reserved.

_____ How about the ones over there? Are they reserved, too?

Group 2

_____ This one is dirty.

_____ Oh, I'm sorry. I'll get you another one.

_____ You can serve yourselves whenever you're ready.

_____ I need another fork.

C CD 2 TRACK **32** Listen again. Answer the questions. Write complete sentences.

1. Where does the man want to sit?

_____

2. Why can't he sit there?

_____

3. What does the man order? What does the woman order?

_____

4. What was wrong with the man's meal the last time?

_____

5. Why is the woman upset?

_____

Grammar to Communicate 1

REFLEXIVE PRONOUNS

Singular				Plural			
Subject Pronoun		Verb	Reflexive Pronoun	Subject Pronoun		Verb	Reflexive Pronoun
I	always	serve	**myself.**	We	always	serve	**ourselves.**
You			**yourself.**	You			**yourselves.**
He			**himself.**	They			**themselves.**
She	always	serves	**herself.**				
It			**itself.**				

A Circle the reflexive pronouns.

1. I've really stuffed myself. No dessert for me!

2. We can't seat ourselves. We have to wait for the hostess.

3. Look at the guy near the window. He's talking to himself.

4. Put that knife down. You could hurt yourself.

5. If your children don't behave themselves, they're going to have to leave.

6. The salad bar is over there. Please help yourselves.

7. It's her birthday, so she's treating herself to lunch in a nice restaurant.

B Complete the sentences. Use the correct reflexive pronoun.

1. I don't go to restaurants by _____myself_____.

2. My friend Anna feels uncomfortable if she sits by _____ in a restaurant.

3. My father never eats out by _____.

4. When I go to a restaurant, I like to pay for _____.

5. My friends and I always enjoy _____ when we eat out together.

6. I never go to restaurants with children that don't behave _____.

7. On their anniversary, my parents treat _____ to a meal in a nice restaurant.

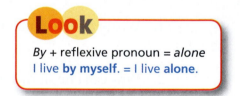

Look

By + reflexive pronoun = *alone*
I live **by myself.** = I live **alone.**

PAIRS. Make the sentences true about yourself or people you know.

Examples: *I don't go to restaurants by myself.* OR *I like to go to restaurants by myself.* OR *My children don't go to restaurants by themselves.*

Complete the sentences. Circle the correct answer.

1. The children stuffed _____ with candy. Now they won't eat dinner.
   a. each other   b. them   c.) themselves

2. Our children started throwing food at _____ in the restaurant last night. It was very embarrassing.
   a. each other   b. them   c. themselves

3. Make _____ at home. Our home is your home. If you're hungry, there's food in the refrigerator.
   a. each other   b. you   c. yourselves

4. My husband hurt his hand, so he can't feed _____.
   a. each other   b. him   c. himself

5. That man ordered three desserts. Do you think that they're all for _____?
   a. each other   b. him   c. himself

6. We haven't seen _____ in months! Let's meet for dinner.
   a. each other   b. us   c. ourselves

7. Come on. You've had a bad day. I'll treat _____ to dinner.
   a. each other   b. you   c. yourself

8. If you stuff _____ like that all the time, you're going to get fat.
   a. each other   b. you   c. yourself

Look

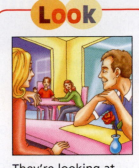

They're looking at **them**.

They're looking at **themselves**.

They're looking at **each other**.

TIME to TALK

ON YOUR OWN. Check (✔) the statements that describe your culture.

❏ 1. People usually seat themselves at restaurants. They don't wait for a waiter.

❏ 2. Children order for themselves. Their parents don't order for them.

❏ 3. When people visit their friends' homes, they help themselves to food.

❏ 4. Children must excuse themselves before they leave the table.

❏ 5. When a couple eats out, the man always treats. The woman never pays.

❏ 6. People often sit by themselves at restaurants.

GROUPS. Compare eating customs in your cultures.

Grammar to Communicate 2

ONE / ONES

	Singular Count Nouns	Plural Count Nouns
THINGS OR PEOPLE IN GENERAL	This **glass** isn't clean. Can you give us a clean **one**?	These **glasses** aren't clean. Can you give us clean **ones**?
SPECIFIC THINGS OR PEOPLE	That's not our **waiter**. Ours is the **one** with the beard.	I don't want these **cookies**. I want the big **ones**.
WITH *THIS* OR *THAT*	I don't want to sit at this **table**. I want to sit at that **one**.	

A **33** **Complete the conversations. Circle the correct words. Then listen and check your answers.**

> **Look**
>
> Use *one* or *ones* to replace singular or plural count nouns.

1. **A:** Do you want your (sandwich) / **sandwiches** with mayonnaise or mustard?

   B: I want one with both, please.

2. **A:** Do you like hot **sandwich / sandwiches** or cold ones?

   B: Hmm . . . That's a good question.

3. **A:** We need more **napkin / napkins**.

   B: I'll get some extra ones.

4. **A:** I can't find my **napkin / napkins**.

   B: Is this one yours?

5. **A:** Which **main dish / main dishes** should we have?

   B: The ones at the next table look good.

6. **A:** Which **main dish / main dishes** did you order?

   B: The one with the potatoes.

B **Complete the conversations. Use *one* or *ones*.**

1. I don't want the chicken dish with peppers. I'll have the _____one_____ with mushrooms.

2. Put the small forks here, and put the big _____ there.

3. You're drinking my glass of water. That _____ is yours.

4. We need two tables. Can we sit at the _____ over there?

5. These knives are dirty. Can you give us two clean _____?

6. This appetizer is good, and that _____ is, too.

7. Are we going to get a large pizza or a small _____?

C Answer the questions. Use *the one* or *the ones*.

1. A: Which waitress is ours?

    B: _____ The short one. _____
            (short)

2. A: Which customers are these for?

    B: _____
            (near the window)

3. A: Which cake do you want?

    B: _____
            (chocolate)

4. A: Which dessert would you like?

    B: _____
            (with bananas)

5. A: Which dishes are good here?

    B: _____
            (on the left side of the menu)

6. A: Which people are waiting for a table?

    B: _____
            (over there)

D Add *one* or *ones* to the sentences.

1. Do you usually eat a big lunch or a small ^one ?
2. Do your children eat a hot lunch or a cold?
3. Do you buy brown eggs or white?
4. Do you use cloth napkins or paper?
5. Do you eat on real plates or paper?
6. Do you shop at a large market or at a small?
7. Which do you buy more often: fresh vegetables or frozen?

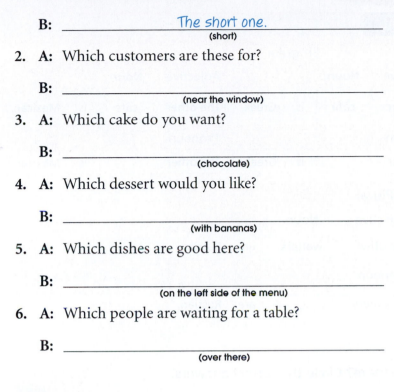

fresh

frozen

TIME to TALK

PAIRS. Ask and answer the questions in Exercise D. Give more details.

Example:

A: *Do you usually eat a big lunch or a small one?*

B: *It depends. On weekends, when I'm at home with my family, I eat a big lunch. But during the week, when I'm at work, I have a small one.*

Let's Eat! **161**

Grammar to Communicate 3

OTHER: SINGULAR AND PLURAL

	Singular				Singular			
	Adjective	Noun			Adjective	Noun		
There are three cafés. One café is French.	**Another**	café	is	Greek.	**The other**	café	is	Mexican.
	Pronoun				Pronoun			
	Another		is	Greek.	**The other**		is	Mexican.

	Plural		
	Adjective	Noun	
There are seven waiters. Two waiters are American.	**The other**	waiters	are	Russian.
	Pronoun		
	The others		are	Russian.

 A   **How many cookies are there? Circle the correct answers.**

1. One cookie is small. The others are big.

   a. 1   **b.** 2   **c.** 3

2. One cookie is small. The other is big.

   a. 1   **b.** 2   **c.** 3

3. One cookie is small. Another is big. The other is medium-size.

   a. 1   **b.** 2   **c.** 3   **d.** more than 3

4. One cookie is small. Another is big. The others are medium-size.

   a. 1   **b.** 2   **c.** 3   **d.** more than 3

B   CD 2 TRACK 34   **Rewrite the answers. Use pronouns. Then listen and check your answers.**

1. **A:** Would you like another cookie?

   B: Sure, I'll have another cookie.

   Sure, I'll have _____.

2. **A:** Are these the forks that you want?

   B: No, I meant the other forks.

   No, I meant _____.

3. **A:** Have you got enough spoons?

   B: No, I need another spoon.

   No, I need _____.

4. **A:** Is one napkin enough?

   B: No, please give me another napkin.

   No, please give me _____.

C Look at the information about different restaurants. Complete the sentences with *another*, *the other*, or *the others*.

	Type of food	Meals served	Open	Location	Price*
China Palace	Chinese	lunch, dinner	7 days a week	341 Main St.	$
Dynasty Inn	Chinese	lunch, dinner	7 days a week	56 Elm St.	$
Jack's Family Diner	American	breakfast, lunch, dinner	7 days a week	658 Main St.	$
La Provence	French	breakfast, lunch	Closed Sunday	10 Park St.	$
Mexico Lindo	Mexican	lunch, dinner	7 days a week	466 Pine St.	$
Napolitana	Italian	lunch, dinner	Closed Sunday and Monday	539 Pine St.	$$$

*$ = inexpensive; $$$ = expensive

1. One is closed on Sundays. ___Another___ is closed Sunday and Monday. ___The others___ are open seven days a week.

2. Two serve breakfast. _____ four serve lunch and dinner only.

3. One serves Italian food. _____ serves American food. _____ serves French food. _____ serves Mexican food. _____ serve Chinese food.

4. Two of the restaurants are on Main Street. _____ restaurant is on Elm Street. _____ restaurant is on Park Street. _____ restaurants are on Pine Street.

5. Five of the restaurants are inexpensive. _____ is expensive.

TIME to TALK

PAIRS. Talk about places near where you work, go to school, and live.

How many restaurants are there? What kind of food do they serve? Which one is your favorite?	How many coffee shops are there? Which one is the most popular? Which one has the best coffee?
How many supermarkets are there? At which one or ones do you shop?	How many places are there to buy fresh fruit and vegetables? Which one has the best prices?

Example:
A: *How many restaurants are there near where you work?*
B: *There are three. There's one next to my office, and the others are across the street.*
A: *What kind of food do they serve?*
B: *The one next to my building is a Greek restaurant. The others are fast-food restaurants.*

Review and Challenge

Grammar

 CD 2 TRACK **35** Complete the conversation with the words in the box. Then listen and check your answers. Be careful. There are extra words.

> | another | herself | me | one | ourselves | the others | ~~yourself~~ |
> |---|---|---|---|---|---|---|
> | each other | himself | myself | ones | the other | you | yourselves |

Amy: Come in. Make ___yourself___ at home. Here, give _____ your jacket.
1.   2.

Jan: Sorry I'm late. I missed the bus and waited an hour for the next _____.
3.

Amy: Don't worry. Two couples, the _____ from Chester, still aren't here.
4.

Jan: Yeah, Chester is far away. Bill, is that you? How are you?

Bill: Oh, Jan, nice to see _____. I'm great.
5.

Amy: How do you two know _____? Did you meet at _____ party?
6.   7.

Jan: Yeah. We met at Lin's. It was great. We really enjoyed _____.
8.

Amy: So Jan, do you know _____ people here?
9.

Jan: Well, I know your boyfriend, of course, but I don't think I know _____.
10.

Dictation

 CD 2 TRACK **36** Listen. You will hear five sentences. Write them in your notebook.

Speaking

PAIRS. Most restaurant owners are *self-employed*. They work for themselves. What do the phrases with *self* in the box mean? Write your ideas.

> | self-addressed envelope | self-cleaning oven | self-made man (or woman) |
> |---|---|---|
> | self-centered person | self-defrosting refrigerator | self-serve restaurant |

WRAP UP. Now share your ideas with the class. Who has the best definitions? Finally, check your definitions in a dictionary or ask your teacher.

Listening

A **37** **Listen to the report. Check (✓) the best title for the report.**

❏ **1.** A History of American Restaurants
❏ **2.** Eating in Your Car: An American Tradition
❏ **3.** The McDonald Brothers
❏ **4.** The Birth of Fast Food

Model-T Ford

B **38** **Listen again. Check (✓) the features of the Speedy Service System.**

assembly line

❏ **1.** There are only a few choices on the menu.
❏ **2.** The food is made to order.
❏ **3.** The waiters are very fast.
❏ **4.** People serve themselves.
❏ **5.** The food is ready very quickly.
❏ **6.** There are no tables. People eat in their cars.
❏ **7.** People seat themselves.
❏ **8.** People clean up after themselves.
❏ **9.** Customers wash their own dishes.

TIME to TALK

GROUPS. Talk about fast-food restaurants in your country. Discuss the answers to the questions.

1. What are the most popular fast-food restaurants where you live? What kinds of food do they serve? Why are they so popular?

2. How often do you eat fast food? What is your favorite kind of fast food? Where do you like to go to eat fast food?

3. Are there American fast-food restaurants in your country? Which ones are there? Which ones are the most popular?

Reading

Getting Ready to Read

Read the introduction and the conclusion of the article. What do you think the main idea of the article is?

_____

Reading

Read the article. Then check your answer to Getting Ready to Read.

SLOW FOOD, SLOW CITIES ... BETTER LIFE?

Life in today's world has been getting faster and faster. Fast food has become very popular because people don't have enough time to cook. The situation has gotten so bad that a group of people in Europe decided to start the Slow Food **Movement**. The goal of this movement is to live an **unhurried** life, beginning at the dinner table.

a truffle

The Movement's **headquarters** are in Bra, Italy, in an area famous for its wine, white truffles, cheese, and beef. There are other Slow Food offices all over the world, including one in Switzerland, another in Germany, and others in the United States, France, and Japan. Slow Food has 80,000 members in more than 100 countries, organized into more than 800 local groups. The leaders of the groups organize special events and they **promote local** products and food growers. In short, they educate the public about good food.

The Slow Food Movement has also **led to** another movement called *Città Slow* (Slow Cities). The Città Slow are a group of towns and cities that try to improve the quality of life for their citizens. According to the Città Slow Web site, the movement is looking for "...towns with **untouched landscapes**...where people are still able to recognize the slow course of the seasons and their...products."

Members of Città Slow have found many ways to make their cities and towns better places to live. One way is to close the center of town to traffic one day a week. Another brings members of the community to markets and town squares—places where local food growers offer their fruits and vegetables.

To sum up, members of the Slow Food Movement and Città Slow try to live like snails. The snail is the **symbol** of the Slow Food Movement because "... it moves slowly and calmly eats its way through life."

After You Read

A   Look at the **boldface** words in the article. Guess their meaning. Match the words with the correct definitions.

<u>h</u>   1. movement   **a.** main office

___   2. unhurried   **b.** made something happen as the result of something else

___   3. headquarters   **c.** help something develop and be successful

___   4. promote   **d.** relating to a particular place or area

___   5. local   **e.** an area of land

___   6. led to   **f.** a picture, person, or object that means or shows
                                something else

___   7. untouched   **g.** slow, not in a hurry

___   8. landscape   **h.** a group of people who share the same ideas and work
                                together

___   9. symbol   **i.** in a natural state or condition

B   Read the article again. Then answer the questions.

1. Why did a group of people start the Slow Food Movement?

_____

2. Where did the Slow Food Movement start?

_____

3. What do the offices and local groups of the Slow Food Movement do?

_____

4. What is the Città Slow Movement?

_____

5. How does the Città Slow Movement make towns and cities better places to live?

_____

6. Why is the snail the symbol of the Slow Food Movement?

_____

Writing

Getting Ready to Write

A Read the sentences from different articles. Write **C** next to the concluding sentences.

__C__ 1. In conclusion, many people are too heavy because they eat too much fast food.

_____ 2. There is a problem with the way we eat today.

_____ 3. One healthy food people can eat is fruit, and another is vegetables.

_____ 4. To sum up, I enjoy cooking dinner at home, but I usually don't have time.

_____ 5. In conclusion, people who eat healthy foods usually feel better about themselves.

> **Writing Tip**
>
> Use words like *in conclusion* and *to sum up* to show readers that you are ending your paragraph.
>
> Examples:
>
> **In conclusion**, members of the Slow Food Movement try to live like snails.
>
> **To sum up**, members of the Slow Food Movement try to live like snails.

B Read the model paragraph.

I agree with some of the ideas of the Slow Food Movement. Of course good, healthy food is better than fast food. But sometimes it is easier to eat fast food. One reason is that many people don't have time to buy and cook good food. When my wife and I both work late, we sometimes fight with each other about who should make dinner. We're too tired to cook for ourselves. Another reason is that our children love fast food. If I cook dinner with good food, they won't eat it. And yet another reason is that good food is often more expensive than fast food. I don't have enough money to buy from local food growers! To sum up, the Slow Food Movement has some good ideas, but I can't live like a snail!

PAIRS. According to the writer, does the Slow Food Movement have good ideas about food? Does the writer use the ideas? Why or why not?

Now discuss your ideas about food. What kind of food do you eat? What are the reasons why you eat certain foods?

Prewriting: Listing Reasons

You are going to write a paragraph about the kind of food you like to eat. Before you write, complete the chart with notes about the topic.

What kind of food do you like to eat?
Reasons: 1.
2.
3.
Concluding Sentence:

Writing

Now write a paragraph about the food you eat. The writing tip, the model paragraph, and your notes will help you. Write in your notebook.

Grammar
- *Can* and *Be able to*
- *Could* and *Be able to*
- *Will be able to*

Vocabulary

CD 2 TRACK 39 Complete the sentences with the words in the box. Then listen and check your answers.

> burn CDs   camcorder   download   record

I love my new _____. I _____
1.   2.
my son Sam all the time. Then I _____
3.
everything onto my computer. Sometimes
I _____ and give them to friends or
4.
family.

> battery   charge   install   software

First, put in the _____. Then
5.
_____ it for twenty-four hours. Finally,
6.
_____ the _____ on your
7.   8.
computer.

> online   operate   remote control   Web

Use the _____ for your TV and DVD
9.
player. It's easy to _____. Just press
10.
the "On" button, and the TV goes on. If you
need help, go _____. There's a lot of
11.
information on the _____.
12.

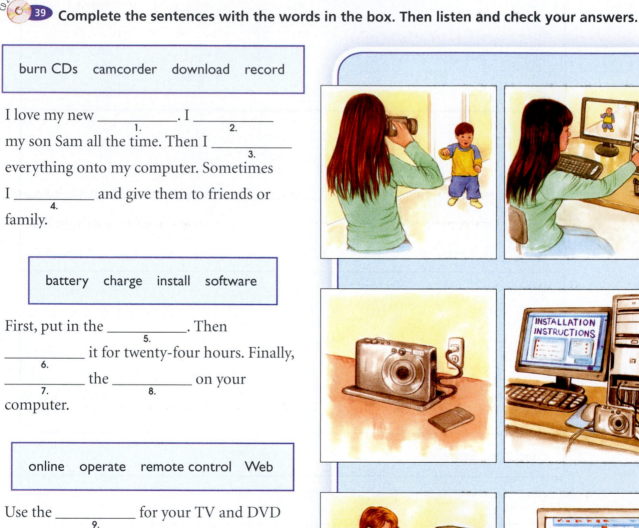

Listening

 A CD 2 TRACK 40 **Listen. What is the woman unhappy about? Check (✓) the sentences.**

❏ 1. Her computer isn't working.

❏ 2. Her husband wanted to fix her computer, but he didn't have time.

❏ 3. Her computer will not be ready tomorrow.

❏ 4. The man is going away on vacation.

Look

access e-mail =
open e-mail

B CD 2 TRACK 41 **Read and listen again. Write the missing words. Use the words in the box.**

able	~~are~~	be	can	couldn't	to	was

Technician: First of all, ___*are*___ you able to turn it on?
 1.

Rashida: Yes, but that's all I _____ do. Two weeks ago I had the same
 2.

problem, but my husband _____ able to fix it. I still couldn't access
 3.

my e-mail, but at least I was _____ to use it for other things. But
 4.

then this morning when I turned it on, I _____ do anything.
 5.

Technician: What do you mean, you couldn't do anything?

Rashida: I mean exactly that. I wasn't able _____ do anything. What do you
 6.

think? Will you _____ able to repair it?
 7.

C CD 2 TRACK 42 **Listen again. Answer the questions. Write complete sentences.**

1. How many times has this problem happened?

_____

2. Who fixed the computer the last time?

_____

3. Why does the woman need her computer?

_____

4. What is the woman going to do?

_____

Grammar to Communicate 1

CAN AND BE ABLE TO

Subject	Can (not)	Verb	
I He We You They	can can't cannot	use	a computer.

Subject	Be + (Not) + able to	Verb	
I	am able to am not able to	use	a computer.
He	is able to is not able to isn't able to		
We You They	are able to are not able to aren't able to		

A Complete the sentences. Write *can* or *can't*.

1. I _____ use a computer.
2. I _____ check the weather online.
3. I _____ send and receive e-mail messages.
4. I _____ install software on a computer.
5. I _____ download pictures from a digital camera to a computer.

Look
Use *can* to talk about present ability. In formal situations use a form of *be able to*.
People **are able to** access the Web from cell phones.

B CD 2 TRACK 43 Complete the speech. Use the correct form of *be able to*. Some sentences are affirmative, and some are negative. Then listen and check your answers.

Many people think that technology _____*is able to*_____ do
1.
everything that humans _____ do. Computers
2.
_____ perform certain tasks better than people. For
3.
example, a computer _____ remember billions of
4.
numbers easily. Most people (not) _____ handle
5.
more than a few numbers at a time. However, computers (not)
_____ do some basic things. For instance, only
6.
very advanced computers _____ remember faces
7.
or voices, and they (not) _____ do it very well. The average person,
8.
however, _____ recognize thousands of faces and voices over a lifetime.
9.
The fact is, we can live without technology, but we cannot live without one another.

PAIRS. Discuss other things that people are able to do better than computers.

C Complete the conversations. Use *can* where possible. Use *be able to* if *can* is not possible.

Look

Use *have* or *has been able to* + main verb to talk about an ability that started in the past and continues into the present.
I haven't been able to go online today.

1. **A:** I _____can pay_____ my bills online.
   (pay)

   B: How long _____have you been able to pay_____ your bills online?
   (pay)

2. **A:** I _____.
   (drive)

   B: How long _____?
   (drive)

3. **A:** People _____ their favorite movies at home.
   (watch)

   B: How long _____?
   (watch)

4. **A:** I _____ programs on my DVD player.
   (record)

   B: How long _____?
   (record)

5. **A:** People _____ by e-mail.
   (communicate)

   B: How long _____?
   (communicate)

6. **A:** People _____ pictures from their cameras to a computer.
   (download)

   B: How long _____?
   (download)

PAIRS. Answer the questions above. Use *people* and the time periods *fewer than fifty years* or *more than fifty years*.

Example:
A: *How long have people been able to pay their bills online?*
B: *I'm not sure, but I know they've been able to pay their bills online for fewer than fifty years.*

PAIRS. How many people in the United States, or in your country, can or cannot do the things in the box? Make sentences with *Most people*, *Some people*, or *Very few people*. Discuss your opinions.

access the Web from home	make their own movies	use a computer
chat with friends online	operate a camcorder	use a DVD player
fix a computer	program a remote control	use e-mail

Example:
A: *I think that most people in the U.S. can use a computer.*
B: *Really? I don't agree. Some people are able to use a computer, but many people can't because they don't have access to one.*

Grammar to Communicate 2

COULD AND *BE ABLE TO*

Affirmative

Subject	*Could*	Verb	Subject	*Be able to*	Verb
I He We You They	could	type.	I He	was able to	type.
			We You They	were able to	

Negative

Subject	*Couldn't*	Verb	Subject	*(Not) Be able to*	Verb
I He We You They	couldn't	help.	I He	wasn't able to	help.
			We You They	weren't able to	

Look

Use *could* or *be able to* to talk about general ability in the past.
I could type well years ago, but now I can't.
I was able to type well years ago, but now I can't.

Use *be able to* to talk about a specific event.
I was able to finish on time.

Look

Couldn't and *(not) be able to* mean the same thing.
I tried, but I **couldn't** help.
I tried, but I **wasn't able to** help.

A   **Complete the sentences. Circle the correct answers.**

1. Four hundred years ago, people <u>were able to</u> make clothes _____.
   a. by hand   **b.** with machines

2. My aunt's sewing machine was broken, but she <u>was able to</u> make the dress _____.
   a. by hand   **b.** with the machine

3. There was a lot of traffic, so we <u>were able to</u> drive only ten miles in _____.
   a. ten minutes   **b.** an hour

4. Fifty years ago, people <u>could</u> communicate with each other by _____.
   a. mail   **b.** e-mail

5. His computer wasn't working yesterday, so I <u>couldn't</u> send him _____.
   a. a letter   **b.** an e-mail message

6. Twenty years ago, people <u>weren't able to</u> talk on the phone when they _____.
   a. were at home   **b.** were walking down a street

7. My cell phone wasn't working, but I <u>was able to</u> use it after I _____.
   a. left   **b.** charged the battery

Change the underlined words where possible.

Example: *Four hundred years ago, people **could** make clothes _____.*

B Write six sentences about people's abilities in the past. Use the words in the boxes and *could, couldn't, were able to,* or *weren't able to*. Write in your notebook.

500 years ago 100 years ago 50 years ago 30 years ago	communicate by cell phone communicate by phone cook food grow food listen to music	listen to music in their cars take photographs take showers in their homes travel by train use batteries in radios

C CD 2 TRACK **44** **Complete the conversations. Write *could* where possible. If *could* is not possible, write *was able to* or *were able to*. Then listen and check your answers.**

1. **A:** You're good with computers. When did you learn to use one?

    B: I don't even remember. I _____ use a computer before

    I _____ read.

2. **A:** Did you repair my printer?

    B: Yes, I _____ repair it, but you really need a new one.

3. **A:** Did your grandfather have a computer for his farm business?

    B: No. It was strange. He _____ learn to operate almost any

    machine, but he was never able to use a computer.

4. **A:** Kids today are amazing. They understand technology so much better than we do.

    B: I know. My son _____ use a cell phone before he _____ read!

5. **A:** Did you put the information on the company's Web site?

    B: Yes. I _____ do it last night.

6. **A:** Did you take a lot of pictures at the wedding?

    B: I _____ take a few before the battery died.

PAIRS. Talk about five things that you were able to do yesterday because of technology. How many of those things could your grandparents do when they were your age?

Example:
A: *I took the subway. I was able to get to work in 15 minutes.*
B: *My grandfather couldn't take the subway because there was no subway in his town.*

WRAP UP. Now think of something that we can't do today because of technology, but most people in the past could do. Then tell the class.

Example:
Most people could ride horses. Now, they can drive, but they can't ride a horse.

Grammar to Communicate 3

WILL BE ABLE TO

Subject	Will / Won't	Be able to	Verb		Question	Answer
I She We You They	will won't	be able to	work	faster.	**Will I be able to** work faster?	Yes, you **will**. No, you **won't**.
					What **will I be able to** do with this?	You**'ll be able to** work faster.

A Look at the pictures and complete the sentences. Write *will be able to* or *won't be able to*.

Look

Use *will be able to* to talk about ability in the future.

All the information in the world in less than a minute.

1. You _____ will be able to _____ get the weather for any city in the world.

Would you like to dance with me?

2. You _____ learn to dance, and your partner will never laugh at you.

Your friend in every room of your house.

3. You _____ turn on everything from any room in your house.

ALARM! Be safe in your home and car.
Install a Safe Alarm today.

4. People _____ steal your car.

ENTER

Keep your kids safe when they're on the Web.

5. Your kids _____ access Web sites for adults.

a b c
SOFTWARE FOR CHILDREN

Do you love books?
Your child will, too.

6. Your three-year-old _____ read in a week.

176 Unit 13

B Write questions customers have about the products in the pictures.

1. _Will I be able to get the weather for my hometown?_
   (the weather / I / will / for my hometown / be able to / get)

2. _____
   (teach me / the robot / will / be able to / dance every dance)

3. _____
   (I / will / use the remote / for everything / be able to)

4. _____
   (be able to / will / hear the car alarm / the police)

5. _____
   (access / which Web sites / my kids / will / be able to)

6. _____
   (be able to / my child / what kinds of things / read / will)

PAIRS. Ask and answer the questions. The person who asks the questions is a customer. The person who answers is a salesperson.

Example:
A: *Will the police be able to hear the car alarm?*
B: *Yes. The alarm has special software. The software will send a message to a computer at the police station.*

C Complete the sentences with *are able to*, *will be able to*, or *won't be able to*.

1. People _____ call their friends with their computers now.

2. People _____ get a college degree and never leave their home now.

3. People _____ eat only one meal a month and stay healthy in 2100.

4. People _____ look young when they are very old in 2100.

5. People _____ live forever in 2100.

6. People _____ travel around the world in one hour in 2100.

7. People _____ take vacations on Mars in 2100.

PAIRS. Compare your opinions. Which of these things would you like to do?

TIME to TALK

GROUPS. Discuss how the items in the box will be different in the future. What will people be able to do with them that they can't do now? Then compare ideas with other groups.

| books | cell phones | clothing | pens | sunglasses | umbrellas | watches |

Example: *Books will be able to talk, so people will be able to listen and read at the same time.*

Review and Challenge

Grammar

CD 2 TRACK 45 Correct the note. There are seven mistakes. The first mistake is corrected for you. Then listen and check your answers.

> Hi,
>
> I have good news and bad news. First, the bad news. I haven't been
> able ∧ fix the TV yet. When I turn it on, I can to see to a picture; but
>   to
> I can't hear a thing. That's strange because yesterday I can hear
> things, but I not able to see anything. I'm going to look at the TV
> again tomorrow. Maybe I could fix it then.
>
> Now, the good news. I could fix the radio yesterday. At first, I'm
> not able to find the problem, but actually there wasn't really a
> problem. It only needed new batteries.
>
> Sam

Dictation

CD 2 TRACK 46 Listen. You will hear five sentences. Write them in your notebook.

Speaking

GROUPS. Make a list of all the things that people in your group can do with technology. Describe what things they can (and can't) do with technology. How long has each person been able to do these things? Think of as many things as possible.

Example:
A: *Sasha, what can you do? Can you use any technology?*
B: *I can do a lot of things. I can use a microwave oven, I can cook very well, I can sew . . .*
C: *Really? Can you use a sewing machine?*
B: *Yes, I can.*

Now tell the class about your group. Which group can operate the most machines or equipment?

178 Unit 13

Listening

A 〔CD 2 TRACK 47〕 **Listen to the report. Check (✓) the picture that best matches the reporter's description.**

❏ **1.**

Where should we go?

The beach!

❏ **2.**

❏ **3.**

B 〔CD 2 TRACK 47〕 **Listen again. Check (✓) the statements that are true about the car.**

❏ **1.** You can have a conversation with the car.

❏ **2.** The car can help people avoid accidents.

❏ **3.** The car knows when the driver is falling asleep.

❏ **4.** If the driver is tired, the car can drive itself.

❏ **5.** The car is able to communicate with other cars.

❏ **6.** Someday, average people will probably be able to buy one.

❏ **7.** The reporter was able to buy one.

TIME to TALK

GROUPS. What will cars be able to do fifty years from now? Check (✓) the correct column. Then share your opinions with the class.

	YES	NO
drive themselves		
fix themselves		
get 70 miles (113 kilometers) per gallon of gas		
go a long distance in a battery-operated car		
go 300 miles (483 kilometers) per hour		
make coffee		
stop accidents from happening		

Example: A: *Will cars be able to fix themselves fifty years from now?*
B: *I don't know. They can't fix themselves now. And I don't think they will be able to fifty years from now.*

Reading

Getting Ready to Read

Skim the article. Check (✓) the main idea of the reading.

❏ **1.** how RFID technology helps pet owners find their lost pets

❏ **2.** how RFID technology is getting more and more useful

❏ **3.** how RFID technology prevents kidnapping

Reading

Read the article. Then check your answer to Getting Ready to Read.

The WONDERS of RFID TECHNOLOGY

For years, pet owners have been able to find their lost pets with the help of radio frequency technology, or RFID. An RFID tag is a very small computer chip. The tag is a little larger than a grain of rice. Veterinarians (doctors for animals) put the tags under the animal's skin. Then someone types the number of the tag into a computer database. Most vets' offices and animal hospitals in the United States have machines to **scan** lost animals. If someone finds a lost animal and takes it to a vet, the vet can scan it and get the contact information of the owner. As a result of RFID technology, many more lost pets go back to their owners today than in the past.

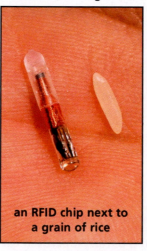

an RFID chip next to a grain of rice

Recently, the use of RFID tags has begun to spread from vets' offices to local hospitals. About 900 hospitals across North America now use RFID tags on the **ankle** bracelets of **newborns**. If someone takes a baby with an RFID bracelet out of the hospital, an alarm rings. A few months ago, the technology stopped the **kidnapping** of a baby from a hospital in North Carolina. Hospital officials were able to catch the kidnapper when the RFID tag on the baby's bracelet **set off** an alarm.

Now some hospitals are putting the chip in their patients. The chips contain information about the patients' medical conditions and medications. If a patient with a chip comes into the hospital, doctors are able to read his or her medical information very quickly. This is especially useful for seriously ill patients who cannot remember the different medications that they are taking. It is also useful for elderly patients with **diseases** that affect their memory, such as Alzheimers disease. These patients often get lost and forget where they are. With the help of RFID technology, their relatives can **locate** them more quickly.

After You Read

A Find the **boldface** words in the article that have similar meanings to the words below.

1. find   *locate*
2. very young babies   _____
3. illnesses   _____
4. make something start operating   _____
5. read or look for information with a special machine   _____
6. "stealing" a person   _____
7. the joint between the foot and leg   _____

B Read the article again. Which uses of RFID technology did you read about in the article? Check (✓) them.

With the help of RFID technology, . . .

❏ 1. pet owners are able to find their lost animals.

❏ 2. sick pets receive faster and better care from the veterinarian.

❏ 3. hospitals are able to protect newborn babies.

❏ 4. parents can check where their children are at all times.

❏ 5. doctors can give patients better care.

❏ 6. relatives can protect their elderly, sick family members.

Veterinarian scans a cat to look for an RFID tag.

Writing

Getting Ready to Write

A Read the sentences. Which happened first, second, and third? Write the time order (*1*, *2*, and *3*) next to the sentences.

1. ____ At first, most Americans couldn't buy a car because it was too expensive.

   _1_ Almost 100 years ago, Henry Ford invented the Model T car.

   ____ Nowadays, most Americans are able to afford a car.

2. ____ Nowadays, some people are able to use their cell phones as computers.

   ____ For many years, computers were very big and expensive.

   ____ Not long ago, most people were not able to operate a computer.

3. ____ For years, people could only watch television in black and white.

   ____ Today, more and more people are buying huge flat-screen TVs.

   ____ Then, stores stopped selling black and white TVs.

B Read the model paragraph.

> In the 1950's, people used transistor radios to listen to music. Transistor radios were small, so people could carry them around easily. In 1980, the Sony Walkman was invented. About five years later, portable CD players became popular. They were light, so people could wear them when they exercised. Now many young people have iPods. With an iPod, you can download hundreds of songs and you don't have to carry any CDs. People can also listen to music on their cell phones these days. How will people be able to listen to music in the future? Maybe they will be able to implant tiny music players in their ears!

PAIRS. Read the model again. How has the way people listen to music changed over the years?

Now choose another type of technology. Talk about how the technology has changed over the years. You can talk about television, telephones, computers, or your own ideas.

Prewriting: Using a Timeline

You are going to write a paragraph about how a type of technology has changed over the years. Read the timelines on cars and computers. Then choose one or make a timeline on another technology you know.

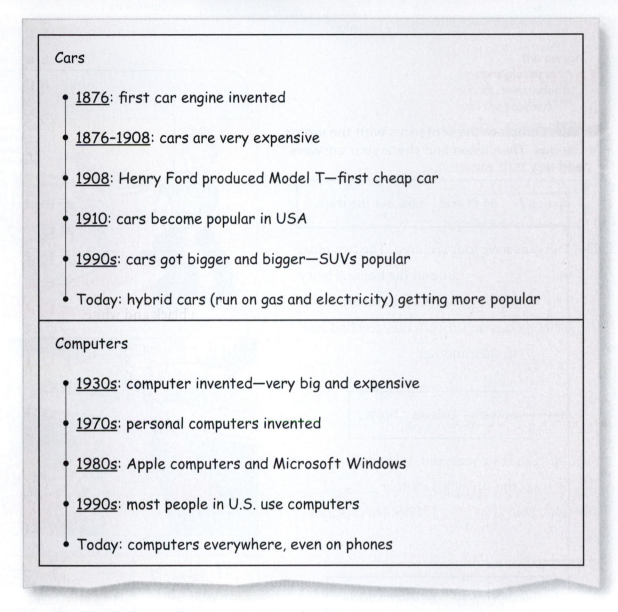

Cars

- <u>1876</u>: first car engine invented

- <u>1876-1908</u>: cars are very expensive

- <u>1908</u>: Henry Ford produced Model T—first cheap car

- <u>1910</u>: cars become popular in USA

- <u>1990s</u>: cars got bigger and bigger—SUVs popular

- Today: hybrid cars (run on gas and electricity) getting more popular

Computers

- <u>1930s</u>: computer invented—very big and expensive

- <u>1970s</u>: personal computers invented

- <u>1980s</u>: Apple computers and Microsoft Windows

- <u>1990s</u>: most people in U.S. use computers

- Today: computers everywhere, even on phones

Writing

Now write a paragraph about a technology and how it has changed over the years. The writing tip, the model paragraph, and your notes will help you. Write in your notebook.

Grammar

● *Have to / Have got to / Must*: Affirmative Statements and *Have to*: Yes / No Questions

● *Does not have to* and *Must not*

● *Had to*: Statements and Questions

Vocabulary

CD 2 TRACK

48 Complete the sentences with the words in the box. Then listen and check your answers.

> apologize   do chores   take out the trash

The Morgans have four children. The two older children _____ around the house. Henry
1.
needs to _____, and Claire usually washes
2.
the dishes. When they forget, they feel bad and _____ to their mother.
3.

> bothers   crosses   holds

Billy Morgan is six years old. When he _____ the street, his mother _____
4.   5.
his hand. This _____ Billy. He's six, not
6.
three!

> behave   obey   punishes   strict

Mrs. Morgan is very _____ with her
7.
children, and they usually _____ her.
8.
When the children do not _____ well, she
9.
_____ them. For example, if they fight or
10.
make too much noise, they can't watch TV.

Listening

A **49** **Listen. What is bothering Nick the most? Check (✓) the correct answer.**

❏ 1. His sister never comes home early.

❏ 2. His mother and father work a lot.

❏ 3. He helps more around the house than his sister.

❏ 4. His father always works late.

B **49** **Listen again. Then check (✓) the things that Nick is unhappy about.**

❏ 1. He's got to go to school.

❏ 2. He must not walk home alone.

❏ 3. His father has to work late.

❏ 4. He's got to cook.

❏ 5. His sister doesn't have to cook.

❏ 6. His sister didn't have to do any chores last month.

❏ 7. He doesn't get any money for doing chores.

❏ 8. His mother had to go back to work.

C **49** **Listen again. Answer the questions. Write complete sentences.**

1. Why does Nick have to cook tonight?

   _____

2. Why does the dinner have to be ready by 6:00?

   _____

3. What did Nick have to do last week?

   _____

4. Why did Nick's mother have to go back to work?

   _____

Grammar to Communicate 1

HAVE TO / HAVE GOT TO / MUST: AFFIRMATIVE STATEMENTS
HAVE TO: YES / NO QUESTIONS

Affirmative Statements

I You We They	have to have got to must	be	on time.	He She	has to has got to must	be	on time.

Yes / No Questions

Do	you we they	have to	buy	books?
Does	she			

Short Answers

Yes,	I you they	do.	No,	I you they	don't.
	she	does.		she	doesn't.

 Look

Use *have to*, *have got to*, and *must* to talk about necessity.

Use *have to* to ask questions about necessity.

 A What do you think? Check (✓) the column you agree with.

Look

respect = be polite to someone because the person is important

	ALL OF THE TIME	SOME OF THE TIME
1. Children have got to respect adults.		
2. Children have to obey their parents.		
3. Children have to behave well.		
4. Parents have got to be strict with children.		
5. Parents must play with their children.		

B These teenagers have responsibilities at home. Write sentences about them.

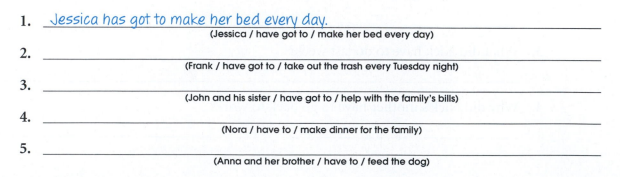

1. _Jessica has got to make her bed every day._
   (Jessica / have got to / make her bed every day)

2. _____
   (Frank / have got to / take out the trash every Tuesday night)

3. _____
   (John and his sister / have got to / help with the family's bills)

4. _____
   (Nora / have to / make dinner for the family)

5. _____
   (Anna and her brother / have to / feed the dog)

1. **Kate:** Esme, it's time for bed.

    Esme: _____ Do I have to go to bed _____ now?
    1. (I / have to / go to bed)

    Kate: Yup. Your mother's note says

    _____
    2. (you / have got to / go to bed)

    at 8, and it's 8 now.

2. **Kate:** Laura, finish your vegetables.

    Laura: _____ his?
    3. (Alex / have to / finish)

    Kate: Yes, but he's already finished.

    _____ yours.
    4. (you / have to / finish)

3. **Kate:** Alex, have you finished your homework?

    Alex: Not yet. _____
    5. (I / have got to / watch)

    the rest of this movie. It's really cool.

    Kate: No, _____ .
    6. (you / have got to / do your homework)

    _____ you?
    7. (I / have to / help)

    Alex: No, you don't. It's really easy.

Look

In casual speech, *have to* is often pronounced "hafta," and *got to* is often pronounced "gotta."

Kate,

Please remember:

Esme must go to bed at 8:00.
Laura must eat her vegetables.
Alex must do his homework.

If there are any problems, call me on my cell phone at 600-555-8760.

Eleanor

TIME to TALK

PAIRS. Talk about the things that schoolchildren have to do in your country. Use the words in the box and your own ideas. Ask and answer questions.

erase the board for the teacher	stand up when the teacher enters the room
go home for lunch	study English
go to school for _____ years	wear school uniforms

Example:

A: *Kids in my country have got to go to school for ten years. Do kids in your country have to go to school for ten years, too?*

B: *No, they don't. They have to go to school for twelve years.*

WRAP UP. Now talk about children in another country you know about. Do they have to do the same things? If not, what do they do differently?

Grammar to Communicate 2

	Does not have to				
I You We They	**don't have to**	walk home. The bus is here.	He She	**doesn't have to**	walk home. The bus is here.

	Must not	
I You He They	**must not** **mustn't**	walk home late at night. It's dangerous.

 A   Complete the sentences with *toddlers* or *teenagers*.

1. _____ mustn't ride in the front seat of a car.

2. _____ mustn't play outside alone.

3. _____ mustn't miss too many classes.

4. _____ don't have to go to bed early.

5. _____ don't have to go to school.

6. _____ don't have to do any chores.

A toddler is a child between the ages of 1 and 3.

B   Complete the sentences. Use *mustn't*, *don't have to*, or *doesn't have to*.

1. You _____*don't have to*_____ wait in line with me, but
   you _____*mustn't*_____ touch anything here.

2. Your daughter _____ stay at home, but
   she _____ run or do a lot of exercise.

3. You _____ hold my hand, but you
   _____ cross the street without me.

4. You _____ eat everything on your plate,
   but you _____ play with your food.

5. Your son _____ sit with you, but he _____ bother
   the other people in the theater.

6. You _____ e-mail us every day, but you _____
   forget to call home once a week.

> ## Look
>
> Use *do not have to* or *does not have to* to say that something is not necessary. Use *must not* to say that something is not permitted.

C Complete the sentences with *don't have to* or *mustn't*. Use the words in the box.

bother	get up early	miss	stay home	~~touch~~
cook	give	obey	tell	walk home

1. The stove is hot. You _____ mustn't touch _____ it.
2. There's no school tomorrow. I _____.
3. The birthday party is a surprise for your mother. You _____ her.
4. I'll pick you up after school if you want. You _____.
5. This medicine isn't for children. You _____ any to your child.
6. My mother makes every meal. I _____.
7. The meeting is very important. Your children _____ it.
8. I'm 14 years old! You _____ with me. I'll be fine alone.
9. Your father is working. You _____ him.
10. You're not my mother! You're just the babysitter. I _____ you.

PAIRS. Talk about the things that children at different ages *don't have to do* and the things that they *mustn't do*. Complete the chart.

	DON'T HAVE TO . . .	MUST NOT . . .
infants (0–11 months)	do any chores.	
toddlers (1–3 years)		cross the street alone.
young children (4–8 years)		
pre-teens (9–12 years)		

Example:
A: *Infants don't have to do any chores.*
B: *Toddlers mustn't cross the street alone.*

Grammar to Communicate 3

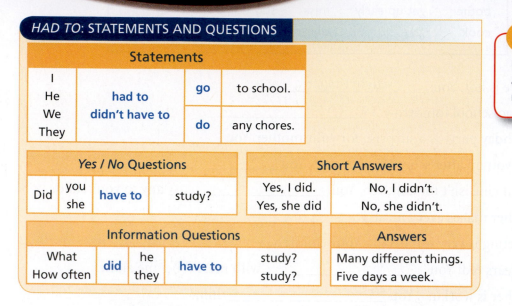

HAD TO: STATEMENTS AND QUESTIONS

Statements			
I He We They	**had to** **didn't have to**	**go**	to school.
		do	any chores.

Yes / No Questions				Short Answers	
Did	you she	**have to**	study?	Yes, I did. Yes, she did	No, I didn't. No, she didn't.

Information Questions					Answers	
What How often	**did**	he they	**have to**	study? study?	Many different things. Five days a week.	

Look

Use *had to* to talk about things that were necessary in the past.

A   **Complete the sentences about yourself. Write *had to* or *didn't have to*.**

1. When I was three, I _____ take a nap every day.

2. When I was six, I _____ drink milk every day.

3. When I was ten years old, I _____ do a lot of chores.

4. When I was twelve, I _____ eat all the food on my plate.

5. When I was fifteen, I _____ work.

B   **Rewrite the sentences. Use *had to* or *didn't have to*.**

1. It was necessary for Bob to go to school six days a week.

   Bob had to go to school six days a week.

2. It was necessary for Sylvia to help her mother clean every Saturday.

   _____

3. It was necessary for my older sister to take care of the younger kids.

   _____

4. It wasn't necessary for my friends to walk to school.

   _____

5. It wasn't necessary for me to do homework on the weekend.

   _____

6. It wasn't necessary for Vera to behave well all the time.

   _____

C Write questions.

1. **A:** I had to work after school.

   B: _Did you have to work after school_ every day?

2. **A:** We had to wear uniforms in elementary school.

   B: _____ in high school?

3. **A:** We had to go to bed early on school nights.

   B: _____ on weekends?

4. **A:** I had to get up very early for school.

   B: What time _____

5. **A:** I had to take a lot of different subjects in school.

   B: Which subjects _____

6. **A:** I had to walk to school.

   B: How far _____

7. **A:** I had to take care of my younger brothers and sisters.

   B: Why _____

Schoolchildren wearing uniforms

PAIRS. Read the sentences that are true for you. Your partner will ask you the follow-up questions. Then switch roles.

PAIRS. Talk about the responsibilities that you had when you were a teenager. Ask and answer questions. Use the words in the box and your own ideas.

Yes / No Questions	Information Questions
…be at home by a certain time?	What time?
…do chores?	What kind of chores?
…go to bed at a certain time?	What time?
…make dinner for your family?	How often?
…spend a lot of time on homework?	How much time?
…take care of an older relative?	Who?
…take care of any animals?	What kind of animals?
…take care of younger children?	Who?
…work?	How many hours a week?

Example:
A: *Did you have to do chores when you were a teenager?*
B: *Of course I did. We lived on a farm, so I had to do a lot of chores.*
A: *What kind of chores did you have to do?*

WRAP UP. Did you and your partner have the same responsibilities? Tell the class.

Review and Challenge

Grammar

CD 2 TRACK 51 Complete the conversation with the words in the box. Then listen and check your answers. Be careful. There are extra words.

didn't	does	get	had	he	I	mustn't
~~do~~	don't	got	have	he's	I've	to

Lee: Why _____do_____ you have to go so early? Let me guess . . . You _____ to
                  1.   **2.**
pick up your sister.

Dan: That's right.

Lee: You _____ to pick her up yesterday, too. Why do you always have
              3.
_____ pick her up?
   4.

Dan: I _____ always have to pick her up. I _____ have to do it last week. It
              5.   **6.**
was Stan's turn.

Lee: So why can't Stan do it today?

Dan: Because _____ got to work.
                      7.

Lee: So, where _____ she have to go this time? Soccer practice? Piano lessons?
                      8.

Dan: She's _____ to go to the dentist. I'm sorry, but _____ really have to
              9.   **10.**
go. She _____ be late for her appointment.
          11.

Lee: And I've got to _____ a new boyfriend — one with no little sister!
                          12.

Dictation

CD 2 TRACK 52 Listen. You will hear five sentences. Write them in your notebook.

Speaking

GROUPS. Compare your responsibilities when you were a teenager and your parents' and grandparents' responsibilities when they were teenagers.

Example: *When I was a teenager, I didn't have to take care of my younger brothers and sisters. My grandmother had to take care of her younger sister and her grandmother.*

Listening

A 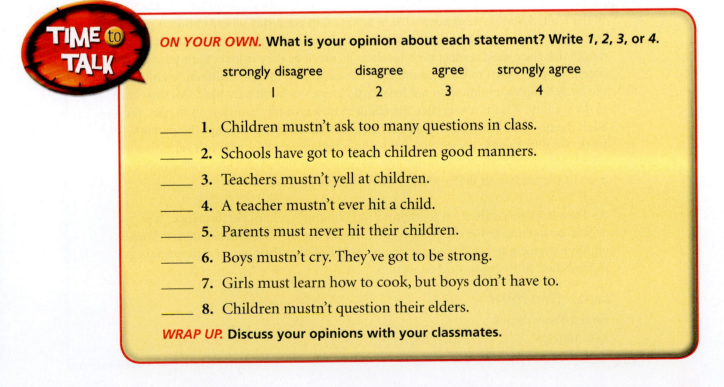 CD 2 TRACK **53** **Listen to the radio interview. What is the main idea? Check (✓) the correct statement.**

❏ 1. Children's lives in the United States and Japan are different from children's lives in other countries.

❏ 2. Children's lives in the United States are different from children's lives in Japan.

❏ 3. Japanese and American parents want to have happy and successful children.

❏ 4. Japanese and American schoolchildren behave differently.

B CD 2 TRACK **53** **Listen again. Check (✓) the statements that are true according to the radio interview.**

❏ 1. American infants and toddlers often sleep in their own rooms.

❏ 2. Japanese infants and toddlers sometimes sleep in their parents' rooms for years.

❏ 3. Many Japanese mothers pick their infants up as soon as they start to cry.

❏ 4. American children do not have to obey their teachers.

❏ 5. Japanese children do not ask a lot of questions in school.

❏ 6. American children do not have to take any exams.

❏ 7. Japanese children spend more time studying than most American children.

TIME to TALK

ON YOUR OWN. What is your opinion about each statement? Write 1, 2, 3, or 4.

strongly disagree	disagree	agree	strongly agree
1	2	3	4

_____ 1. Children mustn't ask too many questions in class.

_____ 2. Schools have got to teach children good manners.

_____ 3. Teachers mustn't yell at children.

_____ 4. A teacher mustn't ever hit a child.

_____ 5. Parents must never hit their children.

_____ 6. Boys mustn't cry. They've got to be strong.

_____ 7. Girls must learn how to cook, but boys don't have to.

_____ 8. Children mustn't question their elders.

WRAP UP. Discuss your opinions with your classmates.

Reading

Getting Ready to Read

Skim the letter. Check (✓) the main topic.

❑ the way to improve the academic performance of American kids
❑ the differences between the United States and other countries
❑ the reasons American kids do better in school than kids in other countries

Reading

Read the letter. Then check your answer to Getting Ready to Read.

To the Editors,

I am a parent of two children in the Lakeville School District. After I read yesterday's **editorial** on the latest "solution" to the **poor** academic **performance** of American children today, I felt that I had to **respond**. Your editorial uses the same arguments that we have been hearing for years. You say the government must provide more money for public schools, and schools have to spend more on teacher training. I am so tired of these arguments! It is time for new ideas. We have got to **come up with** solutions that work.

In the United States, we **ignore** what is going on in countries where children perform better than American kids, such as India and China. In these countries, children are taught that they must respect their teachers as much as they respect their parents. A parent's highest goal in these countries is the education of their children. Unlike in the United States, children do not have to do chores or work part-time. All they have to do is study! This is a **sacrifice** the children make for the family. And in turn, the adult members of the family make sacrifices for the children. Perhaps the parents work two jobs to pay school fees, while the grandparents take care of everything at home. I think that education is not just the responsibility of teachers and schools, or even of the student. It is the whole family's responsibility.

As I see it, if we really want to improve our children's school performance, we should be looking at the differences between our society and those countries where children perform better. I am sure that we will find that the biggest difference is in the families' attitudes toward education.

Emma Vanderbrook
Emma Vanderbrook
Los Angeles

After You Read

A Look at the **boldface** words in the letter. Guess their meaning. Match the words with the correct definitions. Be careful. There are two extra definitions.

__h__ 1. editorial

____ 2. poor

____ 3. performance

____ 4. respond

____ 5. come up with

____ 6. ignore

____ 7. sacrifice

____ 8. as I see it

a. in my opinion

b. how well or badly someone does something

c. not pay attention to

d. very bad

e. think of

f. not having any money

g. opportunity

h. an article in a newspaper that expresses the opinion of the editors

i. something valuable that you decide not to have, in order to get something that is more important

j. say or write something as a reply

B Read the letter again. Check (✓) the statement that best expresses the writer's point of view.

❏ 1. Schools and teachers are not very important to children's academic success.

❏ 2. Parents' attitudes toward education are more important to their children's academic success than the schools or teachers.

❏ 3. If the government does not spend more money on education, children will not be successful in the future.

> **Reading Skill:**
> **Recognizing Point of View**
>
> A writer's **point of view** is his or her opinion about or attitude toward the topic. Look for words like *I think* or *as I see it* in the text. They often come at the beginning of sentences that give the writer's point of view.

Writing

Getting Ready to Write

A **Rewrite each sentence two ways. Use phrases that express a point of view.**

1. As I see it, children need more places to play.

    In my opinion, children need more places to play.

    The point is, children need more places to play.

    _____

2. In my opinion, the schools in our city are terrible.

    _____

    _____

3. The point is, parents must teach their children good manners.

    _____

    _____

4. The point is, children had to do too many chores fifty years ago.

    _____

    _____

> ## Writing Tip
>
> Use *the point is*, *in my opinion*, and *as I see it* to express your point of view:
>
> **Examples:**
>
> **The point is,** children should respect their teachers.
>
> **In my opinion,** children should respect their teachers.
>
> **As I see it,** children should respect their teachers.

B **Read the model letter.**

> To the Editors,
>
> I am writing because there is a serious problem in our community. As I see it, this city doesn't have enough parks. Parks are important because most people in our city don't have yards. Parks are the only places we can sit and enjoy nature. Also, parks are great for kids. Kids love to run and play on the grass. Because there aren't enough parks, our kids have to play in the streets. That can be really dangerous! If parents want to keep their children safe, they have to keep them inside the house. That's not fair to the children. In my opinion, our city has got to start building parks for our children as soon as possible!
>
> Ned Bates
> Centerville

PAIRS. **Read the model again. Why is it important to a community to have parks?**

Now choose a problem in your community. Talk about why it is important to solve the problem. You can talk about housing, traffic, schools, crime, or your own ideas.

Prewriting: Brainstorming

You are going to write a letter to the editor about a community problem. Before you write, look at the brainstorming ideas for the writing model. Then brainstorm, or write down very quickly, as many ideas as you can think of. Check (✓) the ideas you would like to include in your letter.

Writing Model

Problem: the city needs more parks

Ideas:
our city parks are boring and small
our city parks are dirty
not enough parks ✓
people don't have yards ✓
parks only place to enjoy nature ✓
people use parks for exercise
children need to be outside ✓
children play on the street: dangerous ✓
children have to stay inside ✓
children need sunshine

Problem:

Ideas:
_____
_____
_____
_____
_____
_____
_____
_____
_____
_____
_____
_____
_____
_____
_____
_____

Writing

Now write a letter to the editor about a community problem. The writing tip, the model letter, and your notes will help you. Write in your notebook.

Vocabulary

CD 3 TRACK **2** Read the sentences and look at the pictures. What do adults say to children? Match the sentences with the pictures. Then listen and check your answers.

1.   2.   3.   4.   5.   6.   7.   8.

____3____ **a.** "Don't **lick** your fingers."

_____ **b.** "Don't **whisper**."

_____ **c.** "Don't **talk with your mouth full**."

_____ **d.** "**Knock on the door** before you enter a room."

_____ **e.** "Don't **interrupt**."

_____ **f.** "**Cover your mouth** when you sneeze."

_____ **g.** "Don't **put your elbows** on the table."

_____ **h.** "Don't **talk about her behind her back**."

Listening

A CD 3 TRACK 3 **Listen. What is Allen doing wrong? Check (✓) the pictures.**

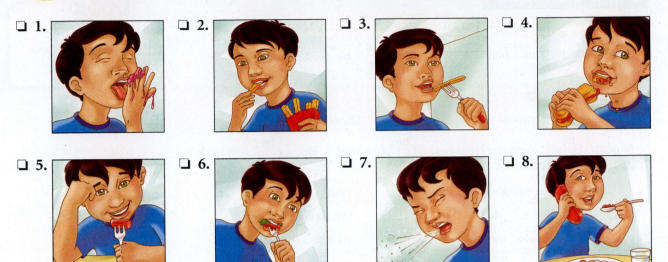

❑ 1.   ❑ 2.   ❑ 3.   ❑ 4.

❑ 5.   ❑ 6.   ❑ 7.   ❑ 8.

B CD 3 TRACK 4 **Listen again. For each pair of sentences, check (✓) the sentence that you hear.**

1. ❑ **a.** You should be asking me that.
   ❑ **b.** You shouldn't be asking me that.

2. ❑ **a.** You should use a fork.
   ❑ **b.** You should be using a fork.

3. ❑ **a.** Why do I have to use a fork?
   ❑ **b.** Why do I have a fork?

4. ❑ **a.** I don't live with them.
   ❑ **b.** I don't have to live with them.

5. ❑ **a.** Should your elbows be on the table?
   ❑ **b.** Your elbows should be on the table.

6. ❑ **a.** I have to talk to her.
   ❑ **b.** I don't have to talk to her.

C CD 3 TRACK 5 **Listen again. Answer the questions. Write complete sentences.**

1. What is Allen's excuse for eating with his hands?

   _____

2. Why doesn't Allen's mother care about his friends' manners?

   _____

3. What is Allen's excuse for putting his elbows on the table?

   _____

4. What is Allen's excuse for answering the telephone at dinnertime?

   _____

SHOULD (NOT) + VERB

Statements							
He They	should	be	polite.	I We	should not shouldn't	be	rude.

Questions		

Yes / No Questions			Short Answers					
Should	he they	apologize?	Yes,	he they	should.	No,	he they	shouldn't.

Information Questions				Answers
What	should	I	do?	Send a card.
When	should	we	call?	At 9:00 P.M.

Look

Use *should (not)* to give advice and opinions.

 A What do you know about manners in the United States? Complete the sentences. Write *should* or *shouldn't*.

1.

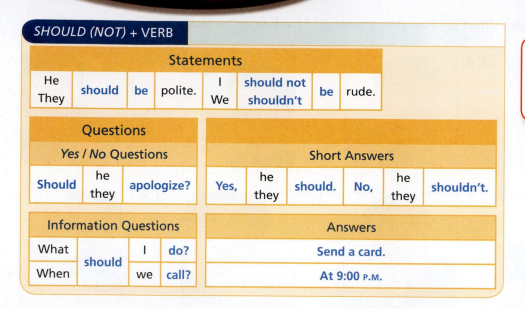

You _____ hold the door open for other people.

2.

You _____ wait for people to get off a bus before you get on.

3.

You _____ look people in the eyes when you talk to them.

4.

You _____ stare at people.

PAIRS. Are these manners the same in your country? Discuss.

B Complete the sentences. Use *should* or *shouldn't*.

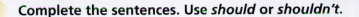

cover your mouth	~~say "please"~~	send a thank-you note
knock on the door	send a card	start eating

1. When you ask for something from someone, you _____*should say "please"*_____.

2. Before you enter someone's room, you _____.

3. You _____ when you cough.

4. After you stay at someone's home, you _____.

5. You _____ before other people at the table start.

6. When someone is in the hospital, you _____.

C Write questions. Use *should*.

1. Paul is going to a co-worker's home for dinner. ___*Should Paul take something?*___
   (Paul / take something)

2. Kevin gave his boss a birthday present.
   _____
   (Kevin's boss / give Kevin a birthday present)

3. Dave and Sheila are going to have a birthday party for their five-year-old daughter.
   _____
   (they / invite children only)

4. Your boss's wife just died.
   _____
   (you / call him)

D Write information questions about the situations in Exercise C. Use *should*.

1. ___*What should Paul take?*___
   (what / Paul / take)

2. _____
   (what / Kevin / give him)

3. _____
   (who / Dave and Sheila / invite)

4. _____
   (when / you / call)

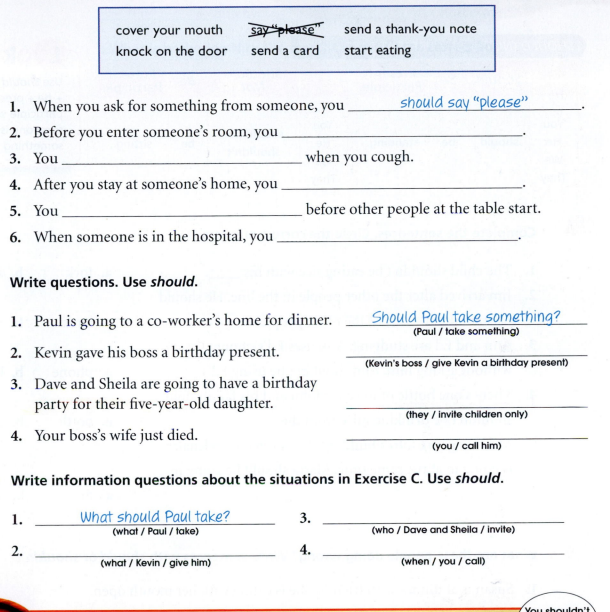

TIME to TALK

PAIRS. Ask and answer questions about the situations on page 305. Discuss what you should do in your culture. Use the words in parentheses and your own ideas.

Example:
A: *Should I go ahead of everyone? I'm in a hurry!*
B: *No, you shouldn't. You should wait in line.*
A: *Should I wait for another bus?*
B: *Yes, if the bus is crowded.*

WRAP UP. Do you know if your answers are correct in American culture? Check with your classmates and your teacher.

You shouldn't go ahead of everyone.

(go ahead of)
(wait for another bus)

Grammar to Communicate 2

SHOULD (NOT) + BE + PRESENT PARTICIPLE							
	Should	*Be*	Present Participle		*Should + Not*	*Be*	Present Participle
I You He We They	should	be	standing.	I You He We They	should not shouldn't	be	sitting.

Look

Use *should (not)* + *be* + present participle when someone is doing something wrong.

A Complete the sentences. Circle the correct answers.

1. The child shouldn't be eating rice with his ____.
   a. fork   b. fingers

2. Jim arrived after the other people in the line. He should be standing in ____ of the other people.
   a. back   b. front

3. Ann and Ed are studying. Ann uses Ed's phone without asking him. Ann shouldn't be using Ed's ____.
   a. phone   b. books

4. There's one bottle of juice for John and his family. John shouldn't be drinking juice from the ____.
   a. bottle   b. glass

5. Marta is going into a building. A man in a wheelchair is going in at the same time. Marta should be going in ____.
   a. first   b. second

B What are these people doing wrong? Write sentences with *should* or *shouldn't*.

1. Susan is at dinner with friends. She is eating with her mouth open.
   Susan shouldn't be eating with her mouth open.

2. Tom is eating dinner with his family. He is reading the newspaper.
   _____

3. Mark is eating chocolate ice cream. He is licking his fingers.
   _____

4. Lucy is with some friends at a movie. She is talking on her cell phone.
   _____

5. David is at a wedding. He's wearing jeans.
   _____

C Look at the picture. People are doing things wrong. Write sentences with *should* or *shouldn't*.

1. The man should be waiting. He shouldn't be getting on the bus before the other passengers get off.

2. _____

3. _____

4. _____

5. _____

6. _____

 TIME to TALK

PAIRS. **Student A:** Act out something that is impolite in your culture.

Student B: Watch your partner. First guess what he or she is doing. Then make a sentence with *should (not) be doing.*

Talk about whether the action is impolite in Student B's culture, too. Then switch roles. Continue until each of you has done three impolite things.

Manners

Grammar to Communicate 3

SHOULD AND HAVE TO

Rule	Example
Use *have to / has to* when something is necessary. There isn't any choice.	A doctor **has to ask** a patient questions.
Use *should* for advice and opinions.	A doctor **should speak** politely to a patient.
Use *don't have to / doesn't have to* when something is <u>not</u> necessary, but there is a choice.	A doctor **doesn't have to go** to patients' homes.
Use *shouldn't* for advice and opinions.	A doctor **shouldn't be** rude to a patient.

A Read the descriptions. What are the jobs? Write *bellhop, cab driver, chauffeur,* or *doorman.*

1. He has to open the door for his boss, and he has to be polite all the time. He doesn't have to do favors for his boss, but he usually does. He shouldn't use the car phone to call his friends. This person is a _____.

2. He doesn't have to open the door for his passengers. He usually opens the door only for elderly passengers. He shouldn't be rude to the passengers, and they shouldn't be rude to him. He has to talk to his passengers at the beginning and end of the ride, but he doesn't have to talk all the time. This person is a _____.

doorman

cab driver

bellhop

chauffeur

B Complete the sentences with *has to, have to,* or *should.*

1. Police officers ___*should*___ have good manners.

2. People who work in expensive hotels ___*have to*___ have good manners.

3. Young people _____ open the door for older people.

4. Ed is a doorman. He _____ open the door for people.

5. Alfred is a bellhop in a hotel. He _____ help people with their bags.

6. You _____ carry your mother's bag. It looks heavy.

C   Write sentences. Use *have to*, *don't have to*, *should*, *shouldn't*, and the words in the boxes.

Classmates	be polite with each other	have dinner together
Co-workers	buy each other presents	invite each other to their homes
Friends	celebrate holidays together	take care of each other
Relatives	eat lunch together	talk behind each other's backs
	get along with each other	talk to each other every day

1.   *Classmates should be polite with each other.* _____

2.   _____

3.   _____

4.   _____

5.   _____

6.   _____

PAIRS. Compare sentences.

Example: A: *Classmates should be polite with each other.*
                     B: *I agree, but classmates don't have to invite each other to their homes.*

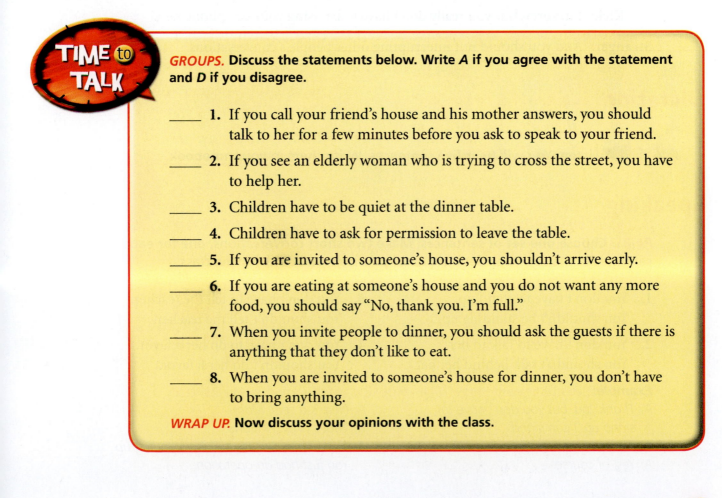

GROUPS. Discuss the statements below. Write *A* if you agree with the statement and *D* if you disagree.

_____ 1. If you call your friend's house and his mother answers, you should talk to her for a few minutes before you ask to speak to your friend.

_____ 2. If you see an elderly woman who is trying to cross the street, you have to help her.

_____ 3. Children have to be quiet at the dinner table.

_____ 4. Children have to ask for permission to leave the table.

_____ 5. If you are invited to someone's house, you shouldn't arrive early.

_____ 6. If you are eating at someone's house and you do not want any more food, you should say "No, thank you. I'm full."

_____ 7. When you invite people to dinner, you should ask the guests if there is anything that they don't like to eat.

_____ 8. When you are invited to someone's house for dinner, you don't have to bring anything.

WRAP UP. Now discuss your opinions with the class.

Review and Challenge

Grammar

6 Correct the conversation. There are seven mistakes. The first mistake is corrected for you. Then listen and check your answers.

   Lori: Listen to that woman with the cell phone. She shouldn't be ~~talk~~ *talking* on her cell phone here. You should be telling her.

   Kirk: What I should say?

   Lori: You should say, "Stop talking on your cell phone."

   Kirk: That's not very polite. I don't think I should to be rude because she's rude.

   Lori: Sometimes you have be rude to people. They don't listen if you're polite.

   Kirk: I don't agree. Watch. Excuse me?

  Stranger: What?

   Kirk: I'm sorry, but you really don't have to be using your cell phone here.

  Stranger: And you should not interrupting other people's conversations.

Dictation

7 Listen. You will hear five sentences. Write them in your notebook.

Speaking

PAIRS. Choose one set of sentences. Make two short conversations, one for each sentence in the set. Then act out one of your conversations for the class.

1. You don't have to stand up.
   You shouldn't be standing up.

2. You don't have to talk to her.
   You shouldn't talk behind her back.

3. You don't have to tell the teacher.
   You shouldn't tell the teacher.

4. You don't have to do her a favor.
   You shouldn't do her a favor.

Example:

A: *Thank you, but you don't have to stand up. I can stand.*
B: *Are you sure?*
A: *Yes, of course.*

A: *Here's a seat, Mom.*
B: *That's okay. I'll stand.*
A: *Come on, you shouldn't be standing up. You just had an operation.*

206   **Unit 15**

Listening

A CD 3 TRACK 8 **Listen to the report. Put the topics in the order in which you hear them in the report. Be careful. There are two extra topics.**

body language	conversation	how to eat	what to wear
children's behavior	food	~~seating~~	

Topic 1: _____seating_____   Topic 4: _____

Topic 2: _____   Topic 5: _____

Topic 3: _____

B CD 3 TRACK 8 **Listen again. Write the number of the correct topic from Exercise A next to each question.**

1. Which utensils should you use? Topic _____
2. Do men and women eat together, or do they have to sit in separate rooms? Topic _____
3. Do you have to eat everything on your plate? Topic _____
4. Which topics should you discuss? Which topics shouldn't you discuss? Topic _____
5. Where should guests sit at the table? Topic _____
6. What should you do if you don't like something? Topic _____
7. What should you do with your legs? Topic _____

utensils

fork

spoon

chopsticks

knife

lap

TIME to TALK

GROUPS. Ask and answer questions about table manners in your countries. Talk about differences between manners at home and manners at a restaurant or at someone else's house.

Example:

A: *In your country, do you have to eat everything on your plate?*

B: *No, you don't. In fact, if you are invited to someone's house, you should leave a little food on your plate. Then the host will know that you are full.*

WRAP UP. Now tell the class about the most interesting thing that you learned.

Reading

Getting Ready to Read

Preview the article. Look at the title and the picture and read the first paragraph. What do you think *etiquette* means? Write a definition.

etiquette = _____

Reading

Read the article. Then check your answer to Getting Ready to Read.

INTERNATIONAL BUSINESS ETIQUETTE

Like social manners, business **etiquette** differs from country to country. Sometimes the rules change only a little, but even small differences can result in a serious **misunderstanding**. Fortunately, there are a lot of books and information on the Internet to help businesspeople **avoid** cultural misunderstandings. If you do business with people from another culture, you should not expect them to understand your culture; instead, you have to learn about their culture and be ready to **adapt** to it.

In American culture, for example, business **colleagues** usually shake hands to **greet** each other. However, they do not always shake hands to say goodbye. In contrast, in many other countries, such as Colombia and Turkey, you must shake hands to both greet and say goodbye to colleagues. If you do not, people will think you are rude.

Let's look at another example. In the United States, if a business colleague invites you out for a meal, you should never try to pay. Everyone understands that the person who invited the other person, male or female, must pay. In the Philippines, however, a businesswoman should never pay the bill for a male colleague. If she does, it might **destroy** their business relationship.

Of course, if your foreign business colleagues are familiar with your culture, they might understand and **excuse** your behavior. However, you should never **assume** that others have such cultural knowledge, because you might be wrong. And you do not want your business colleagues to think that you are rude, or even worse, to imagine that you are trying to **insult** them. In conclusion, you should always learn the cultural rules of your foreign colleagues. It's just good business sense.

After You Read

A   Find the **boldface** words in the article that have similar meanings to the words below.

1. say bad things about someone   *insult*
2. keep away from
3. think that something is true
4. change your behavior to fit a new situation
5. forgive
6. co-workers
7. when you can't understand something or someone
8. say hello to and welcome someone
9. manners
10. damage something so badly that it does not exist anymore

B   Read the article again. Write three supporting details from the article. Look for the words *example* and *such as*.

1. _____

    _____

2. _____

    _____

3. _____

    _____

> **Reading Skill:**
> **Recognizing Supporting Details**
>
> Writers use **supporting details** to give more information about the main idea. When you read, look for words like *example* and *such as*. These words are used to give examples that support the main idea.

Writing

Getting Ready to Write

A   Read the sentences from a paragraph. Check (✓) the supporting details.

❏ **1.** For example, Germans will be insulted if you do not use their titles.

❏ **2.** In the U.S., you do not always have to use titles.

❏ **3.** To sum up, you have to learn the appropriate language to use with businesspeople from other countries.

❏ **4.** American businesspeople are generally less formal than businesspeople from most other countries.

❏ **5.** In fact, in Japan, you must never call your colleagues by their first names.

❏ **6.** The language of business can be formal or informal, depending on the country.

> **Writing Tip**
>
> Use words like *in fact* and *for example* to help readers identify supporting details.
>
> Examples:
>
> In the U.S., **in fact**, colleagues shake hands.
>
> In the U.S., **for example**, colleagues shake hands.

B   Read the model paragraph.

> Both Chinese and American businesspeople like to have business dinners. However, polite behavior at a Chinese business dinner is not the same as polite behavior at an American business dinner. For example, in China, business dinners usually have 20 or 30 courses. You should always taste a little bit of each dish. But at the end of the meal, you have to leave a little food on your plate. In fact, if you don't, the host will think that he did not order enough food. In the United States, in contrast, business dinners usually have only two or three courses. You should finish all the food on your plate because this shows that you liked the food. To sum up, if someone invites you to a business dinner in China or the United States, you should remember these important rules of etiquette.

PAIRS. Read the model again. According to the writer, what are the differences in business etiquette in China and the United States? Why are they important?

Now think about your country. Talk about business etiquette in your country. You can talk about appointments, clothes, giving gifts, or your own ideas.

Prewriting: Using an Outline

You are going to write a paragraph about some aspect of business etiquette in your country. Before you write, complete the outline with notes about your topic.

Writing Model

Main Idea: Polite behavior at a Chinese business dinner is not the same as polite behavior at an American business dinner.

Supporting Details:

1. China—business dinners usually have 20 or 30 courses

2. If you don't leave food, host will think he didn't order enough

3. U.S.—business dinners usually have only one or two courses. Should finish all the food—shows you liked it

Concluding Sentence: To sum up, if someone invites you to a business dinner in China or the U.S., remember etiquette rules.

Main Idea:

Supporting Details:

1.

2.

3.

Concluding Sentence:

Writing

Now write a paragraph about an aspect of business etiquette in your country. The writing tip, the model paragraph, and your notes will help you. Write in your notebook.

Unit 16
Neighbors

Grammar
- *Must* + Verb
- *Must* + *Be* + Present Participle
- *Must not* and *Can't*

Vocabulary

9 Match the numbers with the words. Then listen and check your answers.

__1__ bark	____ driveway	____ gardener	____ musician	____ slam the door
____ chat	____ garden	____ junk	____ shout	____ yard

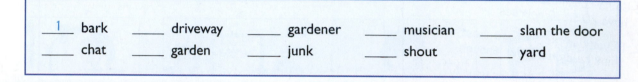

Listening

A **CD 3 TRACK 10** **Listen. Ann and Bob live in a large apartment building. Check (✓) the correct statement.**

☐ **1.** The man has been away for a month and wants to know about his neighbors.

☐ **2.** The woman is not very interested in her neighbors' lives, but the man is.

☐ **3.** The man and the woman don't like their neighbors very much.

☐ **4.** The man and the woman are not very interested in their neighbors' lives.

B **CD 3 TRACK 10** **Listen again. Who said it? Write B (Bob) or A (Ann).**

_____ **1.** You must be tired.

_____ **2.** She must be doing well at work.

_____ **3.** She must not be very happy about that.

_____ **4.** But they can't be getting along.

_____ **5.** He must be at his mother's.

_____ **6.** She can't be staying with Mrs. O'Hara.

_____ **7.** She can't be alone!

C **CD 3 TRACK 10** **Listen again. Write T (true) or F (false). If the statement is false, correct it to make it true.**

__F__ **1.** Bob's grandchildren were visiting him.   _Bob was visiting his grandchildren._

_____ **2.** Emily Rose is doing well at her job.   _____

_____ **3.** Roberta was wearing a new suit.   _____

_____ **4.** Roberta and Andy are fighting.   _____

_____ **5.** Andy is staying at his mother's house.   _____

_____ **6.** Mr. and Mrs. Russel are on vacation with Mrs. O'Hara.   _____

_____ **7.** The Russels' daughter is alone in the apartment.   _____

_____ **8.** Sarah's grandmother has a car.   _____

Grammar to Communicate 1

MUST + VERB				
Fact	**Logical Conclusion**			
	Subject	*Must*	Verb	
The house has a big garden.	You She They	**must**	**like**	flowers.
People are wearing heavy coats.	It	**must**	**be**	cold out.

> **Look**
>
> Use *must* when you are 95 percent sure that something is true. Do not use *must* if you <u>know</u> that something **is** true.
> My neighbor **is** a teacher. He told me.
> NOT My neighbor ~~must be~~ a teacher. He told me.

A   Match the sentences.

___d___ 1. The woman next door has a beautiful garden.

_____ 2. The old people on the other side never have visitors.

_____ 3. The man on the corner is always fixing things.

_____ 4. The neighbors around the corner have four cats.

_____ 5. The man across the street has a lot of parties.

a. He must have a lot of friends.

b. Their family must live far away.

c. They must like animals.

d. She must be a good gardener.

e. He must be good with his hands.

> **Look**
>
> good with his hands = to be good at fixing or building things

B **11** **Complete the answers with *must*. Then listen and check your answers.**

1. **A:** Do the people across the street have a lot of visitors?

   B: _____They must have_____ a lot of visitors. There are always cars in front of their house.

2. **A:** Does Mrs. Cho like children?

   B: _____ them. She babysits all the time.

3. **A:** Is that house empty?

   B: _____ empty. There's never anyone there.

4. **A:** Does John know his neighbors' names?

   B: _____ their names. He talks to them all the time.

5. **A:** Does that woman live near here?

   B: _____ around here. I see her on the bus all the time.

6. **A:** Are Vic and Cindy at home?

   B: _____ there. Their car is in the driveway.

C Barbara and Don are going to buy a home. They're looking in different neighborhoods. Write sentences about the people who live in the homes.

1. (be) _They must be_ _doctors._ 2. (have) _____ _____ 3. (be) _____ _____

4. (have) _____ _____ 5. (like) _____ _____ 6. (love) _____ _____

PAIRS. Which neighbors would you like to have? Why?

TIME to TALK

PAIRS. Read the logical conclusions. Then think of a fact each conclusion could be based on.

Fact	Logical Conclusion
1. _She is always carrying a guitar._	Your neighbor must be a musician.
2. _____	The man next door must love dogs.
3. _____	Your landlord must be single.
4. _____	The woman next door must be a good cook.

Now, read the facts and think of a logical conclusion you could make based on each fact.

5. Her phone rings all the time. _____
6. His TV is always very loud. _____
7. They have a party every weekend. _____
8. She never has any visitors. _____

Grammar to Communicate 2

MUST + BE + PRESENT PARTICIPLE			
Fact	**Logical Conclusion**		
	Subject	*Must + Be*	Participle
The bedroom door is closed, and the lights are off.	He She They	**must be**	sleeping.

Look

Use *must + be* + present participle when you are 95 percent sure that something is happening <u>now</u>.

A Connie's brother Raúl is staying in her apartment. Connie told Raúl about her neighbors. Complete the sentences with the correct names.

> Old Mrs. Bell in 3F doesn't hear well.

> Sylvia in 3H is a music student.

> Tom and Chris in 3C have a noisy dog.

> Mr. and Mrs. Sty in 3A don't get along.

> Joe in 3D loves parties.

1. Raúl hears a dog. _____Tom and Chris's_____ dog must be barking.

2. Raúl hears violin music. _____ must be practicing.

3. Two people are yelling. _____ must be arguing.

4. There's loud music in 3D. _____ must be having a party.

5. Raúl hears someone's television. _____ must be watching TV.

B **12** Answer the questions. Use *must* and the words in the box. Then listen and check your answers.

1. **A:** I hear a child crying. Do your neighbors have kids?

   B: Yeah. Billy Johnson _____must be crying_____. He cries a lot.

2. **A:** What's that strange smell?

   B: Tom Moroney _____. He's a really bad cook.

3. **A:** Do you have a musician in the building? I hear a piano.

   B: Paul Tram _____. He's very talented.

4. **A:** Who's making so much noise?

   B: The Tate kids _____ the door. They go in and out of the house all day long.

5. **A:** Who's that? Her voice is so loud!

   B: Mrs. Norton _____. Her husband doesn't hear well.

cook
~~cry~~
play
shout
slam

C **13** **Lois and Ed are talking about Ed's neighbors. Complete the conversation. Use** *must* **and the correct form of the verbs in the box. Then listen and check your answers.**

be sick	go to work	~~look for her keys~~	visit her mother
fight	~~have a new boyfriend~~	sell	

Lois: A woman across the street is taking everything out of her bag.

Ed: Oh, Linda ___must be looking for her keys___.
1.
She always loses them.

Lois: And the college student is holding hands with a

good-looking young man.

Ed: Katie ___must have a new boyfriend___. Her
2.
last boyfriend wasn't good-looking at all.

> ## Look
>
> Stative verbs do not take *–ing*.
> He must have a dog.
> NOT He must ~~be having~~ a dog.
> She must be tired.
> NOT She must ~~be being~~ tired.
> See page 298 for a list of
> stative verbs.

Lois: A police officer is coming out of the house next door.

Ed: Oh, that's Officer Timmons. He lives there. He _____.
3.

Lois: Your next-door neighbors aren't home.

Ed: Mia and Tom _____. They see her every Monday.
4.

Lois: Some little girls in green uniforms are going from house to house.

Ed: They _____ Girl Scout cookies. They always come
5.
in the spring.

Lois: A nurse is going into the small yellow house.

Ed: Mr. Romero _____.
6.

Lois: Two people are going into the green house. They look very angry.

Ed: Tim and Ann _____. They are not a happy couple
7.
these days.

> ### TIME to TALK
>
> *PAIRS.* **Look at the picture of the neighborhood on page 212. Make logical conclusions about the people you see in the picture.**
>
> *Example:*
> *The people at 10 Vista Drive must be visiting their grandchildren.*
>
> *WRAP UP.* **Now share some of your sentences with the class. Did other students make the same conclusions?**

Grammar to Communicate 3

MUST NOT AND CAN'T	
Fact	**Logical Conclusion**
They don't live together.	They **must not** be married.
They fight all the time.	They **must not** be getting along.
Fact	**Logical Conclusion**
He already has a wife.	She **can't** be married to him.
They are getting a divorce.	They **can't** be getting along.

Look

Use *must not* when you are 95 percent sure that something is <u>not</u> true.

Use *can't* when you think that something is impossible.

A   Complete the sentences. Circle the correct answers.

1. Alan must be _____. He never has time to chat with his neighbors.
   a. busy   **b.** free

2. Stan and Ellen must not be living here anymore. I _____ see them.
   a. always   **b.** never

3. That white car can't be Miranda's. Her car is _____.
   a. black   **b.** white

4. Susan can't be standing in front of her house. She's at _____.
   a. home   **b.** her sister's house

B   Write sentences with *must not*. Use the phrases in the box.

be at home
care about their home
feel very well
go to school
like noise
~~work today~~

1. Ann goes to work at 8:00. It's 9:00, and her car is here.
   She must not be working today.

2. I called Deb a minute ago, and there was no answer.
   _____

3. When Myra's neighbor has a party, she often calls the police.
   _____

4. The Robertsons' yard always has junk in it.
   _____

5. Mrs. Jackson just got out of the hospital. She looks terrible.
   _____

6. I just saw Anya. She was leaving the house without her book bag.
   _____

C   **Joe and Ann are talking about their neighbors. Ann thinks that Joe's conclusions are wrong. Match Ann's statements and Joe's conclusions.**

Ann says . . .

__d__ 1. Your neighbors must be angry with you.

____ 2. Mrs. Lee next door must be moving.

____ 3. Mrs. Jones must be pregnant.

____ 4. Their grandchildren must be visiting.

____ 5. Sue in 1A must be having a party.

____ 6. That must be his girlfriend.

Joe's conclusions . . .

a. She can't be. She's 50 years old!

b. She can't be. She's on vacation.

c. They can't be. It's not school vacation.

d. They can't be. I'm an excellent neighbor.

e. She can't be. He's married.

f. She can't be. She loves it here.

D   CD 3 TRACK **14**   **Complete the conversations. Use *can't*, *must not*, or *must*. Then listen and check your answers.**

1. **A:** Sue and Dave have the same last name. They ____must____ be married.

    B: They ____can't____ be married. Sue's husband's name is Brad. Dave ____must____ be her brother.

2. **A:** Oh look, there's Lena's dog.

    B: That _____ be Lena's dog. Her dog died. That _____ be her son's dog.

3. **A:** Adam's not here. He _____ be out running.

    B: He _____ be running. His running shoes are right here.

4. **A:** The new neighbors _____ love pink. Even their house is pink.

    B: Annie Sullivan across the street _____ be very happy! She hates pink.

PAIRS. You live in the same building. Make conversations about your neighbors from the situations below. Make as many conclusions as you can with *must*, *mustn't*, and *can't*.

Jill isn't paying rent on time.	Pete has a lot of boxes in his apartment.
Luz is going to lose her job.	Sam is working a lot of late nights.
Ms. Yu has stayed home for 3 days.	The Bradys are fighting a lot.

Example:
A: *The Bradys are fighting a lot. They must be getting a divorce.*
B: *They can't be getting a divorce. They've been married for 20 years. They must be going through hard times.*

Review and Challenge

Grammar

 15 **Correct the mistake in each conversation. Then listen and check your answers.**

1. **A:** It ~~can't~~ *must* be difficult to find a good apartment around here.

   B: You're right. It is. I've been looking for a place for three months.

2. **A:** Laura's walking to the bus stop. That's strange.

   B: Her husband must use her car today.

3. **A:** Mrs. Olsen must not be feeling lonely since her husband's death.

   B: I know. We should visit her next weekend.

4. **A:** Look, there's Tommy. He must be going to school.

   B: But it's Saturday. He can't go to school.

5. **A:** Hello? Could I please speak to Donna?

   B: Donna? There's no Donna here. You must be having the wrong number.

Dictation

16 **Listen. You will hear five sentences. Write them in your notebook.**

Speaking

PAIRS. **Choose one of the situations. Make up a story.**

• She can't be paying for that. Her son must be helping her.

• They must be joking. They can't be serious.

• It can't be all her fault. He must be responsible, too.

• He can't be the murderer! The police must have the wrong man.

• That can't be true. She must be wrong.

Now tell your story to the class. Who has the best story?

Example: *Mrs. Ephran is a retired school teacher. She's a widow. One day you see two men carrying a plasma TV into her house. You know that her son makes a lot of money. You say, "She can't be paying for that. Her son must be helping her."*

Listening

CD 3 TRACK 17 **A** Listen to the radio talk show. Check (✓) the pictures that match the stories.

1. ❏ **a.**
   ❏ **b.**
   ❏ **c.**

2. ❏ **a.**
   ❏ **b.**
   ❏ **c.**

CD 3 TRACK 17 **B** Listen again. Match each fact with a logical conclusion.

Fact	Logical Conclusion
(Caller 1)	
____ **1.** He thinks his neighbors are watching him.	**a.** That must be uncomfortable.
____ **2.** There is no reason for the police to be watching him.	**b.** So he can't really be worried about that.
____ **3.** They are trying to be friendly.	**c.** They must not know how he feels.
(Caller 2)	
____ **4.** She didn't think the situation was funny.	**d.** Her husband must not like the neighbor very much.
____ **5.** He shouted at her.	**e.** She mustn't have a very good sense of humor.

GROUPS. Talk about problems you or people you know have had with neighbors.

Example:
A: *My neighbor leaves a light on outside his house all night. It keeps me awake.*
B: *That must be really annoying. Have you ever talked to him about it?*

Reading

Getting Ready to Read

Read only the first paragraph of the article. How do you think the writer will answer the question at the end of the paragraph?

_____ yes   _____ no   _____ The writer will not answer the question.

Reading

Read the article. Then check your answer to Getting Ready to Read.

A Difficult Question

"Why does the richest country in the world have so many people living on the streets?" This is a question that visitors to the United States often ask. Americans **respond to** this question in different ways. Some Americans think that homeless people must not be able to find jobs. Others believe that they must not want to work. Others think that the homeless must all be **addicted to** alcohol. And many believe that the government must not be doing enough to help. However, there is one thing that most Americans agree on: homeless people cannot be working. After all, anyone with a job must be able to afford a place to live, right?

Some of the things that Americans believe about the homeless are true. For example, it is true that some homeless people have a problem with alcohol. It is also true that the government could help more. However, it is _not_ true that all homeless people do not work. According to **advocates** for the homeless, 25 to 40% of homeless people work full-time or part-time. And 38% of the homeless population is **made up of** families with children.

So how does someone with a job and family end up living on the street? The answer to that question is **controversial.** People on both sides have strong opinions about it. However, most advocates say there are three main causes of homelessness: not enough **affordable** housing, jobs that do not pay enough, and the high cost of health care.

Unfortunately, most of the programs for the homeless help mainly with **temporary** solutions, such as housing for a short time, food, clothing, and emergency health care. These temporary solutions are important, but they do not solve the real causes of homelessness.

After You Read

A Look at the **boldface** words and expressions in the article. Guess their meaning. Then complete the sentences with the words in the box.

addicted to	affordable	made up of	temporary
advocates	controversial	~~respond to~~	unfortunately

1. You have to _____respond to_____ this e-mail immediately. They need an answer today.

2. When you are _____ something, you don't stop taking it, even if it is very bad for you.

3. The United States does not have just one culture. It is _____ many different cultures.

4. The job of _____ is to help people.

5. This solution to the problem is _____: it will only work for a short time.

6. Health care needs to be _____. Both poor and rich people should be able to pay for it easily.

7. It's a _____ topic. People feel very strongly about it.

8. _____, the fact is that many homeless people in the U.S. are families with children.

B Read the article again. Then check (✓) the statements that are true.

❏ 1. The U.S. is a rich country, so there aren't many homeless people.

❏ 2. Most people understand the causes of homelessness.

❏ 3. Some homeless people work.

❏ 4. The U.S. government could do more to help the homeless.

❏ 5. Most homeless people are old and sick.

❏ 6. Many homeless people in the U.S. are families with children.

❏ 7. Health care does not cost a lot of money.

Writing

Getting Ready to Write

A   **Read the paragraphs. For each paragraph, underline the question that gets the reader's attention. Then circle the answer to the question.**

> **Writing Tip**
>
> Use questions in your writing to get your reader's attention and highlight important ideas. Your reader will then try to find the answer to your question.
>
> Example:
>
> **So how does someone with a job and family end up living on the street?**

1. Anyone with a job must be able to afford a place to live, right? Well, it is true that many people who live on the streets don't have jobs. But up to 40 percent of homeless people do work full or part-time and still can't afford a place to live.

2. Is the government doing enough to help the homeless? It does pay for some programs to help the homeless. The programs offer homeless people temporary housing, food, clothing, and free emergency health care. However, there are still far too many homeless people, so the government must not be doing enough to solve this problem.

3. Homelessness is a difficult problem to solve in the U.S. Are the homeless people the same in every U.S. city? No, they aren't. For example, in Portland, Oregon, many of the homeless are teenagers who have run away from home. In other cities, the homeless are mostly adult men or single mothers with small children.

B   **Read the model paragraph.**

> There are thousands of homeless people in our city. What is the best way to help them? Some people choose to make free food for the homeless. Others donate clothing that they don't need anymore. The government builds apartments for the homeless to live in for a short time. All of these things are helpful. However, some homeless people have also started helping themselves. They write their own newspapers and sell them to people on the streets. These newspapers must be a good way to help. Why? Because when you buy a newspaper, you are helping homeless people help themselves.

PAIRS. **Read the model again. Are these good solutions to help the homeless?**

Now choose a problem in your country. Talk about ways to solve the problem. You can talk about economic problems, political problems, or your own ideas.

Prewriting: Using Questions

You are going to write a paragraph about a problem in your country. Before you write, make a list of questions to ask about the problem. Write answers to the questions. Then use the best question and answer for your paragraph.

Question 1:

Answer:

Question 2:

Answer:

Question 3:

Answer:

Writing

Now write a paragraph about a problem in your country and a possible solution. The writing tip, the model paragraph, and your notes will help you. Write in your notebook.

Health

Grammar
- *It* + Infinitive
- *Too* and *Enough* + Infinitive
- Infinitives of Purpose

Vocabulary

CD 3 TRACK **18** **Match the sentences with the pictures. Then listen and check your answers.**

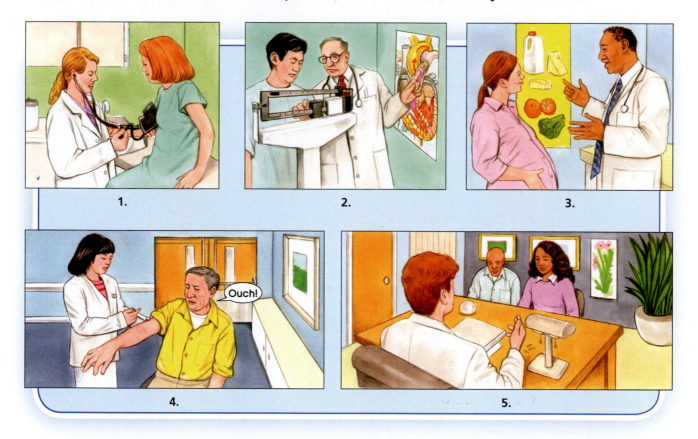

1.   2.   3.

4.   Ouch!   5.

_____ **a.** "You **gained** 15 pounds in six months. You also have **high cholesterol**. You must go on a diet and lose weight, at least 25 pounds."

_____ **b.** "Your **blood pressure** used to be low, but now it's a little high. That's **common** for people your age. You need to **get in shape**. Exercise more."

_____ **c.** "After your grandfather **has surgery**, he's going to be very **weak**. He won't be able to do things for himself, so he'll need your help."

_____ **d.** "Most people hate to **get shots**. They're painful."

_____ **e.** "You and the baby need **vitamin C**. Eat oranges or drink orange juice. You also need **calcium**. Drink milk every day and eat yogurt. You can also take calcium pills, but don't take more than 500 mg. at one time. 1,000 mg. pills are too **strong**."

Listening

A  CD 3 TRACK 19 **Listen. What is Mr. Harris's problem? Check (✓) the correct answer.**

> **Look**
>
> normal = usual, not special

❏ **1.** He is normal for his age.

❏ **2.** His blood pressure is high.

❏ **3.** He goes on too many diets.

❏ **4.** He works two jobs.

❏ **5.** He's very young.

B CD 3 TRACK 20 **Listen again. For each pair of sentences, check (✓) the sentence that you hear.**

1. ❏ **a.** It's unhealthy to go on a diet.

   ❏ **b.** It's healthy to go on a diet.

2. ❏ **a.** You need to eat less and exercise more.

   ❏ **b.** You don't need to eat less and exercise more.

3. ❏ **a.** You're not old enough to make these changes.

   ❏ **b.** You're not too old to make these changes.

4. ❏ **a.** I'm too busy to exercise.

   ❏ **b.** I'm too lazy to exercise.

5. ❏ **a.** I don't have enough time to cook every day.

   ❏ **b.** I don't have enough time to cook today.

6. ❏ **a.** It's easy to do, I think.

   ❏ **b.** It's easier to do than you think.

C CD 3 TRACK 21 **Listen again. Answer the questions. Write complete sentences.**

1. What advice does the doctor give to Mr. Harris?

   _____

2. How does Mr. Harris feel about the doctor's advice?

   _____

3. Do you think that Mr. Harris will follow the doctor's advice? Explain why or why not.

   _____

Grammar to Communicate ❶

IT + INFINITIVE					
Subject	Be	Adjective		Infinitive	
It	is	necessary		to finish	all the medicine

Subject	Be	Adjective	For (someone)	Infinitive	
It	is	important	for patients	to follow	their doctor's advice.

> **Look**
> An infinitive is *to* + a verb. Use an infinitive after *It* + a form of *be* + certain adjectives.

A Underline the infinitives.

1. It's important <u>to brush</u> your teeth after every meal.
2. It's important for you to get a flu shot.
3. It's unusual for a child to have high blood pressure.
4. It's normal to be nervous before surgery.
5. It's important to go to the dentist for a cleaning every six months.
6. It can be dangerous to drive after you take this medicine.

get a cleaning

B **22** Read the conversations. Rewrite B's response with *for*. Then listen and check your answers.

CPR

1. **A:** If I get the job, do I need to take a course in CPR?

   B: Yes. It is necessary to know CPR.

   <u>Yes, it's necessary for all employees to know CPR.</u>
   (all employees)

2. **A:** My dad hasn't been to your office in a year. Should he make an appointment?

   B: Yes. It's important to check his cholesterol once a year.

   _____
   (me)

3. **A:** Should I go on a diet?

   B: Yes, it's necessary to lose weight.

   _____
   (you)

4. **A:** Should he have the surgery soon?

   B: Yes, it's important to have it as quickly as possible.

   _____
   (him)

5. **A:** Should I keep my children home from school?

   B: Yes, it's important to stay away from other children.

   _____
   (them)

228   Unit 17

C **Write sentences. Use a phrase from the box where necessary.**

for babies	for elderly people	for teenagers

1. <u>It is difficult for elderly people to climb stairs.</u>
   (difficult / climb stairs)

2. <u>It is unhealthy to smoke.</u>
   (unhealthy / smoke)

3. _____
   (not healthy / eat a lot of sweets)

4. _____
   (important / get enough exercise)

5. _____
   (important / see the doctor every three months)

6. _____
   (common / take several different pills every day)

7. _____
   (normal / need to eat less)

8. _____
   (good / play sports for exercise)

9. _____
   (normal / spend time with their friends)

PAIRS. **What do you do to stay healthy? What is easy, difficult, and impossible for you to do? Explain your answers. Use the words in the box and your own ideas.**

avoid junk food	gain weight	get enough sleep
eat three healthy meals a day	get a cleaning every six months	lose weight
exercise every day	get a physical once a year	

Example:

A: *It's really difficult for me to exercise every day. I'm so busy.*

B: *I agree. In fact, I think it's impossible for most people to exercise every day.*

Grammar to Communicate 2

TOO AND ENOUGH + INFINITIVE

Too + Adjective	Too + Adjective + Infinitive
Your son is **too weak**. [He can't leave the hospital.]	Your son is **too weak to leave** the hospital.
	Too + Adjective + For (Someone) + Infinitive
Your son is **too weak**. [You can't take him home.]	Your son is **too weak for you to take** him home.

Adjective + Enough	Adjective + Enough + Infinitive
Your son isn't **strong enough**. [He can't leave the hospital.]	Your son isn't **strong enough to leave** the hospital.
	Adjective + Enough + For (Someone) + Infinitive
Your son isn't **strong enough**. [You can't take him home.]	Your son isn't **strong enough for you to take** him home.

A   **Circle the correct words.**

1. The hearing aid isn't **too comfortable** / (**comfortable enough**) for him to use.
2. It's **too painful** / **painful enough** to stand up.
3. The pharmacist is **too busy** / **busy enough** to talk.
4. She isn't **too strong** / **strong enough** to leave the hospital.
5. The baby is **too young** / **young enough** to take adult aspirin.

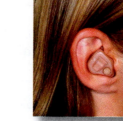

hearing aid

B   **Rewrite the sentences with _too_.**

1. The patient isn't comfortable enough.   _The patient is too uncomfortable._
2. These glasses aren't strong enough.   _too weak._
3. The nurse isn't fast enough.   _is too slow._
4. The hearing aid isn't small enough.   _is too big._
5. The hospital isn't modern enough.   _is too old._

Now rewrite these sentences with _enough_.

6. The patient is too nervous.   _The patient isn't relaxed enough._
7. Your blood pressure is too high.   _isn't low enough_
8. These pills are too big.   _aren't small "_
9. The letters on the bottle are too small.   _aren't big "_
10. The man is too unhealthy.   _isn't healthy "_

C Combine the sentences with *for*. Use *too* or *enough*.

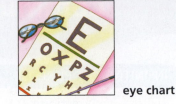
eye chart

1. I can't read the letters in the eye chart. They are too small.
   The letters in the eye chart are too small for me to read.

2. Children can't take this medicine. It's too strong.
   _____

3. You can't go out and play. Your fever is too high.
   _____

4. You can't use that Band-Aid. It's too small.
   _____

5. I can't stay on a diet. It's too hard.
   _____

6. My mother can't take a walk with me. It isn't warm enough.
   _____

D Complete the sentences. Use *too* or *very*.

1. You should see Dr. Norton. He's a ___*very*___ good doctor.

2. My mother's _____ old, but she is still able to live by herself.

3. You're _____ thin. You must gain weight.

4. I couldn't see the dentist yesterday. She was _____ busy to talk to me.

5. They can't be doctors. They're _____ young.

6. I'm upset because Dr. Tran moved. Her office is _____ far away now.

7. I'm _____ tired, but I'll help you.

8. He's _____ weak to walk home. You should call him a cab.

> **Look**
>
> *Too* has a negative meaning. *Very* makes an adjective stronger.
> I'm **too tired**. I can't drive.
> I'm **very tired**, but I can drive.

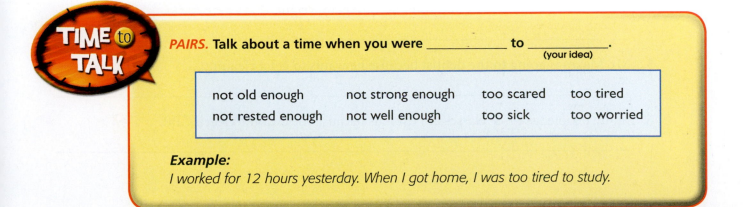

TIME to TALK

PAIRS. Talk about a time when you were _____ to _____.
(your idea)

| not old enough | not strong enough | too scared | too tired |
| not rested enough | not well enough | too sick | too worried |

Example:
I worked for 12 hours yesterday. When I got home, I was too tired to study.

Grammar to Communicate 3

INFINITIVES OF PURPOSE	
Questions	Answers
Why do people go to drugstores?	**To pick up** their medicine.
Why is he going to the drugstore?	He's going to the drugstore **to pick up** his medicine.

A Match the questions and answers.

__d__ 1. Why do people go on diets?

_____ 2. Why do people wear glasses?

_____ 3. Why do people perform CPR?

_____ 4. Why do people wear hearing aids?

_____ 5. Why do people talk to a pharmacist?

_____ 6. Why do people go to emergency rooms?

_____ 7. Why do people get shots?

a. To protect them from diseases.

b. To save a person's life.

c. To get help right away.

d. To lose weight.

e. To see better.

f. To get information about medicines.

g. To hear better.

B Rewrite the sentences. Use *to* + verb.

1. I take vitamins because I want to stay healthy.

   _I take vitamins to stay healthy._____

2. My husband takes pills because he wants to lower his cholesterol.

   _____

3. Anita is swimming four days a week because she wants to get in shape.

   _____

4. I'm drinking a lot of milk because I need to gain weight.

   _____

5. Mr. Maxes is going to the dentist because he wants to get a cleaning.

   _____

6. Many people take free classes at hospitals because they want to learn CPR.

   _____

C   *PAIRS.* Complete the list of Healthy Tips for Children. Use the words in the box and *to*. Some sentences may have more than one correct answer.

be ready to learn	have strong bones	protect your skin
~~get in shape~~	prevent colds	stop germs
have energy during the day	prevent tooth decay	

Healthy Tips for Children

- Exercise every day
  to stay in shape

- Brush your teeth
  _____

- Get plenty of calcium
  _____

- Wash your hands often
  _____

- Wear sunscreen
  _____

- Sleep 10 hours a night
  _____

- Eat a good breakfast
  _____

- Get enough vitamin C
  _____

TIME to TALK

PAIRS. Write a brochure about health for one of the groups in the box. Use the brochure in Exercise C as a model.

babies	middle-aged men	pregnant women
the elderly	middle-aged women	teenagers

Example: *Middle-aged women: Take calcium to make your bones stronger.*

Health   **233**

Grammar

23 Correct the mistake in each conversation. Then listen and check your answers.

1. **A:** You're ~~very~~ *too* sick to go to work.

    B: But I have to go! I have a very important meeting.

2. **A:** Does he need surgery?

    B: No, the problem's for him not serious enough to have surgery.

3. **A:** The doctor's too busy for seeing you today.

    B: But I have an appointment!

4. **A:** What do you take when you have a cold?

    B: Sweet Night. It's too good. It helps me sleep.

5. **A:** Where are you going?

    B: I'm going downtown for to see the doctor. I have an appointment.

Dictation

24 Listen. You will hear five sentences. Write them in your notebook.

Speaking

PAIRS. Look at the pictures. Why do doctors use these things? Make a sentence for each picture. Use the verbs in the box.

give	listen to	protect	take	weigh

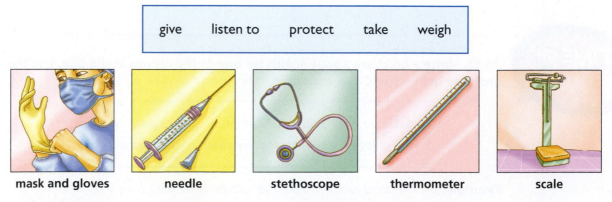

mask and gloves needle stethoscope thermometer scale

Example: *Doctors wear gloves and masks to protect themselves and their patients from germs.*

Listening

A *CD 3 TRACK 25* **Listen to the interview. Check (✓) the questions that the doctor answers.**

❏ 1. What are the secrets to a healthy life?

❏ 2. Which countries in the world have healthy diets?

❏ 3. Who eats more vegetables and fruit: new immigrants or people born in the United States?

❏ 4. Why is fast food unhealthy?

❏ 5. Where can people find out what is in their food?

❏ 6. How much sugar should we eat a day?

❏ 7. How much salt should we eat a day?

❏ 8. How much fat should we eat a day?

❏ 9. How much exercise do most people need to stay healthy?

❏ 10. Which fast-food restaurants serve the healthiest food?

Nutrition Facts
Serving Size 4.5oz (126g/about 1/2 cup
pasta and 1/4 cup cheese sauce)
Makes about 1 cup Prepared
Servings Per Container about 2.5

Amount Per Serving

Calories 400   Calories from Fat 130

	% Daily Value*
Total Fat 14g	22%
Saturated Fat 6g	30%
Trans Fat 3g	
Cholesterol 30mg	9%
Sodium 1110mg	46%
Total Carbohydrate 51g	17%
Dietary Fiber 2g	9%
Sugars 5g	
Protein 15g	

Vitamin A   6%   •   Vitamin C 0%
Calcium   20%   •   Iron   10%

* Percent Daily Values are based on a 2,000
calorie diet. Your daily values may be higher
or lower depending on your calorie needs:

	Calories:	2,000	2,500
Total Fat	Less than	65g	80g
Sat Fat	Less than	20g	25g
Cholesterol	Less than	300mg	300mg
Sodium	Less than	2,400mg	2,400mg
Potassium	Less than	3,500mg	3,500mg
Total Carbohydrate		300g	375g
Dietary Fiber		25g	30g

Calories per gram:
Fat 9   •   Carbohydrate 4   •   Protein 4

B *CD 3 TRACK 25* **Listen again. Answer the questions that you checked in Exercise A.**

_____

_____

_____

_____

_____

_____

_____

TIME to TALK

GROUPS. **Discuss the questions.**

1. Compare what you eat now to what other people your age probably eat in your country. Who has the healthier diet?

2. What kinds of food have a lot of vitamin C?

3. What kinds of food have a lot of calcium?

4. What kinds of food have a lot of protein?

5. What kinds of food are bad to eat if you have heart disease?

Example: I eat a lot of meat and rice. People in my country eat more vegetables. It is unhealthy to eat too much meat, so I am going to try to change my diet.

Reading

Getting Ready to Read

Check (✓) *T* (true) or *F* (false) for each statement.

QUIZ: Things My Mother Taught Me

1. ■T ■F It is dangerous to go swimming right after you eat.
2. ■T ■F It is not good to sit too close to the television.
3. ■T ■F To improve your eyesight, eat a lot of carrots.
4. ■T ■F To avoid colds, never go outside with wet hair.
5. ■T ■F To get over a cold, eat mom's chicken soup.

Reading

Read the article with the answers to the quiz. Then check your answers in Getting Ready to Read.

Answers to this month's quiz

IT IS DANGEROUS TO GO SWIMMING RIGHT AFTER YOU EAT.
False. There is no proof that swimming with a full stomach is more dangerous than swimming at any other time. In fact, there is no **evidence** that anyone has ever drowned because he or she went swimming after eating.

IT IS NOT GOOD TO SIT TOO CLOSE TO THE TELEVISION.
False. It might make your eyes tired, but it doesn't **harm** them because it doesn't cause any permanent damage to your eyesight. It is not good for children to watch too much television, although the distance from the television set is not the problem. The problem is the amount of time children spend watching TV when they should be doing healthier activities such as riding their bikes or playing a sport.

TO IMPROVE YOUR EYESIGHT, EAT A LOT OF CARROTS.
False. Carrots, like all vegetables, are very good for your health, so Mom was right to tell you to eat them. However, no matter how many you eat, they will not improve your ability to see.

TO AVOID COLDS, NEVER GO OUTSIDE WITH WET HAIR.
False. We catch colds from viruses, not from the cold air. If you go outside with wet hair, you might feel cold and uncomfortable, but you won't catch a cold from it. To avoid colds, wash your hands frequently, and stay away from people who are coughing and sneezing.

TO GET OVER A COLD, EAT MOM'S CHICKEN SOUP.
True...sort of. To get over a cold, it helps to drink a lot of liquids, so chicken soup (or anything else that contains a lot of water) is good for you. And since there is strong evidence that people who feel loved recover faster from an illness, homemade soup from your Mom might be just what the doctor ordered!

After You Read

A   Look at the **boldface** words in the article. Find a synonym in the same paragraph. Write the synonyms next to the words below. Be careful. You might need to write more than one word.

Reading Skill:
Recognizing Synonyms

Synonyms are words that have similar meanings, such as *large* and *big*. When you read, look for words or expressions with similar meanings. This will help you understand the writer's main point.

1. evidence

   _____

2. harm

   _____

3. eyesight

   _____

4. avoid

   _____

5. get over

   _____

B   Read the article again. Complete the sentences.

1. Quiz answer 1: It is safe to _____.

2. Quiz answer 2: It is not harmful for children to _____. However, it isn't good for children to _____.

3. Quiz answer 3: It is healthy to _____. However, it doesn't _____.

4. Quiz answer 4: It is not dangerous to _____.

   To _____ a cold, it is important to _____ and _____.

5. Quiz answer 5: To _____ a cold faster, you should _____.

Writing

Getting Ready to Write

A Write as many synonyms for each word as you can. Use a dictionary or a thesaurus (a dictionary that gives synonyms) if you need help.

1. believe = _____ *think, guess* _____

2. sleep = _____

3. important = _____

4. eat = _____

5. exercise = _____

6. safe = _____

7. sick = _____

8. healthy = _____

9. fat = _____

10. thin = _____

> **Writing Tip**
>
> Use synonyms to make your writing more interesting.
>
> Example:
>
> To **avoid** colds, ~~avoid~~ *stay away from* people who are coughing and sneezing.

B Read the model paragraph.

> Many people believe that you should eat most of your food in the morning or afternoon. They claim that if you eat late at night, the food will turn to fat, and you will gain weight. This is not true. Your body does not shut down when you go to sleep. It is important to give your body food so that it keeps working while you rest. However, it is essential to avoid eating junk food. To stay thin, you should eat healthy food, like vegetables, late at night — or at any time of day! And, of course, you should exercise regularly. Experts say that you should try to work out for at least an hour, three or four times a week.

PAIRS. Read the model again. Were you surprised by what was true and what wasn't true?

Now, choose a health myth from your country (something people think is true but is actually false). Talk about what people believe.

Prewriting: Using a Cluster

You are going to write a paragraph about a common health myth in your country. Before you write, look at the cluster for the writing model. Then complete a new cluster to get ideas for your writing. Write any ideas you can think of about your topic.

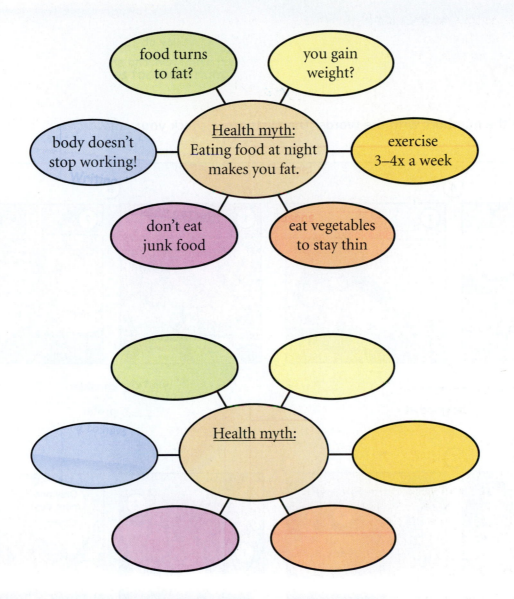

Writing

Now write a paragraph about a common health myth in your country. The writing tip, the model paragraph, and your notes will help you. Write in your notebook.

Unit 18
Free Time

Grammar
- Gerunds as Subjects
- Gerunds as Objects of Prepositions
- Gerunds or Infinitives as Objects of Verbs

Vocabulary

CD 3 TRACK **26** Match the numbers with the words. Then listen and check your answers.

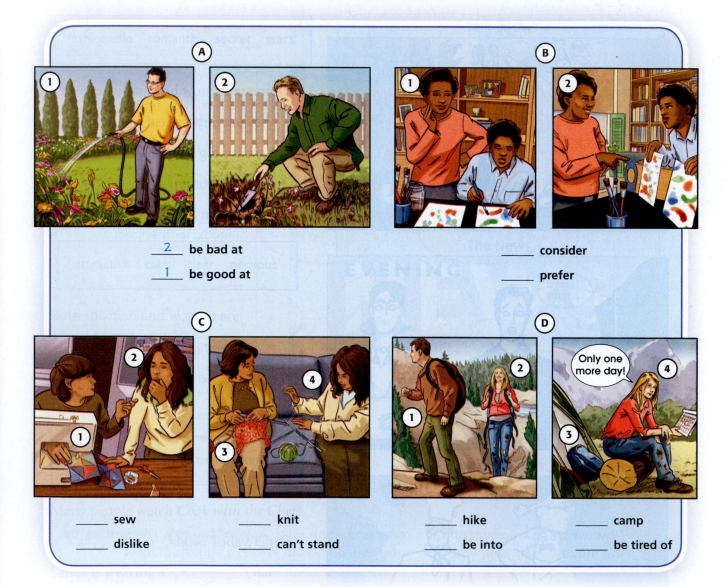

| ___2 | be bad at | ___ | consider |
| ___1 | be good at | ___ | prefer |

| ___ | sew | ___ | knit | ___ | hike | ___ | camp |
| ___ | dislike | ___ | can't stand | ___ | be into | ___ | be tired of |

240   Unit 18

Listening

A 🎵 CD 3 TRACK **27** **Listen. Arinaldo is talking to his friend Mei. Check (✓) the things that Arinaldo is interested in learning.**

❏ how to teach art   ❏ how to draw   ❏ how to paint

❏ how to play the guitar   ❏ how to play the piano   ❏ how to read music

B 🎵 CD 3 TRACK **28** **Listen again. For each pair of sentences, check (✓) the sentence that you hear.**

1. ☑ **a.** I'm tired of just playing computer games and going to the mall.

   ❏ **b.** I'm tired and just play computer games and go to the mall.

2. ❏ **a.** I'm taking some classes.

   ☑ **b.** I'm considering taking some classes.

3. ☑ **a.** Drawing's okay, but I prefer painting.

   ❏ **b.** Drawing pictures is okay, but it's more fun to paint.

4. ❏ **a.** I started drawing when I was little.

   ☑ **b.** I started to draw when I was little.

5. ☑ **a.** I started studying painting there last year.

   ❏ **b.** I started to study painting there last year.

6. ❏ **a.** I'm also thinking about playing the guitar.

   ☑ **b.** I'm also thinking about learning to play the guitar.

C 🎵 CD 3 TRACK **29** **Listen again. Answer the questions. Write complete sentences.**

1. What does Arinaldo usually do in his free time?

   _____

2. Why does Arinaldo want to try something new?

   _____

3. Where does Mei take classes?

   _____

4. What advice does Mei give Arinaldo?

   _____

Free Time **241**

Grammar to Communicate 1

GERUNDS AS SUBJECTS		
Gerund (Subject)	Verb	
Watching TV	is	fun.
Playing cards	isn't	

Look

Verbs in the progressive form end in *–ing*, but they are not gerunds.

I'm knitting a hat for my son. (verb)
Knitting is a fun hobby. (gerund)

A Circle the gerunds.

chair

1. My husband is hiking this weekend. (Hiking) is good for him.

2. Doing crossword puzzles is fun. I've been doing a lot of them lately.

3. I've been singing with a chorus for years. Singing relaxes me.

4. We aren't going on vacation this year. Going on vacation costs a lot of money.

5. Next year, I'm going to swim more. Swimming helps people lose weight.

6. Drawing takes a lot of practice. I've been drawing for years, but I'm not very good.

B Rewrite the sentences. Begin each sentence with a gerund.

1. It takes me a long time to do crossword puzzles.
   Doing crossword puzzles takes me a long time.

crossword puzzle

2. It isn't easy to play the piano.
   _____

3. It is sometimes dangerous to ride horses.
   _____

4. It is expensive to take tennis lessons.
   _____

chess

5. It is fun to play chess.
   _____

6. It takes practice to be a good chess player.
   _____

7. It is sometimes scary to hike alone.
   _____

chorus

8. It takes a lot of work to be in a chorus.
   _____

C Answer the questions. Begin each sentence with *I think*.

1. Which is better for your health: swimming or running?

   I think swimming is better. OR *I think running is better.*

2. Which is more dangerous: riding a horse or hiking?

   _____

3. Which is less expensive: fishing or playing tennis?

   _____

4. Which is harder: knitting or sewing?

   _____

5. Which takes more practice: singing in a chorus or playing a musical instrument?

   _____

6. Which is more important for most boys: being a good dancer or being good at sports?

   _____

D Write sentences with the words in the boxes. Use gerunds.

bake	knit	bad for you	fun
camp	play computer games	boring	good for you
draw	ride a bike	dangerous	popular
fish	ride a horse	difficult	relaxing
hike	sew	easy	scary

1. *Camping is often fun, but sometimes there are mosquitoes.*

2. _____

3. _____

4. _____

5. _____

6. _____

GROUPS. **Make a list of several activities. Describe an activity on your list to a different group. The other group tries to guess what the activity is. Take turns.**

Example:
A: *Learning this is difficult and takes practice.*   C: *Playing the piano?*
B: *Playing chess?*   A: *That's right.*
A: *No. Lessons are very expensive.*

Grammar to Communicate 2

GERUNDS AS OBJECTS OF PREPOSITIONS

Subject	*Be* + Adjective + Preposition	Gerund	Subject	Verb + Preposition	Gerund
She	**is good at**	**baking.**	He	**is into**	**fishing.**
We	**are interested in**	**going.**	They	**thought about**	**joining.**

Look

concentrate on = give most of your attention to one thing

dream of = think about something that you want to happen

feel like = want to have or want to do

give up = quit

look forward to = be excited about something that is going to happen

take up = begin doing a job or activity

 A   Match the beginnings and endings of the sentences.

__c__ 1. I'm dreaming   a. like going swimming.

____ 2. I'm looking forward   b. up knitting.

____ 3. I'm getting old. I am giving   c. of being the best chess player in history.

____ 4. I'm concentrating   d. on winning.

____ 5. I'm hot. I feel   e. up hiking.

____ 6. I'm going to take   f. to being in the chorus.

____ 7. I'm   g. into cooking.

Look

See page 299 for a list of verbs + prepositions + gerunds.

B   Write true sentences about yourself. Add *not* where necessary.

1. __I'm interested in learning new things. OR I'm not interested in learning new things.__
   (I / interested in / learn / new things)

2. _____
   (I / good at / make / things with my hands)

3. _____
   (I / tired of / learn English)

4. _____
   (I / scared of / be / alone in the water)

5. _____
   (I / excited about / go / on vacation)

C Combine the sentences. Take out or change words where necessary.

1. I want to be the star of the team. I dream of it.
   I dream of being the star of the team.

2. We might try out for the chorus. We talked about it.
   _____
   _____

3. I joined a new team. I'm excited about it.
   _____

4. I might take up chess. I'm thinking about it.
   _____

5. We're going to play next week. I'm looking forward to it.
   _____

6. They finished the crossword puzzle. They concentrated on it.
   _____

7. He cooked last night. He felt like it.
   _____

TIME to TALK

GROUPS. Discuss the questions.

1. What kinds of things are difficult for you to concentrate on?

2. What do you feel like doing after class today? Are you going to do it?

3. Have you ever given anything up? If so, what have you given up? When did you give it up? Why?

4. Have you taken anything up in the past few years? What have you taken up? Are you happy that you took it up?

5. Are you looking forward to anything these days? If so, what?

6. What did you dream of doing when you were young?

Example:
A: *What kinds of things are difficult for you to concentrate on?*
B: *It is difficult for me to concentrate on studying. I have two kids, and they are very noisy.*

Grammar to Communicate 3

GERUNDS OR INFINITIVES AS OBJECTS OF VERBS		

Verb + Gerund		Verb + Infinitive		Verb + Gerund OR Infinitive	
I **considered** She **finished** We **stopped**	playing.	I've **decided** We **want** They **expect**	to play.	I **can't stand** You **prefer** They **started**	playing. to play.

Look

Some verbs can be followed only by a gerund, some only by an infinitive, and some by either a gerund or an infinitive.

A Change the names to make true sentences about people you know, or write *Nobody I know*.

My mother   Nobody I know

Example: <u>My nephew Jack</u> loves reading. OR <u>My nephew Jack</u> loves reading.

1. <u>My nephew Jack</u> loves reading.
2. <u>My friend Lynn</u> loves to sing.
3. <u>My mother</u> enjoys knitting.
4. <u>My father</u> likes to fish.
5. <u>My friend Ari</u> likes listening to music.
6. <u>My brother</u> misses being on a team.

7. <u>My friend Bob</u> dislikes going for walks.
8. <u>My sister</u> is learning to play the guitar.
9. <u>My niece</u> hopes to become a writer.
10. <u>My sister-in-law</u> hates to watch TV.
11. <u>My husband</u> hates dancing.

PAIRS. Tell each other your sentences.

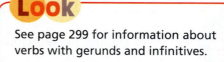

Look

See page 299 for information about verbs with gerunds and infinitives.

B Check (✓) what comes after each verb: gerund, infinitive, or either (gerund or infinitive). Look at the sentences on this page for help.

VERB +	GERUND	INFINITIVE	GERUND OR INFINITIVE
can't stand			✓
consider	✓		
decide		✓	
dislike			
enjoy			
expect			
finish			
hate			
hope			

VERB +	GERUND	INFINITIVE	GERUND OR INFINITIVE
learn			
like			
love			
miss			
prefer			
start			
stop			
want			

C Complete the sentences. Use the infinitive or gerund. Sometimes both the gerund and the infinitive are correct.

1. I like ____being____ with friends. I don't like ____to be____ alone. (be)
2. I love _____ for long walks, but I dislike _____ alone. (go)
3. I dislike _____ in a pool. I prefer _____ in the ocean. (swim)
4. I finished _____ one puzzle, so I started _____ a new one. (do)
5. My husband always wants _____ out, but I prefer _____ at home. (eat)
6. I miss _____. I want _____ with a chorus. (sing)
7. I can't stand _____ chess, but I enjoy _____ computer games. (play)
8. I don't like _____. I stopped _____ when I sold my house. (garden)
9. I love _____. I want _____ well. (draw)
10. I considered _____ art classes, but I decided _____ sewing classes. (take)

PAIRS. Now change the verbs above to infinitives or gerunds where possible.

Example: *I like to be with friends. I don't like being alone.*

TIME to TALK

GROUPS. Talk about your past. Use the words in the boxes. How many of you had the same interests and hobbies?

Example:
A: *When I was little, I hated to play with dolls.*
B: *Really? I loved playing with my dolls.*

doll

When I was little . . .	decided	be alone.
When I was ten . . .	disliked	become a(n) _____.
When I was a teenager . . .	enjoyed	cook.
When I graduated from high school . . .	hated	draw.
When I got married . . .	hoped	exercise.
When I moved to the United States . . .	learned	fish.
When my first child was born . . .	liked	have a dog.
	loved	play the guitar/piano.
	started	play with dolls.
	stopped	ride horses.
	wanted	talk on the telephone.

WRAP UP. Report to the class. Which group has the most similarities?

Review and Challenge

Grammar

CD 3 TRACK 30 Correct the advertisement. There are seven mistakes. The first mistake is corrected for you. Then listen and check your answers.

BAY AREA HIKING CLUB

Do you feel like ~~to do~~ *doing* something new? Are you tired of be in the office all the time? Are you interested in spend time with fun people? Then hike is the answer for you. Being in the fresh air and see all the beautiful flowers and trees will make you feel wonderful. You don't need to be an experienced hiker. You just have to enjoy to go for long walks. If you want getting more information about our group, call (777) 555-3476. Great experiences are waiting for you.

Dictation

CD 3 TRACK 31 Listen. You will hear five sentences. Write them in your notebook.

Speaking

GROUPS. Talk about what you like (and don't like) to do in your free time. Use all the words in the box at least once.

be good at	be terrible at	can't stand	enjoy	look forward to
be into	be tired of	dislike	hate	love

WRAP UP. Now tell the class about the people in your group.

Unit 18

Listening

Look

conduct a poll = ask many people what they think about something

A CD 3 TRACK 32 **Listen to the report about free time in the U.S. Check (✓) the topics that the reporter discusses.**

❏ how adults spend their free time   ❏ how children spend their free time

❏ the most popular activities   ❏ the least popular activities

❏ how many hours a week people work   ❏ how much free time people have every week

❏ changes since 1995   ❏ why people have very little free time

B CD 3 TRACK 32 **Listen again. Complete the chart.**

bowling

Source: Harris Interactive Poll, 2004

Favorite Free-Time Activities

Activity	2004	1995
reading	35%	28%
watching TV	21%	25%
spending time with family	20%	____
going to the movies	10%	8%
_____	8%	10%
using a computer	7%	____
gardening	____	9%
walking	6%	5%
renting movies	____	8%
playing team sports	5%	____
sewing	4%	7%
swimming	2%	____
playing tennis	1%	2%
horseback riding	1%	2%
_____	1%	2%
dancing	1%	1%
bowling	1%	4%

TIME to TALK

GROUPS. **Discuss the questions.**

1. What is the most interesting thing that you learned about free time in the U.S.? What is the most surprising thing? Which information is the same as you expected it to be?

2. How are free-time activities in your country different from those in the U.S.?

Reading

Getting Ready to Read

Preview the article. Read the first and last sentences of each paragraph. Then write questions that you think the article will answer.

1. _____Who were the first surfers?_____

2. _____

3. _____

Reading

Read the article. Then check your questions in Getting Ready to Read. Can you answer them now?

When most people hear the word *surfing,* they think of modern California teenagers in the ocean. However, surfing actually started in Hawaii **centuries** ago. No one knows exactly when Hawaiians began to surf. In 1778, James King, a British **explorer,** saw Hawaiians riding the waves. He wrote about *he'e nalu,* the Hawaiian word for surfing. King was **amazed** by the skill of the surfers. At that time, many people in England couldn't even swim.

Surfing was an important part of early Hawaiian **society.** In Hawaii, a system of laws called Kapu **ruled** everything— including surfing. For example, Hawaiian kings and queens and other members of the **royal family** had their own beaches. Other Hawaiians could never swim on those beaches. The royal family also had longer and heavier boards. The surfboard was a symbol: it showed the owner's **status** in the society.

In 1820, Christian missionaries from the U.S. arrived in Hawaii. They believed that surfing was a waste of time and tried to stop people from doing it. As a result, surfing almost **disappeared.** However, in the early 20th century, a Hawaiian teenager named Duke Paoa Kahanamoku made surfing popular again. Duke was a wonderful surfer and swimmer. He competed in the 1912 Olympics and won almost every medal in water sports. After the Olympics, Duke used his **fame** to promote both Hawaii and the **ancient** sport of surfing all over the world.

statue of Duke Kahanamoku
on Waikiki Beach

After You Read

A Look at the **boldface** words in the article. Guess their meaning. Then match the words with the correct definitions.

_g_	**1.** centuries	**a.**	had power over a country and people
____	**2.** explorer	**b.**	very, very old
____	**3.** amazed	**c.**	did not exist anymore
____	**4.** society	**d.**	very surprised
____	**5.** ruled	**e.**	the state of being known about by a lot of people
____	**6.** royal family	**f.**	a king or queen and his or her relatives
____	**7.** status	**g.**	hundreds of years
____	**8.** disappeared	**h.**	how important a person is compared to others
____	**9.** fame	**i.**	someone who travels to a place where other people have never been before
____	**10.** ancient	**j.**	a group of people who live together and have the same laws

B Read the article again. Then check (✓) the inferences that you can make from the information in the text.

> **Reading Skill: Making Inferences**
>
> An **inference** is a logical conclusion based on information. Often, writers do not say all of their ideas directly. They expect the reader to make inferences, or guesses, based on the information in the text.

❏ **1.** Under the Kapu laws, only men were allowed to surf.

❏ **2.** The members of the Hawaiian royal family were often excellent surfers.

❏ **3.** Duke Paoa Kahanamoku was a member of the Hawaiian royal family.

❏ **4.** Duke Paoa Kahanamoku only surfed in Hawaii.

❏ **5.** Duke Paoa Kahanamoku is a hero for many Hawaiians.

Writing

Writing Tip

When you write a paragraph, make sure that the ideas are in a logical order. Think about what the reader needs to know first, second, ... and last. Start with the main idea, follow with supporting points, and end with a concluding sentence.

Getting Ready to Write

A   **Number the sentences in logical order for a paragraph.**

_____ **a.** Every year, sharks attack at least a few surfers.

_____ **b.** And even for the best surfers, there is a high risk of broken bones and head injuries.

_____ **c.** First of all, you need to be a strong swimmer and have excellent balance.

__1__ **d.** Surfing is a difficult and dangerous sport.

_____ **e.** To sum up, before you take up surfing, you should know the difficulties and risks.

_____ **f.** You also need patience, because becoming a surfer takes years.

_____ **g.** Shark attacks are a final danger.

Now copy the sentences in the correct order to complete the paragraph.

Surfing is a difficult and dangerous sport. _____

_____

_____

_____

_____

_____

B   **Read the model paragraph.**

> Mountain climbing is an exciting sport. Mountain climbers have to be strong and healthy. Knowing how to use equipment such as ropes is also important. Serious climbers usually spend years training. But even for well-trained climbers, climbing the highest mountains—for example Mount Everest—is extremely dangerous. The air has very little oxygen, so breathing is difficult. And when your brain doesn't get enough oxygen, thinking clearly is impossible, and you could easily get lost. To sum up, mountain climbing is an exciting, but serious, sport.

PAIRS. Read the model again. Do you think mountain climbing is an exciting free-time activity? Would you like to do it? Why or why not?

Now choose another free-time activity. Talk to your partner about why it is exciting, interesting, or fun.

Prewriting: Using an Outline

You are going to write a paragraph about a free-time activity. Before you write, look at the outline for the model paragraph. Then complete your own outline.

Writing Model

Main idea: Mountain climbing is an exciting sport.
1. (supporting detail) must be strong, healthy
2. (supporting detail) know how to use equipment
3. (supporting detail) need years of training
4. (supporting detail) breathing difficult
5. (supporting detail) not enough oxygen = confusion; get lost
Concluding sentence = To sum up, mountain climbing is an exciting, but serious, sport.

Main idea: _____

_____

1. (supporting detail) _____

2. (supporting detail) _____

3. (supporting detail) _____

4. (supporting detail) _____

5. (supporting detail) _____

Concluding sentence = _____

_____

Writing

Now write a paragraph about a free-time activity. The writing tip, the model paragraph, and your notes will help you. Write in your notebook.

Grammar
● Verb + Object + Infinitive
● Verb + Noun Clause and Replacing Noun Clauses
● *Make* and *Let*

Vocabulary

CD 3 TRACK 33 Complete the sentences with the words in the box. Listen and check your answers.

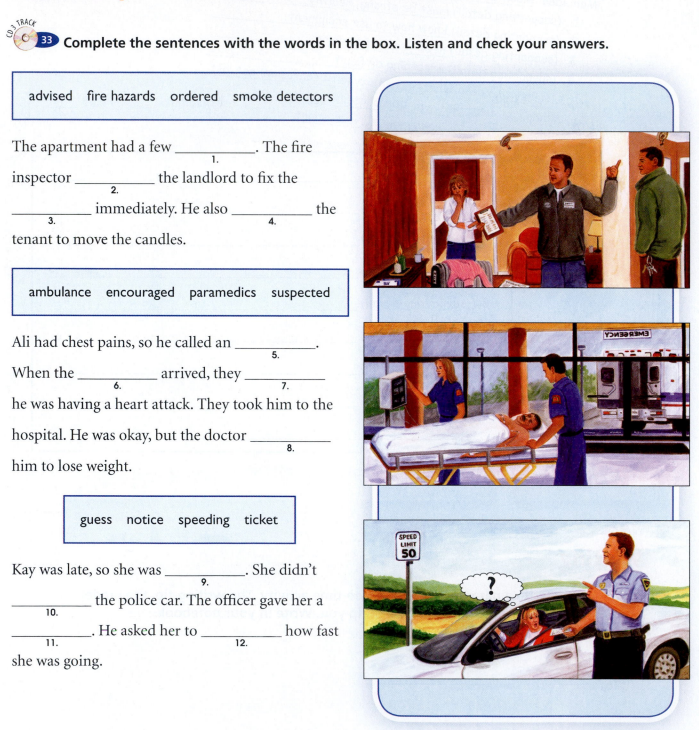

---

advised   fire hazards   ordered   smoke detectors

The apartment had a few _____. The fire
1.
inspector _____ the landlord to fix the
2.
_____ immediately. He also _____ the
3.   4.
tenant to move the candles.

---

ambulance   encouraged   paramedics   suspected

Ali had chest pains, so he called an _____.
5.
When the _____ arrived, they _____
6.   7.
he was having a heart attack. They took him to the
hospital. He was okay, but the doctor _____
8.
him to lose weight.

---

guess   notice   speeding   ticket

Kay was late, so she was _____. She didn't
9.
_____ the police car. The officer gave her a
10.
_____. He asked her to _____ how fast
11.   12.
she was going.

254   Unit 19

Listening

A 🔘 **34** **Listen. What just happened to the woman? Check (✓) the correct answer.**

❏ 1. A man stole her bag and ring when she was at a store.
❏ 2. A man stopped the woman on the street, stole her bag and ring, and drove away.
❏ 3. The woman was walking to the store when a man stole her bag and ring.
❏ 4. The woman was walking home when a man stole her bag and ring and ran away.

B 🔘 **34** **Listen again. Check (✓) the sentences that are true.**

❏ 1. The man made the woman take off her wedding ring.
❏ 2. The man let the woman go.
❏ 3. The woman believes that the man was wearing jeans.
❏ 4. The woman doesn't think that the man has a beard.
❏ 5. The operator told the woman to go to the police station.
❏ 6. The operator expects the woman to wait at the store.
❏ 7. The woman doesn't know if she will get her wedding ring back, but she hopes so.

Look

expect = think that
something will happen

C 🔘 **34** **Listen again. Answer the questions. Write complete sentences.**

1. Where is the woman right now?

_____

2. How long did the woman wait before she called 911?

_____

3. What does the man look like?

_____

4. Where did the man go?

_____

5. Where is the woman going to go?

_____

Grammar to Communicate 1

VERB + OBJECT + INFINITIVE							
Subject	Verb	Object	Infinitive	Subject	Verb	Object	Infinitive
They	advise expect need	me you him	to leave.	He	wants would like	us them Luis	to stay.

A Complete the sentences. Write *The man wants the police officer* or *The police officer wants the man*.

Look

See page 299 for a list of verbs + objects + infinitives.

1. _The police officer wants the man_ to show him his driver's license.
2. _The man wants the police officer_ to come to his home right away.
3. _____ to answer some questions.
4. _____ to get out of his car.
5. _____ to give him directions to a hospital.
6. _____ to move his car.
7. _____ to help him.

B Complete the sentences about each conversation.

1. **Ms. Dennis:** Can you show me your badge?
   Police officer: Sure. Here you are.
   Ms. Dennis wanted _the officer_ _to show_ her his badge.

2. **Mrs. Rivers:** Can I ride in the ambulance?
   Paramedic: Yes.
   The paramedic allowed _____ _____ in the ambulance.

3. **Police officer:** Open the bag.
   Sergei: Okay.
   The police officer ordered _____ _____ the bag.

4. **Monique:** I'm scared.
   Paramedic: Relax. Everything will be okay.
   The paramedic encouraged _____ _____.

5. **Mr. Johnson:** The landlord didn't install smoke detectors in my apartment. What should I do?
   Firefighter: Call the landlord immediately.
   The firefighter advised _____ _____ the landlord immediately.

badge

Look

install = put in and connect equipment

C Read the situation. Then complete the sentences with your ideas.

1. Al is driving on the highway. Suddenly, he sees a police car behind him. The flashing lights are on.

    The police expect ___Al to move over.___

2. Roger smelled smoke and called the fire department.

    Roger wanted _____

3. The firefighter is talking to students about smoke detectors in their homes.

    The firefighter is encouraging _____

4. The paramedic has asked the patient his name three times, but he hasn't answered.

    The paramedic wants _____

5. Rita's elderly grandmother has fallen and can't move. Rita calls 911 for an ambulance.

    Rita needs _____

6. Drivers can't use Beacon Street today. The police are sending drivers to Market Street.

    The police are not allowing _____

    _____

Look

A police officer **is** here.
The police **are** there.

TIME to TALK

PAIRS. Read the situations. Then say what you think happened next. Use the verbs in the box and your own ideas.

advised	asked	didn't allow	ordered
allowed	convinced	encouraged	told

1. Tina was driving the wrong way down a one-way street. She saw a police car behind her. What happened next?

2. The police stopped Jim on the highway because he was driving fast. They thought he was acting strange. What happened next?

3. The police saw some teenagers with cans of spray paint writing on a building. What happened next?

4. It was 2:00 A.M. The fire alarm went off in a hotel. What happened next?

Example: The police officer ordered Tina to pull over. He asked her to take out her driver's license and registration. Then he told her to wait in her car. She had a clean driving record, so he didn't give her a ticket. . . .

VERB + NOUN CLAUSE

Subject	Verb	Noun (Object)	Subject	Verb	Noun Clause (Object)
The police	know	his name.	The police	know	that his name is Jim Smith.
					his name is Jim Smith.

REPLACING NOUN CLAUSES

	Affirmative	Negative
Did the police find him?	I think so. (= I think that the police found him.)	I don't think so. (= I don't think that the police found him.)
	I believe so.	I don't believe so.
	I hope so.	I hope not.
	I guess so.	I guess not.

A This article has seven noun clauses. The first one is underlined. Find and underline the other six noun clauses.

Belmont Pickpocket Steals Again

This time the unlucky person was Ana Fremi. When Ms. Fremi went to pay for her groceries, she noticed <u>that her wallet wasn't in her bag.</u> The cashier saw that she was upset and guessed that the reason was the Belmont Pickpocket. The cashier immediately called the police. The police know that the pickpocket is a young man. They suspect he's from the area. They also believe that he works nearby. The manager at Belmont Market hopes the police catch the person soon.

B Combine the sentences. Use a noun clause.

1. The fire started in an apartment on the third floor. The firefighters know this.
   <u>The firefighters know that the fire started in an apartment on the third floor.</u>

2. Someone was smoking in bed. The firefighters think this.
   _____

3. Mr. Johnson in Apartment 3D was probably the smoker. The firefighters suspect this.
   _____

4. Everybody got out of the building. The police believe this.
   _____

5. There will never be another fire. The people in the building hope this.
   _____

C Write sentences. If you do not agree with the sentence, make the main verb negative.

1. _I think the police work very hard._ OR _I don't think that the police work very hard._
   (I / think / the police / work / very hard)

2. _____
   (I / think / the police / be / always helpful)

3. _____
   (most people / believe / the police / want / to help them)

4. _____
   (people / know / the job of a firefighter / be / dangerous)

5. _____
   (I / believe / firefighters / should make / more money)

6. _____
   (most people / know / paramedics / be not / doctors)

D Answer the questions. If you are sure of the answer, say *Yes* or *No*. If you are not sure, use the verbs *believe*, *think*, *hope*, and *guess*. Use *not* where necessary.

1. Do all the rooms of your home have smoke detectors?   _I think so._ OR _I don't think so._

2. Are the batteries in your smoke detectors old?   _____

3. Do you change the batteries in your smoke detectors every year?   _____

4. Are there any fire hazards in your home?   _____

5. Are there plenty of firefighters in your neighborhood?   _____

PAIRS. Ask and answer the questions. Whose home is safer? How can you and your partner make your homes safer?

TIME to TALK

GROUPS. Ask and answer the questions. Explain your opinions.

Do you think that . . . ?

• the police in your neighborhood are doing a good job

• the emergency services in your neighborhood are good

• the government should build more prisons

• the police should be tougher on criminals

• prisoners should be able to get an education in prison

• prisoners should be able to vote

• most criminals can change and become honest citizens

Example:
A: *Do you think that the police in your neighborhood are doing a good job?*
B: *Yes, I think so. I believe that the police are doing their best. There is less crime in my neighborhood now than there was a few years ago.*
C: *I agree.*

Grammar to Communicate 3

MAKE AND LET

	Make	Object	Verb				Let	Object	Verb	
He	**made** **didn't make**	me them	**go**	to the police station.		She	**let** **didn't let**	him us	**leave**	early.

A What happens in the U.S. when a police officer stops you for speeding? Circle the correct answers.

1. The police officer _____ him your license.
   - **a.** makes you give
   - **b.** doesn't make you give

2. The police officer _____ in your car.
   - **a.** makes you stay
   - **b.** doesn't make you stay

3. The police officer _____ of your car.
   - **a.** lets you get out
   - **b.** doesn't let you get out

4. The police officer _____ for a long time.
   - **a.** makes you wait
   - **b.** doesn't make you wait

5. The police officer _____ to the police station.
   - **a.** makes you go
   - **b.** doesn't make you go

6. After the police officer gives you a ticket, he _____.
   - **a.** lets you drive away
   - **b.** doesn't let you drive away

> **Look**
>
> make someone do something = force someone to do something
>
> let someone do something = allow someone to do something

PAIRS. Are the answers the same in your country? If not, what is different?

B There was a fire alarm at work yesterday. Complete the sentences with *let*, *made*, *didn't let*, or *didn't make*.

1. I couldn't stay in my office because the firefighters ____*made*____ us leave the building.

2. They _____ us use the elevator. We had to walk down the stairs.

3. I forgot my coat, but the firefighters _____ me go back in the building.

4. They _____ us wait a long time outside. We waited for over an hour!

5. They _____ us go far away. We waited across the street.

6. They _____ us show any identification. They didn't need our names.

7. After they were sure there was no fire, they _____ us go back in the building.

8. When we went in the building, they _____ us use the elevator. Some people walked up the stairs, but I used the elevator. My office is on the tenth floor.

C Look at the scenes from a TV show. Write sentences. Use the words in the box and *made*, *didn't make*, *let*, or *didn't let*. Then compare answers with a partner.

get in the police car	make one phone call	~~stop~~
leave	put his hands up	talk

1. _____ *They made him stop.* _____   2. _____

3. _____   4. _____

5. _____   6. _____

TIME to TALK

PAIRS. How can parents help their children stay out of trouble? Complete the chart with your opinions. Write two or more ideas for each column.

To help their children stay out of trouble, parents should . . .

NOT LET THEM . . .	MAKE THEM . . .	NOT MAKE THEM . . .

WRAP UP. Share your ideas with the class.

Review and Challenge

Grammar

CD 3 TRACK 35 Complete the letter with the words in the box. Then listen and check your answers. Be careful. There are two extra words.

> didn't I it let made make me so that ~~think~~ us we

To whom it may concern:

    I'm writing this letter because I ___think___ you should know about my experience

1.
at your hospital last Saturday. My ten-year-old daughter had an accident on her bike,
and I noticed _____ she couldn't move her arm. I thought _____ might

2.   **3.**
be broken, so I drove her to the emergency room. We got there at 1:00. The nurse
saw that my daughter was in pain, but she _____ let us see a doctor right away.

                                 4.
She told the two of _____ to wait in the waiting area and _____ me fill

               5.   **6.**
in four different forms. We waited and waited. Finally, at 4:00 the nurse called my
daughter's name. My daughter wanted _____ to go with her, but the nurse didn't

                                 7.
_____ me go. She was very rude to me. I am writing because I would like to know

8.
your policy on this. Did the nurse have the right to _____ me stay in the waiting

                                                  9.
room? I don't think _____, but maybe there is a new policy.

                     10.

Dictation

CD 3 TRACK 36 Listen. You will hear five sentences. Write them in your notebook.

Speaking

GROUPS. What problems have you noticed in your neighborhood? What would you like the police or other local officials to do about the problems?

Example:
A: *The streets are dirty. I'd like the city to clean them more often.*
B: *I agree. And the police should make people pick up their trash.*

Listening

A 🔘 **37** **Listen to the radio show. What is the caller's problem? Check (✓) the correct answer.**

fire extinguisher

- ❏ 1. He has no smoke detectors in his apartment.
- ❏ 2. There are no smoke detectors in his apartment building.
- ❏ 3. The smoke detectors in the hallway of his apartment building are not working.
- ❏ 4. He doesn't have a fire extinguisher in his apartment.
- ❏ 5. His apartment has only one exit.
- ❏ 6. The sprinkler system in his building isn't working.

B 🔘 **37** **Listen again. Answer the questions.**

sprinkler system

1. Who must make sure that the smoke detectors are working? _____

2. What must there be in every apartment? _____

3. What must there be in all new buildings? _____

4. How many exits must each apartment have? _____

TIME to TALK

GROUPS. Discuss the answers to the questions. Think of four things for each category.

What does the fire department advise people to do to prevent fires?	What do the police advise people to do to protect themselves from crime?	What do the police advise people to do to avoid car accidents?
_____	_____	_____
_____	_____	_____
_____	_____	_____
_____	_____	_____

WRAP UP. Now share your ideas with another group. Do you have any of the same ideas?

Example:
A: *The fire department advises people not to use electric heaters.*
B: *And they also advise people not to smoke in bed.*

Reading

Getting Ready to Read

Make a list of four things that you can do to prevent a fire in your home.

1. _____
2. _____
3. _____
4. _____

Reading

Read the article. Does the writer talk about any of your ideas in Getting Ready to Read?

DON'T

Every year, about 3,500 people in the United States die in home fires. To make sure that you and your family do not have a fire in your home, safety experts advise you to follow these steps:

• Never keep **flammable** chemicals such as gasoline inside your house. If you have a lawn mower or other **equipment** that uses gasoline, you need to keep them outside.

• If you have a fireplace, keep things that are flammable, such as curtains, away from it. Also, keep a screen in front of your fireplace.

• Keep matches and lighters in a locked cabinet.

• Do not allow children to keep candles in their rooms.

• Teach your children to respect fire. Never let them play with dangerous **objects** like matches, lighters, or candles.

• Ask a professional to check your fireplaces and heating system once a year.

• When you are cooking, do not wear **loose-fitting** clothing, for example bathrobes with long sleeves.

• Keep outdoor barbecue grills at least three feet away from other objects, including the house and trees.

The best way to keep your family safe is to prevent a fire in the first place. However, you need to be ready to act quickly if a fire starts at home. Take the following steps:

• Identify two **exits** out of every room, such as a window or door.
• Decide on a meeting place outside of the house if there is a fire.
• Hold a family fire drill (when you pretend there is a fire) at least twice each year.
• Install smoke alarms in your home and test them monthly.
• Teach every family member to "Stop, Drop, and Roll" if their clothes catch fire.

stop, drop, and roll

After You Read

A   Write the examples from the article. Then write a definition of the **boldface** word.
Use a dictionary for help.

1. Things that are **flammable**:
    gasoline, curtains

    Flammable means
    something that burns easily

2. One type of **equipment**:
    _____

    Equipment means
    _____

3. **Objects**:
    _____

    Objects are
    _____

4. **Loose-fitting** clothing:
    _____

    Loose-fitting means
    _____

5. Two types of **exits**:
    _____

    Exits are
    _____

> **Reading Skill:**
> **Understanding Examples**
>
> Writers often use examples to explain their main points. When you are reading, pay close attention to the examples. They will help you to understand the writer's main points.
>
> Never let them play with **dangerous objects like matches, lighters, or candles**.

B   Read the article again. As you read, remember as many of the fire safety tips as you can.
Then take notes. Do *not* look at the article when you take notes.

1. TO PREVENT A FIRE:
no flammable chemicals inside house
_____
_____

2. TO PREPARE FOR A FIRE:
identify exits from every room in your house
_____
_____

Now read the article one more time. How many of the fire safety tips did you remember?

Writing

Getting Ready to Write

A Complete the sentences with examples. Use your own ideas.

1. Products that contain flammable chemicals, including
   _____ *paint and gasoline* _____, can be dangerous.

2. Never store anything flammable near a heating source
   such as a _____.

3. For your bedroom, only buy things made out of non-
   flammable material, for instance, non-flammable
   _____.

4. When you are with your family in a crowded building, identify a meeting place, like
   _____, in case someone gets lost.

5. When you are cooking, pull your hair back to keep it away from hot surfaces, especially
   _____.

6. Keep cleaning products in a place where small children cannot find them, for example,
   in _____.

> ### Writing Tip
>
> When you give advice, be very specific and give examples to make your advice clear and useful. Use these expressions: *for example, such as, like, including, for instance.*
>
> **Example:**
>
> Keep outdoor barbecue grills at least three feet away from other objects, **including the house and trees**.

B Read the model paragraph.

> What are some things that the police advise people to do to protect themselves from crime? First of all, they encourage homeowners to buy security systems, including special window locks and burglar alarms. They also tell people to avoid keeping valuables like jewelry in their homes. They advise car owners to put all of their belongings, including briefcases, backpacks, and shopping bags, in the trunk. The police also tell people to pay attention to their surroundings. In parking garages, for example, they warn people not to park next to vehicles with dark windows. Finally, they tell people to avoid wearing clothes that are difficult to move in, especially high heels or tight clothing.

PAIRS. Read the model again. According to the writer, how can people protect themselves from crime?

Now talk about other ways people protect themselves from crimes or accidents.

Prewriting: Using Examples

You are going to write a paragraph about advice that experts, such as the police or paramedics, give to protect people from crimes or accidents. Before you write, organize your ideas in the chart. Write two pieces of safety advice. Then write at least two examples for each piece of advice.

If you need more information, look in the library or on the Internet. To search the Internet:

- Go to an Internet search engine such as www.google.com

- Choose topics you want to write about. For example, type in "fire prevention".

- Choose a site and click on its Web address.

- Read some of the information on the site. Write notes in the chart.

Writing Model
Topic: Robbery
Expert: Police
Safety advice # 1:
Buy security systems
Examples: special window locks and burglar alarms

Topic: _____ Expert: _____ Safety Advice: _____ _____	Topic: _____ Expert: _____ Safety Advice: _____ _____
Example 1:	Example 1:
Example 2:	Example 2:

Writing

Now write a paragraph about advice that experts give. The writing tip, the model paragraph, and your notes will help you. Write in your notebook.

Unit 20
Taking a Trip

Vocabulary

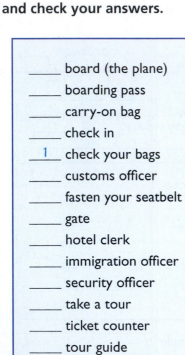 **38** Match the numbers with the words. Then listen and check your answers.

_____ board (the plane)

_____ boarding pass

_____ carry-on bag

_____ check in

__1__ check your bags

_____ customs officer

_____ fasten your seatbelt

_____ gate

_____ hotel clerk

_____ immigration officer

_____ security officer

_____ take a tour

_____ ticket counter

_____ tour guide

NORTHEAST AIRLINES

NORTHEAST AIRLINES

BOARDING PASS FLIGHT 723 ROW 5 SEAT A

FLIGHT 723 ROW 5 SEAT A

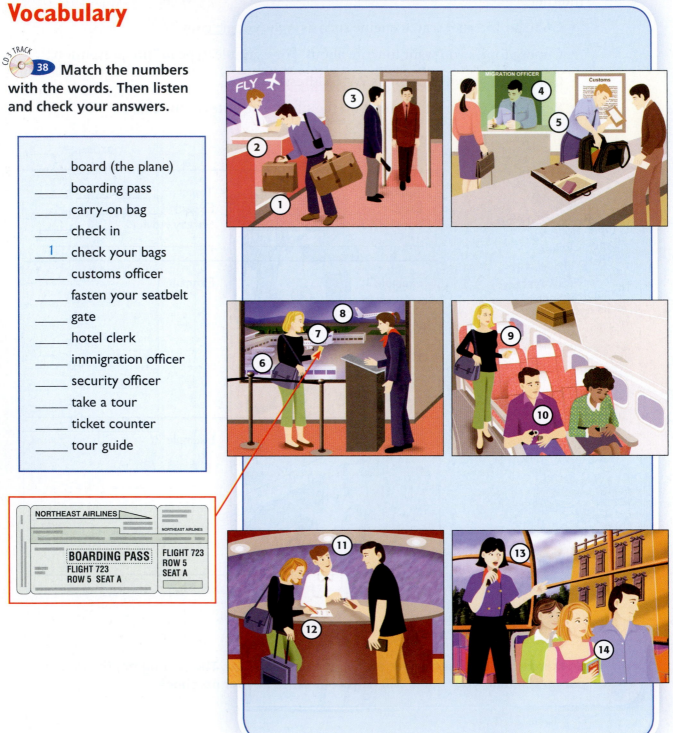

Listening

A CD 3 TRACK 39 **Listen. Check (✓) the statement that is true.**

❏ 1. The man and woman are meeting the Dwyers at the airport.

❏ 2. Rick and Helen Dwyer's flight is going to be late.

❏ 3. Mr. and Mrs. Dwyer are going on a trip.

B CD 3 TRACK 39 **Listen again. Circle the correct answers.**

1. The person from the airline tells the passengers _____.
   a. not to lose their boarding passes   **b.** to have their boarding passes ready

2. The man asks the woman _____.
   a. not to talk so softly   b. to repeat a lot

3. The woman says, _____
   a. "Here, give me your carry-on bag."   b. "Here is your carry-on bag."

4. The man says that _____
   a. he doesn't have the woman's boarding pass   b. he doesn't have his boarding pass

5. The woman tells the man that _____.
   a. he lost her boarding pass   b. he has her boarding pass

6. The man asks, _____
   a. "What's wrong?"   b. "What was that?"

C CD 3 TRACK 39 **Listen again. Answer the questions. Write complete sentences.**

1. What is the flight number, the name of the airline, and the gate number?

   _____

2. What do the passengers on the flight need to do?

   _____

3. Why is the man asking the woman so many questions?

   _____

4. What is in the man's carry-on bag?

   _____

5. Why do you think the Dwyers need to go up to the check-in counter?

   _____

Grammar to Communicate 1

REPORTED SPEECH: PRESENT STATEMENTS

Quoted Speech	Reported Speech	
He says, "The place is very nice."	He says (that)	the place is very nice.
He says, "I'm writing you from my hotel room."	He says (that)	he's writing us from his hotel room.

A Which statements are about each postcard? Which statements could be about both postcards? Write *M* (Miami), *T* (Toronto), or *MT* (Miami and Toronto).

Greetings from Miami

_MT_ 1. She says that she's sent ten postcards.

_____ 2. She says the beaches are beautiful.

_____ 3. She says they're going skiing on Monday.

_____ 4. She says they're having a great time.

_____ 5. She says that it has snowed every day.

_____ 6. She says that they miss us.

_____ 7. She says that she wears two sweaters all the time.

_____ 8. She says she loves the warm weather.

Greetings from Toronto

B Write the exact words from the postcards in Exercise A. Start the sentences with *She says*, and put quotation marks (" ") around the writers' exact words.

1. She says, "I've sent ten postcards."

2. _____

3. _____

4. _____

5. _____

6. _____

7. _____

8. _____

> **Look**
>
> When you report someone's speech, change the verbs and pronouns as necessary.
> He says, "**I am** going to enjoy Miami."
> = He says **he is** going to enjoy Miami.

CD 3 TRACK 40 **A woman and her 86-year-old mother are taking a tour. The mother can't hear well. Complete the conversation with reported speech. Then listen and check your answers.**

> You're going to have lunch soon.
> The restaurant is famous for its soups.
> I'm not going to have lunch with you.
> I need to go to the museum to buy the tickets for today's visit.
> You'll have 90 minutes for lunch.
> This restaurant is great. You're going to enjoy it.

Anna: "I can't understand a word that young man is saying."

Sammi: _He says that we're going to have lunch soon._
1.

Anna: "Where? What kind of restaurant? I hope it's good."

Sammi: _____
2.

Anna: "I hope he's going to sit next to me and explain everything on the menu."

Sammi: _____
3.

Anna: "Huh! The restaurant must not be very good. And what's that about the museum?"

Sammi: _____
4.

Anna: "Why didn't he have the tickets? He's not organized. Anyway, how long is lunch?"

Sammi: _____
5.

Anna: "Do we need 90 minutes? Is the service slow? Oh, look, we're here. What's that about the restaurant?"

Sammi: _____
6.

Anna: "Well, we'll see about that!"

TIME to TALK

PAIRS. **Student A: Look at page 305. Student B: Look at page 306.**

Student A, tell Student B what the writer of Postcard 1 says. Say one sentence at a time. Student B, look at the list of places. Guess which city Student A is talking about. Then Student B tells Student A what the writer of Postcard 2 says, and Student A guesses.

Example:
A: *They say they are really enjoying themselves.*
B: *That could be anywhere. What else do they say?*

Grammar to Communicate 2

REPORTED SPEECH: COMMANDS

Quoted Speech (Commands)		Reported Speech	
AFFIRMATIVE	He told her, **"Open the bag."**	He told her	to open the bag.
NEGATIVE	He told her, **"Don't walk fast."**		not to walk fast.

A **Read what happened to Donna. Underline the reported speech.**

Today wasn't fun. <u>First, I told the man behind me in line not to push.</u> He told me to stop talking on my cell phone and not to let people get in front of me. Then after we sat down, the children started fighting. I told them not to make too much noise, but they didn't listen. Then, a woman behind us told them to behave themselves, so the little one started crying. Finally, he fell asleep. When the movie started, I told the older boy to sit down and watch the movie. But the movie wasn't for children, so he watched it for only five minutes. Then he started to run around. An older man walked over to him and told him to go back to his seat. Then the man came over to me and told me not to let my son run around. The man was very annoyed, and I was embarrassed.

embarrassed
annoyed

Where was Donna? Circle the correct answer.

a. at a restaurant **b.** in a hotel room **c.** on an airplane

B **There are different speakers in Exercise A. Write their exact words.**

1. Donna told the man, "_____*Don't push.*_____"
2. The man told Donna, "_____"
3. Donna told her children, "_____"
4. A woman told the children, "_____"
5. Donna told her older son, "_____"
6. An older man told her son, "_____"
7. The man told me, "_____"

C CD 3 TRACK **41** Look at what Jack said before he and Ruth left on vacation. Then complete Ruth's part of the conversation. Then listen and check your answers.

Before vacation, Jack said to Ruth:

> Take the brown suitcase, not the red one.
> Don't bring my jacket.
> Leave my credit card at home.
> Don't put my cell phone in the suitcase.
> Don't pack too many things for me.
> Buy some new clothes for yourself.

During the vacation, Jack and Ruth are talking in their hotel room.

Jack: Why did you take the brown suitcase?

Ruth: You _____*told me to take the brown suitcase.*_____
1.

Jack: You forgot to bring my jacket.

Ruth: No, I didn't. You _____
2.

Jack: Where's my credit card?

Ruth: You _____
3.

Jack: My cell phone isn't in the suitcase. Where is it?

Ruth: _____
4.

Jack: I have only three shirts. That's not enough.

Ruth: _____
5.

Jack: And what are all these new clothes? I've never seen them before.

Ruth: _____
6.

Jack: I did?

TIME to TALK

PAIRS. Make a conversation. A teenager is going to travel alone. The teenager's parent is telling the teenager what to do and what not to do. Student A: You are Student B's parent. Student B: You are Student A's teenage child.

Example:
　　Parent: *Don't forget your tickets.*
Teenager: *Don't worry. They're in my carry-on bag.*

WRAP UP. Now act out your conversation. Your classmates will report what you said. Then listen to your classmates' conversation and report what they said.

Example:
A: *She told him not to forget his tickets . . .*

Grammar to Communicate 3

REPORTED SPEECH: REQUESTS

	Quoted Speech (Requests)		Reported Requests
She asked,	"Would you sit here, please?"	She asked me	to sit here.
	"Can you please sign your name?"		to sign my name.
	"Could you wait a few minutes?"		to wait a few minutes.

A **What did the people say? Circle the exact words.**

1. She asked us to check our carry-on bags.
   a. "Could you please check your carry-on bags?"
   b. "Are you able to check your carry-on bags?"

2. He asked me to take off my shoes.
   a. "Can you take off your shoes, please?"
   b. "Can you take off my shoes, please?"

3. She asked me to take everything out of my carry-on bag.
   a. "Can I take everything out of your bag, please?"
   b. "Would you take everything out of your bag, please?"

4. She asked me to put my arms up.
   a. "Could you please put your arms up?"
   b. "Are you able to put your arms up?"

B CD 3 TRACK 42 **Complete the conversations. Use *asked*. Then listen and check your answers.**

1. A: Why did you close the window?
   B: The cab driver ___asked me to close___ it.

2. A: Why are you fastening your seat belt? The plane isn't moving.
   B: The flight attendant _____ our seat belts.

3. A: Why is Jack showing his passport to the immigration officer again?
   B: The immigration officer _____ it to her again.

4. A: Why do you want to wait at the gate?
   B: My husband _____ at the gate.

5. A: Why did you give the hotel clerk our credit card?
   B: She _____ it to her.

C Look at the pictures. What requests did the airport workers make? Write sentences in reported speech. Use the words in the box or your own ideas.

answer some questions	~~hand (someone something)~~	show (someone something)
empty (one's) pockets	open (something)	sit down and wait

1. <u>The ticket agent asked the woman</u> <u>to hand him her bag.</u>

2. The ticket agent _____

3. The security officer _____ _____

4. The security officer _____ _____

5. The customs officer _____ _____

6. The customs officer _____ _____

TIME to TALK

PAIRS. Talk about an experience you had at an airport. What did the airport workers and officers ask you to do? What did they tell you to do?

Example: *When I moved to Miami, I didn't speak any English. When the customs officer asked me to show him my passport, I handed him my carry-on bag.*

Review and Challenge

Grammar

CD 3 TRACK 43 **Correct the mistake(s) in each conversation. Then listen and check your answers.**

1. **A:** Why did that man tell us ~~that~~ *to* go to the ticket counter?

   B: Because we need to check in.

2. **A:** Is Annie having a good time?

   B: She says I am.

3. **A:** When do we need to check in?

   B: The travel agent told us to we check in an hour before the flight.

4. **A:** The hotel clerk told us to leave the passports in our room.

   B: No. He told us to not leave them in our room.

5. **A:** Would you sit in the seats near the door, please?

   B: What did she say?

   C: She asked that to sit near the door.

Dictation

CD 3 TRACK 44 **Listen. You will hear five sentences. Write them in your notebook.**

Speaking

PAIRS. Student A: You had a difficult day at work yesterday. Choose a situation and tell Student B what happened.
Student B: Listen and ask questions. Then switch roles.

1. You are a tour guide. A tourist on the bus was not enjoying the tour.
2. You are a ticket agent at the airport. A traveler's flight was cancelled.
3. You are an immigration officer. A traveler forgot his passport.
4. You are a customs officer. A passenger had fruit and meat in a carry-on bag.

Example:
A: *This man came through customs. His bag smelled strange, so I asked him to open it. . . .*
B: *What happened next?*

Listening

CD 3 TRACK 45 **A** **Listen to the report. Check (✓) the best title.**

❏ 1. Enjoying your vacation: It's harder than you think!

❏ 2. Flying: The best part of the trip

❏ 3. Packing for your next vacation: Control yourself!

❏ 4. Traveling: How to get there comfortably

❏ 5. Traveling alone: How to do it safely

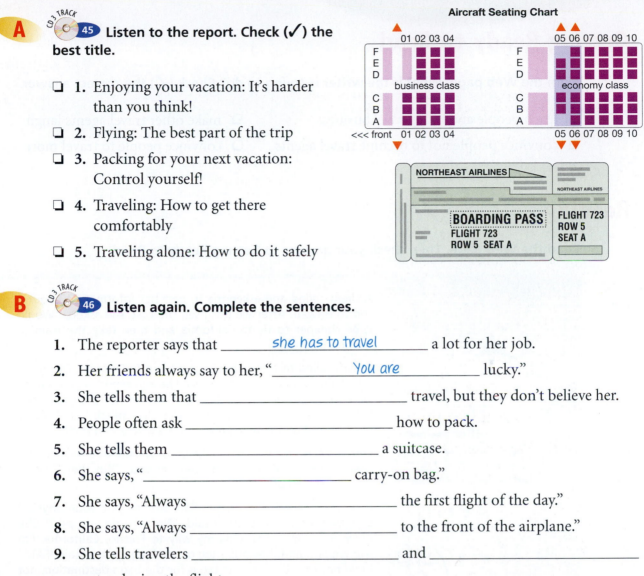

Aircraft Seating Chart

business class

economy class

<<< front 01 02 03 04   05 06 07 08 09 10

NORTHEAST AIRLINES
NORTHEAST AIRLINES

BOARDING PASS
FLIGHT 723
ROW 5 SEAT A

FLIGHT 723
ROW 5
SEAT A

CD 3 TRACK 46 **B** **Listen again. Complete the sentences.**

1. The reporter says that _____ *she has to travel* _____ a lot for her job.

2. Her friends always say to her, "_____ *You are* _____ lucky."

3. She tells them that _____ travel, but they don't believe her.

4. People often ask _____ how to pack.

5. She tells them _____ a suitcase.

6. She says, "_____ carry-on bag."

7. She says, "Always _____ the first flight of the day."

8. She says, "Always _____ to the front of the airplane."

9. She tells travelers _____ and _____ water during the flight.

TIME to TALK

GROUPS. Discuss the questions.

1. Do you like flying? Why or why not? If not, how do you like to travel?

2. When you travel, how much luggage do you usually take with you?

3. Have you ever gone on a tour? If so, where? When? Did you enjoy it?

4. Have you ever traveled alone? If so, tell your group about your experience.

WRAP UP. Now tell the class something interesting about someone in your group.

Example: *Jairo told us that he is scared of flying. When his sister got married in Arizona, his family flew there for the wedding, but he drove all the way by himself.*

Reading

Getting Ready to Read

Skim the Web page. What is the writer is trying to do? Check (✓) the correct answer.

❏ teach people about the travel business

❏ convince people not to become travel agents

❏ make other travel agents laugh

❏ convince people to travel more

Reading

Read the Web page. Then check your answer to Getting Ready to Read.

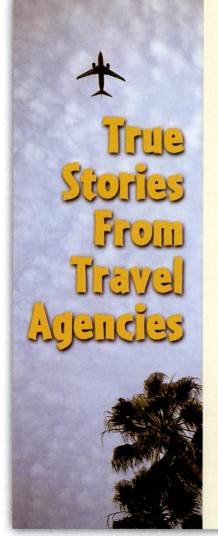

True Stories From Travel Agencies

A client called and asked me to give her information about a trip to Hawaii. After we discussed the cost, she asked, "Would it be cheaper to fly to California and then take the train to Hawaii?"

A man called to complain about his trip to Orlando, Florida. I asked him what was wrong. He said he was expecting an ocean–view room. I tried to explain that that is not possible, since Orlando is in the middle of the state. He **replied,** "Don't lie to me. I looked on the map and Florida is a very thin state."

I got a call from a man who asked, "Is it possible to see England from Canada?" When I answered, he said, "But they look so close on the map!"

A woman called and asked, "Do airlines put your **physical description** on your bag?" I said, "No, why do you ask?" She answered, "Well, I was on my way to Fresno, California. I'm overweight, and they put a **tag** on my **luggage** that said 'FAT.'" I told her that the luggage tag is for the bag's **destination,** not the owner's appearance. The city **code** for Fresno is "FAT."

I just **got off** the phone with a man who asked, "How do I know which plane to get on? They announced that flight 823 was ready for boarding, but none of the planes in the parking lot have numbers on them."

A businessman called with a question about the **documents** he needed in order to fly to China. After a long discussion about passports, I told him to **apply for** a visa several months in advance. He replied, "Oh no, I don't need a visa. I've been to China many times and never had to have one of those." I checked again, and sure enough, his visit **required** a visa. When I told him this he said, "Look, I've been to China four times and every time they have accepted my American Express."

Adapted from http://www.scaruffi.com/travel/jokes.html

After You Read

A   Find the **boldface** words in the Web page that have similar meanings to the words below.

1. ask for _____ _apply for_____

2. what someone looks like _____

3. needed _____

4. the place that you are going to _____

5. a piece of paper that the airlines put on your suitcase _____

6. a set of numbers or letters that represent something, such as the name of a place _____

7. answered _____

8. suitcases and bags for travel _____

9. papers that give information, for example, about a person _____

10. ended a telephone conversation _____

B   Read the Web page again. Write the sentences where the writer reports the statements below.

1. "Apply for a visa."

    _____

    _____

2. "Please give me information about a trip to Hawaii."

    _____

    _____

3. "What's wrong?"

    _____

4. "Get on flight 823."

    _____

> **Reading Skill:**
> **Recognizing Reported Speech**
>
> It is important to understand when the writer is reporting someone else's words. Some common verbs that are used to report speech are *say, ask,* and *tell.*

Writing

Getting Ready to Write

A Read the sentences. Add commas, quotation marks, and capital letters where necessary.

1. She asked him to change the flight number.
2. I told him don't forget to get a visa.
3. The man said your seat is next to the window.
4. He told me to look for a different hotel.
5. I asked him to get a travel guide.
6. She asked me where did you stay in London?
7. They told her to take a train to the airport.

B Read the model paragraph.

> Ten years ago, I flew home for my sister's birthday. I had a big blue bag. When I got off the plane, I waited and waited for my bag, but it never came. All the other people on the plane got their bags and went to line up at the customs desk. I started to get worried. I asked an airport worker to help me find my bag, but he just said, "Look over there, in the corner." Then he walked away. I saw a bag that looked like my bag, but I opened it and it wasn't mine. Then I saw a woman in the customs line. She had a bag that looked just like mine. I asked her to open the bag, but she told me to go away. She was in a hurry. So I grabbed the bag and opened it. My things were inside. The woman looked surprised, but she didn't apologize. She just said, "Have a good trip."

PAIRS. Read the model again. What happened to the writer? How did the writer feel about it?

Now talk about something funny or interesting that happened to you or someone you know while you were traveling.

Prewriting: Using Quoted and Reported Speech

You are going to write a paragraph about something funny or interesting that happened to you or someone you know while you were traveling. Before you write, read the notes for the student model. Then write some of the things that the people in your story said. Use both quoted and reported speech.

**Model Story
My Missing Bag**

<u>Quoted speech</u>
- "Look over there, in the corner."
- "Have a good trip."

<u>Reported speech</u>
- I asked an airport worker to help me find my bag.
- I asked her to open the bag.
- She told me to go away.

My Story:

<u>Quoted speech</u>

<u>Reported speech</u>

Writing

Now write a paragraph about something funny or interesting that happened to you or someone you know while you were traveling. The writing tip, the model paragraph, and your notes will help you. Write in your notebook.

Grammar Summaries

UNIT 1 Getting to Know You

Have got: Statements

1. *Have got* and *have* mean the same thing. We use *have got* more in speaking than in writing.
   Have they **got** any children?
   = **Do** they **have** any children?

2. The contracted forms (*'ve got* or *'s got*) are more common than the full forms.
   I **have got** black hair.   He **has got** gray hair.
   (Full forms)
   I**'ve got** black hair.   He**'s got** gray hair.
   (Contracted forms)

3. Use *have got* with *I, you, we,* and *they*.
   I**'ve got** a lot of free time.
   We**'ve got** a lot of free time.

4. Use *has got* or *'s got* with the third person singular (*he, she, it*).
   He **has got** short hair.   She**'s got** long hair.

5. Be careful! Do not confuse the contraction for *has got* and the contraction for *is*.
   She**'s got** a new boyfriend.
   = She **has** got a new boyfriend.
   She**'s** nice. = She **is** nice.

6. We use *have got* (or *has got*) only in the present.
   He**'s got** gray hair. (present)
   He **had** gray hair. (past)

Present Progressive: Extended Time

1. Use the present progressive to talk about activities happening right now, at the time of speaking.
   Look! The baby**'s walking**. (= right now)

2. Use the present progressive to talk about activities happening these days: this week, this month, or this year.
   Look at the baby! He**'s getting** big. (= these days, not right this moment)

3. Look at page 295 for information about the spelling and forms of the present progressive.

Simple Present and Present Progressive

1. Use the present progressive to talk about activities that are temporary (will probably change soon):
   I can't talk. I**'m eating** dinner. (= now)

   It**'s getting** hot. Summer is almost here. (= these days)

   He**'s smoking**. (= cigarette in his hand at this minute)

2. Use the simple present to talk about activities that are permanent (will probably stay the same for a long time):
   We **eat dinner** at 6 o'clock. (habit or routine)
   It **gets** hot in the summer. (scientific fact)
   He **smokes** (habit) but **he's not smoking** now. (now)

3. Use the simple present with stative verbs. Do not use the present progressive. (Look at page 298 for a list of stative verbs.)
   I **like** this party a lot.
   NOT I'm liking this party a lot.

UNIT 2 The World We Live In

Count and Noncount Nouns: Quantifiers

1. Count nouns are singular (*1 tourist*) or plural (*3 tourists*). Noncount nouns have only one form (*tourism*) and no plural.
   There **are** a lot of tourist**s** in my country.
   Tourism **is** important. (NOT tourisms)

2. Use *some* with noncount nouns and plural nouns in affirmative sentences.
   There is **some traffic** on Pine Street.
   There are **some cars** on Pine Street.

3. Use *any* with noncount nouns and plural nouns in negative sentences and *yes/no* questions.
   There **aren't any** parking spaces here.
   Is there **any** parking on your street?

4. Use *a lot of* with noncount nouns and plural nouns.
   There is **a lot of pollution.**
   Are there are **a lot of cars?**

5. Use *no* with noncount nouns and plural nouns. *No +* noun has the same meaning as *not any +* noun. This form is less common than *not any +* noun.
   We **have no** oil. = We **don't have any** oil.

6. Use *a little* and *little* with noncount nouns. *A little* means *some*. *Little* means *not much*. We often use *very* with *little*.
   We've got **a little** food. (We can give you some of ours.)

   We've got **very little** food. (We can't give you any of ours.)

7. Use *much* with noncount nouns in negative sentences and questions. Use *a lot of*, not *much*, in affirmative sentences.
   How **much** money do you have?
   We don't have **much** money.
   There's **a lot of** oil in Texas.
   (NOT There's much oil.)

8. Use *many, a few, few,* and *several* with plural nouns. *Many* means *a lot of*. *A few* and *several* mean *some*. *Few* means *not many*. We often use *very* with *few*.
   I have **a few** quarters. (I can give you one.)
   I have **very few** quarters. (I can't give you any.)

Count and Noncount Nouns: *Plenty of / Enough / Too much / Too many*

1. Use *plenty of* and *enough* with non-count nouns and plural nouns.

   > There is **plenty of** tourism in Paris.
   > (= a lot; no more needed)

   > There are **plenty of** restaurants.
   > (= a lot; no more needed)

   > There is **enough** parking.
   > (= the correct amount; no more needed)

   > There isn't **enough** parking.
   > (= less than is needed)

2. Use *too much* with non-count nouns. Use *too many* with plural nouns.

   > There is **too much** noise.
   > There are **too many** people.

3. Be careful. *Too much* and *too many* have a negative meaning.

   > I hate big cities. There is **too much** noise.
   > I love big cities. There are **a lot of** things to do.
   > (NOT ~~There are **too many** things to do.~~)

Both / Neither / Either

1. Use *both*, *neither*, and *either* to talk about two count nouns.

   > I like **both** New York and Los Angeles. (I like the two cities.)

   > I like **neither** of them. (I don't like New York or Los Angeles.)

   > I could live in **either** city. (New York is OK; Los Angeles is OK, too.)

2. After *both* and before a plural noun, you can use *of* + qualifier or leave it out.

   > I like **both** boys.
   > I like **both of the** boys.

   With *of*, use a qualifier (*the, those, my*, etc.).

   > NOT ~~I like both of boys.~~

3. Use *neither* + singular noun for a negative meaning.

   > I like **neither** city. (I don't like New York and I don't like Los Angeles.)

4. Be careful. Do not use *neither* with a negative verb.

   > ~~I don't like neither city.~~

5. Use a singular noun after *neither* or *either*, or a plural noun after *neither* + *of* + qualifier or *either* + *of* + qualifier.

   > I like **neither** boy. (I don't like John, and I don't like Bill.)
   > I like **neither of the** boys.

Simple Past: Regular and Irregular Verbs

1. For the simple past tense of regular verbs, add *–ed* to the verb.

   > The Tigers **played** last Sunday.
   > They **play** every Sunday in the winter.

2. Look at page 296 for information about spelling rules for regular simple past verbs. Look at page 300 for information about the pronunciation of the *–ed* endings.

3. Many verbs are irregular. The simple past of these verbs do not have *–ed* at the end. Look at page 298 for information about irregular simple past verbs.

   > catch—**caught**

4. For the negative of past tense verbs, use *did not* (or *didn't*) and the base form of the verb.

   > He **did not score** two goals.
   > (He **scored** one goal.)

   > We **didn't see** Sunday's game.
   > (We **saw** Saturday's game.)

5. Be careful! The past tense of *be* is *was / wasn't* and *were / weren't*. Do not use *didn't* with the past tense of *be*.

   > I **wasn't** at home last night.
   > NOT ~~I didn't be at home last night.~~

Simple Past: Questions

1. To make a *yes/no* question, add *did* before the subject and use the base form of the verb.

   > They **had** two tickets last week.
   > **Did** they **have** two tickets last week?

2. Use *did* or *didn't* in short answers.

   > Did she play last week?
   > Yes, she **did**. OR No, she **didn't**.

3. In information questions, *did* comes after the question word (*what, where, why,* etc.)

   > **Where did** the Tigers **play**?
   > **How many** points **did** they **score**?

4. For questions with the verb *to be*, do not use *did*. Use *was* or *were*.

   > **Was** the game good?
   > Yes, it **was**. OR No, it **wasn't**.

5. When *who* or *what* is the subject of the question, do not use *did* in the question. Use the past form of the verb.

SUBJECT	VERB		
Who	**saw** the game?	We did.	
What	**happened**?	They lost.	

6. When *who* or *what* is the object of the question, use *did* and a subject word in the question.

OBJECT		SUBJECT	VERB	SUBJECT	VERB	OBJECT
Who **did**		you	see?	I		saw the Tigers.
OBJECT		SUBJECT	VERB	SUBJECT	VERB	OBJECT
What team **did you**			see?	I		saw the Tigers.

Clauses with *Because, Before, After, As soon as*

1. A clause is a group of words that has a subject and a verb. Some sentences have just one clause. That clause is the main clause.

   SUBJECT   VERB
   We   won   the game.

2. Some sentences have more than one clause. One clause is the main clause, and the other clause is the subordinate clause.

   After we scored a goal, we won the game.
   [subordinate clause]   [main clause]

3. The subordinate clause begins with a connecting word like *after, as soon as, because,* and *before.* A subordinate clause is not a complete sentence. It needs a main clause.

   After we scored a goal . . .

4. When the subordinate clause comes at the beginning of the sentence, put a comma between the subordinate clause and the main clause.

   After we won the game,   we celebrated.

   [subordinate clause] [comma] [main clause]

5. When the subordinate clause comes after the main clause, do not put a comma.

   We celebrated after we won the game.

   [main clause]   [subordinate clause]

UNIT 4 Accidents

Past Progressive: Statements

1. For the past progressive, use the past of the verb *to be* and verb + *–ing.*

   I **was** play**ing** with the children yesterday morning.

   Joe and Sue **were** visit**ing** Joe's parents at the time of the fire.

2. Use the past progressive to talk about activities in progress at a specific time in the past.

   The children **were sleeping** at 10 last night.
   (= They began sleeping before 10 and continued sleeping after 10.)

3. For the negative, use *was not* (or *wasn't*) or *were not* (or *weren't*) and a verb + *–ing.*

   She **wasn't** iron**ing** early this morning.
   We **weren't** work**ing** at 4 yesterday.

4. Use the simple past with stative verbs. Do not use the progressive. (Look at page 298 for a list of stative verbs.)

Past Progressive: Questions

1. To make a *yes/no* question, change the word order of the subject and the verb.

   They were eating dinner at 6:30.
   Were they eating dinner at 6:30?

2. Use *was/wasn't* or *were/weren't* in short answers.

   Was he driving at the time of the accident?
   Yes, he **was**. OR No, he **wasn't**.

   Were you going home at the time of the accident?
   Yes, we were. OR No, we **weren't**.

3. In information questions, *was* or *were* comes after the question word (*what, where,* etc.)

   What was your neighbor **doing** yesterday?
   Where were you **going** at 7 this morning?

4. When *who* or *what* is the subject of the question, there is no subject after *was.*

   SUBJECT   VERB
   Who   **was smoking?**   Mr. Jackson was.
   What   **was burning?**   Some food in the oven was burning.

5. When *who* or *what* is the object of the question, use *was* or *were* and a subject word in the question.

   OBJECT   SUBJECT   VERB
   What   **was**   he   **smoking?**   A cigarette.
   Who   **was**   he   **talking to?** The doctor.

Past Progressive and Simple Past: *When* and *While*

1. Use the past progressive and the simple past to say that one activity was in progress when another activity happened.

   While we **were watching** TV, Gus **arrived**.
   (= We began watching TV before Gus arrived.)

   When Gus **arrived**, we **were watching** TV.
   (= We began watching TV before Gus arrived.)

2. Use the simple past two times to say that one activity happened *after* another activity.

   We **watched** TV when Gus **arrived**.
   (= First, Gus arrived. Then we watched TV.)

3. Use *while* with the past progressive to say that two activities were in progress at the same time.

   While I **was washing** the dishes, he **was making** the beds.

4. When the subordinate clause with *when* or *while* comes at the beginning of the sentence, put a comma between the subordinate clause and the main clause.

   While they were talking,   I was working.

   [subordinate clause] comma [main clause]

5. When the subordinate clause comes after the main clause, do not put a comma.

   I was working while they were talking.

   [main clause]   [subordinate clause]

Used to: Statements

1. We use *used to* + verb to talk about things that happened often in the past. These things usually do not happen often or at all now.

   > Women **used to wear** skirts all the time.
   > (Now they often wear pants.)

   > I **used to** work downtown.
   > (Now I work in a different place.)

2. The negative of *used to* is *didn't use to*.

   > Women **didn't use to work** outside the home.

3. Be careful! Use the simple past, NOT *used to* + verb for actions in the past that happened once or only a few times.

   > I wore that dress to my brother's wedding.
   > NOT ~~I used to wear that dress to my brother's wedding.~~

   > He took care of the children three times last month.
   > NOT ~~He used to take care of the children three times last month.~~

4. For past habits or customs, both *used to* + verb and the simple past are sometimes possible. The meaning is similar.

   > Women used to stay at home. OR Women **stayed** at home.

   > Men didn't use to do housework. OR Men didn't do housework.

Used to: Yes/No Questions

1. To make a *yes/no* question, add *did* before the subject and use *use to* + verb after the subject.

   > They **used to go out** on Fridays.
   > **Did** they **use to go out** on Saturdays?

   > He **used to feed** the baby.
   > **Did** he **use to feed** the baby?

2. Use *did* in short answers.

   > Did you use to live in London?
   > Yes, I **did**. OR No, I **didn't**.

   > Did she use to be a teacher?
   > Yes, she **did**. OR No, she **didn't**.

Used to: Information Questions

1. In information questions, *did* comes after the question word (*what, how much*, etc.) and *use to* + verb comes after the subject.

   > **Where did** you **use to go** on weekends?
   > We used to go to the movies.

   > **How much did** a movie **use to** cost?
   > A movie used to cost 25 cents.

2. When *who* or *what* is the subject of the question, do not use *did* in the question. Use *used to* + verb.

   > SUBJECT   VERB
   > Who   **used to live** there?
   > A young couple **used to live** here.
   > SUBJECT   VERB
   > What   **used to happen** on dates?
   > Young people **used to go** bowling on dates.

3. When *who* or *what* is the object of the question, use *did* in the question. Use *use to* + verb.

   > OBJECT   SUBJECT
   > What **did** you **use to do** after school?
   > SUBJECT   OBJECT
   > I   **used to do** my homework.

Future: *Will* for Decisions and Promises

1. Use *will* for an action that you decide to do at the time you are talking.

   > A: The phone's ringing.
   > B: **I'll get** it.

2. Use *will* or *won't* when you make a promise.

   > I **won't spend** all the money on clothes. **I'll put** some of the money in the bank.

Future: *Be going to* and *Will*

1. Use *will* for an action that you decide to do at the time you are talking.

   > A: The phone's ringing.
   > B: **I'll answer** it. (= decides to answer the phone at the moment it rings)

2. Use *be going to* for an action that you already have decided to do.

   > A: Why are you calling Joe's Pizzeria?
   > B: **We're going to have** pizza for dinner.
   > (= decided to have pizza for dinner before starting to call)

3. Use *be going to* when you see something now that tells you about the future.

   > Look at the clouds. **It's going to rain.** (The clouds give information about the future.)

4. Use *will* or *won't* when you make a promise.

   > **I'll be** on time. I promise.

5. Use either *will* or *be going to* to make predictions about the future. (You think something will happen, but you aren't sure.)

   > I think they**'ll attend** the meeting.
   > I think they're **going to** attend the meeting.

Future: Present Progressive for Future Arrangements

1. Use the present progressive for the future when the future activity was planned or arranged in advance (= before the moment of speaking).

   > **I'm working** tomorrow.
   > The teacher **is giving** us a test next week.

Grammar Summaries   **285**

2. When we use the present progressive for the future, we usually use a time expression. Without a time expression, people understand the present progressive is for *now*.

> What **are** you **doing** on Saturday night?
> (= a question about the future)

> What **are** you **doing**?
> (= a question about now)

3. You can also use *be going to* + verb instead of the present progressive for future activities that are planned or arranged in advance. Often the meaning is the same. Do not use *will* in these situations.

> **I'm going** to the dentist today. =
> **I'm going to go** to the dentist today. (= I have an appointment.) NOT ~~I'll go to the dentist today.~~

UNIT 7 Education

Future: *If* Clauses for Possibility

1. Sentences with *if* have a subordinate clause and a main clause. The *if* clause is the subordinate clause. It gives a possible situation in the future. The main clause gives the result of the possible situation.

> If you study hard, . . .
> (= It is possible you will study hard.)
> . . . you will do well in the course.
> (= This will be the result of studying hard.)

2. The *if* clause is about the future, but do not use *will* or *be going to* in the *if* clause. Use the simple present.

> If he **doesn't graduate** in June, he'll graduate in January.
> NOT ~~If he won't graduate in June, he'll graduate in January.~~

3. Use *be going to* or *will* in the main clause of the sentence.

> If I get a scholarship, **I'll go** to college full-time.
> If I get a scholarship, **I'm going to go** to college full-time.

4. When the *if* clause comes at the beginning of the sentence, put a comma between the *if* clause and the main clause. When the *if* clause comes after the main clause, do not put a comma.

> If they fail the final exam, they will not pass the course.
> They will not pass the course if they fail the exam.

Future: Time Clauses

1. Future time clauses begin with a time word: *after, as soon as, before, until,* or *when*.

> I will stay in college **until I graduate**.

2. Use the simple present, *not* will or be going to, after future time words.

> Before I **take** the test next week, I'm going to study a lot.
> NOT ~~Before I will take the test next week, I'm going to study a lot.~~

3. Use *be going to* or *will* in the main part of the sentence.

> **I'm going to get** a job after I graduate.
> **I'll get** a job after I graduate.

4. When the future time clause comes at the beginning of the sentence, put a comma between the time clause and the main clause. When the time clause comes after the main clause, do not put a comma.

> As soon as he gets his diploma, he'll start college.
> He'll start college as soon as he gets his diploma.

Future: *May* and *Might* for Possibility

1. Use *may* and *might* + the base form of a verb to talk about future possibility. Use the base form of the verb after *may* or *might*.

> He **may go** to Colson College next year, but he's not sure.
> They **might have** a test next week.

2. Use *may not* or *might not* for negative statements. Do not contract them.

> You **might not pass** the course.
> NOT ~~You mightn't pass the course.~~

3. The forms are the same for all persons (*I, you, he, she, it, we, they*).

> I **may get** a scholarship.
> She **might apply** to college.

4. Be careful. *May* + *be* is a modal + a verb. *Maybe* is an adverb that comes at the beginning of the sentence. It means *possible*. We often use *maybe* with *will*.

> **Maybe** Gloria **will take** another English class.

UNIT 8 Getting a Job

Present Perfect: Regular Verbs [+ *Ever* and *Never*]

1. Use the present perfect to talk about actions at an indefinite time in the past.

> **I've worked** in many restaurants. (= indefinite time: The sentence doesn't say when.)

2. To make the present perfect, use *has* or *have* and the past participle of the verb. To make the past participle of regular verbs, add *–ed* to the verb. Look at page 296 for information about the spelling rules for past participles, and page 300 for information about the pronunciation of the *–ed* endings.

> He **has talked** to the owner.
> I **have contacted** the manager.

3. Use the contracted form of the verb *have* in conversations.

> She**'s applied** for a job.
> They**'ve applied** for jobs.

4. Add *not* to *have* or *has* for negative statements. Use the contracted forms *hasn't* or *haven't* in conversations.

> He **hasn't started** his new job.
> They **haven't finished** the interview.

5. Be careful! Use the simple past, not the present perfect, to talk about actions at a *definite* time in the past.

> I **worked** at that restaurant two years ago.
> (Definite time: We know when—two years ago.)

6. *Never* and *not ever* have the same meaning.

> We**'ve never** worked. = We haven**'t**
> ever worked.
>
> NOT ~~We've not never worked.~~ NOT ~~We've ever worked.~~

Present Perfect: Irregular Verbs [+ *Already* and *Yet*]

1. Many verbs have irregular past participles. The past participles of these verbs do not have *–ed* at the end. Look at page 298 for a list of irregular past participles. Some common irregular past participles are:

> be—**been**   do—**done**   have—**had**
> see—**seen**   take—**taken**   quit—**quit**

2. We often use *already* in affirmative sentences with the present perfect. Put *already* between *has* or *have* and the past participle.

> I've **already** been on an interview.
> (= Before now, but not an exact time)

3. We often use *yet* in negative sentences with the present perfect. Put *yet* at the end of a sentence.

> She hasn't heard from the manager **yet**. (But she will probably hear from the manager soon.)

4. Be careful! The contraction *'s* can mean *has* or *is*. In the present perfect, the contraction *'s* always means *has*.

> It**'s been** hard to find a good job.
> (= It **has** been hard to find a good job.)
> It**'s** hard to find a good job.
> (= It **is** hard to find a good job.)

Present Perfect: *Yes / No* Questions

1. To make a *yes/no* question, add *has* or *have* before the subject and the past participle of the verb. Use *has* or *have* in short answers.

> **Has** she ever **talked** to you about the problem?
> Yes, she **has**.
> **Have** you ever **found** a job online? No, I **haven't**.

2. When we ask someone a question with *Have you ever . . .* , we are asking about the time period from any time in the past until now. The time is indefinite.

> **Have** you **ever worked** as a waitress?
> (= indefinite time, at any time in the past)

3. We can also ask a question with *yet*. Put *yet* at the end of the question.

> Have you found a job **yet**?

Present Perfect: *For* and *Since*

1. Use *for* and *since* with the present perfect to show that something began in the past and is continuing now.

> Joe **has been** here for a month. (= Joe came here a month ago and is here now.)

2. Use *for* with a period of time.

> I've known him **for** a week / **for** a long time / **for** years.

3. Use *since* with a specific time.

> They've been married **since** 2005 / **since** last year / **since** two years ago.

Present Perfect Progressive: *For* and *Since*

1. Use the present perfect progressive to talk about actions that began in the past and are continuing now.

> I**'ve been reading** a lot lately.
> (= I started reading at some point in the past, and I am still reading now.)

2. To make the present perfect progressive, use *has* or *have* + *been* + the present participle of the verb. To make the present participle of verbs, add *–ing* to the verb.

> We **have been sitting** in class for an hour.
> The teacher **has been teaching** for an hour.

3. Use the contracted form of the verb *have* in conversations.

> She**'s** been going out with him for a month.
> They**'ve** been going out for a month.

4. Be careful! The contraction *'s* can mean *has* or *is*. In the present perfect progressive, the contraction *'s* always means *has*.

> It**'s** been raining since 11 o'clock.
> (= It **has** been raining.)
> Look! It**'s** raining. (= It **is** raining.)

5. Add *not* to *have* or *has* for negative statements. Use the contracted forms *hasn't* or *haven't* in conversations.

> It **hasn't been raining** for long.
> We **haven't been waiting** for long.

6. We often use the present perfect progressive expressions with these time expressions: *recently*, *lately*, *for* (+ period of time), *since* (+ specific time).

> Lee and Al **have been fighting** a lot **recently**.
> I**'ve been spending** a lot of time with Americans **lately**.

7. We use the present perfect progressive and *for* and *since* with <u>action</u> verbs (for example, *go*) to show that something began in the past and continues now.
   We **have been dancing** for two hours.
   We use the present perfect simple with <u>non-action</u> (stative) verbs (for example, *know*) to show that something began in the past and continues now.
   I **have known** her for two years.
   Be careful. Do not use the present perfect progressive with stative verbs. Look at page 298 for a list of stative verbs.
8. With some verbs (*work*, *live*, *teach*), you can use either the present perfect progressive or the present perfect simple, with no change in meaning.
   We**'ve been living** here since 1999.
   We **have lived** here since 1999.
   She**'s been teaching** for 35 years.
   She **has taught** for 35 years.

Present Perfect Progressive: Questions
1. To make a *yes/no* question, add *has* or *have* before the subject + *been* + the present participle of the verb. Use *has* or *have* in short answers.
   Has he **been working** a lot lately? Yes, he **has**.
   Have you **been living** alone for a long time? No, I **haven't**.
2. To make information questions, use *has* or *have* after the question word (*how long*, *what*, etc.)
   How long **has** Chris been going out with Steve?
   What **have** you been doing lately?

UNIT 10 Television

Adverbs and Adjectives
1. Adverbs describe verbs. Adjectives describe nouns.
   VERB   ADVERB   ADJECTIVE   NOUN
   She speaks **well**.   She's a **good**   speaker.
2. Some verbs describe our senses. We use adjectives, not adverbs, after these verbs: *feel*, *look*, *smell*, *sound*, *taste*.
   This food **tastes good**.
   NOT ~~This food tastes well.~~
3. Adverbs also describe adjectives and other adverbs.
   ADVERB ADJECTIVE   ADVERB ADVERB
   He is **often   happy**.   She is late **too   often**.

Adverbs of Manner
1. Adverbs of manner answer the question *How*. Put adverbs of manner after the verb.
   (How does he run?)   He runs **quickly**.
   To form an adverb of manner from most adjectives, add *–ly*.
   ADJECTIVE   ADVERB
   quick   quick**ly**
2. For adjectives with two syllables or more ending in *–y*, change the *–y* to *–i* and add *–ly*.
   ang**rily**   [an·gry]   happ**ily**   [hap·py]
             1 2   1 2

3. For adjectives ending in *–ic*, add *–ally*.
   realist**ically**   [realistic]
   romant**ically**   [romantic]
4. For adjectives ending in *–le*, change the *–e* to *–y*.
   terrib**ly**   [terrible]
   comfortab**ly**   [comfortable]
5. Some adverbs are the same as the adjectives.
   She's a **fast** talker.   She talks **fast**.
   He's a **hard** worker.   He works **hard**.
6. The adverb of *good* is *well*.
   They're **good** singers.   They sing **well**.
7. Some adjectives do not have adverb forms. For example, adjectives that end in *–ly* (for example, *friendly*, *lovely*, *ugly*, *elderly*) do not have adverb forms.

Adverbs of Degree
1. Adverbs of degree (intensifiers) change how strong an adjective or adverb is. Put adverbs of degree in front of the adjective or adverb that they describe.
   They're **really** good dancers.
   (= stronger than *good*)

   They dance **very** well.
   (= stronger than *well*)
2. Do not use *very* or *extremely* with words that mean *very*. Use *pretty* or *really* with these words.
   The show's really great.   (great = very good)
   NOT ~~The show's very great.~~
3. Be careful. *Pretty* is an adjective and adverb, but the meaning is different. The adverb *pretty* goes before an adjective and makes the adjective less strong.
                     ADJECTIVE
   She's a very **pretty woman**.
   (= She's beautiful.)
              ADJECTIVE   ADJECTIVE
   She's a **pretty   nice** person.
   (= She's nice, but she's not very nice.)

UNIT 11 The Animal Kingdom

Comparative and Superlative of Adjectives and Adverbs
1. Use the comparative to compare two people, places, or things.
   Elephants are **bigger than** lions.
2. You can put an auxiliary (for example, *is*, *are*, *does*, or *do*) at the end of a comparative sentence, but it is not necessary. The auxiliary depends on the main verb.
   The dog **is** bigger than the cat **is**.
   OR The dog is bigger than the cat.

   A cheetah **runs** faster than a lion **does**.
   OR A cheetah runs faster than a lion.
3. In formal English, use the subject pronoun (*I*, *you*, *he*, *she*, *we*, *they*) after *than*. In informal English, use the object pronoun (*me*, *you*, *him*, *her*, *us*, *them*).
   FORMAL: My brother has more pets than I.
   INFORMAL: My brother has more pets than me.

4. We sometimes put *a little*, *a lot*, or *much* before the comparative of adjectives and adverbs. *Much* and *a lot* have the same meaning.

> A rat is **a little bigger** than a mouse.
> A rat is **a lot more frightening** than a mouse.
> A rat is **much more frightening** than a mouse.

5. The opposite of *more . . . than* is *less . . . than*. Use *less . . . than* with most adjectives and adverbs that have two or three syllables. Use *not as . . . as* with adjectives and adverbs that have one syllable.

> A snake is **more** dangerous **than** a cat. =
> A cat is **less** dangerous **than** a snake.
>
> My cat is small**er than** my dog. =
> My cat is**n't as** big **as** my dog.

6. Use the superlative to compare three or more people, places, or things.

> The blue whale is **the biggest** animal in the world.

7. Look at page 297 for information about the forms of the comparative and superlative.

Comparative and Superlative of Nouns

1. Use *less* or *more* to compare two non-count nouns.

> Cats eat **less food** than dogs. =
> Dogs eat **more food** than cats.
>
> Rabbits make **much less noise** than parrots. =
> Parrots make **much more noise** than rabbits.

2. Use *fewer* or *more* to compare two count nouns.

> Dogs sleep **fewer hours** than cats. =
> Cats sleep **more hours** than dogs.

3. Use *the least* or *the most* to compare three or more noncount nouns.

> Snakes need **the least space** of all the animals in the zoo.
> Gorillas need **the most space**.

4. Use *the fewest* or *the most* to compare three or more count nouns.

> Sharks have **the most** teeth of any animal.
> The snakes had **the fewest** visitors last year.

Equatives

1. Use *as . . . as* to say two people, places, or things are the same.

> A giraffe is **as beautiful as** a bear.
> (= They are both beautiful.)
>
> A giraffe moves **as quickly as** a horse.
> (= They both move quickly.)

2. We use *not as . . . as* for the opposite of *more than*.

> The chimpanzee is **not as dangerous as** the lion.
> (= The lion is more dangerous.)

Reflexive Pronouns

1. We use reflexive pronouns when the subject and the object are the same.

> **He** is looking at **himself** in the mirror.

2. We often use reflexive pronouns after these verbs: *burn, cut, enjoy, hurt*.

> I **hurt myself** when I was cooking.

3. Do not confuse reflexive pronouns and *each other*.

> **Jim and Laura** are talking to **each other**.
> (= Jim is talking to Laura. Laura is talking to Jim.)
> NOT ~~Jim and Laura are talking to **themselves**.~~
> ~~(= Jim is talking to himself and Laura is talking to herself.)~~

4. *By* + reflexive pronoun means *alone*.

> She lives **by herself**. (= She lives alone.)

One / Ones

1. We use *one* or *ones* when we do not want to repeat a noun.

> I want a small glass, not a large **one**.
> (NOT ~~I want a small glass. I don't want a large glass.~~)
> I like red apples, but I don't like green **ones**.
> (NOT ~~I like red apples, but I don't like green apples.~~)

2. Use *one* for singular count nouns. Use *ones* for plural count nouns. Do not use *one* or *ones* for noncount nouns.

> I don't want a hot **sandwich**. I want a cold **one**.
> We don't want hot **sandwiches**. We want cold **ones**.
> I don't want hot tea. I want iced tea. (NOT ~~I want iced one.~~)

3. We often use *the* before *one* or *ones*.

> Which salad would you like?
> The smallest **one**, please.
>
> Which tables are ours?
> **The ones** near the window.

4. Be careful! Use *it* or *they* to refer to "*the* + a noun." Do not use *one* or *ones*.

> A: Where's **the** Italian **restaurant**?
> B: **It**'s on Winter Street.

5. Use *it* or *they* to refer to a possessive adjective (*my, your, his, her*, etc.) + a noun. Do not use *one* or *ones*.

> A: Where are **our menus**?
> B: **They**'re here.

Other: Singular and Plural

1. *One* is a pronoun. We use it when we do not want to repeat a singular count noun.

> They have chicken sandwiches. Do you want **one**?

2. *Another* means "an additional . . ." or "a different . . ." It can be an adjective or a pronoun.

> ADJECTIVE
> There are three places. One place has Chinese food. **Another place** has Italian food.
>
> PRONOUN
> There are three places. One place has Chinese food. **Another** has Italian food.

3. *The other* means "the last one in a group." We use *the other* before singular and plural nouns.

> There are two places. One place has Chinese food. **The other place** has Italian food.
> There are four places. One place has Chinese food. **The other places** have Italian food.

4. *The other* is an adjective or a pronoun. *The others* is a pronoun.

> ADJECTIVE
> This dessert is okay, but **the other** one is better.
> (= the other dessert)
>
> PRONOUN
> This dessert is okay, but **the other** is better.
> (= the other dessert)
>
> PRONOUN
> These eggs are good, but **the others** are better.
> (= the other eggs)

UNIT 13 Technology

Can and Be able to

1. Use *can* or *can't* to talk about ability. *Can* and *can't* are the same for all subjects (*I, you*, etc.).

> I **can download** music.
> I **can't download** pictures.
> She **can download** music.
> She **can't download** pictures.

2. We also use *be able to* and *not be able to* to talk about ability. The verb *be* changes for different subjects (*I am able to, He is able to, They are able to*, etc.).

> I**'m able to access** the Internet at work.
> I**'m not able to access** the Internet at home.
> He**'s able to access** the Internet at work.
> He **isn't able to access** the Internet at home.

3. *Can* and *can't* are more common when we are talking about present ability. We use *be able to* with other forms—for example, the present perfect (*have/has been able to*) and modals (*might be able to*).

> People **have been able to send** e-mail messages for more than ten years.
> I **might be able to help** you, but I'm not sure.

Could and Be able to

1. *Could* and *couldn't* are the past forms of *can't*. Use *could* and *couldn't* to talk about general ability in the past.

> People **could talk** on the phone 30 years ago.
> People **couldn't talk** on cell phones 30 years ago.

2. Use *was/were able to* (<u>not</u> *could*) to talk about a specific event in the past.

> My son fixed my computer yesterday, so I **was able to use it** today.
> NOT I could use it today.

3. We also use *was/were able to* and *was not/were not able to* to talk about general ability in the past.

> I **was able to play** soccer well when I was younger.
> More people **were able to ride** horses a long time ago.

4. *Couldn't* and *wasn't/weren't able to* have the same meaning.

> I tried to fix it, but I **couldn't**.
> = I tried to fix it, but I **wasn't able to**.

5. Be careful! *Could* is also a way to ask a polite question. In this situation, it doesn't mean ability.

> **Could** I sit here?

Will be able to

1. Use *will be able to* and *won't be able to* to talk about ability in the future.

> I **will be able to download** the music next week.
> You **won't be able to access** the Internet tomorrow.

2. To make a *yes/no* question, put *will* before the subject. We use *will* or *won't* in short answers.

> **Will** they **be able to help** me?
> Yes, they **will**. OR No, they **won't**.

UNIT 14 A Kid's Life

Have to / Have got to / Must: Affirmative Statements and Have to: Yes / No Questions

1. Use *have to, have got to*, and *must* to talk about necessity. *Have to* and *have got to* are more common than *must* in conversation.

> You **have to** respect her.
> = You **have got to** respect her.
> = You **must** respect her.

2. Use *have to* or *have got to* with *I, you, we*, and *they*. Use *has to* or *has got to* with the third person singular (*he, she, it*).

> We **have to** be home at 8.
> = We **have got to** be home at 8.
> = We**'ve got to** be home at 8.
> He **has to** be home at 6.
> = He **has got to** be home at 6.
> = He**'s got to** be home at 6.

3. Use *have to* to ask questions about necessity. Use *do/does* or *don't/doesn't* in short answers. Do not use *have got to* or *must* in questions.

> **Do** you **have to** leave now?
> Yes, I **do**. OR No, I **don't**.
>
> **Does** the party **have to** be on Saturday?
> Yes, it **does**. OR No, it **doesn't**.

4. In information questions, *do* or *does* comes after the question word (*where, how often*, etc.).
    Where do you have to go?
    How often does he have to do chores?
5. When *who* is the subject of the question, do not use *do* or *does* in the question. Use *has to*.
    SUBJECT   VERB
    Who   **has to** do the dishes?   I do.
6. When *who* is the object of the question, use *do* or *does* and a subject word in the question.
    OBJECT   SUBJECT   VERB
    Who   **do** you   **have to** tell?   My mother.

Does not have to and *Must not*

1. *Don't / Doesn't have to* means that something is <u>not</u> necessary.
    The children **don't have to** stay in the house. They can go outside.

    Chris **doesn't have to** stay in her bedroom. She can play in the living room.
2. *Must not* or *mustn't* means that something is <u>not</u> permitted.
    The children **mustn't** leave the house. They have to stay in the living room.

    Chris **mustn't** leave her room. She **has to** stay there.

Had to: Statements and Questions

1. Use *had to* to talk about things that were necessary in the past. *Had to* is the past of *have to*, *have got to*, and *must*.
    I **had to** leave early yesterday.
    I **have to / have got to / must leave** early today.
2. For the negative, use *did not* (or *didn't*) + *have to* + the base form of the verb.
    We **didn't have to** go to school on Saturdays.
3. To make a *yes/no* question, add *did* before the subject and use the base form of the verb. Use *did* in short answers.
    Did you **have to go** to school on Fridays?
    Yes, we **did**. OR No, we **didn't**.
4. In information questions, *did* comes after the question word (*what, where, why*, etc.).
    What time did you **have to** leave in the morning?
5. When *who* is the subject of the question, do not use *did* in the question. Use *had to*.
    SUBJECT   VERB
    Who   **had to** take out the trash?   I did.
6. When *who* is the object of the question, use *did* and a subject word in the question.
    OBJECT   SUBJECT   VERB
    Who   **did** you   **have to** wait for?
    My sister.

UNIT 15 Manners

Should (not) + Verb

1. Use *should* and *shouldn't* (*should not*) to give advice and express opinions. *Should, shouldn't* and *should not* are the same for all subjects (*I, you, he, she*, etc.).
    I **should** wait for her.   He **should** wait for her.
    I **shouldn't** be late.   He **shouldn't** be late.
2. Use the base form of the verb after *should* or *should not*. Use *shouldn't* for negative statements when speaking.
    She **should respect** her elders.
    You **shouldn't be** rude to people.
3. To make a *yes/no* question, put *should* before the subject and use the base form of the verb. Use *should* or *shouldn't* in short answers.
    Should I **give** him a present?
    Yes, you **should**. OR No, you **shouldn't**.
4. In information questions, *should* comes after the question word (*when, what*, etc.).
    When should I **go**?
    What should they **bring**?
5. *Who* can be the subject of a question with *should*.
    SUBJECT
    Who **should help**?   You should.
6. *Who* can also be the object of a question with *should*.
    OBJECT
    Who **should** I **help**?   You should help your grandparents.

Should (not) + *Be* + Present Participle

1. Use *should (not)* + *be* + present participle to give advice and opinions about something happening now.
    Why is your grandfather carrying all those bags? You **should be helping**.

    Look at that boy. He's pushing the other children. He **shouldn't be pushing**.
2. Use *should (not)* + *be* + present participle to talk about something happening now. Use *should (not)* + base form of the verb to talk about something that is true all the time.
    You **should be helping** me with the bags. (= now)

    You **should help** older people with their bags. (= all the time)

Should and *Have to*

1. Use *should* to say that it is a good idea for someone to do something.
    You **should be** kind to strangers. (= It's the right thing to do.)
2. Use *has to* or *have to* to say that it is necessary for someone to do something.
    Carly, you **have to be** nice to the other children. (= Carly doesn't have a choice.)

3. Use *shouldn't* to say that it is not a good idea for someone to do something.
> People **shouldn't be** rude to each other.
> (= It's not the right thing to do.)

4. Use *doesn't have to* or *don't have to* to say that it is <u>not</u> necessary for someone to do something.
> My brother's going to help tomorrow. You **don't have to help**. (= It's not necessary.)

Unit 16 Neighbors

Must + Verb

1. Use *must* when you are 95% sure that something is true, but you are not 100% sure.
> Alice and Mark **must need** the money. They both work two jobs.

2. Do not use *must* when you are 100% sure.
> That's George.
> (= I work with him and know him well.)
> That **must be** George.
> (= I've never met him, but he's with Mary and her boyfriend's name is George.)

3. Use *may* or *might* when you are less than 50% sure that something is true. You don't really know. You are just guessing.
> Carly's not in class. She **might be** sick.
> (= Maybe she is, and maybe she isn't.)

4. Remember! *Must* also means "necessary."
> You **must fix** the door today. (= It's necessary.)
> You **must be** tired.
> (= I think so, because of how you look.)

Must + *Be* + Present Participle

1. Use *must* + *be* + present participle when you are 95% sure that something is happening, but you are not 100% sure.
> Barbara **must be cooking**. It smells great in here.
> (Barbara's a good cook, and she lives here.)

2. Do not use *must* + *be* + present participle when you are 100% sure that something is happening.
> Barbara can't come to the phone. She's cooking.
> (You are with Barbara in the kitchen.)

3. Be careful! Do not use *must* + *be* + present participle to say that something is necessary.

Must not and *Can't*

1. Use *must not* when you are 95% sure that something is not true, but you are *not* 100% sure.
> The neighbor upstairs **must not be** home much. I never hear him.

2. We often use the contracted form *mustn't* in conversation.
> He **mustn't pay** a lot in rent. The apartment is very small.

3. Use *can't* when you think that something is impossible.
> She **can't have** four children! She's so young.

4. We also say *couldn't* when we think that something is impossible.
> She **couldn't have** four children! She's so young.

5. Use *be* + present participle with *must not, can't*, or *couldn't* when you are talking about something now.
> Louisa **must not be working** today. Her car is in the driveway.
> Norman **can't be watching** TV. He doesn't have a television.
> The children **couldn't be playing** in the yard. It's raining.

Unit 17 Health

It + Infinitive

1. An infinitive is *to* + verb. Use an infinitive after *It* + a form of *be* + certain adjectives (for example, *important* and *necessary*). Look at page 300 for a list of adjectives that can be followed by infinitives.
> It is **important to exercise** every day.

2. Add *for* + (a person) before the infinitive when you want to say "who".
> It is necessary **for me** to talk to the doctor. = I must talk to the doctor.

Too and *Enough* + Infinitive

1. Use *too* before an adjective. *Too* has a negative meaning. It means "more than is good."
> Your blood pressure is **too high**. You have to take medicine.

2. *Not enough* means "less than the correct amount."
> He **isn't strong enough**. He can't walk alone.

3. Use *enough* after an adjective but before a noun.
> ADJECTIVE + ENOUGH
> Your diet isn't **healthy enough**.
> ENOUGH + NOUN
> You don't eat **enough fruits and vegetables**.

4. An infinitive often comes after *too* or *enough*.
> The doctor is **too** busy **to see** you.
> You're not **strong** enough **to leave** the hospital.

5. Use these patterns with *too* and *enough* when you want to say "who".
> i) *too* + adjective + *for* + (a person) + infinitive:
> Your fever is **too high for you to go** to school.
> (You can't go to school.)
>
> ii) (*too*) + adjective + *enough* + *for* + (a person) + infinitive:
> The doctor's office is**n't close enough for us to walk**. (We can't walk.)

6. You can also use *too* and *enough* before an adverb.
> The doctor speaks **too quickly** for me to understand.
> The doctor doesn't speak **clearly enough**.

7. Be careful. Don't confuse *too* and *very*. *Too* has a negative meaning; it causes a negative result. *Very* makes the meaning of an adjective stronger.
> I'm **too tired**. I can't drive.
> I'm **very tired**, but I can drive.

Infinitives of Purpose

1. We often use an infinitive (*to* + verb) to say the reason for doing something. It answers the question *Why*.

    Why does she take a pill every day?
    She takes it **to lower** her cholesterol.

2. *To* can have the same meaning as *in order to*.

    People go on diets **to lose** weight. =
    People go on diets **in order to lose** weight.

3. You can use *for* + noun to give a reason. You cannot use *for* + verb to give a reason.

    I went to the drugstore **to get** some aspirin.
    I went to the drugstore **for aspirin**.
    NOT ~~I went to the drugstore for get some aspirin.~~

Unit 18 Free Time

Gerunds as Subjects

1. Gerunds are used as nouns. We form a gerund by adding *–ing* to the end of a verb.

    (BE + ING):
    Being on a basketball team is fun.

2. Like nouns, gerunds can be the subject of a sentence.

    GERUND   NOUN
    Playing chess is fun. OR **Chess** is fun.

3. Use the singular form of the verb after a gerund.

    Running 10 kilometers **is** easy.

4. Use the plural form of the verb after two or more gerunds.

    Swimming and **hiking are** popular.

5. Be careful. Gerunds and the present participle of verbs look the same. They both end in *–ing*.

    VERB (present participle form)
    Tom and Jack are **taking** an art class.

    GERUND
    Taking an art class is expensive.

6. Look at page 295 for information about the spelling of gerunds.

Gerunds as Objects of Prepositions

1. Use a gerund after a preposition. The preposition can come after a verb, an adjective, or a noun.

    (verb + preposition + gerund)
    I'm thinking **about taking** a dance class.

    (adjective + preposition + gerund)
    Are you interested **in learning** how to bake?

    (noun + preposition + gerund)
    What's your reason **for being** late?

2. For a negative gerund, add *not* before the gerund.

    I enjoy **not going** to work on the weekend.

Gerunds or Infinitives as Objects of Verbs

1. Use a gerund after some verbs—for example, *dislike*, *finish*.

    I **dislike going** for walks alone.
    I'm going to **finish doing** the puzzle soon.

2. Use an infinitive after some verbs—for example, *expect*, *would like*.

    We **expect to go** to the game.
    I **would like to learn** Chinese.

3. You can use either a gerund or infinitive after some verbs—for example, *love*, *hate*. There is little difference in meaning.

    I **love swimming**.   I **love to swim**.
    Chris **hates cooking**.   Chris **hates to cook**.

4. Look at page 299 for a list of verbs that take gerunds or infinitives or both.

Unit 19 Emergency Services

Verb + Object + Infinitive

1. Use an object + infinitive after some verbs—for example, *advise*, *order*.

    OBJECT   INFINITIVE
    The police advised **him**   **to get**   a lawyer.

2. You can use two different patterns after some verbs—for example, *need*, *want*:

    i) verb + infinitive   I want **to go**.
    ii) verb + object + infinitive   I want **you to go**.

3. Look at page 299 for a list of verbs that take objects + infinitive.

Verb + Noun Clause and Replacing Noun Clauses

1. A noun clause is part of a sentence. It has a subject and a verb, and it is used as a noun. You can use a noun clause as the object of a verb.

    NOUN [OBJECT]
    I know the **police officer**.
    I know **that the police officer's name is Bill**.

    NOUN CLAUSE [OBJECT]

2. Use a noun clause after certain verbs—for example, *think*, *know*, *believe*. You can use *that* after the verb, but you don't have to. Both ways are correct.

    I think **that the firemen are here**.
    I think **the firemen are here**.

3. Look at page 300 for a list of verbs that take noun clauses.

4. When you answer a *yes/no* question, you can use one of these expressions in place of a noun clause.

    I **think so**.   I **believe so**.
    I **don't think so**.   I **don't believe so**.
    I **hope so**.   I **guess so**.
    I **hope not**.   I **guess not**.

    Are the firefighters coming? **I hope so**.
    (= I hope that they are coming.)

    Was the accident serious? **I hope not**.
    (= I hope that the accident wasn't serious.)

Make and Let

1. The verb *make* can mean "to force." When *make* has this meaning, use this pattern:
   make + an object (*someone*) + the base form of the verb

   > The firefighters **made everyone leave** the building.
   > NOT ~~The firefighters made everyone to leave the building.~~

2. The verb *let* can mean "to permit." When *let* has this meaning, use this pattern:
   let + an object (*someone*) + the base form of the verb

   > The firefighters **let us go** back into the building an hour later.
   > NOT ~~The firefighters let us to go back in the building an hour later.~~

UNIT 20 Taking a Trip

Reported Speech: Present Statements

1. Use a form of *say* and quotation marks (" ")when you write someone's exact words. Put a comma (,) after *say* and before the quotation marks.

   > Rick **says, "**The weather's beautiful in Santa Rita.**"**

2. Use a form of *say* and a noun clause when you report someone's statement. Do <u>not</u> put a comma or quotation marks.

   > Rick **says that** the weather is beautiful in Santa Rita.

3. You can use *that*, but it is not necessary.

   > Rick **says** the weather is beautiful in Santa Rita.

4. When you report someone's statement, change the pronouns and verbs when necessary.

   > Susan says, **"I am** really enjoying **myself."**
   > Susan says (that) **she is** really enjoying **herself**.

Reported Speech: Commands

1. When you report an order, use *tell* [someone to do something].

   > The driver said, "Open the door."
   > The driver **told me to open** the door.

2. When you report a negative order, use *tell* [someone not to do something].

   > The flight attendant said, "Don't leave your bags on the floor."
   > The flight attendant **told us not to leave** our bags on the floor.

3. Be careful. After *tell* (or *told*), use an object + infinitive. After *say* (or *said*) use a noun clause.

   >   OBJECT   INFINITIVE
   > They told **us**   **to come** early.
   >   NOUN CLAUSE
   > She says **(that) she's coming** early.

Reported Speech: Requests

1. We use a lot of different language to make requests:

   > "Can you tell me your name, please?"
   > "Could you tell me your name, please?"
   > "Would you tell me your name, please?"
   > "Please tell me your name."

2. When you report a request, use *ask someone to do something*.

   > The woman **asked me to tell** her my name.

Charts

Spelling Rules: Present Progressive and Gerunds

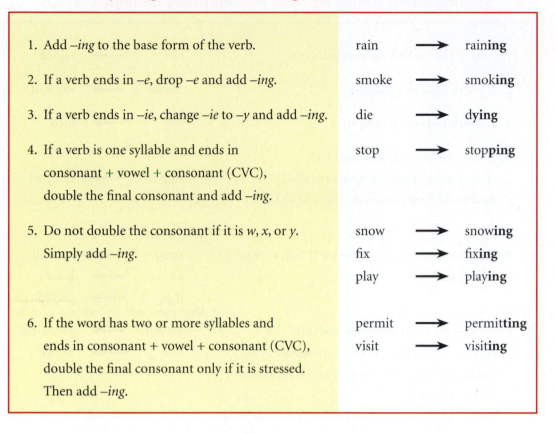

1. Add –*ing* to the base form of the verb.	rain ⟶	rain**ing**
2. If a verb ends in –*e*, drop –*e* and add –*ing*.	smoke ⟶	smok**ing**
3. If a verb ends in –*ie*, change –*ie* to –*y* and add –*ing*.	die ⟶	d**ying**
4. If a verb is one syllable and ends in consonant + vowel + consonant (CVC), double the final consonant and add –*ing*.	stop ⟶	stop**ping**
5. Do not double the consonant if it is *w*, *x*, or *y*. Simply add –*ing*.	snow ⟶ fix ⟶ play ⟶	snow**ing** fix**ing** play**ing**
6. If the word has two or more syllables and ends in consonant + vowel + consonant (CVC), double the final consonant only if it is stressed. Then add –*ing*.	permit ⟶ visit ⟶	permit**ting** visit**ing**

Spelling Rules: Simple Present Third Person Singular

1. Add –*es* to words that end in –*ch*, –*s*, –*sh*, –*ss*, –*x*, or –*z*.	teach ⟶ wash ⟶ miss ⟶ fix ⟶ fizz ⟶	teach**es** wash**es** miss**es** fix**es** fizz**es**
2. Add –*es* to words that ends in –*o*.	do ⟶	do**es**
3. If the word ends in consonant + –*y*, change –*y* to –*i* and add –*es*.	cry ⟶	cr**ies**
4. Add –*s* to words that end in vowel + –*y*.	play ⟶	play**s**

Spelling Rules: Simple Past and Past Participle of Regular Verbs

1. Add –ed to the base form of the verb.   rain ⟶ rained

2. If a verb ends in –e, add –d.   smoke ⟶ smoked

3. If a verb ends in –ie, add –d.   die ⟶ died

4. If the verb is one syllable and ends in consonant + vowel + consonant (CVC), double the final consonant and add –ed.   stop ⟶ stopped

5. Do not double the consonant if it is w, x, or y. Simply add –ed.   snow ⟶ snowed
fix ⟶ fixed
play ⟶ played

6. If the word has two or more syllables and ends in consonant + vowel + consonant (CVC), double the final consonant only if it is stressed. Then add –ed.   permit ⟶ permitted
visit ⟶ visited

Spelling Rules: Plural Nouns

1. Add –es to words that end in –ch, –s, –sh, –ss, –x, or –z.   watch ⟶ watches
bus ⟶ buses
dish ⟶ dishes
pass ⟶ passes
box ⟶ boxes

2. Add –es to words that end in –o.   potato ⟶ potatoes

3. If the word ends in consonant + –y, change –y to –i and add –es.   country ⟶ countries

4. Add –s to words that end in vowel + –y.   day ⟶ days

Comparative Form of Adjectives

<u>One-syllable words</u>

1. If the word ends in a consonant, add –er.   old   ⟶   old**er**

2. If the word ends in 1 vowel + 1 consonant,   thin   ⟶   thin**ner**
   double the consonant and add –er.

3. If the word ends in –e, add –r.   nice   ⟶   nice**r**

<u>Two-syllable words</u>

If the word ends in –y, change –y to –i and add –er.   pretty   ⟶   prett**ier**

Superlative Form of Adjectives

<u>One-syllable words</u>

1. If the word ends in a consonant, add –est.   old   ⟶   old**est**

2. If the word ends in 1 vowel + 1 consonant,   thin   ⟶   thin**nest**
   double the consonant and add –est.

3. If the word ends in –e, add –st.   nice   ⟶   nice**st**

<u>Two-syllable words</u>

If the word ends in –y, change –y to –i and add –est.   pretty   ⟶   prett**iest**

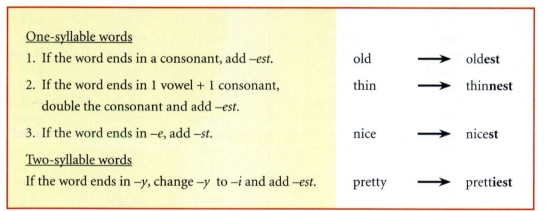

Comparative and Superlative Forms of Adverbs

Comparative

<u>One-syllable words</u>

1. If the word ends in a consonant, add –er.   fast   ⟶   fast**er**

2. If the word ends –e, add –r.   late   ⟶   late**r**

<u>Two-syllable words</u>

If the word ends in –ly, add *more* before the word.   quickly   ⟶   **more** quickly

Superlative

<u>One-syllable words</u>

1. If the word ends in a consonant, add –est.   fast   ⟶   fast**est**

2. If the word ends –e, add –st.   late   ⟶   late**st**

<u>Two-syllable words</u>

If the word ends in –ly, add *the most* before the word.   quickly   ⟶   **the most** quickly

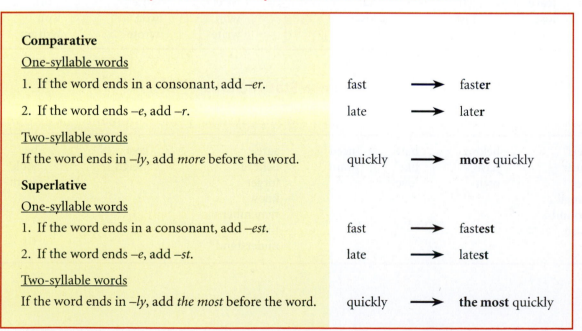

Irregular Verbs

Base form	Simple Past	Past Participle	Base form	Simple Past	Past Participle
be	was	been	make	made	made
become	became	become	meet	met	met
buy	bought	bought	pay	paid	paid
catch	caught	caught	put	put	put
come	came	come	read	read	read
cost	cost	cost	ride	rode	ridden
cry	cried	cried	ring	rang	rung
cut	cut	cut	run	ran	run
do	did	done	say	said	said
drink	drank	drunk	see	saw	seen
drive	drove	driven	sell	sold	sold
eat	ate	eaten	send	sent	sent
feel	felt	felt	shine	shone	shone
find	found	found	sit	sat	sat
fly	flew	flown	sleep	slept	slept
forget	forgot	forgotten	speak	spoke	spoken
get	got	gotten	spend	spent	spent
give	gave	given	stand	stood	stood
go	went	gone	steal	stole	stolen
have	had	had	swim	swam	swum
hear	heard	heard	take	took	taken
hit	hit	hit	teach	taught	taught
hold	held	held	think	thought	thought
hurt	hurt	hurt	try	tried	tried
know	knew	known	wake	woke	woken
leave	left	left	wear	wore	worn
lose	lost	lost	win	won	won
			write	wrote	written

Common Stative Verbs

Senses	Possession	Likes	Needs	Mental States	Measurement	Description
feel	belong	hate	need	agree	cost	be
hear	have	like	want	believe	weigh	look
see	own	love		forget		seem
smell				know		
sound				remember		
taste				think		
				understand		

Verb + Gerund

acknowledge	consider	enjoy	justify	prohibit	risk
admit	delay	escape	keep (*continue*)	quit	suggest
advise	deny	explain	mention	recall	support
appreciate	detest	feel like	mind (*object to*)	recommend	
avoid	discontinue	finish	miss	regret	
can't help	discuss	forgive	postpone	report	
celebrate	dislike	give up (*stop*)	practice	resent	
	endure	imagine	prevent	resist	

Verb + Preposition + Gerund

adapt to	approve of	be into	consist of	engage in
adjust to	argue (with	blame for	decide on	forgive (someone)
agree (with	someone)	care about	depend on	for
someone) on	about	complain (to	disapprove of	help (someone)
apologize (to	ask about	someone) about	discourage (someone)	with
someone) for	believe in	concentrate on	from	

Verb + Infinitive

agree	choose	hesitate	need	promise	want
appear	consent	hope	neglect	refuse	wish
arrange	decide	hurry	offer	request	would like
ask	deserve	intend	pay	rush	
attempt	expect	learn	plan	seem	
can't afford	fail	manage	prepare	volunteer	
can't wait	help	mean (*intend*)	pretend	wait	

Verb + Object + Infinitive

advise	encourage	hire	persuade	tell
allow	expect	invite	promise	urge
ask	forbid	need	remind	want
cause	force	order	request	warn
choose	get	pay	require	wish
convince	help	permit	teach	would like

Verbs Followed by the Gerund or the Infinitive

begin	continue	hate	love	remember	stop
can't stand	forget	like	prefer	start	try

Go + Verb + –ing

go bowling	go hiking	go sailing
go camping	go horseback riding	go shopping
go dancing	go hunting	go skating
go fishing	go jogging	go skiing
go golfing	go running	go swimming

Verbs Followed by a Noun Clause

believe	hear	say
feel	hope	suspect
guess	know	think

It + Adjective + Infinitive

dangerous	embarassing	good	normal
difficult	exciting	important	unhealthy
easy	frightening	necessary	unusual

Pronunciation Rules

Simple Present Third Person Singular

1. If the word ends in a vowel sound or /b/, /d/, /g/, /l/, /m/, /n/, /ŋ/, /ɹ/, /θ/, /v/ or /w/,

   it is pronounced /z/.

   gives   onions   Tom's

2. If the word ends in /f/, /h/, /k/, /p/, /t/ or /ð/,

   it is pronounced /s/.

   walks   maps   Matt's

3. If the word ends in /tʃ/, /dʒ/, /s/, /ʃ/, /z/ or /ʒ/,

   it is pronounced /ɪz/.

   sneezes   watches   Nash's

Simple Past and Past Participle of Regular Verbs

1. If the base form ends in a vowel sound or /b/, /dʒ/, /g/ /l/, /m/, /ŋ/, /ɹ/, /θ/, /v/, /w/, /z/, or /ʒ/,

   it is pronounced /d/.

   snowed   mailed

2. If the base forms ends in /tʃ/, /f/, /h/, /k/, /p/ or /s/,

   it is pronounced /t/, /ʃ/, or /ð/.

   stopped   laughed

3. If the base form ends in /d/ or /t/,

   it is pronounced /ɪd/.

   needed   wanted

Partner Activities

From Time to Talk, PAGE 53

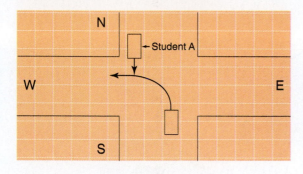

From Time to Talk, PAGE 91

Spring of your junior year
- ☐ Meet with a guidance counselor.
- ☐ Discuss several different colleges.

Fall of your senior year
- ☐ Study for the SAT.
- ☐ Decide on three colleges.
- ☐ Register for the December SAT.

Winter of your senior year
- ☐ Take the SAT in December.
- ☐ Start working on college applications.
- ☐ Start working on financial aid forms.
- ☐ Write college application essays.

Spring of your senior year
- ☐ Ask high school to send your transcript to the colleges.
- ☐ Submit completed application packet before the deadline.
- ☐ Submit completed financial aid form before the deadline.
- ☐ Relax and wait for an answer!

From Time to Talk, PAGE 119

Student A, read each sentence twice.

1. You haven't been listening to me.
2. We didn't speak at your wedding.
3. I haven't heard from them for months.
4. She's known him since college.

Now listen to Student B and check (✓) the sentences you hear.

5. ☐ **a.** They've been arguing for an hour.
   ☐ **b.** They argued for an hour.

6. ☐ **a.** She's been crying all day.
   ☐ **b.** She cried all day.

7. ☐ **a.** We've been getting along better.
   ☐ **b.** We're getting along better.

8. ☐ **a.** She's been talking for hours.
   ☐ **b.** She talked for hours.

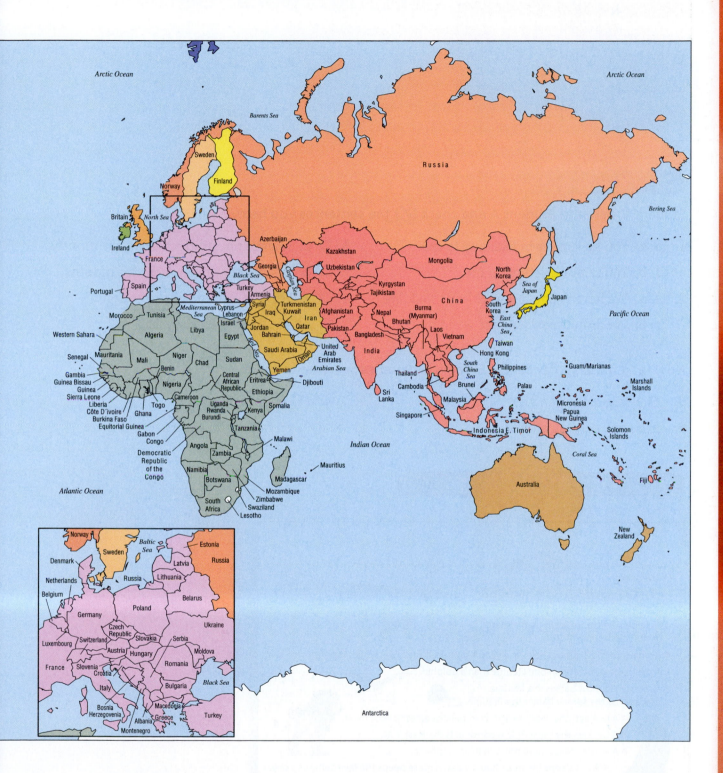

Arctic Ocean

Arctic Ocean

Barents Sea

Bering Sea

Russia

Sweden

Finland

Norway

North Sea

Britain

Ireland

France

Azerbaijan

Kazakhstan

Mongolia

North Korea

Sea of Japan

Japan

Pacific Ocean

Georgia

Uzbekistan

Kyrgystan

Tajikistan

China

South Korea

East China Sea

Portugal

Spain

Black Sea

Turkey

Armenia

Syria

Turkmenistan

Kuwait

Afghanistan

Nepal

Bhutan

Burma (Myanmar)

Morocco

Tunisia

Mediterranean Sea

Cyprus

Lebanon

Iraq

Iran

Pakistan

Laos

Taiwan

Israel

Jordan

Qatar

Bangladesh

Vietnam

Hong Kong

Western Sahara

Algeria

Libya

Egypt

Bahrain

Saudi Arabia

United Arab Emirates

India

Thailand

South China Sea

Philippines

Guam/Marianas

Senegal

Mauritania

Mali

Niger

Chad

Sudan

Yemen

Oman

Arabian Sea

Cambodia

Brunei

Malaysia

Marshall Islands

Gambia

Benin

Eritrea

Djibouti

Sri Lanka

Micronesia

Palau

Guinea Bissau

Nigeria

Central African Republic

Ethiopia

Papua New Guinea

Guinea

Sierra Leone

Cameroon

Uganda

Kenya

Somalia

Singapore

Indonesia E. Timor

Solomon Islands

Liberia

Côte D´ivoire

Ghana

Togo

Rwanda

Burundi

Tanzania

Malawi

Indian Ocean

Burkina Faso

Equitorial Guinea

Gabon

Congo

Angola

Zambia

Mauritius

Coral Sea

Fiji

Democratic Republic of the Congo

Madagascar

Mozambique

Australia

Namibia

Botswana

Zimbabwe

Atlantic Ocean

South Africa

Swaziland

Lesotho

New Zealand

Norway

Baltic Sea

Estonia

Russia

Denmark

Sweden

Latvia

Netherlands

Russia

Lithuania

Belgium

Belarus

Germany

Poland

Luxembourg

Czech Republic

Slovakia

Ukraine

Switzerland

Serbia

Austria

Hungary

Moldova

France

Slovenia

Romania

Croatia

Italy

Bulgaria

Black Sea

Bosnia Herzegovina

Macedonia

Montenegro

Albania

Greece

Turkey

Antarctica

From Time to Talk, PAGE 53

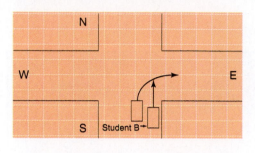

From Time to Talk, PAGE 119

Student B, listen to Student A and check (✓) the sentences you hear.

1. ❑ **a.** You haven't been listening to me.
   ❑ **b.** You're not listening to me.

2. ❑ **a.** We haven't spoken since your wedding.
   ❑ **b.** We didn't speak at your wedding.

3. ❑ **a.** I haven't heard from them for months.
   ❑ **b.** I didn't hear from them for months.

4. ❑ **a.** She's known him since college.
   ❑ **b.** She knew him in college.

Now read these sentences for Student A. Read each sentence twice.

5. They argued for an hour.

6. She's been crying all day.

7. We've been getting along better.

8. She's been talking for hours.

Answers to Time to Talk Quiz, PAGE 147

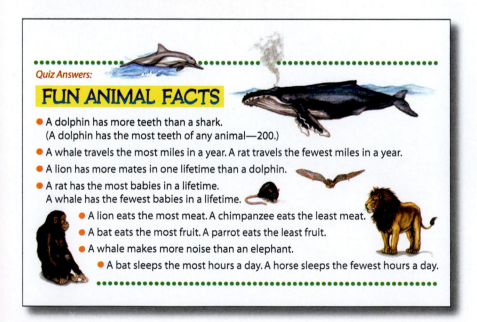

Quiz Answers:

FUN ANIMAL FACTS

- A dolphin has more teeth than a shark.
  (A dolphin has the most teeth of any animal—200.)
- A whale travels the most miles in a year. A rat travels the fewest miles in a year.
- A lion has more mates in one lifetime than a dolphin.
- A rat has the most babies in a lifetime.
  A whale has the fewest babies in a lifetime.
- A lion eats the most meat. A chimpanzee eats the least meat.
- A bat eats the most fruit. A parrot eats the least fruit.
- A whale makes more noise than an elephant.
- A bat sleeps the most hours a day. A horse sleeps the fewest hours a day.

From Time to Talk, PAGE 201

Student A

Peter

(knock)
(apologize)

(offer to help)
(touch the dog)

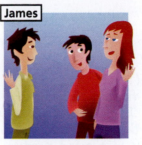

James

(shake her hand)
(kiss her)

Student B

Katie

(cover her mouth)
(say "Excuse me")

Maria

Achool

(say "Sorry")
(say "Bless you!")

George

(interrupt)
(whisper to a classmate)

From Time to Talk, PAGE 271

Postcard 1:

SYDNEY OPERA HOUSE

Dear Linda,
We're really enjoying ourselves. Our hotel is beautiful, and there are many interesting things to do. We go to the beach every day. The people are friendly, but it's hard for me to understand their English. They have a different accent and use different expressions than Americans do. It's also strange to be in a place where it's summer in January, but we love the warm temperatures. Hope you're keeping warm in Chicago.

Love, Jacquie and Paul

International POST
Australia
$1.20

Ms. Linda Wong
28 West Kinzie Street
Chicago, IL 60610

Choices for Postcard 2:

❏ Cairo, Egypt

❏ São Paulo, Brazil

❏ New York, New York, USA

❏ Montreal, Canada

Partner Activities

305

From Time to Talk, PAGE 271

Postcard 2:

Times Square, New York City

Dear Mom and Dad,
I've been here for five days, and it's
been great so far. I've seen many famous
places already. All the skyscrapers are
amazing. My hotel is in a great location,
with a wonderful view of Central Park.
The only problem is the weather. It's
been cold every day, and it's snowed
twice. But that hasn't stopped me from
going out to the theater! I've seen two
Broadway shows, and have tickets for
another one tonight. I miss you!

Love, Annie

Mr. and Mrs. James Nieves
240 Hogan Street
Houston, TX 77009

Choices for Postcard 1:

❑ Hong Kong, China

❑ San Juan, Puerto Rico

❑ Miami Beach, Florida, USA

❑ Sydney, Australia

Answers to Exercise C, PAGE 35

2. The first World Cup took place in Uruguay.

3. People watched the World Cup on TV for the first time in 1958.

4. England won the World Cup in 1966.

5. Brazil won the 2002 World Cup.

6. 1.7 billion people saw the 2002 World Cup on TV.

Answers to Exercise D, PAGE 145

2. T 3. T 4. T 5. T 6. F 7. T 8. F

Audioscript

Unit 1: Getting to Know You

Listening, A, B, and C, page 3

Marco: Hey Betsy! How are you doing?

Betsy: Hi, Marco. I'm great. It's good to see you. What's new with you?

Marco: Oh, you know, the same old stuff. I'm taking classes at Spencer, and working nights at Clarks. Look at all these people! I can't believe that they all live in our neighborhood.

Betsy: I know. A lot of new people are moving in.

Marco: Hey, who's that?

Betsy: The woman in the kitchen? That's Felicia Banks. She lives in the Long's old house.

Marco: What's she like?

Betsy: I'm just getting to know her, but I think she's got a nice personality.

Marco: Is she going out with anyone?

Betsy: Yeah, she's got a boyfriend.

Marco: Oh well, too bad. Hey, is that Amy Parsons?

Betsy: No. Amy Parsons doesn't look like that. Amy's got long hair, and she's a lot shorter.

Marco: Oh, yeah, you're right. So who is she?

Betsy: I don't know her name, but she lives on Elm St., next to the Fosters. She works at the mall.

Marco: Has she got a boyfriend?

Betsy: No . . . but she's got a husband. Hey, what's going on with you? Are you and Jenny fighting again?

Marco: No . . . but we're not going out anymore. We're still friends, but she's going to college now, and she hasn't got time for a boyfriend. So, if you've got any single friends . . .

Grammar, page 10

Stan: Hi, Jack. How are things going?

Jack: I'm pretty busy. I'm taking five classes this semester.

Stan: Really? That's a lot. I'm just taking three. Do you like your teachers?

Jack: Yes. I get along with all of them. I really like my math teacher. He's got a good sense of humor, and he explains things really well.

Stan: I like my teachers, too. So, where are you going now?

Jack: I'm going home. Peggy's waiting for me in the car.

Stan: Oh, are you two going out these days?

Jack: No, we're just friends. She's got a boyfriend.

Dictation, page 10

1. My daughters have got wavy hair.
2. My husband's got a beard and a mustache.
3. She hasn't got a good sense of humor.
4. Who are you going out with these days?
5. These days my sister and I are getting along better.

Listening, A and B, page 11

Reporter: This is Evangeline Lopez with *Spotlight on the City*. People in the city often complain that nobody knows their neighbors anymore. We decided to find out if that's true. We are downtown, standing in front of an apartment building. Excuse me, I'm with *Spotlight on the City*. Do you live in this building?

Woman 1: Here? No. I'm just visiting a friend.

Reporter: Thank you. Excuse me, sir? Have you got time for a few questions? I'm with *Spotlight on the City*, and we're talking to people today about their neighbors.

Man: Their neighbors?

Reporter: Yes. Do you know your neighbor's names?

Man: Hmmm . . . Let me think . . . well, I know the name of my neighbor's dog—it's Lucy—but I don't know *his* name. And the woman next door to me. . . . she's got a cat . . . I think her name is Mrs. Carson . . . or is it Carter? I'm not sure. I guess that's it.

Reporter: And how long have you lived here?

Man: Ten years.

Reporter: Thank you very much.

Man: No problem.

Reporter: Excuse me, ma'am?

Woman 2: Yes?

Reporter: I'm with *Spotlight on the City*. Can I ask you a few questions?

Woman 2: Yes, of course, dear.

Reporter: Do you live in this building?

Woman 2: Yes.

Reporter: And do you know your neighbors?

Woman 2: Of course. I know all of them . . .

Reporter:	Really? All of them? How many are there?
Woman 2:	Well, there's Mr. Rupert on the first floor— He's got a bad heart. And there's poor Jenny in 3A. She's working so much these days. She's making herself sick . . . and then there's Molly in 3B. She's looking for a job. Maybe you've got something for her at the radio station?

Unit 2: The World We Live In

Listening, A, B, and C, page 17

Rita:	I'm sick of living in the city. There are very few good schools, too much crime, and very little open space. I want to move somewhere safe where there's plenty of space for my kids to run around.
Ben:	Let me guess—you're thinking about moving to the suburbs, right?
Rita:	Yeah, why?
Ben:	Don't do it! My wife and I moved out of the city two years ago, and neither of us is happy with the decision.
Rita:	Why do you say that?
Ben:	Well, you're right about the open space— there's plenty. But I don't have any time to enjoy it. I have no time with my kids.
Rita:	Why is that?
Ben:	There are a lot of reasons. First of all, a lot of people are moving out of the city. There aren't enough houses and apartments for them all in the suburbs, so the prices are really high. I have to work extra hours to pay for our new house, and we still don't have enough money to pay our bills. And the traffic is terrible. I spend several hours a day in my car. I'm spending too much on gas, but what can I do?
Rita:	Why don't you take public transportation?
Ben:	Because there are no trains before 7:00 A.M., and only a few after 5:00. There's one at 5:30 and one at 6:30, but as you know, I work until 7.
Rita:	That's a real problem. So where do you park? There's very little parking out back, and the public lots are expensive, aren't they?
Ben:	Well, there aren't a lot of parking spaces here, but there are a few. That's why I get here so early every day.

Rita:	Hmmm . . . I'll think about what you said.
Ben:	Well, if you *do* decide to move to the suburbs, let me know. Maybe we can sell you our house . . . and move into your apartment.

Grammar, page 24

I'm writing from my new home. The neighborhood is safe, and it's quiet most of the time. There's a little noise in the morning, but I get up early anyway. The rent is very cheap, but there is very little public transportation. Just one bus stops on my street. That's not great, but I'm lucky because there are plenty of inexpensive stores and restaurants.

My apartment's fine, but there are a few problems. First of all, the rooms are small, so there isn't a lot of space. Second, there isn't enough light. There isn't much sunshine around here, and my bedroom has no windows, zero! There are two windows in the living room, but both of them are very small. I miss the sunshine back home!

Dictation, page 24

1. We haven't got too much crime.
2. There isn't enough public transportation.
3. There's plenty of sunshine all the time.
4. We've got too many tourists.
5. We have a little traffic and a little crime, but neither problem is very serious.

Listening, A and B, page 25

Good evening. This is Jeff Woodman for *Spotlight on Our World*. Tonight's Spotlight Report is on the island nation of Cape Verde. The Republic of Cape Verde is located in the North Atlantic Ocean. It is about 500 kilometers from the West African coast. There were no people on the islands when they were discovered by the Portuguese in 1460. Today, the islands are home to approximately 400,000 people. Like many other island people, Cape Verdeans eat a lot of fish. However, they sell very little to other countries. It is difficult and expensive to keep the fish fresh. Other than fish, there are very few natural resources in Cape Verde.

Cape Verde is warm and dry all year, with plenty of sunshine. Most Cape Verdeans do not live in the big cities. About 70% live on farms or in small towns. They grow bananas, corn, beans, sweet potatoes, sugarcane, coffee, and peanuts. However, there are very few large farms because there isn't enough water. Most years, there is very little rain. In fact, in the 20th century there was no rain at all for several years. As a result, Cape Verdeans cannot grow enough food to feed their population, so they have to buy food from other countries. They import about 80% of their food.

Cape Verdeans are proud of their culture. Cape Verdean art and music is well known all over the world. Tourism is very important to Cape Verde. There are many beautiful beaches and several great hotels on the islands. Every year, more tourists choose Cape Verde for their vacations. Most of the tourists are from Western Europe, but Cape Verdeans hope there will soon be more tourists from other parts of the world too.

For *Spotlight on Our World*, this is Jeff Woodman. Tune in again tomorrow night, when we visit the beautiful Mexican island of Cozumel.

Unit 3: Sports

Listening, A, B, and C, page 31

Mina: Hi, honey. What time are you picking me up tonight?

Tony: Tonight? I can't go out tonight. I have tickets for the soccer match.

Mina: But you went to a match last night!

Tony: Yeah. And it was great. As soon as we sat down, our team scored a goal. Didn't you watch it on TV? It was . . .

Mina: No, Tony, I didn't. Tony, didn't you promise me something?

Tony: Did I? What did I promise?

Mina: A movie . . . do you remember anything about a movie?

Tony: Oh . . . yeah . . . I remember now . . . You wanted to see a movie because your sister liked it.

Mina: And who did I want to see it with?

Tony: Me? Did you want to see it with me?

Mina: Yes, I did.

Tony: But I didn't know that it was tonight.

Mina: Yes, you did. Before I got the tickets, I called you and asked. You said tonight was fine.

Tony: Uh oh . . . Now I remember. After I talked to you, Barney stopped by and invited me to go to tonight's game with him. I'm sorry, honey. I was so excited that I completely forgot about our date.

Mina: Well, just call Barney and tell him you can't go.

Tony: But, Mina, I'll take you to the movies another night.

Mina: Forget it, Tony. It's either me or soccer . . .

Tony: [silence—thinking]

Mina: Goodbye, Tony.

Grammar, page 38

Inez: I called you last night, but you weren't home.

Anton: I went to the Stars game.

Inez: How did the Stars do? Did they win?

Anton: No, they lost 3 to 1.

Inez: What happened?

Anton: Bond left the game because he got hurt. After he left, they didn't score again.

Dictation, page 38

1. They beat the other team by ten points.
2. Did the game take place at night?
3. How many times did your team lose to them?
4. The fans cheered after the team scored a goal.
5. Because he missed the shot, the player got angry.

Listening, A and B, page 39

Reporter: Good morning. This is June Vero, with *Spotlight on Sports*. Today we are talking about the first team sport with Dr. Ramon Perez, an expert in ancient Mesoamerican civilizations. Dr. Perez, welcome!

Dr. Perez: Thank you, June.

Reporter: So, Dr. Perez, where and when did the first team sport appear?

Dr. Perez: We now believe that the native people of Central America invented the first team sport about 3,500 years ago.

Reporter: What kind of game was it?

Dr. Perez: Well, there were several different versions of the game. We don't know all of the details, but we do know that in most places, the two teams played on a court in the shape of a capital I. They played with a large, heavy rubber ball.

Reporter: And what did they do with the ball?

Dr. Perez: We think that the players tried to pass the ball through a ring high on the wall of the court. They couldn't touch the ball with their hands, and the ball could never touch the ground.

Reporter: So how did they pass the ball?

Dr. Perez: We think they used their hips and elbows.

Reporter: How did the game end?

Dr. Perez: The game ended as soon as one team put the ball through the ring, or as soon as the ball touched the ground.

Reporter: So as soon as one team scored, the game was over?

Dr. Perez: Well, in fact, in most games there was no score. The ball usually touched the ground before any of the players put it in the ring.

Reporter:	But then who was the winner?
Dr. Perez:	The team that touched the ball right before it hit the ground lost the game. The other team won.
Reporter:	What happened after the game?
Dr. Perez:	There was a big celebration for the winning team.
Reporter:	And what happened to the losers?
Dr. Perez:	That was different in different places and at different times in history. In the earliest days of the game, the captain of the losing team was killed.
Reporter:	Well thank you, Dr. Perez, for being here.

Unit 4: Accidents

Listening, A, B, and C, page 45

Emily:	Manny, what happened to you? You look terrible!
Manny:	I had the worst weekend of my life.
Emily:	Why? What happened?
Manny:	Well, I was working with my father-in-law. We were painting his house. I was climbing up a ladder to paint the top of the house, and my father-in-law was standing below me. Suddenly, I heard a loud BANG. I was so surprised that I dropped my paintbrush . . . When I looked down, my father-in-law was standing there with paint all over him.
Emily:	Oh, no!
Manny:	Then my wife and mother-in-law ran out of the house. They were screaming.
Emily:	What was going on?
Manny:	I didn't have any idea at first. While I was climbing down the ladder, I heard another bang. And then I smelled smoke.
Emily:	Where was it coming from? Was it coming from inside the house?
Manny:	No, it wasn't. It was coming from the house next door.
Emily:	Oh no! Was anyone in the house?
Manny:	No, thank goodness. They were away for the weekend, visiting their daughter.
Emily:	Well, that's one good thing. Did the house burn down?
Manny:	Yes, it did. It was awful.
Emily:	How did the fire start?
Manny:	They don't know yet.

Emily:	Did anything happen to your father-in-law's house?
Manny:	No, we were very lucky.

Dictation, page 52

1. I was daydreaming when the teacher called my name.
2. What were you doing when you fell off the ladder?
3. Was he paying attention when the accident happened?
4. Last night at nine I was ironing.
5. She was talking on the phone while she was standing on the ladder.

Listening, A and B, page 53

Insurance Agent:	Capital Insurance. May I help you?
Maddy:	Hello? This is Maddy White. I have an insurance policy with you.
Insurance Agent:	Yes, of course, Mrs. White. Are you OK? You sound a little upset.
Maddy:	I am. I just had an accident.
Insurance Agent:	Oh, that's terrible. Are you okay?
Maddy:	Yes. I was wearing my seatbelt, thank goodness.
Insurance Agent:	Was anyone else injured?
Maddy:	Yes, the driver of the car that hit my car wasn't wearing her seatbelt, and she hit her head. She was bleeding a lot. They took her to the hospital.
Insurance Agent:	I'm sorry, Mrs. White. I know you're upset, but I have a few more questions.
Maddy:	Okay, go ahead.
Insurance Agent:	When and where did the accident happen?
Maddy:	I was driving down Seventh Ave. when—
Insurance Agent:	Were you driving east or west on Seventh?
Maddy:	I was driving east.
Insurance Agent:	And when was this?
Maddy:	About two hours ago.
Insurance Agent:	OK, go ahead.
Maddy:	As I was saying, I was driving down Seventh Ave. There was a red light ahead at the intersection with Grove St. I was slowing down to stop when I saw a car behind me. It was coming very fast— maybe 30 miles an hour. The driver wasn't paying attention, so she didn't see the red light. She was talking on her cell phone while she was driving! Then she hit me, and my car hit a van in front of me.

Insurance Agent:	Was anyone in the van injured?
Maddy:	No, thank goodness. They were wearing their seatbelts.
Insurance Agent:	And how fast do you think you were going when she hit you?
Maddy:	I told you, my car wasn't moving! I was at a stop sign.
Insurance Agent:	Please calm down, Mrs. White. These are just routine questions. Did the police come to the scene?
Maddy:	Yes, they did. They gave me a copy of the accident report.
Insurance Agent:	Great. That will make things a lot easier. Okay, so here's what you need to do . . .

Unit 5: Then and Now

Listening, A, B, and C, page 59

Tina:	Grandma, what were things like when you were young?
Grandma:	What do you mean?
Tina:	I mean, well, between boys and girls. Did you use to go on dates?
Grandma:	Yes, of course we did.
Tina:	Well, what did you use to do?
Grandma:	Well, we used to go bowling, or go out for an ice cream, or go to a movie.
Tina:	Who used to pay?
Grandma:	The boy did. It wasn't like today. In those days, the girl never paid.
Tina:	Did the guy pick you up, or did you meet him somewhere?
Grandma:	Oh, when I was your age, the boy used to pick the girl up at her house and meet her parents. We didn't use to meet at the mall, like kids do today. In fact, there didn't use to be any malls!
Tina:	No malls? You're kidding!
Grandma:	No, I'm serious. All of the stores used to be downtown, on Main Street.
Tina:	Wow. Did you go on dates every Saturday night?
Grandma:	No, I didn't. I wasn't that popular. I used to study a lot.
Tina:	So how did you meet grandpa?
Grandma:	At a dance.
Tina:	Was he your first boyfriend?
Grandma:	I think that's quite enough questions for tonight.

Grammar, page 66

Rob:	Do you always take your son to school?
Dan:	Always.
Rob:	Did your father use to take you to school?
Dan:	No, never.
Rob:	Did your father use to help around the house?
Dan:	My father didn't use to do a thing. He used to come home, have dinner, and watch TV.
Rob:	Who used to take care of the house?
Dan:	My mother, of course.
Rob:	Did you use to help her?
Dan:	No, I didn't. My brothers and sisters and I used to be the same as my father.

Dictation, page 66

1. Men never used to change children's diapers.
2. People didn't use to throw old things away.
3. Women used to make their own clothes, but men didn't.
4. Did men use to wear casual clothes to work?
5. How often did women use to get dressed up?

Listening, A and B, page 67

Reporter:	This is Ellie McDermott for *Spotlight on Women*. On today's program, we are taking a trip back in time with Alice and Lynn Thomas. They are twins. They are 102 years old today, and they are here to talk to us about the changes in women's lives in the past century. First of all, happy birthday!
Alice and Lynn:	Thank you.
Reporter:	So, what can you tell us about life when you were young? How were things different for women then?
Lynn:	Oh, my goodness. Well, life was very difficult for the girls and women of our generation.
Alice:	What do you mean?
Lynn:	Take housework, for example. In those days men didn't use to do any housework at all. And remember, there didn't use to be any washing machines, dishwashers, hot water, vacuum cleaners, electric stoves, or refrigerators.
Alice:	Lynn, do you remember laundry day?
Lynn:	Of course I do!
Reporter:	Why? What happened on laundry day?
Alice:	Every Monday, we had to wash the family's clothes, sheets, and towels—everything by hand.

Lynn:	Oh, we used to hate Mondays, didn't we, Alice?
Alice:	Yes, we certainly did! We used to get up at 4:00 A.M., and we didn't finish until 8:00 or 9:00 at night.
Lynn:	And do you remember how our hands used to hurt?
Alice:	How could I forget??!!! Sometimes they even bled.
Reporter:	Your hands used to bleed?
Lynn:	Oh, yes.
Reporter:	That sounds terrible. Was the rest of the week any easier?
Alice:	Not really. Now, don't get the wrong idea. The men used to work really hard too, but at least they got Sundays off. Not the women! Even on Sundays we had to eat, and there didn't use to be any fast food. My mother used to spend hours preparing the Sunday meal. And of course my sister and I had to help her.
Reporter:	Well, I guess I feel pretty lucky! *Spotlight on Women* will be back after a short break, with more from our guests, Lynn and Alice Thomas, who are 102 years old today . . .

Unit 6: Busy Lives

Listening, A, B, and C, page 73

Mom:	Hurry up! You're going to miss the bus!
Billy:	I'm not taking the bus today. Luz is picking me up.
Mom:	What time is she coming? It's really late.
Billy:	Relax, Mom. We'll get to school on time. I promise.
Billy:	I'll get it. It's probably Luz . . . Hello? Yeah, hi Luz. . . . Uh oh . . . okay, I'll ask. Mom?
Mom:	Yes, Billy?
Billy:	Can you drive Luz and me to school?
Mom:	What? But Luz is picking you up!
Billy:	Her mother needs the car today.
Mom:	Well, too bad. I'm already late for work. Come on. I'll drop you off at the bus stop.
Billy:	That's okay. I'll call Tad. He'll give us a ride.
Mom:	Forget it! It's already 7:30. Now say goodbye to Luz and get in the car.
Billy:	Luz? My mother can't give us a ride. I'm going to take the bus. I'll see you at school.

Mom:	What time are you going to be home tonight?
Billy:	Pretty late. I'm trying out for the soccer team after school.
Mom:	Oh, that's right. Good luck.
Billy:	Thanks . . . What are we having for dinner?
Mom:	I don't know. I need to run some errands after work. I'm not going to have time to cook, and your father's not going to be home. It's just going to be you and me.
Billy:	I'll cook. I'll make pizza.
Mom:	Really? That's great, honey.

Grammar to Communicate 1, B, page 74

1. A: What's fresh today?
    B: Everything's fresh. These muffins are hot out of the oven.
    A: Mmmm. I'll take six.
2. A: Mr. Roberts, Charlie Parker is on the line.
    B: Tell him I'm busy. I'll call him back later.
    A: But he said it was important.
3. A: Hello? Jimmy, it's Mom. I'm working late again tonight.
    B: But what about the movie? You promised.
    A: I'm sorry. Dad isn't busy. Maybe he'll take you.
4. A: Are you dropping off or picking up?
    B: Dropping off. Wow, you're busy. I'll run some errands and come back at noon.
    A: Okay. I'll have your prescription ready for you then.
5. A: A table for two, please.
    B: And your name, please?
    A: Oh, is there a wait? We're in a hurry. We'll get something to go.

Grammar, page 80

1. A: Bye, darling. Have a good day.
    B: Bye-bye. I'll call you later.
2. A: Oh, no! I haven't got my wallet with me!
    B: That's okay. I'll pay. You can pay next time.
3. A: Is Linda pregnant?
    B: Yes, she's going to have a baby in three months.
4. A: So, what did you decide? Are you going to New York this weekend?
    B: No, we haven't got the money.
5. A: Don't forget about tonight.
    B: Don't worry. We won't be late.
6. A: Which days are you going to work this week?
    B: Monday to Saturday. I'm off on Sunday.

Dictation, page 80

1. I'll give you a ride.
2. I'm sorry, but I won't have time to pick you up.
3. When is she going to try out for the team?
4. Are you babysitting on Friday night?
5. My husband and I are attending an important meeting tonight.

Listening, A and B, page 81

CONVERSATION 1

Woman: Oh, that's too bad. So . . . what are you going to do?

Man: I'm not sure. The job market is really bad here. Maybe I'll move.

CONVERSATION 2

Female Passenger: Look at all this traffic! We're going to be late.

Cab Driver: Sorry, lady, but it's rush hour.

Male Passenger: Just drop us off at the next corner. We'll walk the rest of the way.

CONVERSATION 3

Mona: Hello?

Barry: Hi, it's me.

Mona: Oh, hi, Barry. What's up?

Barry: I was just wondering . . . Are you and Dad going to Billy Rose's wedding next month?

Mona: Billy Rose is getting married?

Barry: Yes. Didn't you get an invitation?

Mona: No, I didn't.

Barry: Oh, that's strange.

CONVERSATION 4

Man 1: So, who's going to pick up the cake?

Man 2: I'm off tomorrow. I'll do it.

Man 1: Thanks. And who's going to buy the card?

Woman 1: We're not going to buy a card. Jose and I are going to make one.

Man 1: Oh, that's a great idea. Now remember—don't say a word to the teacher. It's a surprise.

Woman 2: Don't worry, we won't say anything.

CONVERSATION 5

Man: Do you want it for here or to go?

Woman: I'll take it to go.

Man: Do you need plates and forks?

Woman: No, thanks. We're going to eat at home.

Man: Okay then. That'll be $15.75.

Woman: Here you go. I'm going to run some errands. When will it be ready?

Man: In about 15 minutes.

Woman: Okay. I'll be back.

Unit 7: Education

Listening, A, B, and C, page 87

Mrs. Parker: Hello, Mrs. Martin?

Mrs. Martin: Yes?

Mrs. Parker: This is Helen Parker, your son Tommy's teacher.

Mrs. Martin: Oh, yes. Mrs. Parker. How are you?

Mrs. Parker: I'm fine. Is this a bad time?

Mrs. Martin: No, of course not. What can I do for you?

Mrs. Parker: Well, I'm worried about Tommy. He's not doing his work. If something doesn't change, he won't finish the year with the rest of his class.

Mrs. Martin: What do you mean?

Mrs. Parker: He might not be ready for high school next year. And he will definitely need to attend summer school.

Mrs. Martin: Why didn't you call me before?

Mrs. Parker: I did call you Mrs. Martin. And I sent you several e-mails. The principal also tried to contact you.

Mrs. Martin: You're right. You did . , . but I've been so busy . . . Anyway . . . as soon as I get home tonight, I'll take care of this. Tommy's not going to leave the house until he improves his grades. After I talk to him, he'll do his work.

Mrs. Parker: Mrs. Martin, can I make a suggestion?

Mrs. Martin: Yes?

Mrs. Parker: Well, Tommy's a smart boy . . .

Mrs. Martin: I know! He's just lazy. If he tries harder, he'll be fine.

Mrs. Parker: That's not what I was going to say. Tommy's very smart, but I think he might have a learning problem.

Mrs. Martin: A learning problem? What do you mean?

Mrs. Parker: We won't know exactly until we test him.

Mrs. Martin: Test him? What kind of test?

Secretary: Mrs. Martin? Mr. Bradley is waiting for you in the conference room.

Mrs. Martin: I'm sorry, but I have a meeting right now. I'll call you when we finish—in about an hour?

Mrs. Parker: That will be fine. My number is . . .

Dictation, page 94

1. I might major in English.
2. If you cheat on the test, you'll fail.
3. I may not take the final exam.
4. I won't go to college until I get a scholarship.
5. As soon as I get my degree, I'm going to look for a job.

Listening, A and B, page 95

Reporter: Good evening. This is Lisette Bouvier for *Spotlight on Education.* Tonight I am talking with this year's candidates for mayor, Tim Lee and Maureen West, about their views on education. Welcome to the show.

Lee: Thanks. Glad to be here.

West: Thank you for inviting us.

Reporter: As you both know, the public schools in our city are not doing very well. In fact, student test scores in our city are among the lowest in the country. Ms. West, if you become mayor, what will you do about this serious problem?

West: As soon as I become mayor, I am going to meet with the principals of all of the public schools in the city. I will listen carefully to their ideas, but before I do anything, I am also going to visit every school in the city. I want to talk to the teachers and the students directly. We won't be able to find a solution until we talk to all of the people involved.

Reporter: And you, Mr. Lee?

Lee: Ms. West's plan sounds good, but it will take too much time. This is an emergency. If we don't act quickly, hundreds of students will lose another year. And they might not get another chance to get a good education.

Reporter: So what's your plan, Mr. Lee?

Lee: As you know, Lisette, early in my career I was a teacher. I know how important good teachers are. But right now, there aren't enough good teachers in our schools, because we don't pay them enough. When I become mayor, I will work quickly to increase teachers' salaries. If we pay the teachers in public schools more, we will be able to hire the best.

Reporter: Well, let's see what the people who live in the city think of your plans. Our first caller is a teacher at Brookside Elementary School.

Unit 8: Getting a Job

Listening, A, B, and C, page 101

Ignacio: Hey, Natalia. How's the job search going? Have you found anything?

Natalia: No, not yet. I've applied at a few places at the mall, but no one has called me back. Have you heard about any jobs?

Ignacio: In fact, I have. Have you been to Danny's?

Natalia: No, I haven't. Why?

Ignacio: I think they're looking for a cashier.

Natalia: But I haven't ever worked as a cashier.

Ignacio: Don't worry about it. They'll train you.

Natalia: How do you know that?

Ignacio: Because several of my friends have worked there. Have you ever handled money?

Natalia: Just when I sold vegetables at a farm last summer. But I've never used a cash register.

Ignacio: Oh, it's easy.

Natalia: Really? Have you ever used one?

Ignacio: Uh, no, I haven't. But a lot of my friends have. Just go in and apply.

Natalia: Hmmm . . . maybe I will. Thanks for the information. So, how about Tracy? Has she started her new job?

Ignacio: Yes, she has.

Natalia: And how does she like it?

Ignacio: She loves it.

Natalia: Has she gotten her first paycheck yet?

Ignacio: No, she hasn't, but I think she's already spent more than she's made!

Natalia: What do you mean?

Ignacio: Well, she's borrowed at least a hundred dollars from me, and another hundred from her Mom. If she's not careful, she's going to need another part-time job.

Grammar, page 108

Raj: Hi, Liz. How are you and the family? Has Annie found a job?

Liz: No, she hasn't. It's never been easy for her to find a job.

Raj: Has she ever searched for a job online? I've found lots of jobs that way.

Liz: I'm not sure. But she's gone to several employment agencies. How about your new job? Have you started yet?

Raj: Yes, I have. It's a little hard because I have to work the night shift.

Liz: Oh, that is hard. I guess I'm lucky. I've always had the day shift.

1. Have you ever owned a business?
2. I've never hired people.
3. She hasn't quit yet.
4. They've already contacted me.
5. Has the manager fired her yet?

Interviewer: Please, Ms. Yu, have a seat. So, did you have any trouble finding us today?

Ms. Yu: No, not at all. Your directions were perfect.

Interviewer: Good. So, you're interested in our management training program.

Ms. Yu: Yes.

Interviewer: Have you ever worked as a manager?

Ms. Yu: No, I haven't. But I've owned my own business for five years.

Interviewer: Yes, I see that on your application. It's a house-cleaning service, right?

Ms. Yu: Yes, that's right.

Interviewer: I see. And how many workers do you have?

Ms. Yu: Oh, I've always worked alone.

Interviewer: I see. So you've never hired or trained anyone.

Ms. Yu: No, I haven't.

Interviewer: And has your business been successful?

Ms. Yu: Well, I haven't gotten rich, but I'm a single parent and I've made enough to put food on the table and a roof over our heads.

Interviewer: It sounds like you've done very well. If you get into our program, what will happen to your business?

Ms. Yu: My oldest son will take over when he graduates from high school next month.

Interviewer: I see. Have you ever worked for a large company? It's very different from working for yourself. You'll have a lot less freedom. Have you thought about that?

Ms. Yu: Yes, I have thought about it a lot. In fact, I've always wanted to work for a large company.

Interviewer: Why?

Ms. Yu: Well, I've learned a lot in the five years that I've had my own business. One of the things that I've learned is that I don't really like to work alone. I'm a people-person. And I don't want to clean houses my whole life. I'm looking for a job with a future.

Interviewer: You haven't ever been a manager. How do you know that you will be good at it?

Ms. Yu: You're right, I haven't managed people. But I have managed a business. And I've had a lot of experience with different kinds of people. My life hasn't been easy, but when I decide to do something, I give it 100%.

Interviewer: Well, Ms. Yu, I must say that I like your positive attitude . . .

Unit 9: Relationships

Rachel: Hello, Lauren? It's Rachel.

Lauren: Rachel! I've been meaning to call you for days.

Rachel: Well, here I am.

Lauren: So, how have the newlyweds been doing? Have you and John had your first fight yet?

Rachel: Stop it! No, we haven't. We've been getting along great. We've been busy with the new house, and I've been making friends in the neighborhood. And I've been learning how to cook.

Lauren: You've been cooking? Poor John!

Rachel: Come on, Lauren. I'm not that bad, and Mom's been helping me.

Lauren: And have you been running much?

Rachel: No, I haven't. The weather's been awful. It's been raining for weeks.

Lauren: Really? It's been beautiful out here. We've been wearing summer clothes since the beginning of June.

Rachel: That's early. And how are my favorite nephews?

Lauren: They've been out of school for two weeks, and I'm ready to send them back. They've been fighting constantly!

Rachel: You know, I've been thinking . . . Why don't you send them out to visit us? John would really love to get to know them better.

Lauren: Really? But you've only been married since February. You and John haven't had enough time alone together.

Rachel: We have the rest of our lives together, but my nephews won't be young forever.

Lauren: I don't know, Rachel. I'm not sure it's a good idea. Has John ever been around young kids?

Rachel:	No, but it will be good practice for him.
Lauren:	Practice? For what? Rachel, are you trying to tell me something? Are you . . . ?
Rachel:	Yup! Your little sister is going to be a mom!

Grammar, page 122

Kate:	John, how long have we been going out?
John:	Let's see. It's December. I moved back here in June. So we've been going out for six months.
Kate:	And how long have we known each other?
John:	For a year.
Kate:	And have we had any conversations since last year?
John:	Sure. Every day. We're having a conversation right now.
Kate:	No. I mean a real conversation, a conversation about our relationship.
John:	About our relationship?
Kate:	Yeah. This is probably a surprise to you, but I haven't been happy for about a month.
John:	Really? Why not?
Kate:	You've been working a lot and you have not been paying attention to me.
John:	Oh, come on, Katie. You know I love you.

Dictation, page 122

1. How long have you been on your honeymoon?
2. They've been arguing a lot lately.
3. She's hasn't made any new friends since childhood.
4. They haven't had a fight since the birth of their daughter.
5. The newlyweds have been looking for an apartment for months.

Listening, A and B, page 123

Walter:	Good evening. This is Walter Sussman with *Heart to Heart*. Tonight we are taking calls from couples with relationship problems. Our first caller is Mary.
Mary:	Hello?
Walter:	Yes, Mary, you're on the air. Go ahead.
Mary	I'm a little nervous. I've never called your show before.
Walter:	Well, welcome. So, tell us what's going on.
Mary:	Well, my husband and I love each other a lot, but recently, we've been arguing a lot.
Walter:	What have you been arguing about?
Mary:	Everything . . . well, mostly money, I guess.
Walter:	How long have you been married?
Mary:	Just one year—we're newlyweds—but we've known each other since we were kids.

Walter	And do you have any children?
Mary:	No, not yet, but we've been thinking about starting a family soon.
Walter:	Okay, so back to your money problems. You said that you've known each other for a long time. Are these arguments something new, or has money always been a problem?
Mary:	Hmmm . . . well, we've never had much money, but we didn't use to fight about it.
Walter:	Have there been any changes in your situation recently?
Mary:	No, not really . . . except that since our marriage, we've been trying to save enough money to buy a house.
Walter:	You said "we've." Are you sure that your husband wants a house and children?
Mary:	Of course I'm sure! That's why we got married.
Walter:	Okay, so you've been trying to save. Has your husband been helping you?
Mary:	No, not at all. He's a very hard worker, but I've found out that he's also a big spender. He loves music. He buys a lot of CDs. And he goes to a lot of concerts.
Walter:	Do you both work?
Mary:	Yes, we both work full-time. Now don't get me wrong. My husband's a very hard worker. He's been working since he was 15 years old.
Walter:	Has he saved anything?
Mary:	No, he hasn't. I didn't know that before our marriage. I thought he had at least some savings.
Walter:	Well, Mary, I'm glad that you called tonight. It sounds like you really need some help . . .

Unit 10: Television

Listening, A, B, and C, page 129

Lisa:	Oh Brad, this is really romantic. The food looks delicious, and the flowers are wonderful. And look at the sky. It's really beautiful tonight. Everything is just perfect.
Brad:	And you look beautiful. Mmm . . . and you smell pretty terrific, too.
Lisa:	Oh Brad . . . What was that?
Brad:	What? Come here . . .
Lisa:	No, I'm serious. I heard a strange noise. Listen . . . There it is again!

Brad:	Relax, Lisa. It's very safe out here. Now, where were we?
Lisa:	No, Brad, I'm really serious. Be quiet and listen carefully. Don't you hear that? It's pretty loud now. Look, over there, in the water! It's swimming really quickly! And it's pretty big. Oh no! It's coming directly this way!
Brad:	What the heck? Run, Lisa, run! We need to get out of here fast!
Narrator:	And now, scenes from next week's dramatic season finale of "The Secret."
Brad:	Lisa, Lisa, where are you? Answer me, please.

Grammar to Communicate 2, A, page 132

1. Umm . . . I think . . . umm . . . I think the . . . um . . . answer . . . the answer is . . . umm . . . umm . . . it's B . . . the answer is B.
2. Oh darling, I love you. You are so beautiful, so perfect. Come to me.
3. I already told you. I don't know the guy.
4. Leave now. Never come back.
5. Look at those people over there. Do you see them?

Dictation, page 136

1. Stars always dress fashionably.
2. The actor looks really nervous.
3. That talk show isn't very interesting.
4. That newscaster doesn't speak clearly.
5. They did pretty well on the game show.

Listening, A and B, page 137

SCENE 1

Detective:	You look worried. What's wrong?
Suspect:	Nothing. I feel perfectly fine.
Detective:	You don't look fine to me.
Suspect:	Well, I am. Can I call my lawyer now?
Detective:	I told you, you can call in a minute.

SCENE 2

Man:	Let's get out of here. I need to talk to you . . . privately.
Woman:	Right now?
Man:	I can't wait even one more minute. It's extremely important.
Woman:	Well, if it's that important . . .
Man:	It is. Come quickly . . .

SCENE 3

Woman:	This recipe is delicious, and you can prepare it quickly and easily—in about 30 minutes.

Man:	But remember . . . I'm the world's worst cook . . .
Woman:	That is ridiculous. Anyone can learn to cook well. Just watch carefully and learn.

SCENE 4

Man:	The rivers here are already dangerously high, and it continues to rain heavily.
Woman:	Did all of the people in the surrounding neighborhoods get out safely yesterday?
Man:	We are not sure right now. It is extremely difficult to get any information. There is no electricity, and there is almost no telephone service.

SCENE 5

Woman:	Look up there, in the top of that tree. Do you see it?
Man:	Where? I can't see anything.
Woman:	It's right up there. You have to look very carefully. It moves really fast.
Man:	Oh, there it is! It's fantastic.
Woman:	This is really amazing. It is extremely unusual to find this kind of bird so easily in this area.

Unit 11: The Animal Kingdom

Listening, A, B, and C, page 143

Ahmed:	Hi, May. What are you doing?
May:	Hey, Ahmed. I'm reading a report about pets. It says that the most popular pet in the United States today is the cat.
Ahmed:	Really? I was sure that dogs were more popular than cats.
May:	This says that a lot more people own cats than dogs.
Ahmed:	Not in my neighborhood. There are as many dogs as children. Things are really different in Morocco. Pets aren't as popular as they are in the United States. And very few people have dogs. In fact, dogs are the least popular pets.
May:	Why is that? Don't you believe that the dog is man's best friend?
Ahmed:	No, many people think that dogs are dirty.

(continued on next page)

May: That's interesting. In China people like dogs, but our houses and apartments are a lot smaller than in the U.S. We don't have as much space as Americans do, so big dogs are less popular than cats and small dogs. So, what is the most common pet in Morocco?

Ahmed: I'm not sure, but in my family, we have falcons.

May: Falcons? What's a falcon?

Ahmed: It's a bird. In Morocco we keep falcons as pets, and we teach them how to hunt. Hunting with falcons is called falconry. I'm surprised you don't know about falconry. It's one of the oldest sports in Asia.

May: Really? I had no idea.

Ahmed: Falcons are the best hunters of all the birds, and they are the easiest to train. They also fly the fastest.

May: That's really interesting.

Grammar, page 150

I have two parrots, Gertie and Peter. Gertie is older. She's 25 years old. Peter's only 10. He is gray. Gertie is more colorful than Peter. She's green, blue, and yellow. Both parrots talk a lot. Gertie is as talkative as Peter. Gertie knows fewer words than Peter, but Peter doesn't know as many big words as Gertie does. And they both say the funniest things. Parrots are always messy, but Gertie isn't as messy as Peter. He always makes a big mess. I love both my parrots. They cause the fewest problems of any pet, and they are the most fun.

Dictation, page 150

1. Little dogs aren't as frightening as big dogs are.
2. Do lions move as quickly as giraffes?
3. Parrots live a lot longer than other birds.
4. Elephants have the biggest ears.
5. Lions eat the most meat.

Listening, A and B, page 151

Reporter: I'm Liz Baker with *Spotlight on Science*. Today, Dr. Richard Downey of the San Diego Zoo is with us, answering your questions about the animal kingdom. Welcome, Dr. Downey.

Downey: Thanks, Liz. I'm happy to be here.

Reporter: There are a lot of kids out there with questions for you, so let's get started. Our first caller is Jeremy. Go ahead, Jeremy.

Jeremy: Ummm . . . yes . . . Is it true that pigs are the dirtiest animals?

Downey: Well, it isn't really possible to say that one animal is dirtier than another. But I can say that the pig is definitely not the dirtiest. People think that pigs are dirty because they like to roll in mud. In fact, they do that because they don't sweat. It's the easiest way for them to stay cool. They are also very smart animals—almost as smart as the chimpanzee.

Reporter: So which animal is the smartest? Is it the chimpanzee?

Downey: Chimps are certainly very smart, but it's difficult to say which animal is the most intelligent. However, many people are surprised when they hear that whales, elephants, and pigs are some of the most intelligent animals.

Reporter: OK, Jeremy, thanks for calling. Let's go to Alison. Alison?

Alison: Hello?

Reporter: Yes, Alison. What's your question?

Alison: Yes . . . My brother says that cats sleep more than dogs, but I think he's wrong. Am I right, or is he?

Downey: I'm sorry, but I'm afraid your brother is right. Cats sleep about 12 hours a day—about an hour and a half more than dogs do. The animal that sleeps the most is the brown bat. Brown bats sleep 20 hours a day. Giraffes sleep the fewest number of hours—only about 2 hours a day.

Reporter: OK, Alison?

Alison: Yes, thank you.

Reporter: We've got time for just one more call. This is Josh. Do you have a question for Dr. Downey, Josh?

Josh: Uh, yeah. Which animal is the most dangerous?

Downey: That's easy—the mosquito.

Josh: The mosquito? No way!!!

Downey: It's true. Mosquitoes carry a serious disease called malaria. More than 300 million people get sick with malaria every year, and one to three million of them die.

Reporter: And that's all we've got time for. Thank you for being on the show today, Dr. Downey.

Downey: Oh, you're quite welcome.

Unit 12: Let's Eat!

Listening, A, B, and C, page 157

Man: Can we seat ourselves?

Waiter: No, please wait. The hostess will seat you.

Hostess: Two for lunch?

Woman: Yes, please.

Hostess: Right this way. Here you go.

Man: Could we have another table? This one is very noisy.

Hostess: Of course. Which one would you like?

Man: How about that one, over there?

Hostess: The one in the corner? It's reserved.

Man: How about the ones over there? Are they reserved too?

Hostess: By the window? One of them is, but the others are free. Enjoy your meal.

Woman: Thank you.

Waiter: Good afternoon.

Woman: Good afternoon.

Man: We're ready to order.

Waiter: What would you like?

Man: I'll have the lunch special.

Waiter: Which one?

Man: The one on the menu!

Waiter: There are several specials on the menu.

Man: The one that comes with a salad.

Waiter: They all come with salads.

Woman: He'll have the number three, please.

Man: I can order for myself. I'll have the number three. And make sure the soup is warm. The last time it was cold.

Waiter: Of course. And for you, ma'am?

Woman: I'll take the number three, too. Thank you.

Waiter: The salad bar is over there. You can serve yourselves whenever you're ready.

Man: I need another fork. This one is dirty.

Waiter: Oh, I'm sorry. I'll get you another one.

Man: And another glass. This one has a hair in it.

Waiter: Of course.

Woman: Could you behave yourself?

Man: What?

Woman: Why are you always so rude?

Man: Me, rude?

Woman: Oh, forget it. Next time, I'm sitting by myself.

Grammar, page 164

Amy: Come in. Make yourself at home. Here, give me your jacket.

Jan: Sorry I'm late. I missed the bus and waited an hour for the next one.

Amy: Don't worry. Two couples, the ones from Chester, still aren't here.

Jan: Yeah, Chester is far away. Bill, is that you? How are you?

Bill: Oh, Jan, nice to see you. I'm great.

Amy: How do you two know each other? Did you meet at another party?

Jan: Yeah. We met at Lin's. It was great. We really enjoyed ourselves.

Amy: So Jan, do you know the other people here?

Jan: Well, I know your boyfriend, of course, but I don't think I know the others.

Dictation, page 164

1. Please give me the other menu. This one is the lunch menu.
2. The main dish with chicken isn't expensive, but the others are.
3. The ice cream is two dollars, but the other desserts are more expensive.
4. Please serve yourselves at the salad bar.
5. We'd like two hot appetizers and two cold ones.

Listening, page 165

Reporter: These days, there are fast-food restaurants everywhere, in almost every country of the world. But it was not always that way. Today, Bryant Jones reports on the birth of the fast-food industry.

Jones: In the 1940s, as large numbers of Americans began to buy cars, drive-in restaurants became popular. At a drive-in restaurant, customers ordered their food, ate it, and paid for it without leaving their cars. Waiters, called car hops, took orders and served customers in their cars. In all other ways, however, drive-in restaurants were typical restaurants. There were different kinds of food on the menu, and all of it was made-to-order. For example, at a table with two customers, one person might order a rare hamburger with onions, while the other might order a well-done one with tomatoes. One customer's hamburger was cooked differently from the other's.

In the 1940s, two brothers, Richard and Maurice McDonald, owned a drive-in restaurant in California. Like the other drive-in restaurants in the area, theirs had a large menu. However, most of the money that they made came from just three items: hamburgers, French fries, and milkshakes. The McDonald brothers decided to try something new. They limited the menu to those three items, and they developed the "Speedy Service System." The Speedy Service System used an assembly line like the one in the automobile industry. Nothing was made-to-order. One hamburger was exactly the same as all the other hamburgers, just as one Model-T Ford was exactly the same as all the others.

Another feature of the Speedy Service System was that there were no waiters. Customers served themselves. They walked up to a window, ordered, and paid. Within minutes, their order came off the "assembly line." They then chose a table and seated themselves. They even cleaned up after themselves. Cleaning up was easy because there were no dishes, just paper cups and bags. Customers just threw everything away.

Today, fast-food restaurants still follow the McDonald brothers' Speedy Service System—the system that put the "fast" in fast food.

Unit 13: Technology

Listening, A, B, and C, page 171

Rashida: I hope that you can help me. My computer isn't working.

Technician: What's the problem?

Rashida: I don't know. That's your job!

Technician: Ma'am, please calm down. I'm trying to help you.

Rashida: I'm sorry. I know it's not your fault, but I really need my computer.

Technician: First of all, are you able to turn it on?

Rashida: Yes, but that's all I can do. Two weeks ago I had the same problem, but my husband was able to fix it. I still couldn't access my e-mail, but at least I was able to use it for other things. But then this morning when I turned it on, I couldn't do anything.

Technician: What do you mean, you couldn't do anything?

Rashida: I mean exactly that. I wasn't able to do anything. What do you think? Will you be able to repair it?

Technician: I don't know, but we'll do our best.

Rashida: Can you look at it right now?

Technician: Right now? No, I'm sorry, but I can't.

Rashida: Well, when will you be able to repair it? I really need my computer. I can't work without it! Will you be able to look at it later today?

Technician: Lady, I'm not even sure we'll be able to fix it at all. But we won't be able to do it by tomorrow. It's going to take at least a week.

Rashida: A week! Why so long?

Technician: Because the only person that can fix that kind of computer is on vacation.

Rashida: Oh, forget it. I'll take it someplace else.

Grammar, page 178

Hi, I have good news and bad news. First, the bad news. I haven't been able to fix the TV yet. When I turn it on, I can see a picture; but I can't hear a thing. That's strange because yesterday I could hear things, but I wasn't able to see anything. I'm going to look at the TV again tomorrow. Maybe I can fix it then.

Now, the good news. I was able to fix the radio yesterday. At first, I wasn't able to find the problem, but actually there wasn't really a problem. It only needed new batteries. Sam

Dictation, page 178

1. I'm usually able to access the Web from my home.
2. I couldn't install the software yesterday.
3. Can you record my TV program for me?
4. In the future, people will be able to get married online.
5. We were able to repair the DVD player yesterday.

Listening, A and B, page 179

Judd: With *Spotlight on Technology*, this is Judd Newman. With us today is our science and technology reporter, Jasmine Thomas, who is just back from this year's international auto show. So, tell us, Jasmine, what will our cars be able to do next?

Jasmine: Well, Judd, several car companies have come out with concept cars that can interact with the driver, and are able to prevent accidents.

Judd: What do you mean, interact with the driver? Do you mean talk to the driver?

Jasmine: No, not exactly. It's more like listening to or "feeling" the driver. Here's how it works. You're driving and you begin to feel sleepy. Your hand relaxes on the steering wheel, and your car starts to go off the road. The car knows what is happening, and wakes you up by setting off an alarm, moving the seat, or spraying water in your face.

Judd: How can a car know that you're falling asleep?

Jasmine: When we are falling asleep, our heart starts beating more slowly, and our muscles relax. A computer in the car is able to "feel" these

	physical changes through sensors on the driver's seat and the steering wheel.
Judd:	That's pretty amazing.
Jasmine:	Yes, it is. And that's not all. These cars can communicate with other cars that have the same technology. Let's say you're on the east side of Los Angeles and you want to go somewhere on the west side. Your car will be able to communicate with another car on the west side, and find out the driving conditions there; for example, accidents or traffic jams. Your car can then show you the fastest and safest route to your destination.
Judd:	So, where can I buy one of these cars?
Jasmine:	You can't. That's why they're called concept cars. There are only a couple of them. You won't be able to buy one for at least two years. And even then most people won't be able to afford them. But I predict that within 5 years, the prices will come down. Then the average person will be able to own one.
Judd:	Very interesting. Thanks, Jasmine . . .

Unit 14: A Kid's Life

Listening, A, B, and C, page 185

Mom:	So, Nick, remember. You don't have to come home right after school, but you've got to call me on my cell phone and tell me where you are. And you mustn't miss the 5:00 bus. Dad's got to work late, so you have to make dinner.
Nick:	Again? I had to make dinner last week, too. It's Suzy's turn.
Mom:	Suzy has to babysit for the Martin boys. She won't be home until 5:30, so she won't have time to cook. We've got to eat by 6:00 at the latest because she has to get to basketball practice.
Nick:	Does she have to babysit for the Martins every afternoon? Last month she didn't have to do any chores because she was always at the Martins. I have to do everything around here, and I don't get any money for it, but the Martins pay her for babysitting. It's not fair.
Mom:	I'm sorry, Nick, but I haven't got time to argue with you right now. I've got to get to work.
Nick:	Why did you have to go back to work, anyway? Things were so much better when you stayed at home. Then I didn't have to cook or clean.
Mom:	Oh, Nick, you know that I have to work. We have to pay the bills. Besides, I like working. And you don't have to do everything in the house. That's just not true. Everyone in the family has to do chores.
Nick:	Yeah, everybody except little Miss Suzy.
Mom:	OK, Nick, that's enough. You've got to get to school, and I've got to get to work. We'll talk about this later.

Grammar, page 192

Lee:	Why do you have to go so early? Let me guess . . . You have to pick up your sister.
Dan:	That's right.
Lee:	You had to pick her up yesterday, too. Why do you always have to pick her up?
Dan:	I don't always have to pick her up. I didn't have to do it last week. It was Stan's turn.
Lee:	So why can't Stan do it today?
Dan:	Because he's got to work.
Lee:	So, where does she have to go this time? Soccer practice? Piano lessons?
Dan:	She's got to go to the dentist. I'm sorry, but I really have to go. She mustn't be late for her appointment.
Lee:	And I've got to get a new boyfriend—one with no little sister!

Dictation, page 192

1. You've got to be strict with your children.
2. We had to obey our parents.
3. My son and daughter don't have to do chores every day.
4. The children mustn't cross the street.
5. Do you have to take out the trash every day?

Listening, A and B, page 193

Reporter:	This is Doris Hamilton for *Culture Watch*. Today, we are going to compare the lives of children in the U.S. and Japan. Mrs. Eileen Aoaki is here with us. She is a professor of early childhood education, and has lived in both the United States and Japan. Welcome, Mrs. Aoaki.
Mrs. Aoaki:	Thank you, Doris.
Reporter:	So, what are the biggest differences that you've found?
Mrs. Aoaki:	Well, the differences start as soon as the baby is born. In the United States, as you know, most parents believe that children have to learn to sleep alone from a very early age.

If there's enough space in the house, infants in the U.S. usually have their own rooms. That usually doesn't happen in Japan. In Japan, children sometimes sleep in their parents' room for years, often because space is limited. Also, many American doctors tell parents that they mustn't pick up their babies every time they cry, because babies have to learn how to comfort themselves. In Japan, many mothers believe that they must pick up a crying child immediately. If they don't, they are not good mothers.

Reporter: Those are big differences.

Mrs. Aoaki: Yes, they are. And the differences get bigger when children begin school. For example, in Japan, children learn that they must obey their teachers.

Reporter: Wait a minute! Children in the U.S. have to obey their teachers too!

Mrs. Aoaki: Yes, of course, let me explain. Japanese children are taught that they must not question their teachers. This is changing a little, but is still a pretty common way of thinking in Japan. In contrast, American children learn that they have to ask questions in class. And many American parents teach their children that they must speak up if the teacher does or says something wrong.

Reporter: Now I see.

Mrs. Aoaki: Another difference is in the amount of time that children spend studying. In the past, children had to go to school 6 days a week. Today, Japanese children don't have to go to school on Saturday. However, most Japanese parents pay for their children to take classes on Saturdays. That's because kids have to pass very difficult exams to get into a good high school. They've got to start preparing at a young age.

Reporter: Interesting. We have to take a break now, but don't go away. We'll be right back . . .

Unit 15: Manners

Listening, A, B, and C, page 199

Mom: Allen, what have I told you about table manners?

Allen: What? What am I doing wrong now?

Mom: You shouldn't be asking me that. You should know.

Allen: Oh come on, just tell me.

Mom: Well, first of all, you shouldn't be eating with your fingers.

Allen: But I'm eating French fries!

Mom: So what? You should be using a fork.

Allen: Why do I have to use a fork? None of my friends has to eat French fries with a fork!

Mom: As I've told you many times, I don't care about your friends' table manners. I don't have to live with them. You don't have to like my rules, but you have to obey them. And one more thing—you shouldn't be talking with your mouth full. It's disgusting. Allen . . .

Allen: What now?

Mom: Should your elbows be on the table?

Allen: OK, OK, I'm sorry. I forgot. [phone rings]

Mom: Sit back down.

Allen: But, Mom, it's probably Blanca. I have to talk to her. It's important.

Mom: I don't care. She shouldn't be calling at dinner time. She should know better.

Grammar, page 206

Lori: Listen to that woman with the cell phone. She shouldn't be talking on her cell phone here. You should tell her.

Kirk: What should I say?

Lori: You should say, "Stop talking on your cell phone."

Kirk: That's not very polite. I don't think I should be rude because she's rude.

Lori: Sometimes you have to be rude to people. They don't listen if you're polite.

Kirk: I don't agree. Watch. Excuse me?

Stranger: What?

Kirk: I'm sorry, but you really shouldn't be using your cell phone here.

Stranger: And you shouldn't interrupt other people's conversations.

Dictation, page 206

1. You shouldn't talk with your mouth full.
2. You don't have to hold the door open but you should.
3. He should be carrying his grandmother's bag.
4. You should knock on my door before you come in.
5. I have to do a favor for my mother.

Listening, A and B, page 207

Reporter: This is Joanna Bergman for *Culture Watch*. This week's topic is table manners. As anyone who has traveled to another country knows, table manners are quite different in different countries. You don't have to know everything, but you should find out the most important rules before you visit a country. Here are some things you will probably want to find out.

First, seating. Where should guests sit at the table? Should you wait for others to sit down, or should you just sit down in the nearest chair? Do men and women eat together, or do they have to sit in separate rooms?

The second set of rules involves how you eat. Which utensils should you use? How should you use them? How shouldn't you use them? In countries where people eat with their hands, can you use both hands, or should you use only one hand? Which hand?

The third set of rules involves body language at the table. How should you sit? For example, should you put your hands on the table, or in your lap? Is it okay to put your elbows on the table? If you have to sit on the floor to eat, what should you do with your legs?

Next, what about conversation at the table? Should you talk while you are eating, or wait until you finish? Which topics should you discuss? Which topics shouldn't you discuss?

And what about food? Do you have to eat everything on your plate? What should you do if you don't like something? If you want more food, can you ask for it, or do you have to wait for the host or hostess to offer it?

Tomorrow, we will be interviewing people from all over the world to learn the answers to these questions and more. Until then, this is Joanna Bergman for *Culture Watch*.

Unit 16: Neighbors

Listening, A, B, and C, page 213

Ann: Hi, Bob. How was your flight?

Bob: Long. I left Detroit at 7:00 A.M.

Ann: You must be tired. So, how are the grandchildren?

Bob: It was great to see them, but I'm glad to be home. So, what's been going on around here?

Ann: I just saw Emily Rose on the elevator. She was wearing a new suit. She must be doing well at work.

Bob: Are you kidding? She lost her job last week.

Ann: Really? She must not be very happy about that.

Bob: No, I'm sure she isn't. And speaking of unhappy, how's Roberta doing?

Ann: She and Andy must be getting along. I haven't heard them fighting lately.

Bob: But they can't be getting along. Haven't you heard? He moved out. They're getting a divorce.

Ann: Really? So that's why it's so quiet over there. He must be at his mother's.

Bob: Actually, he's staying with his brother. What about the Russels?

Ann: Mr. and Mrs. Russel are on vacation, but I saw little Sarah Russel on her way to school this morning. She must be staying with Mrs. O'Hara.

Bob: She can't be staying with Mrs. O'Hara. Mrs. O'Hara is visiting her son.

Ann: Well then who's taking care of her? She's only 10 years old. She can't be alone!

Bob: Her grandmother must be staying with her. I saw her car when I came in.

Ann: You're amazing. You've been away for a month, and you know more about what's going on around here than I do!

Grammar, page 220

1. **A:** It must be difficult to find a good apartment around here.
   B: You're right. It is. I've been looking for a place for three months.
2. **A:** Laura's walking to the bus stop. That's strange.
   B: Her husband must be using her car today.
3. **A:** Mrs. Olsen must be feeling lonely since her husband's death.
   B: I know. We should visit her next weekend.
4. **A:** Look, there's Tommy. He must be going to school.
   B: But it's Saturday. He can't be going to school.
5. **A:** Hello? Could I please speak to Donna?
   B: Donna? There's no Donna here. You must have the wrong number.

1. My wife isn't answering the phone. She must be chatting with a neighbor.
2. The flowers in that yard are beautiful. The owners must be good gardeners.
3. The kids can't be next door. Our neighbors are on vacation.
4. My dog can't be barking in the yard. He's in the house.
5. The Smiths must not be at home. Their car isn't in their driveway.

Listening, A and B, page 221

Vicki: Good evening, this is Vicki Hernandez for *Your Turn*. Tonight's topic is getting along with your neighbors. Our first caller is Randy. So, Randy, how are things in your neighborhood?

Randy: Not great, I'm afraid. A family moved in next-door a few months ago. The houses in our neighborhood are very close together, and their kitchen window is across from ours. Every time they see me through the window, they wave. At first, I thought it was sweet. But lately it's really started to bother me. I feel like they're watching me all the time.

Vicki: That must be uncomfortable.

Randy: Yeah, especially after someone told me that they are police officers.

Vicki: Is there some reason that the police should be interested in you?

Randy: No, of course not.

Vicki: So you can't be worried about that. They probably just want to be friendly with you. They must not know how you feel. Do you have curtains?

Randy: Uh, no . . .

Vicki: Well, Randy, it's time to get some! Good luck . . . Well, that was easy! Let's take another call. Hello, Sue?

Sue: Yes. Hello. My problem is not my neighbors; it's my husband. He doesn't get along with our neighbors. Take last night, for example. The doorbell rang at dinnertime. My husband thought that it must be someone asking for money. He answered the door, and shouted "Why are you bothering people at dinner time!" and slammed the door. Just then I looked out the window, and saw my next-door neighbor walking away from our house. I opened the door, and found a box of cookies. It was a birthday gift for me!

Vicki: Oh dear. Your husband must not like your neighbor very much.

Sue: He didn't know it was her. It was dark, and he wasn't wearing his glasses . . .

Vicki: Did he apologize?

Sam: Yes, but I don't think she believed him. She hasn't been very friendly to me since then.

Vicki: Really? Your neighbor mustn't have a very good sense of humor. It's a pretty funny story.

Unit 17: Health

Listening, A, B, and C, page 227

Doctor: Mr. Harris, it isn't normal for someone of your age to have high blood pressure. You must lose weight.

Mr. Harris: But, doctor, diets have never worked for me. Maybe it's impossible for me to lose weight.

Doctor: I'm not talking about a diet. In fact, it's unhealthy to go on a diet.

Mr. Harris: If I don't go on a diet, how will I lose weight?

Doctor: It's simple. You need to eat less and exercise more.

Mr. Harris: Isn't that a diet?

Doctor: Usually when people talk about a diet, they're talking about doing something for a few weeks to lose weight. But you need to change your eating and exercise habits—not just for a few weeks, but for the rest of your life.

Mr. Harris: So I have to be on a diet for the rest of my life?

Doctor: No, you need to eat healthy food and exercise regularly. And you're not too old to make these changes.

Mr. Harris: But I'm too busy to exercise. I work two jobs.

Doctor: It isn't necessary to go to the gym and spend hours a day exercising. Just small changes will make a big difference.

Mr. Harris: Like what?

Doctor: Even just a few minutes of fast walking a day will help. Most people can find enough time to take a 15-minute walk.

Mr. Harris: But what about the healthy food part? I don't have enough time to cook every day.

Doctor: You can make a healthy, delicious meal in less than 15 minutes.

Mr. Harris: Really?

Doctor: Yes. It's easier to do than you think.

Grammar, page 234

1. **A:** You're too sick to go to work.
   B: But I have to go! I have a very important meeting.
2. **A:** Does he need surgery?
   B: No, the problem is not serious enough for him to have surgery.
3. **A:** The doctor's too busy to see you today.
   B: But I have an appointment!
4. **A:** What do you take when you have a cold?
   B: Sweet Night. It's very good. It helps me sleep.
5. **A:** Where are you going?
   B: I'm going downtown to see the doctor. I have an appointment.

Dictation, page 234

1. It's important for him to gain weight.
2. You should exercise more to get in shape.
3. She's not strong enough to leave the hospital yet.
4. Your blood pressure is too high for someone your age.
5. He's too weak to have surgery.

Listening, A and B, page 235

Talk Show Host: Please join me in welcoming Dr. Paul Wade. Dr. Wade, what can we do to stay healthy?

Dr. Wade: There are two secrets to a healthy life: a healthy diet and regular exercise. Did you know that new immigrants often have a healthier diet than Americans born in the U.S.?

Talk Show Host: Really?

Dr. Wade: Yes. American-born women eat fewer fruits and vegetables than new immigrants: two and a half fewer servings every day. After a few years in the United States, however, most immigrants have the same diet as people born in the U.S. And that's not a good thing.

Talk Show Host: But the United States is a rich country. Why is the American diet so unhealthy?

Dr. Wade: In the United States it's often cheaper to buy fast food than fresh fruits and vegetables. And people don't have time to cook. So it's faster to pick up dinner from a fast-food restaurant or to buy a frozen meal from the supermarket. The problem is, fast food is unhealthy. It has too much salt and too much fat.

Talk Show Host: How can we find out how much salt and fat is in our food?

Dr. Wade: Learn to read food labels. The chemical name for salt is sodium. Most adults should eat fewer than 2,400 milligrams of sodium a day. There are two kinds of fat—saturated and unsaturated. You shouldn't eat more than 20 grams of saturated fat a day, and not more than 65 grams of total fat.

Talk Show Host: How do we know what's in the food at fast-food restaurants?

Dr. Wade: It's easy to find that information on the Web. But let me save you time. Most of the food at fast-food restaurants is bad for you. The average cheeseburger at a fast-food restaurant has about 10 grams of saturated fat, and over 1,000 milligrams of salt.

Talk Show Host: That is a lot. Now let's talk about exercise.

Dr. Wade: Most people need about 30 minutes of exercise a day, five days a week. People think that they don't have time to exercise. But on average, Americans watch 2 to 3 hours of TV a day. . . . So they have free time. They just don't use it to exercise.

Talk Show Host: It's time for a short break, but don't go away.

Unit 18: Free Time

Listening, A, B, and C, page 241

Arinaldo: I'm bored. I'm tired of just playing computer games and going to the mall.

Mei: Well, what else are you interested in?

Arinaldo: Lots of things. I'm considering taking some classes.

Mei: In what?

Arinaldo: Well, drawing, for example. I'm good at drawing, but I've never taken any classes.

Mei: You like drawing? I didn't know that. Drawing's okay, but I prefer painting.

Arinaldo: I started to draw when I was little. Anyway, I'm thinking about taking a class at the community center.

Mei:	I started studying painting there last year. It's great. I love going . . . And it's not very expensive.
Arinaldo:	Yeah, that's what I've heard. I'm also thinking about learning to play the guitar. I've taken piano lessons, so I can read music, but I've never really liked to listen to piano music. I prefer to listen to the guitar.
Mei:	Playing is very different from listening, though. It's pretty difficult to play the guitar.
Arinaldo:	Harder than playing the piano?
Mei:	Maybe not. So, do you want to take both guitar and drawing classes?
Arinaldo:	Oh no, I don't want to do both. I'm trying to decide between them. What do you think?
Mei:	Hmmm . . . well, if you've decided to take classes at the community center, then you should take drawing.
Arinaldo:	Why?
Mei:	Because I know they have great art teachers, but I haven't heard good things about the music teachers.
Arnaldo:	That's good to know. Thanks!
Mei:	No problem.

Grammar, page 248

Do you feel like doing something new? Are you tired of being in the office all the time? Are you interested in spending time with fun people? Then hiking is the answer for you. Being in the fresh air and seeing all the beautiful flowers and trees will make you feel wonderful. You don't need to be an experienced hiker. You just have to enjoy going for long walks. If you want to get more information about our group, call (777) 555-3476. Great experiences are waiting for you.

Dictation, page 248

1. I can't stand knitting because I'm not good with my hands.
2. I'm good at drawing, but I don't like painting.
3. I'm considering taking up chess.
4. I'm tired of being alone all the time.
5. When I got sick, I gave up singing in the chorus.

Listening, A and B, page 249

Reporter: Good morning. This is Martha Hong reporting. Today we are looking at the ways that adults in the United States spend their free time. The information in this report comes from a poll of 1,014 adults conducted by Harris Interactive in the year 2004.

According to the poll, reading, watching TV, and spending time with family were the three most popular free-time activities in the U.S. in 2004—35% of adults in the poll said reading, 21% said watching TV, and 20% said spending time with family. Next on the list were going to the movies—10%; fishing—8%; and using a computer—7%. Gardening, walking, and renting movies were all equally popular, at 6%.

And what were the least popular activities? Playing tennis, horseback riding, running, dancing, and bowling were at the bottom of the list, with only 1% each.

Since the poll was first conducted in 1995, the biggest increases in popularity have been in spending time with family—from 12% in 1995 to 20% in 2004; reading—from 28% to 35%; and using computers, from 2% to 7%. The biggest decreases in popularity from 1995 to 2004 were in swimming (from 7% to 2%), TV watching (from 25% to 21%), and playing team sports (from 9% to 5%).

And how about the amount of free time people have per week? That has not changed at all since 1995—19 hours a week. But if you go back to 1973, you'll see a big difference. On average, adults in the U.S. had 26 hours a week of free time in 1973. For *Spotlight on Culture*, I'm Martha Hong.

Unit 19: Emergency Services

Listening, A, B, and C, page 255

Operator:	911. What's your emergency?
Woman:	A man just stole my bag! I was walking home . . . He told me to give him my money and jewelry. He made me give him my wedding ring!
Operator:	Are you safe now? Did he hurt you?
Woman:	No, he didn't. He let me go when I gave him my bag and my ring.
Operator:	Where are you now?
Woman:	In a store on the corner of 16th Avenue and Babcock St.
Operator:	How long ago did this happen?
Woman:	Just a minute ago.
Operator:	Can you describe him?
Woman:	I think so. He was about 17-years-old, white. He was tall and thin. I believe he was wearing a black sweatshirt and jeans.
Operator:	Did you notice anything else? Did he have a mustache or a beard?
Woman:	I don't think so.

Operator:	Did you see where he went?
Woman:	Yes, he ran down Babcock St.
Operator:	Okay, ma'am. I've contacted the police.
Woman:	Please, make them come right away. You can't let him get away with my wedding ring!
Operator:	I can only report the emergency, ma'am. Now, can I have your name, address, and telephone number?
Woman:	Marianne Jackson, 230 Westfield Terrace, 555-660-2050. Will the police expect me to wait here?
Operator:	No, ma'am. You need to go to the police station and fill out a report.
Woman:	But shouldn't I wait here for the police?
Operator:	No, you should go to the police station.
Woman:	Okay, thank you. You've been very kind.
Operator:	You're welcome. I hope you get your wedding ring back.
Woman:	Thank you. I hope so, too.

Grammar, page 262

To whom it may concern,

I'm writing this letter because I think you should know about my experience at your hospital last Saturday. My ten-year-old daughter had an accident on her bike, and I noticed that she couldn't move her arm. I thought it might be broken, so I drove her to the emergency room. We got there at 1:00. The nurse saw that my daughter was in pain, but she didn't let us see a doctor right away. She told the two of us to wait in the waiting area and made me fill in four different forms. We waited and waited. Finally, at 4:00 the nurse called my daughter's name. My daughter wanted me to go with her, but the nurse didn't let me go. She was very rude to me. I am writing because I would like to know your policy on this. Did the nurse have the right to make me stay in the waiting room? I don't think so, but maybe there is a new policy.

Dictation, page 262

1. I hope that you don't get another speeding ticket.
2. The firefighter advised us to look for fire hazards in our home.
3. The woman wants an ambulance to come right away.
4. The paramedic didn't let me go in the ambulance with my friend.
5. I made the police officer show me his badge when he stopped me.

Listening, A and B, page 263

Reporter:	It's Fire Prevention Week. I'm Cynthia Steiner and Captain Will Farrell is with us to talk about fire safety. Thank you for coming in, Captain Farrell.
Captain:	Thank you for inviting me.
Reporter:	I know that there are several listeners waiting to talk to you, so let's get started.
Caller 1:	Hello? Captain Farrell?
Captain:	Yes?
Caller 1:	I live in a large apartment building, but I have noticed that the smoke detectors in the hallways are not working.
Captain:	How do you know that they aren't working?
Caller 1:	The other night my wife was cooking, and she burned our dinner. There was a lot of smoke. The smoke detectors in our apartment went off, but the ones in the hallway didn't. I suspected that they weren't working, so I checked them.
Captain:	Well, I hope that you called the landlord right away.
Caller 1:	Yes, I did, but he hasn't called me back yet.
Captain:	Well, I advise you to call him again, and tell him to fix the problem immediately or you will call the fire department. If he doesn't call you after that, I want you to call your local fire station, and ask them to call him, okay? I'm pretty sure he will listen to them.
Caller 1:	Okay. Thank you very much.
Captain:	You're very welcome. You know, Cynthia, not enough tenants know that they have rights. They can make their landlords fix fire hazards like the one that the caller described.
Reporter:	What other things should tenants know?
Captain:	By law, there must be a fire extinguisher in every apartment. And in all new buildings, there must be a sprinkler system.
Reporter:	I understand that every apartment must also have two exits. Is that correct?
Captain:	Yes, absolutely. That's very important.
Reporter:	So, if any of our listeners have problems with their landlords, what do you advise them to do?
Captain:	First they need to talk to their landlords, and ask them to fix the problem. Then, if they don't, they need to call their local fire department.

Reporter: Thank you, Captain. In a minute we'll be back to take more of your calls.

Unit 20: Taking a Trip

Listening, A, B, and C, page 269

Announcer: National Airlines flight #650 is now boarding at gate 23. Passengers, please have your boarding passes and identification ready.

Man: What's that? What's he saying?

Woman: Our flight must be leaving. He told us to take out our boarding passes and identification. Here, give me your carry-on bag.

Man: What?

Woman: I asked you to give me your carry-on bag.

Man: Why do you need my carry-on bag?

Woman: I need to find our boarding passes.

Man: You need to find what?

Woman: Our boarding passes . . . I said that I need to find our boarding passes.

Man: Your boarding pass? I don't have your boarding pass. I only have mine.

Woman: What did you say?

Man: I said that I have my boarding pass, but I don't have yours.

Woman: You're kidding.

Man: What?

Woman: Oh, never mind. Just give me your carry-on bag.

Man: What?

Woman: I told you to give me your carry-on bag.

Man: But I told you that I don't have your boarding pass.

Woman: Yes, you do. It's right here. See?

Announcer: Would passengers Rick and Helen Dwyer please check in at the ticket counter?

Woman: That's us! He just asked us to check in.

Man: What? What's wrong? We already checked in.

Woman: I don't know. We'd better go up and see.

Grammar, page 276

1. A: Why did that man tell us to go to the ticket counter?
    B: Because we need to check in.
2. A: Is Annie having a good time?
    B: She says she is.
3. A: When do we need to check in?
    B: The travel agent told us to check in an hour before the flight.
4. A: The hotel clerk told us to leave the passports in our room.

B: No. He told us not to leave them in our room.
5. A: Would you sit in the seats near the door, please?
    B: What did she say?
    C: She asked us to sit near the door.

Dictation, page 276

1. The woman says that your carry-on bag is too big.
2. My wife says she doesn't want to take a tour.
3. The hotel clerk told us not to leave the key in the room.
4. The immigration officer asked me to wait in a small room.
5. I told you to ask the tour guide.

Listening, A and B, page 277

This is Karen Saunders with *Spotlight on Travel*. As you know, I have to travel a lot for my job. My friends always tell me that I'm lucky. They don't believe me when I tell them that I don't like to travel. But it's true. I love visiting new places, but I don't really enjoy getting there. I especially dislike flying. However, over the years, I have found some ways to make my trips a little easier.

First, let's talk about what I do before I get to the airport. People often ask me to tell them how to pack. My advice? Don't pack a suitcase. Yes, you heard me . . . I said, "Never pack a suitcase." When I travel, I pack everything in my carry-on bag. That way, I don't have to check any bags. At the end of the flight, I can just leave the airport. I don't have to wait, and I don't have to worry about losing my suitcase.

My next piece of advice? Always take the first flight of the day. It usually leaves on time. And when you make your reservation, ask the ticket agent to give you your seat assignment. That way you will be able to choose your seat. If you wait until you get to the airport, you won't have a choice. Always ask for a seat close to the front of the airplane. That way, you can get off the plane more quickly.

Now let's talk about the flight. Make sure that you get up and walk around, especially on a long flight. It's good for you. It's also good to drink a lot of water, because the air on an airplane is very dry. You will look and feel much better at the end of the flight.

Finally, I definitely agree with the saying, "When in Rome, do as the Romans do." If you are traveling into a new time zone, don't forget to change your watch on the airplane. And don't think about what time it is back home. Even if you are very tired, wait until it is nighttime to go to bed. Likewise, go to bed at a normal hour, even if it feels very early to you.

For *Spotlight on Travel*, I'm Karen Saunders. Have a great trip!

Index

Writing

LIFESKILLS

Business and Employment